A Question of Silence?

A Question of Silence?

The Sexual Economies of Modern India

edited by

MARY E. JOHN AND JANAKI NAIR

kali for women

A Question of Silence? The Sexual Economies of Modern India
was first published in 1998 by

Kali for Women
B 1/8 Hauz Khas
New Delhi 110 016

All the papers in this collection, except
the Introduction, were presented
at the XXVI Interdisciplinary Research
Methodology Workshop at the
Madras Institute of Development Studies,
Chennai, 1–3 August 1996.

Grateful thanks to MIDS and
all the participants

Cover design: Ayesha Abraham

ISBN: 81-86706-08-9

Typeset by Scribe Consultants, B 4/30 Safdarjung Enclave
New Delhi 110 016
Printed at Pauls Press E 44/11, Okhla Phase II
New Delhi 110 020

Contents

Preface

This volume has a history and a pre-history. Kali for Women had been interested in bringing out a book on sexuality for some time, but initial efforts in that direction did not bear fruit. When Urvashi Butalia approached one of us, Janaki Nair, with a proposal to edit such a volume in 1995, it soon became obvious that the project would have to be reframed. With some trepidation, Janaki agreed, invited Mary John to join as co-editor, and a fresh beginning was made.

The idea of first holding a workshop on the subject of sexuality came up at the Madras Institute of Development Studies during conversations between Janaki, M S S Pandian and Padmini Swaminathan. The workshop was envisaged as the inaugural moment for work on the book. Held during August 1996, the 26th Inter Disciplinary Research Methodology Workshop (an annual event at MIDS), was also one of three special seminars to commemorate MIDS' Silver Jubilee Year. The entire administration worked long and hard to make the workshop a success, and several faculty members and students were enthusiastic participants. Our thanks go out to all of them, especially to Padmini Swaminathan, Manabi Majumdar, S. Subramanian, C.T. Kurien, T. Maheswari, Dharma Perumal, Ajit Menon, M. Prashanti and M.S.S. Pandian.

All the papers in this volume were first presented at the MIDS workshop. We regret that not all of the papers presented there could be included. We also regret other gaps and omissions in our collection. In spite of considerable effort on our part, all of whom we contacted for papers on the theme of alternate sexualities were unable to attend the workshop. We also hoped to have a paper on Kerala, given its long and ongoing history of having been sexualised as a region, but here, too, we were unsuccessful. These disappointments apart, we are grateful to all our contributors for their participation in this venture. They responded to our comments, and to the occasional cracking of the editorial whip, constructively and with good humour. Our special gratitude goes to T.Maheswari, who has most efficiently and enthusiastically turned papers produced in several disparate word processing programmes into a coherent format on the computer, thus significantly facilitating the task of the editors.

Thanks to Madhava Prasad and Satish Deshpande, whose encouragement and assistance helped in the organisation of the workshop and the subsequent editing of the volume. Urvashi Butalia has been very supportive of all our ideas. This volume has also benefited considerably from Jaya Banerji's editorial assistance.

Finally, it remains only to thank each other. Both of us have been involved in every aspect of the book, in spite of the logistical problems due to distance. Bringing different disciplinary perspectives and inputs into the project, this intellectual collaboration has been a mutually enriching experience and deepened our friendship, despite disagreements. What we have learnt in the process of putting this volume together is now a resource for future efforts, whether in this field or elsewhere.

A Question of Silence?

An introduction

MARY E. JOHN AND JANAKI NAIR

Is there a way of charting sexuality in India that does not begin with the *Kamasutra* (the text) and end with 'Kama Sutra' (the condom), separated by an intervening period of darkness illumined fleetingly by the laborious pieties of erotic temple sculptures or miniatures? Can there be a history of our sexual economies which breaches the status enjoyed by these 'anomalies', emblems perhaps of artistic licence, but lodged within an overarching narrative of repression? If Michel Foucault's celebrated insights into the history of western sexuality, particularly of the Victorian era, may be usefully invoked in the Indian context at all, it is his suggestion that the common sense of Victorian puritanism must be read afresh as an incitement to discourse.[1]

A focus on the conspiracy of silence regarding sexuality in India, whether within political and social movements or in scholarship, blinds us to the multiple sites where 'sexuality' has long been embedded. In the spheres of the law, demography or medicine, for instance, sexuality enjoys a massive and indisputable presence that is far from prohibited. How, then, may we thematise this crucial but neglected field, in order to dislodge prevailing opinions regarding the irrelevance of sexuality as an object of investigation, barring, say, alarmed reactions to the obscenity being so assiduously nurtured by commercial cinema? Only by insisting that, far from signifying biological genitality, 'sexuality' must connote a way of addressing sexual relations, their spheres of legitimacy and illegitimacy, through the institutions and practices, as well as the discourses and forms of representation, that have long been producing, framing, distributing and controlling the subject of 'sex'. This would also extend our enquiries beyond those disciplines within which sexuality currently enjoys a safe, public existence to include potentially provocative questions about the heterosexual norm, the 'arranged marriage' and emerging alternate sexualities. Our aim is to make space for more wide-ranging approaches towards understanding the sexual politics of desire and violence among men and women in modern India.

Mapping this vast and treacherous terrain in a way that takes account of regional differences as well as disciplinary competences can hardly be accomplished in the space of one volume. Yet, given the relative newness of the field,[2] it is imperative that these introductory remarks address inclusions and exclusions not only within this collection but elsewhere, problematics and questions that may have been raised but not always adequately answered, in order to indicate some of the directions that future research may profitably take.

'Sexuality': A Short Conceptual Genealogy

Before proceeding further, it may be useful to provide a very quick history of the term and uses of 'sexuality' itself. A nineteenth century, western concept, initially used in botany and zoology in connection with the reproduction of living things (whether amoebae, plants or insects), it soon came to be more closely associated with the peculiarities of the intercourse of people: In 1879, it was noted that "in removing the ovaries, you do not necessarily destroy sexuality in a woman."[3] The terms 'homosexuality' and 'heterosexuality' were also first invented at this time; 'heterosexuality', especially, developed many different connotations in the medical establishment, encompassing at first an 'inclination to both sexes' before contracting into a more exclusive, and increasingly normalised 'other-sex attraction' outside of procreation.[4]

In terms of theoretical influences in the twentieth century, five important moments in the thematisation of sexuality in the West may be signposted: the work of Sigmund Freud; the radical 'sexual politics' of the women's movements of the 1960s and '70s; Jacques Lacan and 'French' feminist theory; Michel Foucault's histories of sexuality; and the more recent designation of sexuality as sexual preference.

It is Freud, still very much the grand theorist of sexuality, who has been credited with major reconceptualisations of the field in the course of demarcating the boundaries of psychoanalysis. Controversy, but also growing authority, surrounded his work, from the early collaborative studies on the nature of hysteria begun in 1893, his subsequent pronouncements on the realities of 'infantile sexuality' in *Three Essays on the Theory of Sexuality* of 1905, to the more explicitly formulated focus on femininity and female sexuality that was to occupy him later.[5] This wide-ranging corpus was to influence succeeding generations of medical experts and psychologists, and, in the process of its popularisation, has been variously reformulated, repudiated and misconstrued. Freudian theories of sexuality have also extended into—and been reconstituted by—the field of comparative ethnography and the study of non-western peoples in disciplines such as anthropology. The work of Bronislaw Malinowski represents an initial moment in what continues to be a fraught relationship between sexuality, psychoanalysis and the study of *culture*.

The decade of the 1960s—also the years of the so-called 'sexual revolution' in many western societies—saw the culmination of a number of theories on sexuality that had been proliferating from the turn of the century, if not before. Many of the first feminist groups that emerged at this time transformed forever the debates on sex—free or repressed—by *politicising* the issue. The subject of sex, it was forcefully argued, could only be approached as a political institution—involving questions of power and an understanding of patriarchy—which structures the denial of abortion rights, the fear of rape, or the sexual politics of literature. Feminists such as Susan Brownmiller referred somewhat dismissively to a complicity of silence on the part of theorists, including Freud, on the question of rape, "the real life deployment of the penis as weapon."[6]

With the waning of radical feminism from its initial position of dominance, interest in the work of Freud, among others, grew. This was mediated in large measure during the present phase of western feminism by the 'return to Freud' announced by Jacques Lacan. Beginning in the early '70s, feminists such as Luce Irigaray in France, and Juliet Mitchell, Jacqueline Rose and Laura Mulvey in Britain, made brilliant, provocative or, at times, defensive interpretations of Freud, Lacan and female sexuality, as they variously set out to determine just what kinds of insights an engagement between feminism and psychoanalysis might yield.[7]

Is it, as Luce Irigaray seemed to suggest, that Freud's theories are irredeemably confounded by their own contradictions, since it is the very postulate of a single libidinal economy under the law of the phallus that turns 'woman', her femininity, sexuality, and so on, into an unanalysable, intractable problem? From a remarkably different point of departure, Juliet Mitchell has recalled that her pioneering work on psychoanalysis in the 1970s was meant to serve as a bridge between feminism and the project of socialism, by demonstrating "that sexual difference is a dynamic in social life as well as in personal life."[8] A decade later, Jacqueline Rose went so far as to suggest that psychoanalysis and feminism need to conceive of themselves as part of one and the same project, given the Lacanian emphases on the precariousness of feminine sexuality and the undermining of sexual identity by the unconscious.

As debates on the relation between feminism and psychoanalyis raged on, with positions hardening while work expanded, Foucault launched his polemic against the (Freudian) 'repressive hypothesis'. It is Foucault who aroused the general suspicion of a much longer and deeper deployment of sexuality in the West, however modern the term itself might be. Nothing could be more misleading than the belief that some earlier time was more enlightened or less pre-occupied with sexual activity as a 'problem'. He planned (and was partially able to realise) an exploration into a history of the experiences of sexuality beginning with Roman and Christian antiquity, through the formation of knowledges, regulation of practices and production of subjects, all of which were laboriously modified and transformed over the centuries.[9] Influential and, indeed, indispensable as Foucault has now become, feminists have been frustrated by the absence of 'technologies of gender' in his elaborate incursions into 'the technologies of sex'.[10]

Since the 1980s, especially in the United States, sexuality has increasingly tended to condense into the more specific question of sexual preference associated with identity politics of the gay and lesbian communities. It is thus commonly alluded to in references to 'race, class, gender and sexuality'. Sharp lines have come to be drawn between positions that view heterosexuality as the very core of women's oppression,[11] on the one hand, and more liberal lesbian criticisms that see a focus on sexual violence alone as being unduly alarmist, an obstacle to speaking about women's pleasure.[12] This has often led feminists to take opposing stances on issues such as censorship, pornography and prostitution. However unresolved they remain, these debates provide an inkling of how intense the subject of sexuality is in other parts of the world.

This brief sketch is but a foray into the western feminist literature. That this literature is voluminous, however, does not imply that it has been an unqualified success. The effect of turning the lights on to sexuality, and from various angles, has too often cast long shadows elsewhere, turning everything else into background. In fact, in a broadly sympathetic review essay written ten years ago, B. Ruby Rich has this to say:

> Looking back over the sexuality debates of the last decade [of the 1980s], it often seems that a crowd is gathered in one corner of a very large house oblivious to the many places left unexplored. We need to ... open up the debates, to look elsewhere in order to find different answers and, even, different questions.[13]

Among other things, she believes that a 'geo-politics' of sexuality would be necessary in order to develop a more active feminist theory on the subject.[14]

If, in retrospect, the issues and 'sex-wars' of the 1980s in the United States seem to have been somewhat constricted, the 1990s may be witnessing a broadening of political and theoretical agendas: The Anita Hill–Clarence Thomas hearings and the subsequent confirmation of Thomas as Supreme Court Judge, in spite of the accusation of sexual harassment against him, threw up especially urgent challenges. Questions of sexuality, race, governance and the law were entangled in a situation of unprecedented confusion and volatility.[15] From the apparently more secluded spaces of the academy, Judith Butler has shown that Foucauldian and psychoanalytical perspectives must be interwoven, rather than opposed, if a political understanding of 'deviant', marginal, sexual subjectivities is to make further headway.[16]

Alluding to the western literature inevitably produces a further set of questions, anxieties and expectations. What about 'Indian' theories of sexuality, quite apart from an Indian sexuality? Why bring up western theories at all?

To begin with the last question, our response would be that 'the West' is at once a particular geographical place, and a *relation*. From where we are, this relation is one of domination, and about as complicated as they come; to all intents and purposes, we are effectively located in the West. It is to the credit of feminists in India that they have refused to be silenced by accusations of being western-identified, and so unable to deal with the real India. Ironically enough, the very conception of the other of the West as being something to which western concepts do not apply (or only as an act of violation from which one must be redeemed) is itself a western legacy. Such constructions of cultural difference leave the West firmly in command. So too, do notions that theory is produced in the West, while we provide the local colour—an Indian Oedipus in contrast to its generic counterpart, for instance.

In our view, the theoretical questions before us are both more daunting and more exciting. We cannot but draw upon western theories, since they "determine at an unconscious level, the reading practices we bring to bear" on our work.[17] But this still leaves us with the task of theorisation, which can never take the form of the application of a theory that one possesses in advance, but must resemble a process, a historical and political mode of conceptualising sexual economies that would be true to our experiences of an uneven modernity, calling for multiple levels of analysis and the forging of articulations between the global and local.

We would therefore like to think that the paucity of preconceived notions about sexuality in our context is less a weakness to be overcome and more a potentially positive sign. Sexuality is not an object to be retrieved, much less a coherent one; neither is it an essential cultural emblem, whether this be the 'bisexuality of the cosmic feminine principle' put forward by Ashis Nandy, or the 'sexual mother' (for Indian men) and the *jodi* or pair (for Indian women), discovered everywhere by Sudhir Kakar.[18] The reference in the sub-title of this volume to 'sexual economies' instead of 'sexuality' is meant to underscore our concern with the materiality of the sites where discussions of 'sex' are laid out and contested, rather than with abstract positions. This is also why this volume shares little with those efforts that seek to isolate or qualify some unique 'Indian sexuality', in whatever guise.

The rest of this introduction attempts to identify and open up some of the major domains in our recent past and present that have accommodated questions of sexuality. In the sections that follow—from the elaboration of the private and the discovery of golden ages to representations of 'sex' in specific disciplines and fields—we have no unifying thesis to offer. This is not because we seek to recover and celebrate the diversity of our sexualities. The production of rigorous and insightful generalisation, we believe, requires the prior exploration of current work, without papering over the gaps, silences and incommensurabilities that remain.

The Initiatives of Feminism

Questions of sexuality have been raised during a number of critical periods in modern India and clearly pre-date explicit feminist concern. Among the more well-known moments when sexuality became politically visible and controversial was during Gandhian nationalism, of which we shall have more to say later. But, as the contributions of Tejaswini Niranjana, Anandhi S. and U.Vindhya in this volume clearly indicate, new protocols of sexual modernity were being defined and placed in circulation at other equally important sites, sometimes as far afield as Trinidad, whose resonances are still felt today.

Sexuality has recently gained more prominence as a subject of political movements or academic discourse as a result of growing feminist involvement with the rights of women to their lives and bodies. For too long, it was not women's sexual experiences that were at stake, but the elaborate codes of honour inscribed on their bodies. Women bear the marks, sometimes violent marks, of caste, ethnic and national imaginations. Not only has the middle class, upper caste woman been the ground on which questions of modernity and tradition are framed, she is the embodiment of the boundaries between licit and illicit forms of sexuality, as well as the guardian of the nation's morality. Susie Tharu and K.Lalita have shown, for instance, that colonial and national agendas were not always opposed when it came to delegitimising the easy depiction of sexual desire by Muddupalini, a non-upper caste artist and writer at the Thanjavur courts during the eighteenth century.[19]

But women are also 'reproductive beings'. It was the dangerous sexuality of the 'non-mother' that motivated the 'social reform' legislation of the nineteenth century.[20] It was, and continues to be, the 'irresponsible promiscuities' of the poor which prompted national programmes for the control of a growing population. If these programmes have evolved considerably from the excesses of the male sterilisation drives associated with Indira Gandhi and Sanjay Gandhi during the Emergency years, 1975–77, it is by affixing reproductive responsibility, but not sexual desire, solely on women. And today, it is the 'menacing' sexuality of the commercial sex worker as a potential bearer of AIDS that has heightened concern for and engendered campaigns about 'safe sex'. Here too, safe sex has primarily been promoted through the aggressive sale of condoms, as a way of protecting (unavoidable) male promiscuity, in an ironic departure from monogamy as an ideal.

This brief overview may already indicate that it is not enough to discover the variety of instances and historical moments when the intemperate and unpredictable force of female sexuality was so named in order to be subjected to institutions of containment, technologies of surveillance, or laws of prohibition. What is needed is a better sense of the specific and historically mutable sites where such modes of incitement and control were deployed, and an exploration of how women and men were being sexualised and desexualised in the process.

It is perhaps because Hindu metaphors and icons of an active female sexual power have enjoyed considerable if not enduring influence, to the point of being used to prove the irrelevance of a women's movement in our context,[21] that feminism in India has overwhelmingly highlighted women as victims. Women have been the victims of patriarchal sexual practices, whether through the exploitation of landlords, during caste atrocities, in marital rape, in state policies concerning reproduction, or as bearers of the violent marks of political change.[22] It is no coincidence that the only entries on 'sexuality' in the index of a recent history of Indian women's movements are grouped under the head "Sexual Assault".[23] Only more recently have spaces opened up for talking of female desire, or of alternate sexualities.[24] In the context of the early campaigns against rape and sexual violence, Flavia Agnes' analyses are an indication of the pressures on women's groups to come up with 'alternatives', even as the legal sphere became the only place where women could seek redressal.[25] As a consequence, the Indian women's movement, to the extent that it specifically foregrounds sexuality, has usually concentrated on the question of enforcing laws that would act as a restraint on long sanctioned male privileges over the bodies and lives of women, and this too, primarily as they affect poor or working class women. One of the most recent successes of the movement is the Supreme Court directive announced in August 1997 which makes the sexual harassment of women at the work place

a punishable offence. At some remove from questions of the law,
V. Geeta's paper in this volume takes up the difficult theme of
battering, in order to try and probe directly into the dynamics
of masculine sexuality and violence.

The other major context within which the women's
movement has discussed issues of sexuality is that of women's
health. Health workshops have been repeatedly thwarted by
'textbook' assumptions in topics such as fertility or menstruation,
which often diverge radically from most women's experiences.
Though Gabriele Dietrich may be right in noting that many
Indian feminists have found the book *Our Bodies, Ourselves*,
produced by the Boston Health Collective, as too "obsessed with
the intricacies of sexual intercourse and with bodily
consciousness in general",[26] it is equally true that it has served
as an inspiration for feminist health books in a number of
regional languages, such as *Savalaaksha Sandehaalu* in Telugu.[27]
In recent years, the movement has shown itself more willing to
address women's tastes and desires (if largely within the middle
classes), often as a way of outlining the possibility of political
opposition to the agencies of globalisation, which seek to
aggressively 'modernise' Indian society while keeping democracy
at bay.

The Question of Modernity

An organising theme of a volume such as this is therefore the
problematic of 'modernity', which encompasses both the
elements of 'modernisation', as well as democratic and more
thoroughgoing forms of social transformation. Feminist politics
as well as scholarship have been aligned, over the years, with
both aspects of Indian modernity, with deeply ambiguous
results. The frameworks of modernity are absolutely essential
since it is from within our location in the modern that the
'traditional' has been identified and so named, and golden ages
have been constructed: Kumkum Roy's discussion of the
emblematic status of the *Kamasutra* outlines successive modern
attempts to produce, circulate or confine this text. Our purpose

is not to suggest a unidirectional assertion of new sexual moralities by the agencies of colonial rule, much less to lay everything at the door of colonialism. Rather, the European masters, nurtured by pornographic fantasies that had long been in circulation, were inordinately interested in and exercised about sexuality in the tropics so that "sexual prescriptions by class, race and gender became increasingly central to the politics of colonial rule",[28] as well as resistance to it. Mrinalini Sinha's work even suggests that the 'manliness' of the colonial master was contingent on the 'effeminacy' of the Bengali babu, both constructs of the colonial period that had substantial material and ideological effects.[29] Fears about the sexual health of the European subalterns in the colonial army subtended a number of arrangements engendered during colonial rule, and in many ways ran counter to congealing attitudes about promiscuous Indian males or the need to assert and maintain racial difference.[30] If, then, the colonial period constitutes a provisional beginning for some of the investigations in this book, it is not in order to suggest the relative immutability of traditions before this time, but to emphasise the profound and radical rupture in all domains that colonialism entailed, especially as it ushered in an uneven Indian modernity.

Recovering a Golden Age

Specifying the modernity of the sites where traditions and pasts are constructed is crucial for a related reason. Feminist narratives that characterise the colonial period as one that homogenised a rich array of familial and sexual practices, so that certain pockets of 'resistance' to patriarchal power declined or were irretrievably lost, seem to stem from a yearning for a 'golden age'. For instance, over the past ten years, studies of the social arrangements within which devadasis worked and flourished in the period before colonial decline have burgeoned into a veritable cottage industry.[31] The Devadasi system has attracted scholars searching for women who enjoyed a measure of economic, sexual and social independence. As keepers of the

Bharatanatyam tradition, attached to the temple complexes of southern India, devadasis survived within the bosom of the upper caste/class family as adjuncts rather than as competitors of the rural household.[32] By the late nineteenth century, they were increasingly identified by the colonial judicial system as 'aberrations' in what became identified as (textual) Hindu law.[33] Soon devadasis became the focus of reform initiatives launched by colonial authorities as well as indigenous elites, who together undermined both the material as well as the ideological foundations of the system.[34]

The narrative of 'decline', or at least displacement, inflects writing on other erotic performance traditions as well. For Bengal, Sumanta Banerjee has recovered the process by which the wandering Vaishnavs, whose robust and sexually explicit songs had an assured appreciation in the homes of privileged Bengali women, were gradually marginalised by the development of new middle class morals.[35] Similarly, Sharmila Rege constructs a narrative of decline for lavani composers and their troupes in Maharashtra, who were considered far too licentious and immoral; their cultural spaces were usurped by the altogether new desire machines of the film industry.[36] Perhaps the high point of these golden age narratives was reached in feminist recuperations of courtesanal cultures, where not only financial and social autonomy has been uncovered, but a genealogy of modern lesbianism as well.[37] By way of contrast, the recovery of unromanticised accounts of the devadasi system by dasis themselves serves as a useful and timely corrective, although such accounts deny devadasis any subjectivity other than that of victim.[38] Taken together, it is clear that many of the feminist narratives fail to acknowledge the ways in which wife/non-wife are constituted by the same patriarchal authorities, so that they are structurally yoked in fundamental ways, making the securities and pleasures of one domain unavailable to the other.

Within the broad contours of this regionally differentiated colonial/nationalist context, it would be vital to have a fuller historical grasp of how concepts of the "public" and the "private", the proper and the scandalous, have hinged so decisively on questions of sexuality. Dagmar Engels' study of Bengal at the close of the nineteenth century, for instance, follows Meredith Borthwick in ascribing a distinct change amongst Hindu middle class women from their confinement within the zenana as "sexual servants", wearing nothing more than a "thin, virtually see-through sari", to their emergence beyond the home following the austere Brahmo style of "sari-cum-petticoat, blouse, and, for some, even shoes."[39] That this entry into public life was no simple process of desexualisation is obvious from Engels' discussion of new conjugal codes and practices, including the novel development of an active market in marriage manuals, proof that "at least for the Bengali or English-educated middle classes, sex was of great *private* interest."[40] Neither is it possible to view such changes as an unambiguously positive step towards a more egalitarian order, given Engels' acknowledgement that male orgasmic satisfaction remained the unchallenged focus. Moreover, according to Tanika Sarkar, the sphere of Hindu conjugality was at the "very heart of the formative moment for militant nationalism in Bengal", but in such a way that, for a group of Hindu revivalists at least, non-consensual, indissoluble infant marriage became the last site of autonomy from colonialism.[41] In the face of such conflicts, therefore, a fuller examination of changing developments around sexual norms and forms of desire among men and women, especially in relation to the elaboration of the private and public spheres, would be indispensable for constructing a genealogy for the present.

While adultery among Bengali women had none of the sanctions that men from "respectable circles" continued to enjoy, given that "if an affair became public, a woman was regarded as a prostitute and treated as an outcaste", prostitution, on its part, was not simply a degraded profession. Prostitutes existed at different social and economic levels; they were established professionally, but at the bottom of the Hindu hierarchy. Many responded to Gandhi's campaign against untouchability, took up spinning and wore khadi; a few even joined as volunteers. Gandhi, on his part, refused to acknowledge them.

If it is thus not clear how changes in modernising Bengal are to be plotted, recent work on the history of private life in Kerala is equally unsettling of commonly held assumptions: Udaya Kumar's discussion of the secret and scandalous pleasures of wearing a blouse by bare breasted Kerala women confirms that the coordinates of *our* Victorian period, if it can be so designated, must be defined afresh.[42] Drawing from the oral confession of an Ezhava woman in the late 19th century, which dwells on the unique role of putting on a blouse at night, Kumar brings together "concealment of breasts, concealment from the mother's surveillance, concealment from the day, and the lover merging with the image of the gandharva. What we see here is a new internal configuration that links attire and the body to an individual private desire and an individual act of volition".

The Emergence of New Sexual Economies

The feminist narrative of 'decline' from an earlier, less confined sexual order falters for another reason. For if some sexual economies were cast in the shadows by the agencies of modernisation, yet others were in the process of being formed at new sites such as the mines, mills and plantations that were set up under the aegis of colonial rule. It is at such locations that we may observe most clearly the state's interest in controlling the relationship between the productive and reproductive capacities of the worker, particularly the woman worker. Nothing so starkly underlines the links between a concern about lower class sexuality on plantations and objective structures of emerging labour regimes than the colonial response to 'wife murder', namely, the assertion of the family as a legal construct.[43] Neither the colonial authorities nor the plantation management of Assam, for instance, where nearly half the workforce consisted of women, were particularly perturbed by the 'unorthodox' sexual and living arrangements that emerged among workers, until, that is, the supply of labour to the plantations was severely affected, producing fresh anxieties that were expressed in pro-natalist policies at the turn of the century.[44] The indifference to sexual arrangements among jute mill workers similarly, was quite marked as long as the supply of labour was assured and undisturbed.[45] But a regulation of the sexuality of working women was prompted by colonial concerns about sustaining family-based farm production as well; if in rural Bengal this led to a category of 'offences against marriage', in rural Haryana, it had quite the opposite effect of asserting the legality of remarriage customs which prevented inheriting widows from partitioning husbands' property.[46]

The sexuality of the working class was cause for anxiety at certain other times as well, as when the troops stationed in India, who had neither the material resources to support their families nor the moral resources to abstain from sex, had to be provided with safe and assured ways of satisfying their sexual appetites.[47] These were clearly the moments when the colonial regime came closest to equating European lower classes with colonised subjects, although racial difference was asserted afresh by commercialising sex work. But what was the status of the commercial sex workers themselves, whose activity was progressively criminalised, tolerated as a necessary evil for the preservation of the emergent monogamous family, but regulated in order to keep adverse medical and moral consequences at bay?[48] Narratives of the historical 'independence' of courtesans or devadasis notwithstanding, contemporary feminist politics alone has enabled the sex-worker to claim political rights and security at work. And once more, it is feminist scholars and activists who caution against too easy an identification of sex work as wage labour, given the difficulties of separating 'sex' from the bodies and personalities of women.[49]

The Ideal of Celibacy

Paradoxically, yet predictably, questions of male sexuality have rarely been a focus of scholarly analysis, except for celebrated instances of celibacy. Celibacy has been long valorised as a cultural ideal for men, especially among Hindus, and was usually advocated as a phase in the life cycle, a temporary abstention that conserves life giving fluid (semen) for superior physical and political tasks. Male wrestlers of North India are required to practice brahmacharya to strengthen and empower their bodies.[50] Gandhian politics gave celibacy a new charge. Despite a general acknowledgement of male sexual need, even promiscuity, male celibacy has thus been valorised as an indisputable (upper caste) ideal. To take a very recent example, the deity Ayyappa's avowed abstinence from sex has recently been upheld in court against the right of women to public worship.[51]

Celibacy received a fresh lease of life with Vivekananada's call to sexual abstinence for building a nation of heroes, one which anticipated in many ways the more publicised embrace of celibacy by Gandhi.[52] But if Gandhi's step to take up brahmacharya and become a 'eunuch for the nation' is considerably more well-known than the efforts of others before and after him, the reasons are not far to seek. For it would be difficult to find a more obsessive concern with male genital sex as a 'problem' in the fully Foucauldian sense of the term. Its very repudiation demanded that sexual desire be talked about endlessly and confessed to at the slightest sign of its arousal, displaced onto other practices, food habits and relationships, and vigorously policed in everyday life. Here was a 'technology of the self' by which the male libido could be repeatedly named and reviled as "poison", "the enemy within", and so on, in order that Gandhi might become the subject of the nation.

One can fully empathise with Sudhir Kakar's acknowledgement of the difficulties that beset the analysis of a man who is "the foremost culture-hero of modern India"; moreover, from a feminist perspective, we cannot remain unaffected by Gandhi's repeated emphasis on the violence which constitutes such a ready ingredient of male sexual desire, one which men can and must transform. But we are still baffled by Kakar's discussion of Gandhi's sex-life and relationships with women, which reproduces Gandhi's own confessions and beliefs in explicit detail, but as proof, merely, of his "candor and honesty", of the truthfulness and purity of Gandhi's search for truth. In an account of the younger Gandhi's self-driven jealousies and suspicions towards his wife, which even included breaking her bangles and sending her back to her natal home, this is what is offered by way of analysis: "Purists can be cruel, especially to those dependent women who threaten to devour their virtue."[53]

More detailed discussion of the implications of Gandhi's attitude towards sexuality is beyond the scope of this introduction, particularly in terms of understanding his special political concern for two groups of people—women and "untouchables". Tejaswini Niranjana's paper in this volume invites us to rethink the nationalist resolution of the women's question by exploring Gandhi's political campaign to end overseas indenture, and redeem the sexually 'depraved' woman worker. In the context of his own life, it appears that women shifted from being the recipients of his projections, fantasies and sexual needs to being required as proof of his successes in the cause of celibacy, since they were capable of inciting male lust even when desire was absent.[54] From the perspective of Gandhi's stance on issues of caste, it seems not just patronising but in some way offensive that self-mortification for a "sexual lapse" in later life should have taken the form of leaving the "luxury" of his ashram to live in a "remote and poverty-stricken, untouchable village."[55] Not only does this seem to suggest a shared revulsion, it places Gandhi's pre-occupations with himself at the centre of the entire exercise.

At the same time, Gandhi's unflinching call for the reform of male sexuality and his use of the figure of the celibate woman, often the Hindu widow, as an ideal to be emulated rather than contained, also inspired early feminists to campaign against 'double standards'. This has gradually been fashioned into the legal ideal of monogamy, rearticulated today in demands for gender just codes. However, it is not virginity that is upheld as an ideal for women so much as the notion of the chaste wife, an empowered figure in (Hindu) myth who functions as a means of taming or domesticating the more fearful aspects of the woman's sexual appetite.[56] It is only of late that feminists have begun envisaging and articulating ways of dismantling patriarchal privileges without necessarily limiting the rights or freedoms of women themselves through self-imposed codes of asexuality. The enforced norm of celibacy both within and outside marriage for women within religious orders, recent research has revealed, holds ambiguous possibilities for women, enabling some women to refuse marriage altogether or at least to redefine its terms.[57]

Although there are some discussions today on male sexuality as a sign of masculine virility, (rather than on the links between celibacy and power), the strongest suggestion of the sexual anxieties undergirding contemporary political movements is in Anand Patwardhan's film *Father Son and Holy War*. Indeed, if Gandhian nationalism deployed the metaphors of celibacy as a (male) ideal, the contemporary phase of the movement of the Hindu Right is marked by complex negotiations of the powers of masculine virility, drawing as much from Vivekananda as from Gandhi, and expressing both envy and fear of the imagined sexual abilities of the (demonised) Indian Muslim. The TV serial *Chanakya*, Uma Chakravarti argues in this volume, succeeded in 'saffronising' the historical character, and lionised his celibacy against the 'debauched', and therefore, weakened, power of the Nanda King, who embodies an emasculated Indian 'nation'. This is in keeping with the broader Hindu nationalist ideal of a citizenry that must quite literally gird its loins in order to undertake the task of nation-building.

Disciplines and Discourses

Over the past two hundred years, sexuality has been present in at least three significant sets of discourses: as an unenunciated ground of demographic discourse, as the site of bitter contention in the discourses of social reform through legislation and in the courtroom, and in the detailed anthropological investigations into forms of marriage and family across the sub-continent. It was not, therefore, the confessional couch or the hystericised woman that generated knowledge and anxieties about sexuality in modern India so much as, on the one hand, the administrative urgency of the colonial power to make sense of and thereby govern a baffling array of 'types and classes' and their family systems, and on the other, the nationalist need to define the dutiful place of the citizen/subjects of the incipient nation. The nineteenth century was one in which the unfamiliar sexual practices and institutions of India were the object of reform by colonial administrators, missionaries and scholars alike; it coincided with state-initiated pro-natalist policies that policed pregnancies in various parts of India, for what were clearly economic ends.[58] By the twentieth century, the Indian elites themselves trained their attention on the sexuality of the lower castes and classes as detrimental to the health and well-being of the nation. As the essay written by Anandi S. explains, there was startling unanimity between the neo-Malthusians and nationalists, and even the first wave feminists, as to which Indian classes should be the targets of contraceptive measures.

Demography

Such world historic changes as the widespread availability of contraception, which transformed the link between sexuality and reproduction, were annexed to the needs of the Indian nation. Today, however, the discourse of demography is symptomatic of a wider hesitation to take on sexual issues, even though there is no way of disentangling them from the counting of populations and the tabulation of fertility rates. In a recent study on culture, women's status and demographic behaviour, for instance, the author refers to "effective marriage" as a way of signalling the onset of sexual relations, and mentions only in passing what the costs of later marriages would be in terms of maintaining norms of "chastity" and countering a longer "exposure to temptation". All this is discussed in a short section on "the initiation of childbearing".[59] The possibility that differences in cultural background must include questions of family forms and sexual practices is never addressed.

Matters are more complicated in the field of family planning programmes. Even though the nuclear family is obviously the ideological frame of the programme, it is individuals who are targeted, and the mode of this targeting has changed over the last two decades. Statistical evidence of changing trends, as provided by figures on sterilisation (increasingly the backbone of the family planning programme), indicate a massive switch from men to women following the Emergency.[60] But this information remains meagre and partial. The assumptions about male and female sexuality and promiscuity, not to speak of contemporary constructions of Muslim lust and polygamy, or lower caste licentiousness and easy divorce, that are harnessed in the theory and practice of population control are urgently in need of exposure.

Critiques of Indian demographic discourse have primarily been aimed at uncovering the enduring influence of Malthus amongst policy makers, making the case instead for increased attention to social and economic inequalities.[61] Even where the critiques have emerged out of feminist perspectives, they have been overwhelmed by a focus on the links between population growth and poverty, although gesturing towards a need for policies to be sensitive to women's bodies and their very right to life.[62] Facile equations between economic backwardness and high fertility rates, for instance have been seriously undermined by regional differences and specificities (as between Kerala and Tamilnadu) but despite growing scepticism about such links, only hesitantly is a role assigned to changing sexual practices and relationships.[63]

If 'reproductive health' has begun to command the attention of the state, it is partly due to the efforts of such feminist critiques even as they have been appropriated by international agencies. It may not be entirely surprising that the more recent demand for replacing an exclusive concern about reproductive health with a broader focus on 'sexual health' has come from grass roots health care providers working in non-governmental organisations.[64] This clearly signifies a shift away from statist discourse to one that insists that questions of reproduction cannot be delinked from changes in sexual practices. Providing quite a different optic on the ongoing eulogisation of the 'Kerala Model of Development' are the health care workers and activists who are more willing to acknowledge the existence of multiple sexual partners (and not just among men), adolescent sexuality, the consequences of split families amongst workers in the Gulf, and the emergence of a thriving pornography industry. It is not fortuitous that such developments have come together with rising levels of violence against women both within and outside the home.

Anthropology

The control, exchange and marking of women's sexualities within marriage and the family has, at least since the beginning of the nineteenth century, been the object of social anthropological discourse, concerned as it is with the production and reproduction of caste, kinship, family and community. The multiplicity of marital and familial arrangements in India has provided generations of scholars with opportunities for 'legitimate' discussions of sexuality, especially as it is embedded in the 'symbolics of alliance'. Within this domain, those islands of sanctioned promiscuity among women, in what is otherwise a sea of confining patriarchal sexual arrangements, have attracted an unusually high degree of interest and scholarship: Nair matriliny comes easily to mind.[65] Yet here, too, older as well as more recent scholarship has tended to focus on the material structures of which these sexual arrangements were a part, rather than the shifts in female subjectivities that were enabled by the agencies of change in the nineteenth century, a period when families and marriages were being formed and reformed.[66]

A related resource in the anthropological archive is that of folklore, which, as A.K. Ramanujan discovered, quite simply and commonly, consists of old women's stories. Startling in their sexual explicitness, their humour and their absurdity, as such stories so often are, anthropology has managed to reify them within ultimately sterile discussions about the power of the mother-son bond in Hindu society, or the relativism of culture.[67] The fact that "all these tales have been told by elderly women, expressing their point of view ranging from the tragic to the ludicrous"[68] seems to have been of no significance. Why not, instead, view them along the lines of, say, black women's blues, as a skilled, performative activity, not to be romanticised, but placed within their scenes of enactment?

Anthropological discussions of the exchange of women (and thereby their productive and reproductive capacities) within castes and clans have articulated questions of sexuality in muted and hypostatised ways. Conventional ethnographic descriptions of 'rites of passage' that mark the sexualisation of men and women respectively have rarely addressed the question of emerging subjectivities and historical change: Kalpana Ram's contribution in this volume represents a pioneering attempt at moving away from these conventions of ethnographic writing. Ram's earlier and ongoing scholarship on femininity in rural and coastal Tamilnadu, moreover, would be an indispensable counter to the frameworks and assumptions of demography and family planning, which are now part of a middle class 'common sense'. In a discussion of the female body of possession, Ram shows that women's inability to conceive, sustain a pregnancy or successfully deliver a live birth cannot be disengaged from women's sexual embodiment, nor from their experiences of the arbitrary powers of female deities. Fertility is neither a simple biological nor an economic issue.[69] Parallel ethnographic work by Karin Kapadia provides important glimpses into the powerful discourses of 'proper' female sexuality and 'proper' fertility amongst all the castes she studied, though, perhaps at the cost of overemphasising the centrality of fertility for 'lower caste' women, in contrast to that of sexuality for 'upper castes' and upwardly mobile groups.[70]

Going against the grain of anthropological models of marriage and family among, say, the Nairs or the Coorgs is the insistent voice of transgression, which also speaks of the deployment of alliance. Prem Chowdhry's essay provides an account of the extremely violent reprisals invited by such transgressions in contemporary rural Haryana; elsewhere, K. Gnanambal has compiled a richly detailed set of case studies which point to far more benign negotiations of the violation of caste boundaries by religious and caste panchayats of southern India.[71] There are a multiplicity of levels at which transgressive relationships are forged, and are in turn pardoned, punished or sanctioned by the religious and caste authorities; it thus appears that the maintenance of caste boundaries can be enabled, rather than hindered by a certain degree of flexibility when sexual codes are broken.

The anthropological literature, however, has far too little to say about the sexual dynamics underpinning the maintenance of caste boundaries and inequalities.[72] Moreover, efforts at analysing the complex sexual politics embedded in recent caste atrocities, such as the socio-cultural context of the Chunduru massacres in Andhra Pradesh in 1990, have, significantly enough, come overwhelmingly from outside the discipline.[73] Could it be that the caste/community/gender nexus framed by anthropology, so critical for any approach to conceptualising sexuality in rural and urban India, has largely turned into a lost opportunity?

The Spheres of the Law

Gnanambal's monograph referred to above also confirms that one of the richest archives for mapping a history of sexuality in India is that of the law, not just the realm of state law and its apparatuses but the adjudications of caste and religious institutions. The courtroom and the legislature have provided legitimate spaces for the most detailed and unembarrassed discussions of male and female sexuality from the colonial period into our own.[74] Throughout the nineteenth century, new technologies of power were brought to bear on the marriage of female children, the sexuality of widows, the inbuilt promiscuities of matrilineal marriage systems, and the widespread practice of abortion or infanticide as a form of family planning among labourers. These were discussed in courtroom, legislature and popular press alike as part of a programme of 'social reform'. A matrix of abstract legality was gradually brought to bear on the range of existing and emerging forms of sexuality among all sections of society, though the focus of colonial surveillance was usually the lower classes, as Samita Sen's article in this volume confirms. Ranajit Guha's discussion of Chandra's Death describes in detail customary ways of coping with sexual transgression within the community (though usually through the exercise of feudal patriarchal power); by the early nineteenth century, they were criminalised and invoked the severely punitive responses of the state.[75] On the other hand, the 'aberrant' sexual practices of the upper castes/classes increasingly became the target of ideological reform, which in turn urged indigenous elites to campaign for social changes: the reform of Nair matriliny decisively demonstrates emerging new divisions between licit and illicit sexual relationships. Throughout the twentieth century, when initiatives for social reform were seized from the agencies of the colonial state by cultural nationalists, the distinction between the licit and illicit domains continued to be defined and maintained, as in the Suppression of Immoral Traffic acts, and in the gradual legal prohibition of the devadasi and her dance.

More than ever before, therefore, it is the legal domain today that has produced some of the most detailed discussions of sexuality. Legal activists and feminists have also discovered the extremely problematic nature of the 'sex talk' and overall ambience of the courtroom during rape trials. This has led to situations where rape victims have suffered a 'second rape', so to speak, at the hands of defence lawyers and judges during the process of interrogation; considerable rethinking is now underway in the women's movement and amongst civil rights lawyers about the advisability of 'in camera' trials, especially in cases involving the sexual abuse of minors.

Interestingly enough, it is in the legal sphere rather than the anthropological one, that the mediations of sexuality by the structures of gender, caste and class are most clearly revealed. Judicial discourse on rape, Veena Das' recent work tells us, tends to devalue the speech of women, looking instead for signs whether the woman's body has been so sexualised as to make her unexchangeable in marriage. Judgements "lie at the intersection of the discourse of sexuality and the discourse of alliance."[76] The recent acquittal of the alleged rapists of Bhanwari Devi, a lower caste sathin of Rajasthan's Women's Development Programme, was predicated on the belief that middle-aged, upper-caste men could not possibly have desired sex with a younger lower-caste woman. This, despite widespread knowledge of the structural access that upper caste males have had to lower caste/Dalit women. As the Mathura and the Rameeza Bee rape cases amply proved, the class and/or ethnic status of the woman more or less automatically places her in the category of inviting rape while consistently denying the status of 'victim' to women with a sexual past.[77] At the same time, while judicial discourse can be more tolerant of the sexual transgressions of those women who identifiably belong to a tiny upper class crust, and act more leniently as a result, it is not always in ways that favour the woman, since here, too, female desires are only admitted as they pose a threat to patriarchal controls.[78] If, indeed, a woman's desire is positioned elsewhere within judicial discourse at all, it is as it psychologically and emotionally bonds a woman to her husband or as it serves to fulfil a woman's desire for motherhood.[79]

Much current research on changes in marriage forms and sexualities has tended to emphasise the 'flexibility' of customary (non-state) law, pointing to the nineteenth century as the period when Hindu law was codified and brought more in line with scriptural or textual readings. The attribution of flexibility to customary law is not entirely unjustified, since caste and religious institutions at the village level have displayed a sensitivity to the dynamics of local power arrangements in ways that were not always possible in the courtroom, though with deeply ambiguous results for women.[80] But the narrative that suggests only flexibility before the period of colonial rule and increasing rigidity thereafter is more difficult to sustain,[81] particularly in a context where colonial and post-colonial law has made its accommodations with local Indian patriarchies, frequently co-operating with, rather than replacing, the realms of their jurisdictions.

Taken together, the discourses and practices of the law, of

anthropology and demography leave us with a mixed legacy of hesitations, of questions opened up in one domain only to be shut out elsewhere, but also with an explicit concern over the details of sex that in any other context would be pornographic. Going by popular prejudice, the real place to look for more full-blown representations of 'sex' would be the spheres of the arts and the media, the one aesthetic and the other commercial, sometimes also alluded to as the domains of 'high' and 'popular' culture respectively. The mediations of 'culture'—literary, performative, visual or technological—do indeed appear to have a special place for sexuality, whether this be understood as a matter of the unique insight and freedom of the artist, or, on the contrary, as a sign of the perversion fuelling the very desire of depiction. Since this overview cannot hope to deal comprehensively with the full range of questions that have been raised within literature, art, performance and the media, we have chosen to limit ourselves to two broad areas—first, the domain of sculpture, emblematic of modern negotiations of a bygone erotic era, and second, the more loosely defined field for addressing that quintessentially contemporary apparatus for the production of pleasure, the cinema.

Representations of 'Sex': The Case of Sculpture

The explicit representations of sexuality in ancient and medieval Indian texts and sculptures fed the fantasies of many European scholars who had long nurtured dreams of the exotic east. Richard Burton's recovery of the *Kamasutra* was one such moment. At the same time, the abundant insistence with which heterosexual and homosexual couplings, female auto-eroticism, fondling or titillation, and group sex were elaborated in frieze after frieze, both within and outside Hindu temples of different periods, was cause for fascinated horror among puritanical colonial explorers, seeking out and restoring 'History' to the Indian people. Khajuraho's sculptures, though, "exquisitely carved" were "extremely indecent and offensive" to T. S. Burt in 1839; James Fergusson found much to praise in Konarak's architecture (1837) while condemning its statuary; and when Percy Brown later reluctantly acknowledged the scandalous realism of erotic sculpture at Konarak, he was quick to conceal his admiration by suggesting that it was a definite indication of decadence. The widespread evidence of such erotic 'excess' to which temples as far apart as Belur/Halebid or Tirunelveli bore ample witness, made it difficult for the intrepid colonials and their nationalist heirs to isolate or 'exceptionalise' such art.

But the more or less exclusive embellishment of religious structures—never secular ones—with erotic sculptures, easily lent itself to mystical interpretations, an approach that continues to enjoy an enduring influence. If E.B. Havell decided that such 'indecency' served primarily to ward off the 'evil eye', Stella Kramrisch's painstaking schematic analysis of 'The Hindu Temple' tries to come to grips with the "limbs conjoined in close embrace" adorning the temple walls as the symbolic union of 'Purusha' and 'Prakriti', namely, "the state of being a couple" (Mithuna).[82] Ananda Coomaraswamy echoed similar sentiments while suggesting that the temple necessarily represented all forms of life and activities as manifestations of the deity; any neglect of the Erotic, therefore, was "tantamount to the denial of god".[83]

If the nationalist aesthetic that was forged in the early years of the twentieth century studiously averted its eyes from such ample evidence of sexual indulgence, carving a spiritualised (and sanitised) sphere for itself, embarrassed negotiations of this erotic heritage resonate even in contemporary scholarship.[84] Others have explained the sexual excesses on temple walls as signs of Tantric cult rituals. There are also more literal readings of the placement of such sculptures on wall surfaces and joints, such as Devangana Desai's assertion that the 'unions' are visual puns appropriate to the juncture walls of major temples and are part of "the intentional language of the sculptor".[85]

Insofar as they consider sculpture in isolation of other representations of Indian erotica, in painting, myth or poetry, such explanations are necessarily partial and even misleading. Not even the Indian nation state is able to offer an authoritative interpretation, and continues to be plagued by the contradictory consequences of exploiting this erotic past, while devising new protocols in the field of vision through censorship of various kinds. To the extent that these contradictions are resolved at all, it is by segmenting the receivers, namely those who are culturally equipped to view/consume erotic images, and those for whom such images are needlessly inciting.[86]

Meanwhile, feminist reinterpretations of this complex heritage are few and far between, some of them even disturbing in their appropriations of, say, homoerotic sculptures as testimony of bygone sexualities.[87] How literally may we read this rich and complex heritage? Can they be taken as signs of freedom and female desire? Malathi de Alwis suggests, for instance, that the Sigiriya Frescoes in neighbouring Sri Lanka are a celebration of women's 'erotic festivals' in painting.[88] Feminists must necessarily confront the possibility that such representations of male and female sexuality, whether in myth, stone or painting, tell us more about the fears and fantasies of their male creators or patrons, than the symmetries of male and female desire. Certainly, the complex world of Hindu myth and iconography reveals male fears about female sexualities much more explicitly than the subtler sculptural and pictorial accommodations of the male gaze. The dominant woman is dangerous in Hindu mythology, whether as erotic woman who drains the man of life, or as the maternal woman, who conjures up fears of incest.[89] What fit, then, may be assumed between this sculptural provenance, and the recurrent metaphors of Hindu myths, including the demonic (female) 'vagina dentata', as well as the (male) lolling, threatening tongue (phallus) of Kali,[90] both evoking fears of an excessive, threatening female sexuality?

Cinema and the Media

Whatever else might have been at work, no doubts have been raised about the artistic provenance of this sculptured past. When it comes to questions of our cinema, however, a whole gamut of preconceptions crowd in—its very popularity and commercialism being sufficient proof of its debased status.

Working out a more measured response to questions of gender and sexuality on the screen has proved particularly elusive for feminists. The first campaigns of the 1970s included the blackening of film hoardings, and picketing cinema halls where obscene films were being viewed. K. Lalita has described how the anti-obscenity demonstrations organised by the Progressive Organisation of Women—as early as January 1975 in Hyderabad—came "as a bolt from the blue for the public in the city".[91] These important initiatives against the ubiquity of sexual imagery for male consumption were launched elsewhere as well—in cities as far apart as Patna, Madras and Pune. Adopting a somewhat different tone, however, historians of the women's movement, Nandita Gandhi and Nandita Shah have lamented that "after eight years of tarring obscene posters, women's groups had not moved even an inch in [their] conceptualisation of obscenity and pornography."[92]

In one of the first discussions of the state's anti-obscenity laws, Shahnaz Anklesaria has sought to make a distinction between gender violence and the depiction of sex, since it is the former rather than the latter which should be the object of feminist protest. However, she then runs into the problem of ascribing causative powers to images of violence and sexual abuse, which, according to her, "spill over into reality" and result in bride-burning, sexual harassment and rape.[93] The regular film reviews provided by *Manushi* have worked within a different frame: the value of a film seems to lie in its ability to adhere to everyday realities. Thus, for instance, the 'shades of grey' masculinity of Om Puri in a film like *Ardh Satya* is preferable to that of the fantastic, invincible persona accruing to Amitabh Bachchan. Shyam Benegal's *Mandi* is questioned for depicting voluntary 'joyful' enslavement to prostitution, when it is well-known that most women go into this profession as victims of circumstance.[94] But if films are to be judged according to criteria of their approximation to the 'real', couldn't it then be argued that there is room for much more gender violence and sex on screen? Madhu Kishwar and Ruth Vanita's arguments against the amendments made to the Indecent Representation of Women

(Prohibition Bill) 1986 are more useful for having pointed out that the bill was so "ridiculously vague and all encompassing" in its definitions that it was clearly not meant to be an implementable law at all; in all likelihood it would only enhance the arbitrary powers of the State.[95]

Important first efforts were also made during the 1980s to theorise Indian cinema against the backdrop of 'film theory', a burgeoning body of work drawing on psychoanalysis, feminism and the tradition of Hollywood cinema. As a consequence, critics appear to have been overwhelmed by the norms of narrative realism set up by Hollywood, becoming forced into inadequate formulations about the Indian cinematic 'difference'. For Rosie Thomas, this difference became encapsulated in our demand for "emotion and spectacle", and the high tolerance of overt phantasy.[96]

In an early exploratory essay, Ravi Vasudevan has analysed the 'family romance' at work in Hindi films from the 1950s, where the cinematic narrative is structured by the conflictive authority of the father, and the successful establishment of the couple (interpreted as the fusion of mother and son). Depictions of female desire in these films set off a disturbance and become caught within characteristic oppositions—"good and evil, country and city, Indian and Western, purity and sexuality, duty and desire."[97] In his contribution to this volume, Vasudevan returns to Raj Kapoor's film *Awaara* in order to reinvestigate the sexuality in and of the film apparatus.

Compared to the 1980s, the '90s are witnessing fresh energies and approaches for analysing the institution of the cinema. Whatever their differences from one another, these analyses can be distinguished by being in a better position to investigate the theoretical and political challenges of cinema in different contexts, by their insistence on the complexity of popular culture in the production and resolution of ideology, and in their concern with the successful establishment of heterogeneous mass audiences. Though obscenity per se is not an issue, questions of sexuality are approached, as in a recent collection of essays in film studies, for what they might offer towards a conceptualisation of the current changes overtaking Indian society.[98]

Some of the explorations into the politics of censorship and banning might provide an indication of the kind of rethinking that is underway. Madhava Prasad's essay 'Cinema and the Desire for Modernity', for instance, makes an important distinction between representations of private sexual intimacy and the spectacle of the female body. The peculiar ban on kissing in Indian cinema (unlike the more familiar one against nudity) only becomes intelligible, in his view, by accounting for the lack of autonomy of the couple vis-a-vis the authority of the traditional family.[99] Where Vasudevan opts for a more formalist film criticism and the resolutions of sexual difference that it offers, Prasad's horizon is conditioned by the complex relationships between ideology and the changing contours of capitalism. Tejaswini Niranjana has pursued a different tack in order to investigate the banning of Mani Ratnam's '*Bombayi*' in Hyderabad on the grounds of offending Muslim sentiments. She takes issue with the liberalism of the film to indicate how the very focus on an eroticised Hindu-Muslim couple as the means for overcoming communal hatred could well be 'offensive' for its flawed view of what communalism is.[100]

Approaches to the cinema and to the media more generally have clearly traversed a significant distance from the first campaigns against obscenity. At the same time, old problems seem to persist even as new ones are being posed. Is obscenity no longer an issue, or is it rather, that the term may need to be abandoned in favour of a more nuanced sense of the multiple issues at stake in representations of sex, desire and violence? Mary John's paper in this volume tries to tackle this question, beginning with a discussion of the Miss World pageant held in Bangalore in 1996.

If it is imperative to examine the power of the image as precisely as possible (neither belittling nor exalting it), it is also necessary to follow up on the less obvious relationships between sexuality and the written word. While the valorisation of the Telugu writer Chalam is one example which is discussed in this collection, Susie Tharu's essay offers another. On the basis of an analysis of the Gujarati writer Saroj Pathak's journalism and fiction, Tharu reveals how sexuality emerges as a crucial site for divergent articulations of citizenship in the nation-state of the '50s and '60s.

Sexuality in Political Movements

If the nationalist movement in the past made attempts to harness sexual energies to the tasks of nation building, what of other political movements in modern India? What were the prohibitions, taboos, or ideas about sexual desire that animated movements for more total and democratic transformation, such as the left movement, or the non-Brahmin movement? In the Indian context, the interface between official Marxism and feminism has been a troubled one, even though Indian feminism in the post 1970s was grounded in Marxism. For its part, the left movement enabled a greater visibility for women in all spheres of political activity, including armed struggle. Yet the celebrated narratives of women in the Telengana movement show that male cadres had no hesitation in sending women out of the party on the mere suspicion of 'immorality'.[101] Here, as in other social movements, there was little attempt to rethink sexual relationships, so that male and usually upper caste transgressions were more readily tolerated, while women laboured under the terrible burden of upholding the moral order, even in conditions of guerilla warfare. U. Vindhya's essay seems to indicate that today there is a more productive dialogue between women within the radical left movement in Andhra and progressive writers such as Chalam, who have inspired women to challenge structures of authority through both political activity and theoretical critique. However, a recent attack on feminist poetry in Telugu for being pornographic or 'blue', launched by literary critics including those on the left, would indicate that questions regarding the appropriate subject matter of women's writing remain unresolved and controversial.

A radical rethinking of the relations between men and

women, Anandhi S. argues, was also a feature of the non-Brahmin movement. A leader of such iconic stature as E.V. Ramaswami Naicker (Periyar) was able to mark a distinct shift in the terms of the debate on contraception. What distinctive features of the politics of sexuality are rendered visible by its location within an anti-casteist frame, unlike the writings of Chalam or those inspired by him, where such issues remain largely occluded? In a recent paper, V. Geeta has suggested that Periyar campaigned vigorously against Gandhi's convoluted politics of piety and sacrifice, while reworking the very spaces of civil society Gandhi had laid claim to—"the interlinked realms of consciousness, communication, sexuality and identity."[102] One of the significant practices to emerge out of the Self-Respect Movement was the Self-Respect marriage, a social contract animated by a vision of chosen reciprocity, based on mutual desire and, especially, on reason. But the interventions of Gandhi, Chalam and Periyar also give us cause to pause, and to ask: what were the conditions of possibility of a female figure, whether as political activist or as writer, being able to command the kind of authority that these men have enjoyed in re-envisaging fundamental social relationships and actively retailing them? Would a feminist re-imagining be recognisably different?

Alternate Sexualities

Perhaps because of all the uncertainties affecting approaches towards the subject of 'sex', whether within social movements or as a field of investigation, the dominant and exclusionary structures of heterosexuality (as distinct from patriarchy or gender) have rarely been a focus of explicit critique. As in other parts of the world, India has seen a growing lesbian and gay movement, one which has also come to receive its share of media attention.

In early 1988, when two policewomen in Madhya Pradesh decided to get married, the news was picked up by the press and created something of a furore. This was perhaps the first occasion when lesbianism became a matter of widespread public debate, and, in such a way, that the issue could not so easily be dismissed as yet another Western aberration. As a political event, however, it also raised troubling questions for the women's movement and for a fledgling gay and lesbian politics, whose relationship to each other was far from clear. An important article highlighted the "elaborate apparatus of explication" evident in most reports of the marriage, which explained away the decision of the two women in terms of their suffering and victimisation at the hands of a patriarchal society, never allowing for the possibility of an affirmative, let alone sexual, relationship.[103]

Over the last decade, the gay and lesbian movement has grown in visibility, with a mushrooming of groups and publications in India, and among South Asians in the West. Legal activism has extended from ongoing efforts to change the discriminatory legislation embodied in the anti-sodomy laws, to proposals to amend the Special Marriages Act to permit same-sex marriages. In a recent overview, Sherry Joseph has tried to plot the emergence of the identity politics of the gay and lesbian movement in its relations with similar movements in the West, as well as the specific dilemmas faced by lesbians within a movement that is male-dominated.[104]

Feminists such as Flavia Agnes are among the spokespersons of the women's movement who have gone on record to claim that "lesbianism is an integral part of the women's movement for liberation. It constitutes an important area of their struggle against the exploitative principles and institutions of patriarchy."[105] Hostility, if not homophobia, however, is not uncommon, as was witnessed when the Vice-President of the National Federation of Indian Women appealed to the Prime Minister in 1994 to cancel permission to host a South Asian Gay Conference in Mumbai. In a widely circulated and endorsed letter of protest against the Vice-President's demand, the women's organisation Jagori stated that it was particularly disturbing that someone who had worked so actively in the women's movement should make virulent and uninformed public statements against homosexuality, notwithstanding the possible class and gender biases of the conference organisers.[106]

For its part, the media has revealed its changeling role in the business of representing gay and lesbian issues. The 1990s have seen a spate of newspaper and magazine articles that, on the face of it, seem to be taking lesbian identities and sexual choices seriously. A second look, however, would reveal that these pieces have managed to evade being homophobic by exoticising and essentialising their theme; however sympathetic the portrayal, lesbians become a breed apart.[107] With films like *Dayra*, *Tamanna*, and *Fire*, gay themes and lesbian relationships have entered the portals of respectable art cinema. In the film *Bombay*, a hijra provides protection to one of the twin sons of the Hindu hero and Muslim heroine during the communal riots, and becomes the mouthpiece for the impossibility of identity. But in other box office hits such as *Hum Aap Ke Hai Kaun*, Giti Thadani has pointed out that whereas the hero is able to cross-dress and successfully access the women-only space that precedes the wedding, a 'butch-looking woman' is denied entry, and humiliated by the transvestite male.[108]

As debates within and across gay and lesbian organisations, the women's movement and a broader public gradually gain ground, scholarly initiatives are also in evidence. A longstanding theme to have exercised scholars both at home and abroad concerns the status of the hijras. In Serena Nanda's ethnographic study of this community, hijras are homosexual men who take on a female persona, living apart from mainstream society under the leadership of a guru, while remaining economically dependent as traditional performers, sex-workers or by receiving alms. In spite of all the evidence of their marginality, Nanda believes that, since "Hinduism ... has always been more able to accommodate gender variation, ambiguity and contradictions" (in contrast to the West), hijras in effect have a place in Indian society as a viable and recognised "third gender".[109] Others have had reason to dispute this view of our great and ancient 'tolerance'.[110]

In part, perhaps, because of unflagging accusations that gay and lesbian sexualities could only be western imports, history has become a crucial site for retrieving an erased past. Ancient texts, medieval court customs, epics and Tantric rituals have been investigated for their representations and descriptions of homosexual acts and relationships. However, difficult questions of methodology also crowd in, since the interpretative frameworks adopted cannot but be modern ones. Thus, for instance, Giti Thadani's important study of lesbian sexuality constructs a narrative of ancient "autonomous gynefocal cosmological traditions" centred in lesbian relations, which were disrupted by the advent of Islam and British colonialism, and lost as Hinduism became more monolithic and heterosexual.[111] Such grand historical accounts run into genuine dangers, however unintended, in a field underdetermined by evidence and severely overdetermined by current agendas, including those of the Hindu Right. But this is not to suggest that the archives of history—ancient, medieval and modern—should therefore be relinquished.[112]

From the perspective of this volume, it is not enough to provide an account of 'alternate sexualities' that closes with a readiness to acknowledge the Indianness of gays and lesbians. (Sometimes this 'Indianness' is posed in terms of justifying the absence of a more strongly demarcated public identity politics compared to the West.) As Nivedita Menon has argued, "to consider homosexuality as an 'alternative' lifestyle is to leave unquestioned heterosexuality as a norm."[113] Rather than endeavour to make room for more and more sexual identities, Menon wonders whether simply expanding the domain of the natural is a sufficient strategy for destabilising the dominant sexual order. What would be required to denaturalise, then, the sedimented structures of our bodies and desires, such that the taken-for-granted aspects of our sexual economies are open to question?

Conclusion

The essays in this collection seek to extend, revise or argue against existing conceptions of the 'sexual', and from diverse perspectives. The prominent position occupied by sexuality in the self-understanding of the West has prompted at least one theorist into the belief that "the lyricism and religiosity that long accompanied the revolutionary project have, in Western industrial societies, been largely carried over to sex."[114] It has neither been our brief to determine how close some of the essays might be to reproducing such a faith, nor to suggest a counter-thesis concerning our non-western character. Though the determining force of sexuality has not been calibrated with any precision, this is not because some other reality is understood to be more pressing. By concentrating on certain specific instances when sexuality emerges as a scandal, an apparatus of power, a form of violence, or a sign of freedom, as the case may be, many essays have, instead, drawn attention to questions of context and the mediating links between issues as key modes for grasping the significance of their engagements within this field.

One of the more interesting aspects of the collection as a whole, we feel, is the overwhelming desire to address our *present* and its history. Though our introduction could be questioned for dwelling so long on colonial/national frames and moments, this is not a major theme in the essays that follow. Only three of the essays—by Kumkum Roy, Samita Sen and Anandhi S.— have had reason to direct more exclusive attention to earlier times, whether this be the precolonial and colonial contexts of the *Kamasutra*, or the considerably more recent histories of nineteenth century Bengal and early twentieth century Madras. Other historically oriented essays weave across time with an explicit anchor in the contemporary—these include Tejaswini Niranjana's discussion of the politics of race and sexuality in Trinidad, Uma Chakravarti's reconstruction of the narrative resources available to the television serial *Chanakya*, and U.Vindhya's account of the legacy of Chalam in Andhra today.

Two essays, by Susie Tharu and Ravi Vasudevan, shed unusual light on the post-independence decades of the 1950s and '60s, by engaging with the media of writing and the cinema respectively. The remaining essays, by Kalpana Ram, V. Geeta,

Prem Chowdhry and Mary John, are more fully absorbed by the problems of analysing sexuality and modernity in contemporary India—for young women "coming of age" in rural Tamilnadu, for the perpetrators of domestic violence in a city like Madras, for the rural-urban caste-classes of Haryana, and for the more cosmopolitan fractions of the 'new middle class'.

Given the wide reach of the essays, both regionally and socially, what generalisations and distinctions can be drawn? At a conceptual level, one might point to a certain open-endedness that is evident in a field which is neither locked within adversarial stances, nor over-determined by other concerns. Is sexuality a 'problem' for some groups, classes or regions more than others? It has been our hunch that the middle classes—as distinct from those above or below them—are especially prone to the fantasies, obsessions and prohibitions commonly associated with sexuality, and that northern India would be more circumscribed by experiences of shame, dishonour, transgression and violence than the south. But such assessments remain somewhat premature, too prone, moreover, to sentimental recuperations of freer, unrepressed zones or peoples. In a field still so undeveloped, we may be better off, therefore, staying with the specifics of the scenes staged in the essays, testing for ourselves how conceptions of patriarchy are analytically and politically enriched—and questioned—by the lens of sexuality provided by the contributors. To take some examples, in what ways might one read Chalam's women characters as bearers of sexual liberation, the break down of Saroj Pathak's ladies' tailor, the scandal of East Indian chutney-soca music in Trinidad, or Periyar's call to end the regulation of desire? What aspects of our received knowledges of male sexual aggression and female suffering are deepened, what must be thought anew?

This introduction was written in tandem with the essays of the volume. We are grateful to Jasodhara Bagchi, Indira Choudhury, Uma Chakravarti, Kumkum Roy, Samita Sen, Susie Tharu and V. Geeta for their comments—both critical and encouraging—on an earlier version.

Notes

1. Michel Foucault *The History of Sexuality: An Introduction,* New York: Peregrine Books, 1984, p. 18.

2. There has been a significant stirring of collective, scholarly interest in the field of sexuality in the last few years. Some efforts, however, have been unable to shake free of the paradigm of social reform efforts and the role of the state in defining, advancing and controlling the position of women in the modern period. See, for instance, *Social Reform, Sexuality and the State,* ed. Patricia Uberoi, New Delhi: Sage, 1996.

   Recent workshops and seminars include 'Gender Constructions, and Alternate Sexualities', December 1993, (organised by Sakhi and NAZ at the Indian Social Institute, Delhi), 'Femininity, the Female Body and Sexuality', (Nehru Memorial Library, Delhi, November 1994, and published under the title *Embodiment: Essays on Gender and Identity,* (ed.) Meenakshi Thapan, Delhi: Oxford University Press, 1997) and a sub-theme on sexuality and the family at the VIIth meeting of the Indian Association of Women's Studies, Jaipur, December 1995.

   Embodied Violence: Communalising Women's Sexuality in South Asia, Kumari Jayawardena and Malathi de Alwis (eds.) New Delhi: Kali for Women, 1996, despite its title, remains for the most part a general history of women in South Asia. Few of the articles included in the justly renowned volume *Recasting Women: Essays on Colonial History,* Kumkum Sangari and Sudesh Vaid (eds.), New Delhi: Kali for Women, 1989, focus on questions of sexuality in modern India.

3. See *The Compact Edition of the Oxford English Dictionary,* Volume II, Oxford: Oxford University Press, 1971, p. 582.

4. Jonathan Ned Katz, 'The Invention of Heterosexuality', *Socialist Review,* Vol. 20.1, January–March 1990, pp. 7–33.

5. See especially, Sigmund Freud and Joseph Breuer, *Studies on Hysteria,* London: Pelican Library, Vol. 3, 1974; Sigmund Freud 'Three Essays on the Theory of Sexuality' (1905), 'Some Psychological Consequences of the Anatomical Distinctions between the Sexes' (1925), 'On Female Sexuality' (1931) reproduced in *On Sexuality, Three Essays on the Theory of Sexuality and Other Works,* London: The Pelican Freud Library, Vol. 7, (ed.) James Strachey and Angela Richards, 1977; and 'Femininity' (1933)

in *New Introductory Lectures on Psychoanalysis*, London: Pelican Library, Vol. 2, 1973.

6. Susan Brownmiller, *Against Our Will: Men, Women and Rape*, New York: Bantam Books, 1976, p. 1. See also Kate Millet, *Sexual Politics*, New York: Doubleday, 1969; Alice Echols *Daring to be Bad: Radical Feminism in America 1967–1975*; Minneapolis: University of Minnesota Press, 1989.

7. Early well-known texts included Luce Irigaray, *Speculum of the Other Woman*, trans. by Gillian C. Gill, Ithaca: Cornell University Press, 1985 (orig. French publication 1974); Juliet Mitchell, *Psychoanalysis and Feminism: Freud, Reich, Laing and Women*; New York: Vintage, 1975 (orig. 1974); Laura Mulvey, 'Visual Pleasure and Narrative Cinema' *Screen*, Autumn 1975, Vol. 16.3, pp. 6–18; Jacqueline Rose, *Sexuality in the Field of Vision*, London: Verso, 1986.

   Laura Mulvey's work, amongst others, was to become instrumental in setting up the field of feminist film theory, an enormous body of work which brought together feminism, psychoanalysis and Hollywood cinema, and where female sexuality functioned as a unique point of focus.

8. Toril Moi, 'Psychoanalysis, Feminism and Politics: A Conversation with Juliet Mitchell', *South Atlantic Quarterly*, Vol. 93.4, Fall 1994, p. 931.

9. Michel Foucault, *The Uses of Pleasure: The History of Sexuality, Volume Two*, New York: Pantheon Books, 1985; and *The Care of the Self: The History of Sexuality, Volume Three*, New York: Vintage Books, 1986.

   As he explains, 'the object was to learn to what extent the effort to think one's own history can free thought from what it silently thinks, and so enable it to think differently.' (Foucault, *The Uses of Pleasure*, p. 9).

10. For some early responses see Martha Vicinus, 'Sexuality and Power: A Review of Current Work in the History of Sexuality', *Feminist Studies*, Vol. 8.1, Spring 1982, pp. 133–55; and Teresa de Lauretis, *Technologies of Gender: Essays on Theory, Film and Fiction*, Bloomington: Indiana University Press, 1986.

11. The classic statement in this regard is Catherine MacKinnon's: "Sexuality is to feminism what work is to marxism: that which is most one's own, yet most taken away... Heterosexuality is its structure, gender and family its congealed forms, sex roles its

qualities generalized to social persona, reproduction a consequence, and control its issue." MacKinnon, 'Feminism, Marxism, Method, and the State: An agenda for theory', in Nannerl O. Keohane, Michelle Z. Rosaldo and Barbara C. Gelpi (eds.), *Feminist Theory: A Critique of Ideology*, Chicago: Chicago University Press, 1981, pp. 1–2.

12. See especially the introduction to Carol Vance (ed.), *Pleasure and Danger: Exploring Female Sexuality*, Boston: Routledge and Kegan Paul, 1984.

13. B. Ruby Rich, 'Review Essay: Feminism and Sexuality in the 1980s', *Feminist Studies*, Vol. 12.3, Fall 1986, p. 558.

14. At least one effort in this direction has not been particularly successful, if only because the editors do not seem to know what to make of nationalism: Andrew Parker, Mary Russo, Doris Summer and Patricia Yaeger (eds.), *Nationalism and Sexualities*, New York and London: Routledge, 1992.

   More useful, if somewhat preliminary, have been attempts to map the enmeshed histories of sex and race. Indeed, a major shortcoming in Foucault's work has been his complete blindness to race and colonialism in the very constitution of sexual practices and discourses. See, for instance, Nancy Leys Stepan, 'Race and Gender: The role of analogy in science', in David Theo Goldberg (ed.), *Anatomy of Racism*, Minneapolis: University of Minnesota Press, 1990, pp. 38–57; Sander L. Gilman, 'Black Bodies, White Bodies: Toward an iconography of female sexuality in late nineteenth century art, medicine and literature', *Critical Inquiry*, Vol. 12.1, 1985, pp. 204–42; Donna Haraway, *Primate Visions: Gender, Race, and Nature in the World of Modern Science*, New York and London: Routledge, 1989.

15. Among the many efforts to evaluate and analyse the Anita Hill–Clarence Thomas hearings and its aftermath, see especially Toni Morrison (ed.), *Race-ing Justice, En-gendering Power: Essays on Anita Hill, Clarence Thomas, and the Construction of Social Reality*, New York: Pantheon Books, 1992. As Morrison points out in her introduction, 'as is almost always the case, the site of the exorcism of critical national issues was situated in the miasma of black life and inscribed on the bodies of black people.' (p. x).

16. Judith Butler, *Bodies that Matter: On the Discursive Limits of 'Sex'*, London and New York: Routledge, 1993.

17. This description of our relation to western theories comes from

Madhava Prasad's discussion of the problems besetting current analyses of Indian cinema. (See Madhava Prasad, *The Ideology of Hindi Cinema: A Historical Construction*, Delhi: Oxford University Press, 1998.) For an extended discussion of issues related to the westernness of theory in the context of feminism, see Mary E. John, *Discrepant Dislocations: Feminism, Theory and Postcolonial Histories*, Berkeley: University of California and Delhi: Oxford University Press, 1996.

18. Ashis Nandy, 'Woman versus Womanliness in India: An essay in social and political psychology', in *At the Edge of Psychology*, Delhi: Oxford University Press, 1980; and Sudhir Kakar, *Intimate Relations: Exploring Indian Sexuality*, New Delhi: Penguin Books, 1989.

19. Susie Tharu and K. Lalita, 'Introduction', *Women Writing in India, 600 B.C. to the Present, Volume I: 600 B.C. to the Early 20th Century*, Delhi: Oxford University Press, 1993, p. 1–12.

20. Law Commission of India, 1979, *Eighty First Report on Hindu Widows Remarriage Act of 1856*, Delhi: Govt. of India, 1979.

21. In an early essay, Veena Das has contrasted the structurally inferior positions of Indian women to their access to certain forms of cultural power, such as those associated with female sexuality in Hindu thought. In her concluding remarks, Das alludes to 'the isolation of women in the narrow world of domestic life and the use of women as primarily sex symbols' in the West (p. 145) to account for the rise of a political movement to combat women's condition. Das' barely veiled implication seems to be that feminism, therefore, belongs only there. (Das, 'Indian Women: Work, power, status' in *Indian Women from Purdah to Modernity*, (ed.) B.R. Nanda, Delhi: Radiant Publishers, 1976, pp. 129–45.)

22. See for instance, Ritu Menon and Kamla Bhasin, 'Abducted Women, the State and Questions of Honour: Three perspectives on the recovery operation in post-partition India'; and Kalpana Kannabiran, 'Rape and the Construction of Communal Identity' both in Jayawardena and Alwis (eds.), *Embodied Violence*, op. cit., pp. 1–41.

23. Radha Kumar, *The History of Doing: An Illustrated Account of Movements for Women's Rights and Feminism in India, 1800–1990*, New Delhi: Kali for Women, 1993, p. 202.

24. 'A Report: Fifth National Conference of Women's Movements' (January 1994) esp. pp. 57–59. See also Meenakshi Thapan,

'Images of the Body and Sexuality in Women's Narratives on Oppression in the Home', *Economic and Political Weekly*, Vol. 30.43, October 28, 1995, pp. 72–80; and *Female Sexuality: A Journey Within...*, New Delhi, Sakshi, 1997. The booklet brought out by Sakshi, meant to initiate discussion among young, urban, middle class women, relies overwhelmingly on a notion of female sexuality as shrouded in 'taboos, secrecy, shame, guilt and doubt', which has to be nudged into a more 'positive acceptance'. (p. 25)

25. Flavia Agnes, 'The Anti-Rape Compaign: The struggle and the setback', in Chhaya Datar (ed.), *The Struggle Against Violence*, Calcutta: Stree, 1993, pp. 99–150; and Flavia Agnes, 'Violence in the Family: Wife beating', in Rehana Ghadially (ed.), *Women in Indian Society*, New Delhi: Sage, 1988, pp. 151–66.

26. Gabriele Dietrich, 'Discussing Sexuality', in *Reflections on the Women's Movement in India: Religion, Ecology, Development*, New Delhi: New Horizon Books, 1992, p. 39.

27. Hyderabad Women's Group, *Savaalaksha Sandehaalu: Streelu Arogya Samasyulu*, Hyderabad: Stree Shakti Sanghatana, 1991.

28. See Ann L. Stoler, 'Making Empire Respectable: The politics of race and sexual morality in 20th century colonial cultures', *American Ethnologist*, Vol. 16.4, 1989, pp. 634–60.

29. Mrinalini Sinha, *Colonial Masculinity: The 'Manly Englishman' and the 'Effeminate Bengali' in the Late Nineteenth Century*, New Delhi: Kali for Women, 1997.

30. Kenneth Ballhatchet, *Race, Sex and Class under the Raj: Imperial Attitudes and Policies and their Critics, 1793–1905*, London: Weidenfeld and Nicholson, 1980.

31. Saskia Kersenboom Story, *Nityasumangali*, Delhi, 1987; Frederique Apffel Marglin, *Wives of the God King: The Rituals of the Devadasis of Puri*, Delhi: Oxford University Press, 1985; Kay K. Jordan, 'Devadasi Reform: Driving the priestesses or the prostitutes out of Hindu temples?' in Robert D. Baird (ed.), *Religion and Law in Independent India*, Delhi: Manohar, 1993, pp. 257–78. Also Srividya Natarajan, 'Another Stage in the Life of a Nation: Sadir, Bharatanatyam and feminist theory', Ph.D. Dissertation, University of Hyderabad, 1997.

32. Amrit Srinivasan, 'Reform and Revival: The devadasi and her dance', *Economic and Political Weekly*, Vol. 20.44, November 2, 1985, pp. 1869–76.

33. Kalpana Kannabiran, 'Judiciary, Social Reform and Debate on

"Religious Prostitution" in Colonial India', *Economic and Political Weekly*, Vol. 30.43, October 28 1995, pp. 59–71.

34. Janaki Nair, 'The Devadasi, Dharma and the State', *Economic and Political Weekly*, Vol. 31.50, December 1994, pp. 3157–68.

35. Sumanta Banerjee, 'Marginalisation of Women's Popular Culture in Nineteenth Century Bengal' in Sangari and Vaid (eds.), *Recasting Women*, op. cit., pp. 127–79.

36. Sharmila Rege, 'The Hegemonic Appropriation of Sexuality: The case of the Lavani performer of Maharashtra', in Uberoi (ed.) *Social Reform, Sexuality and the State*, op. cit., pp. 23–38.

37. Veena Talwar Oldenburg, 'Lifestyle as Resistance: The case of the courtesans of Lucknow', *Feminist Studies* 2, 1990, pp. 259–97.

38. Anandhi S., 'Representing Devadasis: 'Dasigal Mosavalai' as a radical text', *Economic and Political Weekly* Annual Number, March 1991, pp. 739–46.

39. Dagmar Engels, *Beyond Purdah? Women in Bengal 1890–1939*, Delhi: Oxford University Press, 1996, p. 84, 85.

40. Ibid., emphasis added.

41. Tanika Sarkar, 'Colonial Lawmaking and Lives/Deaths of Indian Women: Different readings of law and community', in Ratna Kapur (ed.) *Feminist Terrains in Legal Domains: Interdisciplinary Essays on Women and Law in India*, Delhi: Kali for Women, 1996, pp. 210–42.

42. Udaya Kumar, 'Self, Body and Inner Sense: Some Reflections on Sree Narayana Guru and Kumaran Asan', paper presented at the Workshop 'Social Criticism, Cultural Creativity and the Contemporary Directives of Transformation', MIDS, Madras, December 1996, and forthcoming in *Studies in History*.

43. Prabhu Mohapatra, 'Restoring the Family: Wife murders and the making of a sexual contract for Indian immigrant labour in the British Caribbean colonies 1860–1920', *Studies in History*, Vol. 11.2 (n.s.), 1995, pp. 225–60.

44. Janaki Nair, *Women and Law in Colonial India*, Delhi: Kali for Women, 1996, pp. 99–104.

45. Nirmala Banerjee, 'Working Women in Colonial Bengal: Modernization and marginalization', in *Recasting Women*, pp. 269–301.

46. Prem Chowdhry, *The Veiled Women: Shifting Gender Equations in Rural Haryana 1880–1990*, Delhi: Oxford University Press, 1994. See also Radhika Singha, 'Making the Domestic More Domestic:

Criminal law and the head of the household, 1772–1843', *Indian Economic and Social History Review* (IESHR), Vol. 33.3, July-September 1996.

47. Ballhatchet, *Race, Sex and Class under the Raj,* op. cit.

48. Janaki Nair, 'From Devadasi Reform to SITA: Transforming sex-work in Mysore, 1892–1937', *National Law School Journal* Special Issue, 1993; Pauline Rule, 'Prostitution in Calcutta, 1880–1940: Pattern of recruitment' in Gail Pearson and Lenore Manderson, (eds.), *Class Ideology and Women in Asian Societies,* Hong Kong, 1987.

49. Carole Pateman, *The Sexual Contract,* Stanford: Stanford University Press, 1988, Chapter 7. For a recent consideration of the links between prostitute rights, legal reform and consequences for feminist politics, see Rajeswari Sunder Rajan, 'The Prostitution Question(s): (Female) agency, sexuality and work', in Ratna Kapur (ed.), *Feminist Terrains in Legal Domains,* op. cit., pp. 122–49.

50. Joseph Alter, 'The Celibate Wrestler: Sexual chaos, embodied balance and competitive politics in North India', in Uberoi (ed.) *State, Sexuality and Social Reform,* op. cit., pp. 109–34.

51. See the discussion of S. Mahendran vs. The Secretary Travancore Devaswom Board, Thiruvananthapuram, in Ratna Kapur and Brenda Cossman *Subversive Sites,* Delhi: Sage, 1966, pp. 215–16.

52. See for instance, Indira Choudhury, 'Spiritual Masculinity and Swami Vivekananda', in *The Frail Hero and Virile History: Gender and the Politics of Culture in Colonial Bengal,* Delhi: Oxford University Press, 1998, pp. 120–49.

53. Sudhir Kakar, 'Gandhi and Women', in *Intimate Relations,* op. cit., pp. 85–86, 92.

54. See also Pat Caplan, 'Celibacy as a Solution? Mahatma Gandhi and Brahmacharya', in Caplan (ed.) *The Cultural Construction of Sexuality* London: Tavistock, 1987, pp. 270–95.

55. Cited in Kakar, *Intimate Relations,* op. cit., pp. 106–07.

56. See Emily Kearns, 'Indian Myth', in *The Feminist Comparison to Mythology,* (ed.) Carolyn Larrington, London: Harper Collins, 1992, pp. 204–05.

57. The example of Sadhvi Rithambara, who is able to draw upon her religious authority as a celibate, but in order to incite Hindu men to violence against Muslims, often in the most sexually explicit terms, indicates just how complex the play of power, sexuality, and agency can be. For an astute analysis, see Kumkum Sangari,

'Consent, Agency and the Rhetorics of Incitement', *Economic and Political Weekly*, Vol. 28.18, 1 May 1993, pp. 867–82.

In a recent article, Madhu Kishwar has proposed female celibacy as the only effective strategy for women, mainly against profligate husbands, since it is the sexually chaste woman, in direct contrast to the promiscuous one, who can command respect. The entire trend of the essay, which draws from individual examples, is one of suspicion toward sexual activity per se. (Madhu Kishwar 'Women, Sex and Marriage: Restraint as a feminine strategy', *Manushi*, no. 99, 1997, pp. 23–36.) Rather than question sexual norms, Kishwar's essay first magnifies sexuality and its potency, in order then to claim superiority for those who can claim control over its power dynamics versus the ones who appear helplessly caught within its web. It is the very framing of sexuality, and the assignment of positions within it, that are therefore problematic.

58. Supriya Guha, 'The Unwanted Pregnancy in Colonial Bengal' *Indian Economic and Social History Review*, Vol. 33.4, 1996, 403–36, esp. pp. 416–19.

59. Alaka Malwade Basu, *Culture, the Status of Women and Demographic Behaviour*, Oxford: Clarendon Press, 1992, pp. 77–82.

60. As a percentage of total sterilisations, tubectomies stood at 66 per cent in 1956 when the programme began. After declining significantly in the 1960s and early 70's as the programme expanded (falling as low as 10 per cent in 1968), tubectomies shot up after the Emergency to reach the figure of 92 per cent by 1990. (Department of Family Welfare, *Family Welfare Programme in India*, New Delhi: Government of India, 1991, p. 190.)

61. For instance, Mohan Rao, 'An Imagined Reality: Malthusianism, neo-Malthusianism, and population myth', *Economic and Political Weekly*, Vol. 29.5, January 24, 1994, PE 40–52. Deepa Dhanraj's film *Something like a War*, includes discussions about sexuality amongst rural women, although her later film *The Legacy of Malthus* places far more emphasis on the critique of Malthusian policies.

62. V. Geeta and Padmini Swaminathan, 'Politics of Population and Development', *Economic and Political Weekly*, Vol. 29.38, September 17, 1994, pp. 2470–72. See, however, Susie Tharu and Tejaswini Niranjana, 'Problems for a Contemporary Theory of Gender', *Social Scientist*, Vol. 22.3–4, March-April 1994, pp. 93–117. On the politics of demography as a discipline, see Susan Greenhalgh, 'The Social Construction of Population Science:

An intellectual, institutional and political history of twentieth century demography', *Comparative Studies in Society and History*, Vol. 38.1, January 1996, pp. 26–66.

63. For example, Padmini Swaminathan, 'The Failures of Success? An analysis of Tamilnadu's recent demographic experience', MIDS working paper No. 141.

64. Meera K. and Anandhi S., 'Report of the Workshop on Gender and Women's Health', mimeo, Madras: IWID and Health Watch 1996, esp. pp. 11–19.

65. K. Saradamoni, 'Changing Land Relations and Women' in *Women and Social Transformation*, Delhi: Concept Publishing House, 1982; K.N. Panikkar, 'Land Control, Ideology and Reform: A study of the changes in family organisation and marriage system in Kerala', *Indian Historical Review*, Vol. 4.1, July 1977.

66. G. Arunima, 'Multiple Meanings: Changing conceptions of matrilineal kinship in nineteenth and twentieth century Malabar', *IESHR*, Vol. 33.3, July-September 1996, pp. 283–308.

67. A.K. Ramanujan, 'The Indian Oedipus', in *Oedipus, A Folklore Casebook*, (ed.) Lowell Edmunds and Alan Dundes, New York: Garland Publishing Company, 1983, pp. 234–61.

68. Gananath Obeyesekere, *The Work of Culture: Symbolic Transformation in Psychoanalysis and Anthropology*, Chicago: Chicago University Press, 1990, p. 77.

69. Kalpana Ram, 'The Female Body of Possession: A feminist phenomenological perspective on rural Tamil women's experiences', Anveshi, Hyderabad, February 1996 and forthcoming in Bhargavi Davar (ed.), *Perspectives: Women in Mental Distress*. See also *Mukkuvar Women: Gender, Hegemony and Capitalist Transformation in a South Indian Fishing Community*, Delhi: Kali for Women, 1992.

70. Karin Kapadia, *Siva and Her Sisters: Gender, Caste and Class in Rural South India*, Delhi: Oxford University Press, 1996, especially p. 169.

71. K. Gnanambal, *Religious Institutions and Caste Panchayats in South India*, Delhi: Anthropological Survey of India, 1973. Gnanambal's cases clearly point to innumerable sexual transgressions by women of lower castes (pp. 27–28) which generate enormous anxieties about the very maintenance of caste ways, although there is acknowledgement that among communities such as the Yadavas or

the Vishwakarmas, there are more pressing everyday anxieties than the policing of female morals (p. 29).

72. An exception would be André Béteille's essay, 'Race, Caste and Gender', reprinted in *Society and Politics in India*, Delhi: Oxford University Press, 1996, which is discussed in Mary John's contribution to this volume.

73. Samata Sanghatana, 'Upper Caste Violence: Report from Chunduru carnage', *Economic and Political Weekly*, Vol. 26.36, September 7, 1991; Vasanth Kannabiran and Kalpana Kannabiran, 'Caste and Gender: Understanding the dynamics of power and violence', *Economic and Political Weekly*, Vol. 26.37, 1991, pp. 2130–33; Tharu and Niranjana, 'Problems for a Contemporary Theory of Gender', op. cit.

74. There is a growing body of research by feminist scholars on questions of laws and social reform: see Nair, *Women and Law in Colonial India* for a summary. See also Tanika Sarkar, 'Rhetoric against Age of Consent: Resisting colonial reason and death of a child wife', *Economic and Political Weekly*, Vol. 28.36, 1993; Dagmar Engels, *Beyond Purdah?*, Oxford and SOAS: Oxford University Press, 1996; Geraldine Forbes, 'Women and Modernity: The issue of child marriage in India', *Women's Studies International Quarterly*, 1979; Janaki Nair, 'Prohibited Marriage: State protection and the child wife', pp. 157–86 and Uma Chakravarti, 'Wifehood, Widowhood and Adultery: Female sexuality surveillance and the state in 18th century Maharashtra', pp. 3–22 both in Uberoi (ed.), *Social Reform, Sexuality and the State*, op. cit.

75. Ranajit Guha, 'Chandra's Death' in R. Guha (ed.) *Subaltern Studies V*, Delhi: Oxford University Press, 1987.

76. Veena Das, 'Sexual Violence, Discursive Formations and the State', *Economic and Political Weekly* Special Number, Vol. 31.35–37, 1996, p. 2416; see also, Ratna Kapur and Brenda Cossman, *Subversive Sites: Feminist Engagements with the Law*, op. cit.

77. Kannabiran, 'Rape and the Construction of Communal Identity' in Jayawardena and Alwis (eds.) *Embodied Violence*, op. cit.

78. Kapur and Cossman, *Subversive Sites*, op. cit., pp. 105–06.

79. Patricia Uberoi, 'When is a Marriage not a Marriage? Sex sacrament and contract in Hindu marriage' in Uberoi (ed.) *Social Reform, Sexuality and the State*, op. cit., pp. 319–46.

80. For instance, lower castes of Mysore argued that their law ways usually permitted widow remarriage making it unnecessary for the

state to prohibit child marriage. Nair, 'Prohibited Marriage' in Uberoi, (ed.) *Social Reform, Sexuality and the State*, op. cit.

81. As in Veena Poonacha, 'Redefining Gender Relationships: The imprint of the colonial state on the Coorg Kodava norms of marriage and sexuality' in Patricia Uberoi (ed.) *Social Reform, Sexuality and the State*, op. cit., pp. 39–64.

82. Stella Kramrisch, *The Hindu Temple*, Calcutta: University of Calcutta, 1946, pp. 346–48.

83. Ananda Coomaraswamy, *Introduction to Indian Art*, Madras: Theosophical Publishing House, 1956.

84. Thus Shobita Punja strongly favours interpretations that suggest sexual union as a metaphor for the bond between human and God, reading Khajuraho as a celebration of the divine union of Shiva and Parvati. See her *Divine Ecstasy: The Story of Khajuraho*, Delhi: Viking, 1992.

85. Devangana Desai, *Erotic Sculpture of India: A Socio-Cultural Study*, Delhi: Tata McGraw-Hill, 1985, second edition, pp. 135–37.

86. The recent uproar over the use of Mohenjo Daro figurines in the 1997 Delhi Diary put out by the DTTDC clearly reveals this.

87. An example of this trend is found in the work of Giti Thadani *Sakhiyani: Lesbian Desire in Ancient and Modern India*, London: Cassell, 1996, which we discuss in the section below on alternate sexualities.

88. Malathi de Alwis, 'Sexuality in the Field of Vision: The discursive clothing of the Sigiriya frescoes', in Jayawardena and de Alwis (eds.) *Embodied Violence*, op. cit., pp. 89–112.

89. O'Flaherty, *Women, Androgynes and other Mythical Beasts*, p. 77.

90. Wendy Doniger, 'Sexual Masquerade in Hindu Myths: Aspects of the transmission of knowledge in ancient India' in Nigel Crook (ed.), *The Transmission of Knowledge in South Asia: Religion, History and Politics*, Delhi: Oxford University Press, 1996, p. 46.

91. K. Lalita, 'Women in Revolt: A historical analysis of the progressive organisation of women in Andhra Pradesh', in *Women's Struggles and Strategies*, (ed.) Saskia Wieringa, Aldershot: Gower, 1988, pp. 61–62.

92. Nandita Gandhi and Nandita Shah, *The Issues at Stake: Theory and Practice in the Contemporary Women's Movement in India*, New Delhi: Isis International and Kali for Women, 1992, p. 13.

93. Shahnaz Anklesaria, 'Obscenity, Media, and the Law', in *Women and Media: Analysis, Alternatives and Action*, (eds.) Kamla Bhasin

and Bina Agarwal, New Delhi and Rome: Kali for Women and ISIS, 1985, pp. 55–60.

94. Madhu Kishwar and Ruth Vanita, 'Mandi', *Manushi*, Vol. 4.3, 1984, p. 45.

95. Madhu Kishwar and Ruth Vanita, 'The Indecent Representation of Women (Prohibition Bill) 1986", *Manushi*, Vol. 7.1, 1986, pp. 2–8.

96. Rosie Thomas, 'Indian Cinema: Pleasures and Popularity', *Screen*, Vol. 26.3–4, May-August 1985, pp. 116–31. According to Vijay Mishra, the only way to interpret Bombay cinema is via 'the narrative paradigm established over two millenia ago in the Sanskrit epics,' namely the *Mahabharata* and the *Ramayana*. (Vijay Mishra, 'Towards a Theoretical Critique of Bombay Cinema', *Screen*, Vol. 26.3–4, May-August 1985, p. 133.)

97. Ravi Vasudevan, 'The Melodramatic Mode and the Commercial Hindi Cinema: Notes on film history, narrative and performance in the 1950s', *Screen*, Vol. 30, 1989, p. 39. For subsequent essays on this period see also Ravi Vasudevan, 'Shifting Codes, Dissolving Identities: The Hindi social film of the 1950s as popular culture', *Journal of Arts and Ideas*, no. 22, 1993, pp. 51–84; Ravi Vasudevan, '"You cannot live in society—and ignore it": Nationhood and female modernity in *Andaz*' in Uberoi (ed.) *Social Reform, Sexuality and the State*, op. cit., pp. 83–108; and Patricia Uberoi, 'Dharma and Desire, Freedom and Destiny: Rescripting the man-woman relationship in popular Hindi cinema', in Meenakshi Thapan (ed.) *Embodiment: Essays in Gender and Identity*, pp. 145–69.

98. See the issue of the *Journal of Arts and Ideas* entitled *Filmstudies*, no. 29, 1996.

99. Madhava Prasad, 'Cinema and the Desire for Modernity', *Journal of Arts and Ideas*, nos. 25–26, 1993, pp. 71–86.

100. Tejaswini Niranjana, 'Banning "Bombayi": Nationalism, communalism and gender', *Economic and Political Weekly*, Vol. 30.22, June 3 1995, pp. 1291–92.

101. See the testimony of 'Regalla Acchamamba' in *We Were Making History...*, Stree Shakti Sanghatana, New Delhi: Kali for Women, 1989.

102. V. Geeta, 'Periyar, Women and an Ethic of Citizenship', paper presented at the seminar 'The Early Years of Indian Independence: Women's perspectives', August 9–11 1997, Baroda.

103. Anu and Giti, 'Inverting Convention', *The Indian Post*, March 13 1988.

104. Sherry Joseph, 'Gay and Lesbian Movement in India', *Economic and Political Weekly*, Vol. 31.33, August 17 1996, pp. 2228–33.

105. Cited in S.K. and P.J., 'Lesbianism as a Political Act', *Observer*, 29 July 1990.

106. Jagori, circular letter dated November 10 1994.

107. Consider, for instance, 'Gay is a Sad Word: Should Indian women come out of the closet?' *Femina*, September 8 1992, pp. 7–11; Sangeeta Jain, 'I'm a Lesbian. So What?' *Network* Magazine, January 1993, pp. 20–23; Parvez Sharma, 'Emerging from the Shadows', *Miscelleny: The Sunday Statesman Review*, July 3 1994, pp. 5–9.

108. Giti Thadani, *Sakhiyani*, op. cit., p. 100.

109. Serena Nanda, 'The Third Gender: Hijra community in India', *Manushi*, no. 72, 1992, pp. 9–16.

110. See, for instance, Anuja Agrawal, 'Gendered Bodies: The Case of the "Third Gender" in India', in *Contributions to Indian Sociology*, Vol. 31.2, July–December 1997, pp. 273–97.

111. Giti Thadani, *Sakhiyani*, op. cit.

112. By all accounts, considerable work is currently underway. Among other forthcoming studies, see Ruth Vanita and Salim Kidwai (eds.) *Love Between Women, Love Between Men: Readings in Indian Literature and History*, and Paola Bacchetta, "Some Identitory Positionalities of Women Who Love Women in India", unpub. mss.

113. Nivedita Menon, 'Destabilising Feminism', *Seminar*, 437, January 1996, p. 100.

114. Foucault, *The History of Sexuality*, Vol. I, op. cit., p. 8.

Unravelling the *Kamasutra*

KUMKUM ROY

The blurb of one of the most recent English translations of the *Kamasutra*, that by Danielou,[1] describes the text as "the world's oldest and most widely read guide to the pleasures and techniques of sex". Further:

> Realistic and pragmatic in its approach, the *Kamasutra* deals without ambiguity or hypocrisy with all aspects of sexual life—including marriage, adultery, prostitution, group sex, sadomasochism, male and female homosexuality and transvestism. The text paints a fascinating portrait of an India whose openness to sexuality gave rise to a highly developed expression of the erotic.

In a sense, this eulogy summarises some of the most widely accepted readings of the text, many of which have crystallised over the past century or so.

The *Kamasutra* was highly visible some years ago in an advertising campaign for a condom. The images which accompanied the text almost invariably depicted a jean-clad man (whose face was barely visible) embracing a young woman, whose eyes were more often than not closed (presumably in ecstasy) and who was more obviously exposed to the gaze of the (male?) observer. While the imagery deliberately and somewhat obviously modernised the text, it also captured one of its dominant strands, namely, its definition of gendered sexuality.

More recently, the *Kamasutra* provided the title (and, it would seem, little else) to Mira Nair's controversial film, which was not released in India at the time of writing. Going by available information, it was initially titled *Tara and Maya* after the two main women protagonists.[2] Supposedly set in the sixteenth century, at least a thousand years after the *Kamasutra* was compiled, Nair's film "is about female friendship and female rivalry, but is ultimately about female solidarity".[3] These are themes that can be read into the Sanskrit text with great difficulty, if at all. That the film was so renamed and then censored is in a sense suggestive of the meanings attributed to the text, which is both perceived and portrayed as being synonymous with notions of sexuality, at once unrestrained and sophisticated.

Undeniably then, the *Kamasutra*, a text which was probably compiled at least one thousand five hundred years ago, is still with us. The text can be located within the tradition of *sutras* or *sastras* of early erotic literature, and within the contemporary context, where the proliferation of translations of the text has, in a sense, transformed it.

It is obvious that these levels are by no means mutually exclusive. For instance, the definition of the text as normative or prescriptive (a feature typical of a sastra) provides the underpinning and justification for many present-day translations. In fact, a somewhat unique feature of the text, which has permitted its exploration at many levels, is that although it is located within the corpus of prescriptive literature and includes a range of injunctions, these are rarely backed up by suggesting rewards for conforming to norms or threats of punishment for violating them. Thus, provisions for enforcing norms are not explicitly laid down, although, as we will see below, these are occasionally implicit. While such anomalies are not uncommon in the sastras, their existence creates a space for varied readings. It is also obvious that the text has had a long and complicated history, which can be only partially recovered.

What I will attempt is rather more limited—an examination of the form and content of the text as constituted during the second and fourth centuries AD, as well as the implications of its more recent appropriation within a context of modernity.

Questions of Context and Form

The *Kamasutra* was probably composed or compiled between the second and fourth centuries AD in north India.[4] While it is traditionally ascribed to Vatsyayana, it is in all likelihood a composite work, a feature fairly typical of Sanskrit texts. It was probably composed after, and in connection with two other major works, the *Dharmasastra* ascribed to Manu (also known as the *Manusmrti*) and the *Arthasastra* assigned to Kautilya. Stylistically, the *Kamasutra* is particularly close to the latter text.

The composition and compilation of the three works were evidently part of a complex process. Each embodies a confrontation with and a resolution of what was defined as its subject—*dharma* (ethical norms), *artha* (means of livelihood) and *kama* (desire) respectively, which were collectively identified as constituting the three crucial dimensions of a man's life, the *trivarga*, encompassing the totality of social existence. Consequently, the texts represent elaborate but not always consistent attempts at codifying social norms and practices.

Each of the texts contains references to predecessors, authors whose opinions were either accepted and elaborated, or, alternatively, rejected. The texts represent the culmination of earlier traditions, and are only partly innovative. As far as the *Kamasutra* is concerned, citing earlier authorities may have been a device for locating the text as a sastra rather than as a *kavya* or literary work. In other words, while the subject matter of the text can and often has been projected as erotic,[5] the manner in which it is treated is closely bound to the structures and concerns of the normative tradition.

The process of codification may be located within a specific socio-political context. In north India (and elsewhere in the subcontinent), the period following the disintegration of the Mauryan empire (around the second century BC) witnessed the growth of regional polities. Their emergence coincided with, and was related to, the intensification of processes of social stratification, and the growing importance of urban centres. These were significant in political, religious and cultural terms, apart from being centres of craft production and increasingly complex exchanges. It is likely that these developments generated pressures for regulating social intercourse, which could have been potentially complicated. The sastras may be viewed as part of this complex process of defining social relations, although, as we will see, this was by no means uncontested or homogeneous.

Codification raised almost as many problems as it attempted to resolve. To start with, the right to codify had to be delimited. In the case of sastras such as the *Kamasutra*, the right to create codes was implicitly or explicitly vested in or claimed by men, more often than not brahmanas well-versed in Sanskrit. This was justified in terms of divine sanction. Effectively then, participation in the process of codification would have been denied to all women and most men. While this provided an apparent resolution, there are indications that the text was in fact open to other influences, especially in the process of transmission (see below).

The programme of the author(s) of the *Kamasutra* seems to have been at least two-fold. On the one hand, kama or desire was to be accorded legitimacy by being made the subject of a sastra. This is evident in the very first, introductory statement: "Salutations to dharma, artha, and kama,"[6] a statement in consonance with the customary invocation of the gods which marks the beginning of most Sanskrit works. Thus, at one stroke kama is located in conjunction with dharma and artha and elevated through an implicit equation of all three with the gods. More explicitly, Vatsyayana states that some sages felt that whereas dharma and artha, given their complexity, were legitimate subjects for discussion, kama was natural and universal and hence did not require codification.

Repudiating this, Vatsyayana argues that women, unlike females of other species, do not have a specific mating season. Consequently, unions between the sexes are governed by other considerations (*upaya*),[7] which need to be regulated. In Vatsyayana's understanding then, human sexuality is socially constructed rather than rooted in the natural order. At the same time, desire is understood to be basic to human existence, comparable to food.[8]

On another level, and more obviously, the text focuses on the legitimation of a (or some) particular form(s) of desire, that is to say, it delimits the contents of kama, in effect recognising and centralising the heterosexual desires of upper class men vis- a-vis all women (directly) and lower class men (indirectly). Desires, thus constructed, are no longer amorphous or inchoate—in fact, we are faced with 'Desire', which acquires definitional status and in terms of which other manifestations are classified as subordinate, irrelevant, or even disruptive. Clearly then, the definition of desire codified in the *Kamasutra* was integrated, ideally, into relations of power, so that it could be viewed as an expression of power.

As an extension of this, positions within the realm of desire are carefully located—one is either capable of experiencing desire or being an object of desire, a man or a woman, powerful or powerless. The specific desire which is privileged is embedded in a context where differences are worked out at length and asymmetrically—that is to say, women are differentiated almost ad infinitum, from men and from each other, whereas powerful men are consolidated into an almost homogeneous category.

Yet this neat hierarchising tendency had its problems as well. An attempt seems to have been made to make the text comprehensive and universal. As a result, a wide range of sexual practices attributed to different regions are listed. While the normative thrust of the text ensures that such practices are ordered hierarchically, the very process of listing would have accorded recognition to diverse practices, which need not necessarily have been in harmony with one another.

Moreover, to acquire validity, any code had to be implemented. This in turn rested on its ability to persuade and/or coerce women and men who were denied access to the process of codification to believe that its end product, normative sexual behaviour, was indeed applicable and valid for all. In other words, the contents of each code had to be communicated and enforced.

The text as available at present is divided into seven sections. The first deals with general practices and precepts (*sadharana*), the second with heterosexual intercourse (*samprayogika*), the third with obtaining a bride (*kanyasamprayuktaka*), the fourth with the duties of the wife (*bharyadhikarika*), the fifth with relations with wives of other men (*paradarika*), the sixth with courtesans (*vaisika*) and the last with secret formulae (*aupanisadika*) designed to ensure success in sexual activities. Not surprisingly, the second section, with its vivid if somewhat monotonous details on physical positions, has attracted the most attention in recent years in spite of the fact that this comprises approximately only a quarter of the text. An analysis of the text[9] suggests that the second, sixth and seventh sections were probably independent of each other and of the remaining sections. These were collated in order to arrive at a comprehensive definition of sexual relations.

While the text is both composite and complex, there is a central concern with defining desire in order to develop a specific understanding of gender relations. This in itself was by no means easy, and its transmission, in particular, may have been fairly complicated.

The first section of the *Kamasutra* lays down, amongst other things, channels for the proper communication of its contents. Access was granted to both men and women.[10] This is somewhat surprising in view of the general tendency to exclude women from sastric knowledge. What is interesting is the argument advanced for opening up the text to women: they ought to acquire knowledge of the sastra as they were involved in its practice.[11] However, women's access to the text was simultaneously circumscribed. A married woman could acquire knowledge with the permission of her husband, whereas others had to learn it from trustworthy people, specifically married women, kinswomen, or servant women.[12]

Clearly, women could not be taught by men versed in the Sanskrit sutra version of the text, as the very proximity of women and men outside certain regulated contexts would have opened up the possibility for alternative expressions of desire. If women were to be taught by other women, who were by definition excluded from direct access to the sastras and Sanskrit learning, the complexities of the text in terms of both style and content would have had to be simplified. In other words, the text would have to be converted into oral formulae or dicta, suitable for transmission to a non-scholastic audience. However, once this was undertaken, the introduction of non-sastric elements was possible within the framework of the text. In fact, the text may have been modified in the process of communication, by less 'scholarly' men as well as women. Thus circumscription was possible only up to a point, beyond which both access to and the construction of the text could become relatively open-ended activities.

It is in this context that the juxtaposition of prose and verse (*sloka*) in the text assumes significance. While the bulk of the text is composed in prose sutras or sentences which are, more often than not, burdened with technical jargon and require careful elucidation, each subsection ends with a set of one or more sloka. These were composed in the popular *anustubh* metre, used in the epics, for instance. The difference between prose and verse elements is not simply stylistic: while in some cases the verses summarise the contents of the preceding prose, in others, the message of the verses is barely in line with the more weighty prose, while in yet others, prose and verse stand in sharp contradiction to one another.

This is obvious, for example, in the section on toothmarks.[13] While the prose sutras elaborate the kinds of toothmarks to be made by the male protagonist and the parts of the woman's body on which they should be made, the concluding verses refer to women biting men.[14] In other words, the agency ascribed to men in the prose section is substantially reversed.

An equally interesting disjuncture between prose and verse occurs in the second section, which deals with the varieties of physical contact. Here,[15] after somewhat tedious classifications of types of embrace, we are assured rather abruptly that the sastras are valid only so long as passion is not aroused—once the threshold is crossed, even that which is not mentioned in the sastras is permitted. Such verses are somewhat anti-climatic to say the least, as they negate, at one stroke, the very elaborate endeavour to classify and codify, apparent in the construction of the rest of the text.

The contradictions posed between verse and prose sections are not explicitly resolved within the text. For example, we are not told whether it is better for men to bite women or vice versa. We can either assume that the prose sutras were considered more authoritative than the sloka, as the former were regarded as typical of prestigious scholastic works, or we can conclude the terminal verses, by their very location, are literally and figuratively the last word in the matter.

The implications of the disjuncture between prose and verse are interesting. We need to remember that only a limited audience would have had access to both prose and verse sections, and that for this audience, given its likely construction in terms of caste, class, and of course gender, the prose formulations would have tended to carry more weight. On the other hand, those who had access only or primarily to the versified text, which was amenable to oral transmission, would not have had the choice of comparing their received wisdom with the more complex and inaccessible prose sastras. This group would have included many men and almost all women.

Given that the messages of the prose and verse sections are not always identical, and can at times have been contradictory, the implementation of the norms codified in the text may have posed problems. It is likely that high status men were able to enforce their definition of sexual relations through their access to other kinds of power—economic, social, ritual or political. However, the very fact that the verses, with their somewhat distinctive message, survive within the 'high' sastric tradition points both to the strength and vitality of alternative definitions of sexual relations, and to the fact that the message of the sastra may have been substantially modified in the course of its transmission to a wider audience.

It is also likely that the composition of the verses was relatively open; the simple verse-structure could have been learnt fairly easily. As such, verses may have been added and deleted, or modified in the course of transmission. In this context, the verses may well have incorporated alternative perspectives on questions of sexuality and gender relations, thus providing us with a glimpse into the complexities of enforcing the sastric definitions of kama.

Locating Socio-sexual Relations

The *Kamasutra* is primarily directed towards the *nagaraka* (citizen), who is often equated with the *nayaka* or actor.[16] While the nayaka is by definition male, he is also expected to be prosperous and "cultured". Besides, his caste affiliations are considered to be relatively unimportant; any man, if sufficiently wealthy, could aspire to proficiency in the precepts and practices advocated in the text.

The structure of the text can, in fact, be envisaged in terms of concentric circles, centring on the nagaraka and moving outwards through wider social relations. The work begins by constructing the ideal life style of the male protagonist, and follows this up by defining the norms of heterosexual intercourse. This is then located within the context of marriage, defined in terms of stratified relations between men and women. Control over women within the patriarchal household is extended to control over women in other households. Finally, the prostitute is accommodated, although, as we shall see, this is somewhat tangential to the perspective of the text.

The construction of the nagaraka as a man who is the focus of socio-sexual relations and in control of them required as its corollary that women, as the object of such relations, be classified and objectified. This resulted in defining ideal women in terms of physical and mental attributes, and classifying them according to region. There is a striking dichotomy between the construct of the nagaraka or nayaka, where the ideal seems to be a single, uniform, universal man, and the sheer plurality and diversity of types of women enumerated. Not surprisingly, there is no feminine equivalent for the nagaraka.

Besides, while we do have references to nayikas (the female counterpart of the nayaka) the attributes and roles of the two categories are not envisaged as identical. The former were classified according to their relationship with men —they could, for instance, be virgins, remarried women, or prostitutes.[17] What differentiates women from one another, and from men, is whether they are accessible to a single man, to two men, or to all men. Thus, the basic definition of women as accessible to men is elaborated. Further, the construction of the nayakas as the embodiment of masculinity was reinforced by the classification of eunuchs, defined as the *trtiya prakrti*, literally the "third nature",[18] the first two types being men and women. Eunuchs could be feminine or masculine in attire and manner, but were defined as feminine vis-a-vis the nayakas.

Distinct constructions of masculinity and femininity are also evident in the description and classifications of forms of physical intercourse. The naming of kinds of genital contact seems to be almost exclusively in terms of the position or role ascribed to the female partner. Some of the names suggest a passive construction of female sexuality; for instance, the *irmbhitaka* or the yawning position[19] was so named as it involved holding up the legs of the woman. Other names, such as the *vadavaka* or mare-like position, in which the woman was expected to hold the penis firmly, suggest an understanding of more active female participation.[20] However, such activity was implicitly viewed as exceptional; the woman astride the man was classified as *purusayita*, literally the woman who assumes the position of the man.[21] On a more basic level, the male partner was defined as the doer (*karta*), with the female counterpart as the *adhara* or base. We are assured that both experience pleasure through their complementary roles.[22]

As important as the kinds of genital contact which are named are those which are either not named or viewed with a certain amount of ambiguity. These include same-sex genital or anal intercourse. References to lesbian relations, for instance, occur not in the context of kinds of sexual unions but in the section dealing with the means of winning over the wives of others.[23] Further, lesbian sex is defined in terms of categories of heterosexual intercourse, with one of the women involved being classified as *purusavat*, literally, man-like. Thus, at one level, such relations were either obliterated or marginalised from the discussion. While at another level, recognition was accorded by assimilating them to heterosexual roles which were legitimised within the dominant tradition.

As interesting is the notion of the 'realm of women'—the *grama nari visya* or the *stri rajya*. This was seen as a land where social and sexual relations were reversed. A number of young men were expected to have intercourse with a single woman. Although this may have suggested a dominant role for the sole female protagonist, such an understanding was undermined by equating the woman with a prostitute, *vasya* and with a woman in the royal harem who would, by definition, have been one amongst a number of women who were expected to compete for the king's favour. While such women may have been able to define sexual relations somewhat differently from others, they were nonetheless constrained in a variety of ways. As such, the sexual 'freedom' ascribed to them was not even a mirror image of what men were allowed.

Also, the region where such sexual practices may have prevailed seems to have been deliberately mythicised; unlike other instances, where we have specific references to the practices of the peoples of Andhra, or Maharashtra,[24] the location of stri rajya is either unspecified or it is transferred to Bahlika or Balkh,[25] to the north-west of the subcontinent, a land which was relatively remote and unknown, and hence could be viewed as exotic. Thus, the reversal of sexual relations was recognised as a theoretical possibility, while being at the same time marginalised as something relatively remote.

On yet another level, violence within sexual relations was both recognised and structured. This is evident in the terms used to classify sexual contact. A particular type of kiss, for instance, required the forcible pulling of the virgin (*kanya*) towards the man. The woman is described as forcibly engaged (*balatkarena niyukta*).[26] Besides, the beating of a woman by a man was recognised as a legitimate part of sexual intercourse. This was justified on the understanding of sex as *kalaharupam* or combat.[27] While men were permitted to indulge in four or possibly eight types of beating, women were expected to respond with various kinds of shrieks and other sounds.[28] Thus, the outcome of the combat was ideally regulated. More insidious was the understanding that if a woman protested against being beaten, this was simply what was expected of her in the game. Thus, her cries could be viewed not as expressions of pain but as indications of conforming to the code. At the same time, the *Kamasutra*[29] warns against the 'excessive' use of violence which could and evidently did occasionally result in the death of the woman.

While violence was recognised as intrinsic to masculine sexuality, women's anger was permissible only within limits. This is evident from the range of actions permitted to the *nayika* who lost her temper; she could shout, scream, even kick the nayaka, but was then expected to go to the door and cry and permit the nayaka to conciliate her.[30]

The legitimation of violence in sexual relations is evident in the discussion on selecting a wife. Eligible women were to be on display like articles of merchandise (*panyasadharmatvat*).[31] Once the man had made his choice, he was expected to initiate the bride into sexual relations. The mechanisms permitted ranged from pleading to threats.[32] The woman was expected to respond shyly to such overtures. As in the case of responses to overt male violence, women's silences or reluctance to participate in the structured patterns of behaviour could be explained away or understood as a shy response. The woman who was reluctant to get married could be persuaded or pressurised through a variety of means, through women known to her, through kinsfolk, through deceit or force.[33] In other words, the expression of masculine heterosexual desire was valorised to the point that it was envisaged as all-powerful—the woman who was the object of such desire could not hope to escape from the web of matrimony. Recourse to force was also considered legitimate for the man who was attempting to seduce another's wife, especially when other means proved ineffective.[34]

In the ultimate analysis, then, resorting to overt or covert violence by the male protagonist was legitimised by being located within the framework of the sastra. Given that the position of the nayaka and nayika were carefully structured, the definition and projection of male violence as acceptable would have provided the means for enforcing what was conceived as the structure of sexual relations. We had noted earlier that the *Kamasutra*, unlike other sastras, does not contain any explicit mention of punishments for violating the code. To an extent, the sanction accorded to routine violence in heterosexual relations may have provided an alternative means of enforcing at least some of the provisions of the code.

If the construction of wifehood rested implicitly on an acceptance of violence as a possibility within sexual relations, the wife's subordination was envisaged in less dramatic ways as well. She was expected to treat her husband as a god,[35] look after the household, maintain a garden, serve her husband by dressing for him, cooking according to his tastes, sleeping only after he had slept, waking before him, performing rituals for his welfare, seeking his permission before going out, avoiding the company of "disrespectable" (and possibly threatening) women including mendicants, renouncers of the world, witches, fortune-tellers and unchaste women. The dependence of the wife was foregrounded particularly in the context of polygyny. The *Kamasutra* urges women not only to accept, but to actively forge relations which would underscore their subordination. For instance, a childless woman was expected to encourage her husband to remarry, while the junior bride was advised to defer to her senior.[36]

What emerges as normative, then, is a nayaka-centred household, where all sexual relations were traced through and revolved around him. In such a situation, heterosexual genital intercourse was only partly dyadic—it was located firmly within a context of gender stratification. The circle of accessible women was widened almost indefinitely beyond the nayaka's own household to include the wives of other men. This is justified on the ground that unsatiated kama could lead to mental and physical agony, culminating in death. The pros and cons of the endeavour are discussed, not in terms of ethics, but in terms of pragmatic considerations.[37]

This preoccupation with desire was not explicitly connected with concerns of procreation. This may seem somewhat surprising, given the sastric status accorded to the text. However, it is perhaps explicable within the overall framework of sexual relations envisaged within the text. The potential or actual availability of women to the male protagonist would have ensured procreation. Besides, given that even in texts such as the *Manusmrti* there is no notion of absolute illegitimacy, but of more or less legitimate offspring, any progeny produced through the satiation of kama could have been accommodated.

As an extension of this, the last section of the text, which lists a variety of aphrodisiacal recipes, does not contain references either to contraceptives or to aids for abortion. Once again, the emphasis is on ensuring a certain kind of sexual success for the male protagonist. The reproductive implications of such success were considered irrelevant.

If procreation was viewed as not directly significant, neither were rituals. While their performance was included amongst the duties prescribed for the ideal housewife, they were not of central importance for the nayaks. To the extent that the attitude towards rituals was pragmatic, there is a certain correspondence between the *Kamasutra* and the *Arthasastra*.

While women were defined as accessible, access to women was construed as an index of male status. Thus, the village chief was supposed to have access to village women, and could have intercourse with them while they were engaged in forced labour, when they entered the granary, when they were transporting, buying or selling things, when they were working in the fields or cleaning the house.[38] In other words, such women could be subjected to sexual advances during virtually all their routine activities. The officer in charge of cattle was permitted similar access to wives of shepherds and so on.[39]

Not surprisingly, such access was envisaged as most complete in the case of the king. If he desired a woman, a slave woman and/or his wife were expected to assist him in his pursuit.[40] However, the king was warned of the dangers of attempting to enter another man's house[41] and of other men gaining access to his own harem. The latter situation was one where the neat ordering of hierarchies evidently collapsed. Were high status women defying their covertly powerful husbands in inviting low status men? If so, this constituted an explicit challenge to gender stratification. On the other hand, if the problem was posed in terms of low status men gaining access to high status women, a gender-based hierarchy would remain inviolable. However, the king's power over his male subjects would be called into question. Neither possibility was perceived as desirable. The solution offered was pragmatic, and consisted in guarding women.[42]

The sixth section of the text was supposed to have been compiled at the request of the courtesans of Pataliputra (modern Patna).[43] This section is somewhat intriguing, in that the protagonist is no longer the nayaka but the prostitute, and the issue at stake is not the fulfilment of kama but the question of profits. The prostitute was advised to observe a semblance of wifehood.[44] This included pretending to learn the sixty-four erotic arts from the man, as well as adopting his likes and dislikes.[45] These were recognised as strategies for extracting wealth from her sexual partner.[46] As such, the prostitute merely appeared wifelike.

At another level, we find a discussion on the qualities expected of both the nayaka and the prostitute.[47] For instance, the man who was solicited was ideally expected to be wealthy, ambitious, learned, skilled in the various arts, healthy, virile, etc. While the woman was expected to be beautiful, desirous of physical union, charming, skilled in the arts, far-sighted, intelligent, and bereft of attributes like anger, greed etc. While these qualities were not symmetrical, the enumeration of the ideal requirements of both partners in the transaction contrasts significantly with that envisaged in the context of marriage. Unlike the wife, moreover, the prostitute was permitted to expel an indifferent or poor man by humiliating him in a variety of ways.[48] In effect, what distinguished the prostitute from the wife was the former's recognised access to income, and control over expenditure.

Translation and Modernity

Texts related to or explicitly derived from the *Kamasutra* continued to be composed till the seventeenth century.[49]

However, many of the later versions omitted the section on prostitution and genital-oral contact, elaborating instead on the second section:

> Thus we come across as many as 50 varieties of union in the supine posture, 12 in the sidal, 13 in the sitting, 17 in the standing, 21 in the bent and 12 in the opposite.[50]

Among the earlier versions in a regional language was the *Sringaramanjari* composed in Sanskritised Telugu in the eighteenth century. This was the work not of a pandit but of a certain Ali Akbar Shah.[51] Significantly, truncated and variously reconstituted versions of the text were available even before its "rediscovery" by Burton in 1883, which was followed by its prolific propagation in the colonial and post-colonial context. However, as of now, there have been virtually no studies on the kinds of audience to whom these versions of the text may have been addressed.

Burton's translation of the *Kamasutra* launched the text into an entirely new level of popularisation. Born in 1821, Richard Burton travelled widely through France, Italy, Arabia and India. He evidently combined a 'love for the Orient' with an aversion for 'the rigid hypocrisy of Victorian sexuality' possibly stemming from his own interest in homosexuality.[52] Besides the *Kamasutra*, he translated the *Arabian Nights*, and an Algerian text, *The Perfumed Garden*. The diverse reactions which Burton's work aroused point to the complexities which surrounded (and continue to surround) discussions on sexuality. On the one hand he was knighted in 1886; on the other hand, his wife burnt the manuscript of his translation of the section on homosexuality in *The Perfumed Garden* after his death.

Burton was probably the first to define the *Kamasutra* as a 'work on love'.[53] He may also have begun the process of representing the subject of the text as 'natural'. This in turn provided the basis for universalising its message. We are told that "the human nature of today is much the same as the human nature of long ago."[54] Moreover, the text was recommended as a "work that should be studied by all, both old and young."[55]

The actual dissemination of the contents of the text on an unprecedented scale was made possible through the medium of print. The process of printing also ensured that the text was standardised in a way which was not possible with a hand written and/or orally transmitted work.

The carefully built up claim of the Sanskrit version regarding social status and the location for desire, and its direct concern with specificities were now glossed over. Burton extended his use of the text to comment on the 'nature of women'. We are informed that:

> ...while some women are born courtesans, and follow the instincts of their nature in every class of society, it has been truly said by some authors that every woman has got an inkling of the profession in her nature and does her best as a general rule to make herself agreeable to the male sex.[56]

Burton's translation and its subsequent editions were directed primarily towards a western audience, who were offered the options of both confronting and escaping from questions of sexuality through explicit, literal translations of what were understood to be erotic practices, which could at the same time be distanced by being regarded as exotic or oriental. Consequently, the specific social context of these practices, delineated in the original, was pushed into the background or accepted as unproblematic. This may have been partly due to a tendency to generalise from superficially similar patriarchal values.

Some of the strategies which underlay Burton's endeavour continue to be resorted to by Indian translators of the *Kamasutra*. Once again, they raise questions of sexuality, but locate this within a variety of other concerns such as those of science, modernity, or even salvation. Virtually every translation contains an introduction which encloses the text and attempts to circumscribe the meanings we are expected to read into it. For instance, Upadhyaya's translation,[57] which is explicitly meant for "members of the medical and legal professions, scholars, and research students of Indology, Psychology, and

Social Sciences"[58] is accompanied by an introduction designed to collapse the distinctions between a specific definition of desire and a more universalistic notion of love. This is achieved by juxtaposing a number of statements on the *Kamasutra* by Indologists and sexologists, and on love by Mahatma Gandhi and Rabindranath Tagore. A cheap version of the text (priced at Rs.12.50) and explicitly meant "for youth on the threshold of married life"[59] includes in its introduction comments by highly placed government officials and academicians evidently intended to serve a similar purpose.

In his lengthy introduction (running to over sixty pages) Upadhyaya legitimates the text by tracing the origin of the discourse on desire back to the earliest category of literature in India, the *Rg Veda*. Besides, parallels are drawn from the epics, the *Puranas* and from Jain and Buddhist literature, as well as from the works of Kalidasa.[60] The reader is thus assured that although the *Kamasutra* is outstanding, it does not stand alone. To antiquity is added continuity and stability—we are in fact confronted with an unchanging (and unchangeable?) sexual order. This is achieved by ignoring the specificities of different literary genres and historical contexts by extracting and collating erotic passages from all of them.

On another level, Upadhyaya attempts to justify the preoccupation with kama on the grounds that this is conducive to procreation. Interestingly enough, this professed interest in procreation is not found in the *Kamasutra* itself, so Upadhyaya's suggestion that desire, if properly channelised, could lead to the production of sons tells us more about the ideal concerns of twentieth century professional men and their values than about earlier notions of sexuality.

At the same time, there is an increasing preoccupation with the physical, and as a result, the second section of the text is privileged by being commented on at length. Moreover, almost every act mentioned in the text is justified by citing parallels from Sanskrit literature, Greek or Roman practices, and/or those of tribal societies, and/or western works on sociology. Besides, data are frequently tabulated[61] to convey the impression, in the words of a medical sociologist, that the *Kamasutra* is indeed "precise, objective and scientific."[62] The attempt to define the *Kamasutra* as scientific is often buttressed by defining it as modern as well. For instance, Khanna[63] suggests that the description of the nayaka's bedroom can serve as a model for five star hotels.

Given this preoccupation with projecting the *Kamasutra* as scientific, it is alarming to note that some present-day commentators tend to justify sexual violence as natural. We are informed that "males now definitely know that the manifestation of tears and cries in a female are quite normal ones and inwardly she desires the opposite of what she expresses by tears and cries and her withholding of favours from the male."[64] Simultaneously, female sexuality is understood in almost mechanistic terms. Thus, clitoral stimulation is discussed in terms of the "adequate amount of pressure on that electric button which normally sets the whole mechanism in operation."[65] In other instances, the underlying assumptions of the *Kamasutra* are accepted and updated. For instance, Khanna[66] dismisses the methods for reducing the size of the vagina recommended in the text, suggesting plastic surgery instead. In other words, the goal of modifying the female body, in literal terms, remains unquestioned; the difference lies only in the methods which are advocated.

There have also been some ingenious attempts to link kama with *moksa* or salvation, the privileged goal attributed to and claimed for diverse early and (by extension) contemporary Indian traditions. According to Mulk Raj Anand,[67] for instance, knowledge of the *Kamasutra* was expected to "lead not only to healthy enjoyment of the variegated pleasures of the body but also clarify the mind of all filth attached to the secret act. Also no hidden longings should remain in the mind of the seeker after *moksa*."

Most printed versions of the *Kamasutra* tend to be illustrated. This is especially true of the more expensive, glossy, coffee-table editions. What is interesting is that even the professedly scholarly or academic translation produced by Upadhyaya[68] contains as many as fifty plates, apart from other illustrations. There are two striking features about these illustrations. First, they are assembled from diverse traditions of sculpture and painting. We have, for instance, depictions from the sculpture of the 3rd century Nagarjunakonda[69] as well as Pahari paintings of the eighteenth and nineteenth centuries.[70] We have representations from Khajuraho[71] and the Deccan[72] as well as from Konarak[73] and Bikaner[74].

Each region and epoch represented in these illustrations is characterised by distinctive stylistic elements. These are held together by an enforced, thematic unity. Almost all the illustrations centre around heterosexual pairs, more often than not shown locked in a close embrace. There is also an implicit understanding that the meanings ascribed to such depictions are uniform and universal. Thus, Mughal court paintings are implicitly equated with the temple architecture of Khajuraho and aesthetic expressions specific to complex traditions are reduced to a kind of equivalence.

The illustrations chosen focus exclusively on the concerns of the second section, in spite of the fact that they are placed throughout the translation. This results in a certain incongruity between text and illustration. For instance, the section on payment to courtesans contains pictures of lovers in a garden.

This focus on and reworking of the text through illustrations blurs the distinction between the erotic and the pornographic, and is obviously useful as a sales strategy. Then again, the illustrations have the effect of valorising, and to an extent isolating, the heterosexual dyad from the web of social relations within which they are embedded. As such, the translation implicitly appeals to the individual/heterosexual pair, and legitimates a certain 'modern' individualism by creating an illusion of social sexual relations.

The fate of the terminal verses, mentioned in Section II, is also interesting. The existence of these verses is more often than not veiled in translations. Although they are translated, they are rendered in English prose like the rest of the text, and their original style is masked. Therefore, the discrepancies between verse and prose, evident in the Sanskrit version, are concealed, and the translated text is relatively homogenised.

With the growing accessibility of translations the fate of the Sanskrit version has been one of steady marginalisation. The nineteenth and twentieth centuries have witnessed the conversion of Sanskrit learning into an activity conducted generally in state-run schools, colleges and universities. As a consequence, traditional methods of imparting and acquiring skills in the language have been marginalised. What has also happened, especially in the decades since Independence, is that the institutionalised learning of Sanskrit has increasingly been perceived as a typically 'female' activity. In other words, the discipline has 'attracted' more women than men, is regarded as less prestigious than most other options, and is often considered a means of getting a university degree rather than acquiring proficiency in the language.

Not surprisingly, the study of the *Kamasutra* in Sanskrit is not open to students in most modern departments which teach the language. The reason, ostensibly, is the nature of the text. Thus, access to and understanding of the text are structured. In effect, the Sanskrit text has become increasingly inaccessible, especially for women.[75]

For all practical purposes, we are now left with translated versions of the text which project it as both ancient and modern, peculiarly Indian as well as universal, scientific as well as aesthetic. In other words, the text has been empowered by relating it to and locating it within a range of discourses—historical, sociological, medical, philosophical and artistic. As such, a critique becomes increasingly difficult, as the social and sexual ideals of the text have been validated and popularised on an unprecedented scale. Literate men now have easy access to the role model of the nayaka—a model which promises both power and the fulfilment of delimited desire.

The access which literate women (who, in any case, are vastly outnumbered by literate men) have to the text is probably somewhat different. As we have seen, women who understand the language of the original text are tacitly denied the opportunity to study it. Besides, there are problems in gaining access even to translations. As such, the book gets read, if at all, in the company or under the guidance of a male companion. In the process, the authoritative character ascribed to the text over the last century or so tends to be reinforced. The weight the text has acquired means that if we feel uncomfortable with what it says we run the risk of being labelled as antiquated or too modern, unscientific, petty, un-Indian, crude, unsophisticated, irrational. Thus, at long last, the text becomes truly prescriptive.

Besides, the text spills over into a variety of other media— it is no longer a work in Sanskrit accessible only to the limited few, but extends in all directions; its ethos pervades our films, songs, dances, advertisements, the new mass culture. In other words, the barriers of illiteracy are transcended in the process of transmission. In the process, the *Kamasutra*'s definition of both male and female sexuality acquires a hegemonic power which the original may have aspired to but never acquired.

Thus, the last hundred years or so have witnessed a dramatic change in the means of transmission of the text. This can be visualised on two levels—on the one hand, the languages of transmission have proliferated; on the other, the technologies of transmission have diversified, including the use of print and other media. While this can and has been viewed as a democratisation of access to what was previously the preserve of a few, this is only partly true.

As we have seen, the Sanskrit sutra composition was in all likelihood open to modification and reworking in the course of the oral transmission of its contents, especially amongst women. Such modifications were accommodated somewhat uneasily within the composite Sanskrit text, possibly through the simple terminal verses, which, as we have seen, did not always match the prose sutras. Thus, both the form and the content of the sutras were open to contestation.

By contrast, the distilled message of the *Kamasutra*— disseminated through print and other media, suggesting that it is concerned centrally with a uniform, universal heterosexual norm—appears less open to contestation, partly because the processes of transmission have become industrialised and mechanised. To an extent, the fate of the *Kamasutra* is symptomatic of that of questions of sexuality in general. Having attained a certain visibility, sexuality is often viewed as symbolic of liberal attitudes, yet in the process of acquiring this visibility, its social context has often deliberately been obscured. It may not be possible to retrieve the potential for critique and contestation inherent in oral transmission, but we need to create its equivalent so as to ground our discussions on contemporary sexualities within a complex reality.

An earlier version of this paper appeared in the *Indian Journal of Gender Studies*, Vol. 3.2.1996. pp. 155-70. I am grateful to the discussant and participants at the workshop, and especially to the editors, Mary John and Janaki Nair, for their comments and suggestions.

Notes

1. Alain Danielou tr., *The Complete Kamasutra*, Rochester: Park Street Press, 1994.
2. *Times of India*, 29 December 1996.
3. Mira Nair, cited in *The Telegraph*, 1 December 1996.
4. N.N. Bhattacharya, *History of Indian Erotic Literature*, Delhi: Munshiram Manoharlal, 1975, p. xii; T.R. Trautmann, *Kautilya and the Arthasastra*, Leiden: E.J. Brill, 1971, p. 6.
5. For instance, see Shobhita Punja, *Divine Ecstasy*, New Delhi: Viking, 1992, p. ix, where the text is described as a work on "the art of love-making".
6. *Kamasutra*, I.1.1. all references to the *Kamasutra* are from Madhavcharya (ed.), *The Kamasutra*, (2 parts), Bombay: Laxmi Venkateshwara Steam Press, 1934.
7. *Kamasutra*, I.2.20.
8. Ibid., I.2.37.
9. Trautmann, *Kautilya and the Arthasastra*, op. cit., p. 169.
10. *Kamasutra*, I.3.1.
11. Ibid., I.3.3.
12. Ibid., I.3.2, 12, 13.
13. Ibid., II.5.
14. Ibid., II.5.37 ff.

15. Ibid., II.2.29–31.
16. Ibid., I.4.1.
17. Ibid., I.5.3.
18. Ibid., II.9.1.
19. Ibid., II.6.25.
20. For the mare as a symbol of active and hence threatening female sexuality in some strands of early Indian mythology see W.D. O'Flaherty, *Sexual Metaphors and Animal Symbols in Indian Mythology*, Delhi: Motilal Banarsidass, 1980, p. 164.
21. *Kamasutra*, II.8.
22. Ibid., II.1.9–30.
23. Ibid., V.6.2.
24. Ibid., II.6.47.
25. Ibid., II.6.45.
26. Incidentally, the term *balatkara* has the connotation of rape in a number of modern Indian languages.
27. *Kamasutra*, II.7.11.
28. Ibid., II.7.3–21.
29. Ibid., II.7.25–30.
30. Ibid., II.10.30–31.
31. Ibid., III.1.14.
32. Ibid., III.2.11–24.
33. Ibid., III.5.2, 16, 19, 27.
34. Ibid., V.3.4.
35. Ibid., IV.1.11.
36. Ibid., II.2.4, 16, etc.
37. Ibid., V.1.
38. Ibid., V.5.5–6.
39. Ibid., V.5.7 ff.
40. Ibid., V.5.13, 24.
41. Ibid., V.5.28.
42. Ibid., V.6.39 ff.
43. Ibid., I.1.11.
44. Ibid., VI.5.36.
45. Ibid., VI.2.13, 22.
46. Ibid., VI.3 ff.
47. Ibid., VI.1.10–14.
48. Ibid., VI.3.
49. Bhattacharya, *History of Indian Erotic Literature*, op. cit., p. 102.
50. Ibid., p. 105.

51. Ibid., p. 122.
52. All biographical details on Burton are from R. Burton and F.F. Arbuthnot tr., *The Kamasutra and The Perfumed Garden*, England: Omega Books Ltd., 1987.
53. Ibid., p. 5.
54. Ibid., p. 229.
55. Ibid.
56. Ibid., p. 173.
57. S.C. Upadhyaya, tr., *Kamasutra of Vatsyayana*, Bombay: Taraporevala, 1961.
58. Ibid., p. iv.
59. V.C. Bandhu, tr. *Vatsayana Kamasutra*, Delhi: Universal Publications, p. 12.
60. Upadhyaya, *Kamasutra of Vatsyayana*, op. cit., pp. 51 ff.
61. Ibid., p. 36.
62. G. Khanna, *Kamasutra: Its Relevance Today*, Bombay: Jaico, 1985, p. 2.
63. Ibid., p. 16.
64. Upadhyaya, *Kamasutra of Vatsyayana*, op. cit., p. 22.
65. Ibid., p. 19.
66. Khanna, *Kamasutra*, op. cit., pp. 166–67.
67. Mulk Raj Anand, *Kama Kala*, Geneva: Nagel Publishers, 1958, p. 26.
68. Upadhyaya, *Kamasutra of Vatsyayana*, op. cit.
69. Ibid., opposite p. 128.
70. Ibid., opposite p. 48.
71. Ibid., opposite p. 128.
72. Ibid., opposite p. 48.
73. Ibid., opposite p. 72.
74. Ibid., plate XVI.
75. This was brought home to me very sharply when I tried to read the Sanskrit text in a public library. The title page of the book contained the words *Nitantam gopaniyam* (literally, extremely confidential or top secret), with "For Private Circulation Only" added in English for good measure. This was evidently taken fairly seriously. The book disappeared from my desk and when I asked for it I was told that young girls who used the library often flipped through the pages in my absence, and that the librarian (also a woman) felt that this was improper, so the books were kept under lock and key.

Offences Against Marriage

Negotiating custom in colonial Bengal

SAMITA SEN

In 1819, the East India Company's government passed Regulation VII introducing two separate provisions—one regarding the employment of labour and the other the enticement of women. The regulation brought 'civil' matters like labour contracts and marriages under criminal jurisdiction. These seminal interventions developed, separately, after 1857. Employers were able to use the police and criminal courts to control workers. Also, husbands could use instruments in criminal law to enforce marriage obligations on wives.

Both employment and marriage were deemed to be governed by the principle of contract. The contraventions of these contracts, in both cases, were given criminal implications and were made penally enforceable. However, in neither case did the contracting parties have analogous rights. Both these contracts were, from the beginning, unequal. The employers' right to enforce a contract implied no equivalent right for the worker. Similarly, the 'wife' had limited power to enforce 'maintenance' that was considered the husband's only contractual obligation in marriage. The 'worker' and the 'wife' were both constituted as legal inferiors. The laws governing employment and marriage concentrated on disabling both the worker and the wife from revoking the contract. Thus the criminal offence of 'enticement' was not an offence against the woman who was being enticed but against the husband to whom the 'wife' was already contractually bound and from whom she was being 'unlawfully' enticed.

The issue became complicated when employers were accused of 'enticing' women away from their homes to distant workplaces. Were these 'enticements' or voluntary migration? Were women legal subjects capable of entering labour contracts on their own behalf? If so, they were bound by the contractual obligation to serve the employer for the stipulated period. Or, was a prior marriage contract for service to the husband violated by a wife entering a labour contract? By this latter argument, the employment contract could be declared invalid at any stage and the employer forced to surrender the contract. These were contentious questions about the deployment of women's labour and sexuality which cropped up throughout the nineteenth century. This paper attempts to address some of these. It will focus on some of the responses of the colonial state which was pulled in different directions by capitalists, imperialists and the indigenous elite. Since many controversies stemmed from the difficulty of determining the actual nature of the marital contract, the first section deals with some of the issues involved in the definition and categorisation of plural marriage practices in India. The second section will focus on the problems faced in implementing the criminal provisions regarding marriage that were codified in the mid-nineteenth century. The third section discusses the overlap between criminal/penal enforcement of the marriage contract and emigration legislation. The prioritisation of the marriage contract placed many restrictions on women's mobility. In both penal and emigration law, the marriage contract was privileged in favour of the husband, and wives were denied the right to escape unhappy marriages by flight, divorce or migration.

Towards a Definition of Marriage—Law and Custom

Criminal law began to intercede into marriage at the beginning of the nineteenth century. The first concern was to protect the husband against the 'seduction' or 'enticement' of wives and against voluntary desertion by wives. It was the former that drew more attention. In 1815, the Magistrate of the Suburbs of Calcutta reported:

[R]epeated representations [are] made to me of the miseries to which families are exposed, particularly the poorer classes of society, from their wives, children and the female relations of their families being seduced away from them for the purpose of prostitution.... [T]he delicacy of the subject requires some remedy to be applied that shall not in its consequences be so dreadful a scourge on society as to render them out-casts [sic] from the act of seeking redress in so heinous a crime.[1]

The Magistrate's concern was not singular. There was a general feeling that the expansion of Calcutta and the congregation of adult men without their families—workers, soldiers and traders —created an 'unnatural' demand for prostitutes. A supply too became available—the procurement of women for prostitution was facilitated by the destruction of traditional occupations. Upto the beginning of the nineteenth century, a large majority of women in Bengal and Bihar were engaged in spinning and grain processing. These activities were usually undertaken as part of the daily routine of housework and could in addition provide an independent means of livelihood.[2] By the 1830s, hand-spinning was practically destroyed. From roughly the middle of the nineteenth century, the unpaid component of women's labour increased at the cost of the paid component.[3] Women became more dependent on land to which their access was mediated by the family.

As women became more economically vulnerable, the role of the family in distribution of resources heightened. As a result, along with 'enticement', the Magistrate also addressed the question of family maintenance. He dwelt on the plight of deceived and deserted mothers of illegitimate children and wives deserted by their husbands. Regulation VII of 1819 addressed some of these problems. It provided for imprisonment not exceeding six months and a fine not exceeding Rs 200 for those found guilty of 'enticing away' women for prostitution. It also provided for imprisonment not exceeding one month to persons found guilty of deserting their wives and families and wilfully neglecting to support them.

To begin with, the concept of 'enticement' as a criminal

offence assumed that women were enticed from their husbands and families for the purpose of prostitution. It became an offence at par with 'procurement'. The two concurrent concerns were to restrict the induction of women into prostitution and to protect the rights and claims of families to 'their' women. In the course of implementing these laws, however, British officials found that these two concerns did not always concur. Women were 'enticed' for purposes other than prostitution and women sometimes defied familial rights and claims without being enticed. What further confused the issue was a wide range of sexual and marital behaviour which defeated administrative efforts to categorise women into 'wives' and 'prostitutes'.

From the early nineteenth century, the British began to investigate and categorise Indian marriage practices. In the usual course, marriage was dealt with under civil law. Warren Hastings' 'bridge over the ocean of litigation' had culled some principles from a body of religious precepts interpreted by pundits and moulvis. From these gradually evolved notions of fully formed 'Hindu' or 'Muslim' laws regarding marriage and inheritance. The so-called personal laws were demarcated as a special area of law to be governed primarily by religious prescription in 1860–61, in the first and second Law Commissions. At the same time, the Regulation VII (of 1819) provisions against 'enticement' and 'willful negligence' to maintain wives and children were developed in criminal law. The Indian Penal Code and the Code of Criminal Procedure were being framed and they contained several sections regarding marriage, the Penal Code containing a separate chapter entitled 'Offences against marriage'. These criminalised adultery and bigamy in particular.

The penal/criminal offences against marriage assumed a singular definition of marriage. This, on the face of it, was opposed to the basic principle in the civil governance of marriage which separated 'personal' laws and recognised variations in custom.

The administration's futile efforts towards a singular definition of marriage caused a variety of problems. In 1868, two years after the Indian Penal Code first came into operation, concerns over the health of soldiers led to the Contagious Diseases Act. The need to police prostitutes made problems of identification and categorisation more urgent. Over time, many marriages, invalidated by the new laws, were dubbed 'clandestine prostitution'; and larger numbers of poor women came under the purview of this blanket term.[4] In Calcutta, where 'the Act was longest in force and has been worked more actively', a daily average of 12 women were arrested by the police.[5] The registering authorities found it difficult to deal with married women, wives of itinerant traders, 'seafaring men' and *kulin* wives who 'practised prostitution' with the 'connivance' of their husbands to augment the 'family income'.[6] Moreover, 'Muslim prostitutes may marry and relapse several times' and many Hindu 'prostitutes' converted to Islam in order to get married.[7] It seemed to colonial officials that compared to Brahminical codes, Islam offered women greater flexibility. Since Muslim women were allowed divorce and remarriage, and followed 'not so rigid a social code', this facilitated the 'rehabilitation' of prostitutes within their own community. In contrast, not only were Hindu women compelled to become prostitutes 'to pursue extra-marital relations', once they had done so they would not be readmitted into their communities. The Sanitary Commissioner felt that extra-marital relations led to the spread of venereal diseases among 'husbands', but felt unable to tackle such a widespread practice.[8] The Secretary of the Bengal Municipal Department admitted that an accurate but effective definition of the 'common prostitute' would continue to elude the government unless they were able to define 'marriage'.[9]

The only acceptable legal definition of marriage would be one that conformed to upper class and high caste norms and could be interpreted through the prism of textual prescriptions of Hinduism and Islam. The social reform debates of the early nineteenth century had already initiated the process of amalgamating a bourgeois Victorian morality, a puritan Brahmo ethic and brahminical norms. The specific target of these reforms was the marriage system of the Hindus. The high-caste, middle-class reformers usually addressed, selectively, issues relating to upper-caste Hindu women. However, the legal and institutional innovations of colonial society empowered these elite men to speak on behalf of the 'Hindus' in their widest definition. As a result, low-caste peasants, labourers and artisans were coopted as participants in upholding the putative Hindu ideal of womanhood. The process involved a legal and ritual brahminisation of marriage. In the only accepted brahminical view, marriage was a sacrament and, therefore, irrevocable. Neither men nor women could revoke marriage though they could dispense with some of the usual observances of marital life. There could be separation, but no divorce. The problem was that while men could marry several times, women were tied to the one irrevocable marriage, ideally, even beyond the death of the husband.

The brahminisation of marriage was a means of denying poor and lower caste women their customary rights of divorce and remarriage and thereby ensuring the control of the male head of the family. But, the criminal/penal laws on adultery and bigamy were of doubtful value in securing these ends. The implementation of these laws forced the colonial state into a delicate balancing act. By application of (Brahminical or Islamic) textual definitions of 'marriage', they were outlawing low caste marital practices which were designated 'immoral'. Their common sense notions about low caste immoralities were shared by elite Indian men, especially those in the lower echelons of colonial administration, who were often required to adjudicate the marital disputes of the poor. At the same time, to bring the lower castes under the purview of criminal jurisdiction, their usual forms of marriages had to be given some status in law.

These problems were often sought to be circumvented by taking refuge in 'custom' which was given the force of law. But custom had to be constantly negotiated. If a customary deviation from the ritual formalisation of marriage was accepted in order to prove adultery or bigamy, it opened the possibility of women affirming their customary rights. The confusion lay in the attempt to constitute some customary marriages as 'adultery' and 'bigamy' and give some others the status of legal marriage. Poor women's attempts to assert their customary rights of separation, divorce and remarriage came into conflict with the provisions of the penal/criminal law. The courts were rarely in sympathy with customs that weakened or threatened male control with the family. While some of the criminal/penal laws did have some provision for customary exceptions, customs were extraordinarily difficult to establish procedurally. The legal-juridical system was biased in favour of customs that privileged male control which could be judiciously applied to favoured and upheld brahminical orthodoxy. In the hands of judges and administrators, custom, because of its amorphous nature, became a useful resource. A selective appropriation of custom (as well as textual prescriptions) and its flexible deployment helped elevate the status of the male head of the family. The colonial legal system squared off custom and text against each other allowing primacy to one or the other according to convenience.

In the case of male polygamy, 'custom' justified non-intervention and inaction. The state argued that polygamy was practised across castes, regions and religions. Colonial administrators, despite their periodic Victorian revulsions, pragmatically accepted and legalised these practices.[10] In the 1860s when the Penal Code was being formulated, the excesses of 'coolin' (kulin) polygamy also received a great deal of attention from social reformers. The state, however, rejected outright the possibility of introducing checks on polygamy. Local bureaucrats from various provinces of Bengal warned the Lt. Governor against a petition from the Maharaja of Burdwan and 21,000 'other Hindus' to legislatively bring 'the practice of polygamy strictly within the limits prescribed by ancient Hindu law'.[11] They argued that polygamy was a 'social and religious institution prevalent, to a large extent, throughout the whole country' and 'it is not only a few scattered individuals who advocate and practise polygamy, but the largest proportion of all classes, Hindoos and Mahomedans, who are in a position to maintain a plurality of wives...'[12] One official went as far as to write, 'A plurality of wives is as suited to the people [of the East] as a strict rule of monogamy is in the West... I would, therefore, strongly disapprove of any extension of the Christian law against bigamy as retrograde and unsuited to the people.'[13]

A confusion arose over 'custom' which tacitly sanctioned male polygamy—even among Christian Santhals and Brahmos. But wives of Christian converts, poor and low caste women were rarely given such benefit of doubt regarding 'custom'.[14] In the case of women, marital arrangements that violated the principle of a life-long sacrament, that allowed divorce and remarriage, and did not prescribe strict monogamy were to be considered illegitimate and presumed 'deviant'. By these standards, the sexual 'customs' of the poor and the lower castes appeared particularly promiscuous. By extension, poor and low-caste women were characterised as sexually deviant. The formalisation of sexual relations varied enormously across social groups and regions. Official expectations were confused by the ease and lack of ceremony with which some 'marriages' were entered into and dissolved. The centralised legal-juridical system could not reconcile these protean practices within the framework of the 'Hindu law' which brahminical interpretations of texts had provided. Their response was to define marriage more rigidly in accord with high caste norms and to increase men's control over their wive's labour and sexuality.

A singular definition of marriage, however, continued to be elusive. British officials attempted to grope through, what appeared to them, a bewildering range and variety of cohabitation practices. Many different terms, haphazardly translated and torn from their social contexts, were used in an attempt to distinguish among these. The term 'temporary' marriage was one of these, originally supposed to describe the more stable but legally invalid cohabitation arrangements that had widespread currency. But applied with assiduous regularity, as it was, the term soon began to include an equally random assortment of practices. Originally coined for the relatively informal systems of separation, divorce, remarriage and multiple marriages current among low caste Hindus and poor Muslims, it soon became a blanket expression, obscuring a diverse set of changing sexual relations. The problem with 'temporary' marriage referred more particularly to women entering such arrangements. The privileging of brahminical norms of sacral marriage began to delegitimise the very notion of women's 'temporary marriage'. Legally, a 'temporary' marriage, like a second marriage, was concubinage; morally, it seemed akin to prostitution.

The designation of some marriages as 'temporary' compounded the problems of administering the penal law. On the one hand, these arrangements were recognised as customary, on the other they were decreed illicit. Colonial officers further confused matters by highlighting their deviations from high caste norms, as though to demonstrate their invalidity. It is unlikely that the marital arrangements of the poor and low castes were completely autonomous from the values of the dominant Hindus and Muslims, but their negative evaluation ignored the existing differences in codes of formalising sexual relations.

Throughout the nineteenth century, colonial officials documented various aberrations in marriage practices in the district gazetteers and census records. Administrative exigencies often prompted a practical tolerance towards the more widespread 'customs', even when they were in conflict with newly established laws. More importantly, however, the emphasis on deviation from high caste practices and textual prescriptions provided increasingly greater 'evidence' both to prove low caste women's promiscuity and to whittle their access to divorce and remarriage. L.S.S. O'Malley's description of Bagdi marriage customs is notable particularly in the way he deploys the notion of 'Hindu'. In Bankura, Manbhum and north Orissa, Bagdis were considered 'more semi-aboriginal', they accepted adult marriages and permitted pre-marital sexual relations. East of Bhagirathi, however, the rule was infant marriage. Thus they were supposed to be more 'Hinduised'.[15] The Bholla claim to superior caste status over the Bagdi was by subjecting divorce to greater restriction in their community.[16]

Vaishnava women were particularly denigrated because they appeared to dispense altogether with the formalisation of sexual relationships. The relative sexual freedom enjoyed by many Vaishnava women outraged Indian and British moralists. By the late nineteenth century, they came under systematic attack from reformers. The *akharas*, always a refuge for destitute women, became associated with prostitution. In Dinajpur, it was believed that 'Hindu prostitutes call themselves Boshtami'.[17] Bankim Chatterjee, the Deputy Magistrate of Murshidabad (better known for his essays, satires and novels) agreed that the Baishnabis were akin to prostitutes. He argued that 'the loose morality of... [the] sect is separated by a very slight line from the utter negation of female morality which constitutes prostitution'.[18] British officials by and large concurred with this view.[19] The Census of 1881 found Vaishnavas to have a larger proportion of women. The officer discovered a semantic confusion between vaishnavis and prostitutes.

> [I]t is a common practice among public women to assume the style of Baishnabs, while the similarity between the name and the word Vaisya [or, more commonly, beshya, meaning prostitute] which denotes their profession is near enough to have led to some mistakes.[20]

The chamars of Bilaspur were also believed to indulge in illegal divorces and remarriages. Apart from the ordinary Bihao or Sadi (arranged marriages) they had other, equally common and accepted forms of marriages. Churi represented the right of the first husband's brother to the widow. But, 'very often, she runs away with someone else'. Only rarely did such affairs end up in prosecution for adultery. Paithoo allowed a married woman to go 'away to the house of her seducer and [begin] to live with him as his wife, and [obtain] the privileges and rights of one... her new husband might have to pay compensation, generally measured by the marriage expense.' It was pointed out by the Census Commissioner that 'the children of both the latter classes of marriage succeeded equally with those of the married wife and such succession is often recognised by our courts.'[21]

The monetary exchanges customarily regarded as adequate settlement of marital disputes, though quite consistent with prevailing brideprice practices, nevertheless did not legalise these marriages. The Census Commissioner ruefully noted that where aberrations were the norm, the law was helpless.

> [I]f the Indian Penal Code be strictly administered in Chhatisgarh, almost one-tenth of the Chamars might be amenable to one or the other sections relating to marriage, and a good many women would go to jail for bigamy. But laws which are above the working level of society can scarcely be effectively administrated, and the law is almost a dead letter in the face of facts, which are held to be quite consistent with good sense and Chhatisgarh morality.[22]

Such sanguine and pragmatic recognition of variable marital and divorce practices became rare by the end of the nineteenth century. The new laws changed gender equations in the community. Neither 'good sense' nor erstwhile morality survived intact the changes in the legal-juridical system. For poor and lower caste men there were new options in penal/criminal law. They could use the courts to curtail women's customary access to divorce and remarriage. Thus the processes of denigrating Vaishnava women and stigmatising Bagdi and Chamar marriages were reinforced. As far as men were concerned, the Government rejected demands to restrict polygamy to narrower textual prescriptions of Hinduism or Islam on grounds of custom. It argued that polygamy was too widely practised and there would be too great an outcry against legislation on such issues. In the case of women, however, a move towards brahminical orthodoxy was relatively easy. British habits, judicial temper and Indian elite convictions converged to condemn and outlaw all female polygamous practices. Hindu women found all options of a second marriage closed. Despite the Widow Remarriage Act (1856), widows of lower and intermediate castes found it more difficult to remarry.[23] The Madras High Court ruled that Hindu marriages were to be monogamous for women. Government admitted that the law of divorce among the Hindus was not properly worked out, but they decreed that divorce did not set a Hindu woman free to marry again.[24] For Hindu women, all second marriages were declared to be 'not marriages at all' and a 'woman contracting a second marriage would know... that the Government did not recognise her condition as that of a wife living in marriage but in concubinage'.[25]

Such blanket application of brahminical norms did, as has frequently been argued, divest lower caste women of their customary rights and freedoms in marriage. However, the colonial rulers did not fully understand the implications of these customary rights. The relative fluidity and flexibility of marriages among the lower castes not only indicated a greater freedom for their women, but also a greater sexual access of upper caste men to lower caste women. There were, as Kumkum Sangari points out, 'partial, erratic quasi-functional connections' between low caste women's relative freedom and upper caste women's lack of it. Brahminical law was not, in fact, premised on 'uniformity' or the universalisation of one patriarchal arrangement. The lower castes lacked inheritance, property and corollary lineage concerns. Their 'looser attachment' to the written word, to orthodox religion and political power permitted their women to have customary access to divorce and remarriage.[26] Their marriages were not marked by the same emphasis on women's chastity that characterised higher caste Hindu and upper class Muslim marriages. Poor men were thought to turn a blind eye to their wives' extra-marital affairs, either through indifference or for gain. Husbands were thought to 'connive at the defilement of their wives'.[27] Apparently, among some low castes (notably the Magahiya Doms) it was considered commonplace to ignore the infidelities of wives, as long as 'she brings grist to the mill'.[28] Rural labouring groups, in particular, attached greater importance to controlling the returns of women's labour and sexual services. As a result, marriages between the poor sometimes resembled forced labour arrangements and new restrictions on divorce gave these arrangements more teeth.

'Offences Against Marriage'—Problems of Implementation

As peasant women lost their traditional means of independent subsistence, they became vulnerable to more intensive extraction of labour on the family farm. The new legal constraints supplemented existing economic constraints on women's mobility. The courts gave men more power to secure and retain wives against their will. But, the contradictions built into these laws often defeated the purpose for which they were meant. At the core of the problem was the ambiguous status of custom. There was, first, a question of the range of customs accepted in the legal validation of marriages. What ceremonial and ritual sanction would establish the legal validity of the 'first' marriage? If customary second and subsequent marriages were outlawed, then the right of husbands based on these marriages also became invalid. Sometimes the men seeking redress of criminal law found themselves vulnerable to charges of adultery and enticement in second marriages which were sanctioned in custom. In addition, there was the problem of new procedures of 'evidence'. The application of penal/criminal laws depended on actual 'proof' of marriage which was difficult to furnish given the absence of records and registration.

Local administrators found that they had to settle for less than full implementation of the IPC chapter on marriage. In Midnapur and Burdwan, magistrates realised that penalising all second marriages was an impossible task. They argued that 'second marriage is concubinage but it is not penal and there is no need to make it penal'.[29] The Commissioner of Burdwan argued that the new laws of bigamy and adultery would play havoc with the *nikka* marriages of the divorced women of the low castes in some parts'. Despite the widespread prevalence of nikka among low castes, it was held to be 'a Muhammedan institution and when the lower class of Hindus get nikka wives, the word is but another name for concubinage'.[30]

According to the Commissioner, the term nikka was derived from Arabic and meant marriage. In nineteenth century Bengal, many Muslims called the first marriage shadi (meaning delight) which was ritually celebrated. The second marriage was called nikka and, even among Muslims, influenced by Hindu notions of disgrace attached to second marriages, performed with less ceremony.[31] Many lower castes and especially Vaishnavas also used the term. Both divorced and widowed women called their second marriage nikka.[32] The Commissioner agreed that these second marriages constituted concubinage, especially in the case of divorced women. Even so, he resisted penalising these marriages because they were so widely practised and so easily accepted within the communities in which they occurred.[33]

So far as the penal/criminal laws were concerned, however, women contracting more than one marriage, and their second (and all subsequent) husbands, became criminally liable. The provisions of adultery and bigamy were framed on the assumption that marriage was monogamous for Hindu and Muslim women. And against the weight of the formidable evidence furnished by their own officials, colonial courts accepted the principle that in case of Hindu women monogamy was a life-long bond. A Hindu woman, even if separated from her husband, could be punished for bigamy (IPC Section 494-5) if she married again during the lifetime of her first husband.

The other instrument given to husbands was the law of restitution of conjugal rights. Men were thereby allowed the use of courts to restrain and recover their runaway wives. Initially, the government was unclear as to how rigorously to apply the restitution of conjugal rights. In 1800, A. Sconce, a member of the Legislative Council raised the question of 'rights in persons' (wives and children) in marriage as opposed to the 'rights in things' (dower and inheritance). The courts were faced with applications for 'restitution' of wives, against unwilling detention of wives and against forcible abduction of children. Of these, 'restitution' proved the most complicated issue. Muslim men had already begun to sue for restitution on grounds of 'enforcing the contract of marriage'. In the Hindu case, the law was less clear because the question of divorce and its validity had not been settled. Sconce felt that Hindu men would also 'benefit' by a law of restitution 'in occasional claims to enforce contracts of which the evasion is attempted'. There was, of course, resistance from various quarters against the notion of Hindu marriage being regarded as a contract rather than a sacrament. Moreover, the Lieutenant Governor refused 'to uphold the justice and [was] less prepared to uphold the expediency in any country, least of all in India, of empowering any court to force one grown-up person to live with another, on a suit for the restitution of conjugal rights'.[34] In 1867, however, restitution was introduced by a judicial decision and later incorporated in the Code of Civil Procedure (1882) Section 260 and 1908 CCP (Order 21 Rule 32). But this provision did not prove effective. As a Deputy Magistrate noted, even if the husband won a declaratory decree, 'the wife cannot be bodily *delivered* over to the husband'. She could at best be charged with contempt of court which was a tedious and expensive procedure.[35]

In many cases, even a declaratory decree proved difficult to obtain. The courts' inability or reluctance to grant restoration decrees resulted from a loophole in the law. Both civil and criminal suits hinged on the definition of 'marriage'. In the case of bigamy and adultery, 'even when the fact of marriage is not disputed, the law requires strict legal proof of the performance of the first marriage'.[36] Thus courts often found themselves unable to enforce fidelity on women: 'very often cases of enticing away married women and other offences relative to marriage are... thrown away since the validity of the marriage could not be proved by any authenticated records'.[37] In most cases, the legal proof of either marriage or divorce could not be easily furnished. There was no provision at all for registration of Hindu marriages. The government refused to countenance any intervention into the accepted manners of solemnising Hindu marriages.[38]

In eastern Bengal, another set of complications arose. In these areas, the mainstay of the agrarian system was the small family farm largely dependent on unremunerated family labour. Also, the gender division of labour in agriculture was relatively more clearly defined. Women from peasant families rarely undertook field labour, but they provided the critical post-harvest input in long-drawn processing activities. Their work was, by and large, compatible with physical seclusion which was more strictly enforced than in northern and western Bengal. While the lower caste and labouring women were in much the same position as elsewhere in Bengal, peasant women had fewer options outside marriage. Their relative economic vulnerability made them more susceptible to the pressures of the new penal/criminal laws. In the 1870s, soon after the IPC came into operation, several controversial questions arose regarding the implementation of the laws of enticement, adultery and bigamy.

The eastern Bengal peasantry was predominantly Muslim. In Islamic law, women's divorce and remarriage were valid. However, as in the case of the Hindu nikka, the Shia Muslim *mota* was recognised as customary, but considered concubinage rather than marriage. Though the father took responsibility for children born of such marriages, '[a] mota or temporary wife is nothing but a legalised kept mistress'.[39] The mota was unacceptable because it empowered women to leave their marriages. Even the *khula* divorce, which women could initiate, was replaced with the unilateral male *talak*.[40] As a result, if a man wished to divorce his wife, 'he gets rid of her by simply informing his neighbours that she is at liberty to go where she pleases, and he refuses to support her any longer'.[41] However, if women left their husbands, they could be charged with desertion. If they subsequently contracted another marriage, they became liable to charges of bigamy and adultery, and their new husbands to charges of enticement or kidnapping.

Muslims could, voluntarily, register their marriages under the Muhammedan Marriage Registration Act and the Kazis Act of 1876 and 1880.[42] In fact, registration of marriages or divorces was by no means common in eastern Bengal. The poorer Muslims almost never drew up a talaknamah. At most talak was verbally delivered 'in the presence of a moulvie or some principal inhabitants of the place'. The upper classes took care to register the *dain mohur* (*kabinnamah*) or deeds of dower, but among poorer Muslims marriage registration was rare. Moulvi Mahomed, Deputy Magistrate, Furreedpore urged that, for the purpose of proving adultery or bigamy, women living with and under the protection of a man for a period be presumed married. This, he argued, would 'put a stop to a great deal of prostitution and social degradation'. And, moreover, by Muslim law and pratice, if a man and a woman lived together before the 'village public', they were presumed married unless the matter was disputed.[43]

The penal/criminal laws, however, required the fact of marriage to be proved by at least three witnesses. If the husband did produce three witnesses to prove 'marriage', technically at least, the wife too could bring witnesses to prove that she had been duly divorced and therefore had the legal right to enter a second marriage by nikka. Some moulvis recommended that in such cases, the requirements of proof be relaxed in favour of husbands and that judges be allowed greater discretionary powers.[44]

Many local officers and magistrates argued for compulsory registration to solve the problem of proof. For instance in Howrah, a rapidly expanding satellite town of Calcutta, 'the omission to register Mahomedan marriages or divorces has led to a very loose system of morality as regards marriages'.[45] The magistrates asked for an extension of the Muhammendan Marriage Registration Act and Kazis Acts. Howrah, with a large migrant population, suffered special difficulties regarding evidence by witness. But the Commissioner of Burdwan recognised the generality of the problem. Muslim peasant women denied their right to initiate divorce, were able to capitalise on the informality of the verbal talak to legitimise a second marriage. The commissioner thus wished to expedite the process of extending the Acts regarding registration.[46] In the Muslim majority districts of eastern Bengal, however, compulsory registration, even at especially lowered fees, would discourage marriage altogether, argued local officials. 'More people will keep women as concubines than now do so rather than be put to trouble and an expense that has not been customary'.[47]

Syed Mahomed Israil, a well-to-do Muslim and a Deputy Magistrate of Mymensingh, indignantly argued the case for poorer Muslim husbands. They were, he argued, really aggrieved by the requirement of proof. Their attempts to recover deserting wives were usually defeated. Wives, bent on desertion, he went on to explain, often complained in court that they had been wrongfully confined and desired to be set free. A wife could thus leave 'the poor man to whom she has been lawfully wedded' and 'go to a paramour who may then be served the same turn'. If the wife charged with bigamy disputed the fact of the first marriage, Israil argued, she did so because '[s]ome crafty man of an immoral character puts temptation in her way and prevails upon her to forsake her lawful husband, and then he manages to elope with her and steal a match'. It was the 'paramour behind the scenes' who organised these defences for immoral or misled wives of injured husbands.[48]

The courts often refused to recognise that such aborted cases constituted a miscarriage of justice. In general, their sympathy lay with the 'injured husband' unless his misconduct could be proved. The colonial judicial system—by legislation and through the courts—attempted to safeguard men's control over wives and daughters. But magistrates believed that such cases were often settled out of court. In cases of adultery and bigamy, the 'seducer' finding himself liable under 'enticement' and/or adultery settled with the 'husband' who 'let the case drop if he gets the woman back, and especially if the accused pays the expenses of the case'. Also, often, husbands brought false cases of adultery and bigamy or sued for restitution merely to create pressure on their wives and relatives.

> In many cases it is found that the woman has gone to the protection of her own father or brother, or a married sister's house, and then her husband makes a 498 case against all her relations, male and female, and at the same time he promises all sorts of things; and to get out of trouble and expense her friends persuade the woman, she will be forced in the end to go back, so it is better to go with good grace. Then the complainant disappears from the court, and it appears as if there has been a failure of justice.[49]

While, in general, British Indian courts favoured the 'injured husband', Government officers sometimes argued against polygamous husbands taking recourse to courts. Since polygamy was associated more strongly with Muslim men, official sympathy for Muslim men's rights over their wives was not always unequivocal. To complaints that deserted Muslim husbands found no redress in the courts, H.J. Reynolds, a Magistrate of Mymensingh, replied,

> I was forcibly struck with the entire one-sidedness of the views.... The subject is fully as much a woman's question as a man's; but... [the Moulvi] seemed to me to handle it entirely from the husband's point of view, and altogether to omit to notice the injustice to the other sex which the present state of the conjugal relation among Mahomedans so frequently involves.... [T]he only remedy is for Mahomedan husbands to realise that the married state implies duties as well as rights.[50]

The British felt the real problem—'the plurality of wives permitted'—was beyond remedy. One officer asserted that 'very rarely do women desert unless another wife is brought to the house'. H.S. Beadon, an Undersecretary to the Government of Bengal, rebutted Syed Mahomed Israil's hypothetical scenario with one of his own. He argued that 'in the great majority of cases the charges are not brought in good faith, and that the process of the court... [is] turned into a mere engine of extortion'. Muslim men who married two or three wives were liable to ill-treat at least one of them. If she ran away to her father or bother, the husband usually made no attempt to bring her back. The relatives, forced to maintain her, would urge a nikka marriage with another man 'who may or may not know that she has been married before'. Then the first husband would sue the wife and the second husband for bigamy and adultery. The aim was to force the second husband to settle a lump sum out of court. Beadon believed this was a 'very common occurrence'.[51]

The Commissioner of Rajshahye added that such situations could be averted by a provision that when a man contracts a second marriage 'he should be bound to make proper provisions for the wife under the first contract before the marriage tie is dissolved and he is permitted to enter into a second contract of marriage which would be recognised by law'.[52] But for most local officers this went a little too far. First, in essence polygamy meant that a second marriage did not require the dissolution of the first marriage—the two could co-exist. L.B.B. King from Noakhally pointed out that a man's second marriage was by no means a revocation of the first marriage contract. Nor could it be assumed that 'the first marriage contract was entered into by the woman only on the understanding that it was to be monogamous'. Rather, the consent of the first wife in her husband's second marriage was considered 'immaterial'. The obligation to maintain a first wife could not then be admitted as a condition for a man's second marriage. The matter was considered to be adequately dealt with the CrPC provision for maintenance.[53]

It has been argued that among the lower and many intermediate castes, peasant and labouring groups, marriage was a means of extracting women's labour. Moreover, the relative fluidity of marriage practices and the comparatively lower emphasis on women's chastity was related to upper caste men's sexual access to lower caste women. In these circumstances, access to divorce could represent an escape for women and the possibility of remarriage provided them room for negotiation. It appears as though women frequently took recourse to flight. They ran away with other men or went to plantations, mines, cities and towns. The women who went to live with other men found themselves and their new husbands vulnerable to restitution proceedings and criminally liable under sections 494, 495 and 498 of the Indian Penal Code relating to enticement, adultery and bigamy.

In course of the actual implementation of these laws, the doubts expressed by local officials proved justified. These laws could not quite serve their purpose. A narrower definition of marriage turned many of these laws, which were meant to enhance men's control over women, into an instrument which women could use against men they wished to leave. To do so they had to admit to concubinage, bigamy or adultery. In cases where a notion of honour was not closely linked to chastity and lifelong monogamy these admissions may not have been so difficult. I have argued that these admissions were easier in migrant and urban situations where women had already lost 'honour' by the very fact of flight or migration.[54] In any case, in communities where adult marriages, divorce and remarriage were informal and frequent, the application of upper class norms in the definition of concubinage, adultery and bigamy may have rendered these terms meaningless. So, some women could manipulate the law to deny men the rights these legal innovations were supposed to guarantee.

Poor women found a stronger imperative to deny men an exclusive right to their labour, services and sexuality. Besides, women of labouring communities, those who worked for daily hire, risked less. They could and often did themselves deny the fact of marriage. Where women repudiated their husbands (by denying the fact of marriage and admitting thereby to concubinage) the courts were unable to uphold the rights of the men who demanded restitution of their 'wives'. Some women found in this provision for 'proof' a way round the many disabilities that hedged their attempts at escaping oppressive marriages. Often, it proved very difficult to decide which marriage came first and complied with the legal requirements. The administration of marriage laws became fraught with difficulties. As the Census Commissioner had so acutely noted of Chhatisgarh, 'laws which are above the working level of society' stood in danger of remaining a 'dead letter'.[55]

Women's ability to manoeuvre the law must not, however, be overestimated. While some women were able to utilise the loopholes of the law, many found themselves in prison for committing 'offences against marriage'. Moreover, for every case that went to court and found its way into official returns and newspaper reports, many did not. Men did not depend only on courts to bend recalcitrant women to their will. Social pressure and socially sanctioned violence was used more frequently and to greater effect.

Women's Migration—An Offence Against Marriage?

Towards the end of the nineteenth century, women's

long-distance migration assumed a new significance, with increasing demand for women in plantations, in overseas colonies and in the Assam tea gardens. The question of women's migration became enmeshed in concerns similar to those relating to the penal 'offences against marriage'. Indeed, by the twentieth century, women's long-distance migration, especially the recruitment of married women, became constituted as an offence against marriage.

In the mid-nineteenth century, when the 'enticement clause' in Regulation VII (1819) was being developed to be incorporated in the IPC, the 'labour clause' which bound workers to contracts was also acquiring fuller shape. The labour clause in Regulation VII made the desertion by workmen before the expiry of the term agreed upon punishable by a term of imprisonment. The question of labour control had assumed significance from the closing decades of the eighteenth century when the expansion of Calcutta hiked the demand for labour. European employers were constantly complaining of their inability to retain workers over a reasonable length of time. The punitive measures against workers were justified by the claim that in cases where the employer paid an advance, the employment contract assumed that the worker would work long enough to allow the employer to recover his advance.

In cases where employers were forced to recruit workers from distance areas and required to pay for the costs of migration, a formal mechanism to ensure workers' adherence to employment agreements became more necessary. Planters—in overseas colonies and in the tea gardens of north Bengal and Assam—were, in particular, interested in harnessing state machinery to reinforce a coercive system of labour control. These new employers operating within the colonial system influenced the labour market and the pattern of migration. The earlier social modes of labour control, which operated through the ritual hierarchies of caste, were no longer adequate. As a result, the penally enforcible contracts became a fully blown indentureship system through the Workmen's Breach of Contract Act of 1859.[56]

To some degree, the issue of the organisation of labour—whether in industry, plantation, mines or agriculture—impinged on the marriage system. Alongside caste and other localised institutions, the family was an important means through which work was organised—in pre-colonial India, it was a legal and ideological instrument for legitimising coercive labour arrangements. In an earlier section of the essay it has been pointed out that the colonial state was also highly dependent on familial deployment of labour for the survival of peasant small-holdings. By and large, the family remained the vehicle for the quotidian application of labour. Work in the household was organised hierarchically by gender and age. In agrarian society, the male head of the household's interest in the control of family labour increased as the already low surplus dwindled further. The household tasks towards consumption, subsistence and social production gained in importance.[57] Women's labour, not just of mothers but of other women especially those widowed, became vital for the poor rural household. Since women's tasks were associated with familial roles, they could be rewarded with a disproportionately low share of the social product. Moreover, since their access to resources was conditional on their familial role fulfilment, heads of families could respond to market opportunities by intensifying the use of family labour.[58]

Generally speaking, the so-called modern sector—factories, plantations and mines—was too limited to require any major intervention into these gender and generational controls. The major industries and urban employers found the family useful in making labour cheaper. Men came to the cities and towns to earn wages, women and children remained in the village to eke out a living from declining rural resources. This classic 'peasant-proletariat' provided for the physical reproduction of the labour force outside the capitalist sphere and required no contribution from the employer by way of wages or as revenue. Employers found the flexibility of the adult male worker who was able to command the labour of his wife and children in the village home more useful than a labour market augmented by young men and women 'free' from familial control. Instead, the family itself became a cheap and informal mechanism of recruitment, often operating within other local caste and community affiliations.[59]

The family continued to play a role in recruitment even when labour was required in greater quantities, as in the case of migrations to Assam and the overseas colonies. But the planters could not depend on informal recruitment. The Assam plantations were situated in distant, inaccessible, labour-scarce areas; and West Indian planters required, quickly, a substitute for African slaves. As a result, both sought the protection of an indentureship system to offset the expenses of organised recruitment. Towards the end of the nineteenth century, both these sets of planters became particularly interested in women's migration. Ideally, the planters wanted to relocate entire families. But they found that adult men seeking migration alone far outnumbered families seeking migration together. They thus resorted to recruitment of single men and single women with the intention of establishing families in the plantations.[60]

The recruitment of 'single' women raised a host of questions. Who were 'single' women? Legally speaking, unmarried women were subject to paternal authority. Besides, the universality and low age of marriage left very few adult women who were technically 'single'. The predominant familial idiom was resistant to the very notion of 'single' women capable of migration outside the family context. Even widows and deserted women were presumed to be part of an extended family—fathers and brothers in the conjugal and/or natal family could lay claim to, and exercise authority over, such women. Indian middle class public opnion disputed the possibility of women's voluntary migration. Women's extra-familial migration became constituted as 'forced' and 'illegal' by definition, not necessarily because the woman migrant was being 'forced' but because the male head of the family was being 'forced' to relinquish his claim on the woman. From the 1870s, the issue caused many a flutter in Calcutta's press. '[A] certain class of writers in the Vernacular Press' harried the Government, exhibiting 'bitter hostility' to planters and carrying hair-raising stories of rape and murder of women workers by plantation managers.[61]

It did not help when British officers in the recruiting districts added their voices to these condemnations. Many local officers in labour catchment districts argued that women's migration outside the family context was deviant. They believed that such migration, voluntary or involuntary, threatened familial control over women's labour and sexuality. They had to deal with increasing numbers of cases of missing wives and daughters. Many district level functionaries began to call for stringent legislative restraints on recruiters to protect the interests of fathers and husbands. A magistrate wrote from Chhotanagpur, 'to protect husbands from the wiles of the coolie recruiter, there should be some... order... regarding the registration of married women'.[62] The arguments advanced by officials to restrict the emigration of women clearly spelt out the two most problematic aspects of unregulated recruitment. The possibility of emigration, it was asserted, widened women's sexual choices, thereby undermining their control and containment within marriage. In such arguments the line between illegitimate and exploitative sexual relations were often blurred: exploitation was seen to be the invariable and inevitable consequence of illegitimate sexual liaisons. The other line of argument concentrated on the domestic role of women. The concerned elite men and British officials drew moving and poignant portraits of the deserted husband, the uncared home and the abandoned child. In both these arguments, the key was marriage and the deployment of women's labour and sexuality which were thought to be threatened by women's emigration.

The existent Inland Emigration acts were proving ineffective. Clearly, the very definition of 'fraudulent' recruitment needed to be extended to include not only 'kidnapping' but also voluntary migration of women. The Government of India resisted fresh legislation because it believed that 'abuses' like 'enticement by fraudulent means' were 'inevitable under any system of emigration on a large scale'.[63] This was especially so in the case of women, argued some Bengal and Assam officers, because of the difficulties of recruiting them.[64] The Government was being pulled in different directions. The planters needed women and were willing to coax, cajole and coerce women into contracts. The Indian Government was committed to protect the interests of the tea-planters. Meanwhile, the coercive recruitment tactics of plantations and emigration agents hardened patriarchal opposition to women's migration. Objections to women's recruitment poured forth from various quarters. The government was enmeshed in alliances with various segments of the rural elites who resisted plantation recruitment of women. Neither the government's economic nor its political interests would be served through undermining the household economy.

In the course of these debates women, rather than men, emerged as critical to the integrity of the household economy. The increased importance of women's labour in the rural subsistence sector meant that the planters and their agents were confronted by formidable competition in their attempts to recruit women. Plantation employment offered women an extra-familial option, the very existence of which the rural 'family' resisted for fear of erosion of its authority. Plantation recruitment was particularly complicated because it involved a prolonged contract. Legally, such a labour contract could be held against the family's claims. Consequently, a great deal of the debate about women's recruitment turned on the issue of women's ability to enter labour contracts. While planters, backed by some British officials, pressed for 'greater freedom' of women to migrate and to enter work agreements, other officers, especially those in the recruiting districts, were supported by the local elites and the bhadralok reformers to press for women's 'protection against fraudulent recruitment' and to safeguard the family against women's migration.

The enticement of married women 'for immoral purposes' was already a cognisable offence under the Indian Penal Code. It was not clear, however, how such a clause could be used against recruiters. In the 1870s, there were several cases where these confusions became apparent. A recruiter, Jaggo Mahato, was charged with the abduction of 11-year old Geerdharee Bhooyan. Nothing could be proved. But the judge felt that these were, in effect, cases of 'enticement'. He argued that the women, thus leaving their husbands, go into the keeping of other men, and the act of enlistment though not illegal at the time becomes tantamount to inducing a married woman to leave her husband for an immoral purpose which the recruiter knows full well will be the result and he can recruit such a woman with perfect impunity.[65]

There were obviously two sides to this argument. The first involved 'inducing a married woman to leave her husband' which was a civil problem remediable by restitution proceedings, but not a penal offence by itself, the second involved the 'immoral purpose' which brought in the penal law. If the woman was 'induced' for prostitution, the law against enticement would apply, if she was 'induced' by another man for marriage, the laws of adultery and bigamy could be invoked; but if she was 'induced' into entering a labour contract, penal law had no remedy. The laws of adultery and bigamy could not be very effectively used in these cases. There were many women recruiters 'inducing' married women, as in the cases of prostitution. Besides, the adultery and bigamy laws were themselves running into problems when applied in courts. Similar problems were faced by judges in emigration cases. Sheikh Panchoo, a recruiter, was charged with the kidnapping of Nobin Mochi's wife. The woman in question was about 20 years old. She testified that she had left Nobin 'voluntarily'. Moreover, it could not be proved that she was related to Nobin, 'even by nikka marriage'. The judge, unable to convict, was sympathetic to Nobin's plight. Such recruitments, he felt, were 'against law and morality', but until the law was clearer in the matter, little could be done.[66] The question was whether the enticement law could be interpreted thus: if a married woman was enticed for a second marriage, the laws of adultery and bigamy would apply, enticement for any other purpose must necessarily be 'immoral' and therefore covered by Section 366 of the IPC. A district migistrate of Chhotanagpur argued that the spirit of the law would be violated if a clause designed to deal with the sale of women into prostitution was stretched to cover labour contracts. But to him, as to many others, there was little difference between the practice of prostitution and the non-marital or extra-marital sexual relationships into which women entered when they reached the tea gardens or the colonies. He argued that separate legislative or administrative measures had to be taken to prevent 'enticement' of women away from their husbands into labour contracts.

> The magistrate should be prohibited from registering as coolies wives who have husbands living without first obtaining the sanction of the husbands—as the law stands now, it is not a penal offence for a coolies recruiter to entice away a married woman over 16 years of age, merely to send her as a coolie to the tea districts. It would... be too great a stretch of the law to hold the doing so to be an offence under section 366, IPC, as the recruiter could hardly be supposed to know that a wife was likely to be seduced to illicit intercourse, though there would be every probability of such a result if she went without her husband.[67]

Charges of enticement were, however, easier to handle than 'abduction' and 'kidnapping'. A charge of enticement could occasionally be made to stick even if the women's willingness to be thus 'enticed' remained questionable. Many cases of kidnapping and abduction were, however, brought to nought because women were willing to declare their consent before the magistrate. By definition, 'abduction' and 'kidnapping', except when they involved minors, assumed forcible apprehension against the will of the victim. Thus when a recruiter was charged with the kidnapping of three young women, the registering officer recorded that though there had '... undoubtedly been great deceit practised by the accused... the offence of kidnapping had not been established...'[68] Many cases came to hinge on proof of the nature and extent of deceit practiced by recruiters.

The needs of the family and the household economy could not be subordinated, on principle, at least, to the planters' requirements of cheap female labour. Thus, the arguments that upheld the father's and husband's right over daughters and wives won against the exigency of 'freeing' female labour. The control and containment of women within marriage appeared the most critical issue. The representations of the indigenous men and local British officers prevailed—women's ability to enter labour contracts on their own behalf was significantly curtailed. Several clauses were included in the Assam Labour and Emigration Act (Act VI of 1901) to prevent women's entering labour contracts without the 'consent' of male guardians. The legal ground for these was found in the marriage contract: '[a] married women may be said to have entered into a contract with her husband which precludes her from engaging in services to another party for a term of years without his consent'.[69]

Conclusion

Colonial laws helped buttress the key role of the household economy which depended on the deployment of unremunerated family labour. It was really the supposed immunity of the family from legislative regulation that made its labour arrangements more coercive and exploitative. But to reinforce family authority for a more efficient and intensive use of family labour, colonial laws had to repeatedly intercede in its legal arrangements. In any case, legislative intervention in the direction of brahminical orthodoxy was never ruled out and happened relatively quietly. Since marriage remained fundamental in household formation, a great deal of emphasis was laid on defining marriage and extending its legal scope. The trend was towards elevating family authority i.e., the authority of male heads of household, over other members of the family. Fathers and husbands were given the aid of civil and criminal instruments to move court to enforce their will on daughters and wives.

In this relation, the state was willing to abrogate the rhetoric of a 'free' labour market. The protection of 'family' and 'marriage' allowed questions of labour to be partially displaced from the market discourse. The state helped to restrain capitalist inroads on labour from the household economy to 'save the family'. But the plantation demand for women workers was resisted by constituting marriage as a contract—a contract that precluded women entering a labour contract after marriage.

Implicitly, the contract for marriage and for labour were posed as conflictual.

The state was moving towards a draconian marriage regime. Women were not to resist or escape marriage by flight, divorce or migration. A new range of offences were constituted under the criminal/penal system—bigamy, adultery and enticement were some of those regularly invoked in the courts. Through these, the state helped men to restrain women within the more narrowly defined norms of marriage. In the case of lower castes, these laws overrode women's customary access to separation, divorce and remarriage which were often the only way they could escape unhappy and oppressive marriages. Since marriage usually provided husbands a means of appropriating the rewards of women's labour and sexual services, such escape routes were important.

The denial of some customary rights produced a host of contradictions in the legal-juridical regulation of marriages which were not always resolved. By and large, the colonial state was able to selectively appropriate custom in upholding brahminical norms and men's rights over women's. But the negotiation of customs and its incompatibility with the new rules of evidence also produced loopholes which women could use to foil the intentions of the state and the men who sought to use its new laws. The criminal/penal laws foundered on a rigid legal definition of marriage which women could deny and husbands found impossible to prove. If the courts found it difficult to restrain runaway wives, divorces and multiple marriages, the registering authorities entrusted with the task of restraining wives bent on migration found themselves in an even greater quandary. Women were attracted by the possibility of independent wage-earning, they wished to escape unhappy marriages; or they wanted to run away with (other) men. To go to the colonies or to the tea districts, they were aided by agents, arkathis and sardars to present 'false' husbands, or they could declare themselves widowed and destitute. Usually, the law failed to pursue them to far away cities, towns and plantations.

Notes

1. West Bengal State Archives [henceforth WBSA], Bengal Jurisdiction, 9 July 1819, Letter of the Magistrate to the Registrar of the Nizamat Adalat, 10 July 1815.

2. Nirmala Banerjee, 'Working Women in Colonial Bengal: Modernisation and marginalisation' in Kumkum Sangari and Sudesh Vaid (eds.) *Recasting Women: Essays in Colonial History*, New Delhi: Kali for Women, 1989. pp. 283–8, Mukul Mukherjee, 'Impact of Modernisation on Women's Occupations: A case study of rice husking industry in Bengal' in J. Krishnamurty (ed.) *Women in Colonial India: Essays on Survival, Work and the State*, New Delhi: Oxford University Press, 1989.

3. Sugata Bose, *Peasant Labour and Colonial Capital, Rural Bengal Since 1770*, New Cambridge History of India, III–2, Cambridge: Cambridge University Press, 1993, pp. 66–111.

4. The Census of 1881 assumed that all unmarried women above the age of 15 years must be prostitutes since it was accepted that every member of the female population were married by then. WBSA, General, April 1886.

5. National Archives [henceforth NA] Home Sanitary 20 February 1883, Municipal, March 1993, 47. Collection 2–3, Letter from A Mackenzie to the Secretary to the Government of Bengal.

6. WBSA, Judicial Judicial, October 1872, B252–79, letter from Sanitary Commissioner to Government of Bengal, 16 July 1872, p.7.

7. Ibid.

8. WBSA, General Sanitation, August 1872.

9. N.A, General Sanitation, June 1888, B106.

10. The existence and legality of male polygamy was established in the Natives Converts' Marriage Dissolution Act. WBSA, General Miscellaneous, August 1866, A38–9.

11. WBSA, General Miscellaneous, January 1867, A3; another petition came from Mymensingh, WBSA, General Miscellaneous, June 1866, A24–5.

12. WBSA, General Miscellaneous, January 1867, A3.

13. L.B.B. King, Magistrate, Noakhally, WBSA, General Miscellaneous, April 1874, B1–15.

14. WBSA, General Miscellaneous, April 1874, B1–15; NA, Home Judicial July 1876, pp. 65–9.

15. L.S.S. O'Malley, *Bengal District Gazetteers*, Birbhum, Calcutta, 1910, p. 38.

16. Ibid., Burdwan, 1910 and Hooghly, 1912. Also see R.K. Ray, 'The Kahar Chronicle', *Modern Asian Studies*, 21, 4, 987, pp. 711–49.

17. WBSA, Judicial Police, October 1872, B252–79, Kashikinkar Sen, Deputy Magistrate, Rajshahi to Government of Bengal.

18. Ibid., B.C. Chatterjee, Deputy Magistrate, Murshidabad to Government of Bengal.

19. O'Malley, *Bengal District Gazetteers*, 24 Parganas, 1914, p. 78.

20. H Beverly, *Report of the Census of the Town and Suburbs of Calcutta*, 1881, p. 139.

21. *Census of the Central Province*, 1881, II, T. Dryadale, pp. 38–45.

22. Ibid., p. 45.

23. Lucy Carroll, 'Law, Custom and Statutory Social Reform: The Hindu Widows' Remarriage Act of 1856', *Indian Economic and Social History Review*, XX, 4,, 1983, pp. 363–88.

24. M.R. Anderson, 'Work construed: Ideological origins of labour law in British India to 1918' in Peter Robb (ed.) *Dalit Movements and the Meaning of Labour in India*, New Delhi, 1993, pp. 87–120. The abolition of divorce for Hindus was reversed by legislation in 1856. But the courts continued to block the operation of local arrangements which permitted women to divorce and remarry.

25. The Moorshedabad Magistry, WBSA, General Miscellaneous, April 1874, B1–15.

26. Kumkum Sangari, 'Politics of diversity: religious communities and multiple patriarchies', *Economic and Political Weekly*, 23 and 30 December 1995.

27. WBSA, Judicial Police, May 1894, Petition from R.C. Mitter and 33 others.

28. *Bihar and Orissa District Gazetteers*, Champaran (revised ed.) R.E. Swanzy, Patna, 1938 quoting Geoffrey R. Clarke, *Outcastes*, 1903.

29. Magistrate, Midnapur, WBSA, General Miscellaneous, April 1874, B1–15.

30. Commissioner of Burdwan, Ibid.

31. There were other opinions. Nikka was also used to denote the First (and any subsequent) marriage contract as distinct from the ceremonial celebration of marriage called shadi.

32. These were also termed 'sagai' or 'sanga'.

33. Commissioner of Burdwan, WBSA, General Miscellaneous, April 1874, B1–15.

34. WBSA, Home Judicial, August 1800, 72–3.
35. NA, Home Judicial, March 1873, 66–8.
36. Ibid.
37. NA, Home Judicial, October 1888A 15–7.
38. Ibid.
39. S.K. Mukherjee and J.N. Chakrabarty, *Prostitution in India*, Calcutta, c. 1945, p. 73
40. Anderson, 'Work Construed', op. cit.
41. NA, Home Judicial, March 1873, 66–8.
42. NA, Home Judicial, October 1888, A105–7.
43. WBSA, Home Judicial, May 1894, A6–12.
44. NA, Home Judicial, March 1873, 66–8.
45. Ibid.
46. WBSA, Home Judicial, May 1894, A6–12.
47. NA, Home Judicial, March 1873, 66–8.
48. Ibid.
49. Ibid.
50. Ibid.
51. Ibid
52. WBSA, General Miscellaneous, April 1874, B1–15.
53. Ibid.
54. Samita Sen, 'Honour and Resistance: Gender, Community and Class in Bengal, 1920–40' in Sekhar Bandopadhyay et al (eds.), *Bengal: Communities, Development and States*, New Delhi, 1984, pp. 209–54.
55. See fn 29.
56. Further strengthened by Act VII of 1873 and Act 1 of 1882.
57. Mukul Mukherjee, 'Women's work in Bengal, 1880–1930: A historical analysis' in Bharati Ray (ed.) *From the Seams of History: Essays on Indian Women*, Delhi: Oxford University Press, 1995.
58. Samita Sen, 'Women Workers in the Bengal Jute Industry, 1890–1940: Migration, motherhood and militancy', Ph.D dissertation, Cambridge University, 1992. Chapters II and IV; Uma Chakravarti, 'Social Pariahs and Domestic Drudges: Widowhood among Nineteenth Century Poona Brahmins', *Social Scientist*, 21, 9–11, 1993, pp. 130–58; and Rosalind O' Hanlon. Introduction, *For the Honour of My Sister Countrywomen: Tarabai Shinde and the Critique of Gender Relations in Colonial India*, Delhi: Oxford University Press, 1994.
59. Sen, 'Women Workers in the Bengal Jute Industry'. Also see

R.S. Chandavarkar, *The Origins of Industrial Capitalism in India: Business Strategies and the Working Classes in Bombay, 1900–1940*, Cambridge, 1994; and Anderson, 'Work Construed', op. cit.

60. Samita Sen, 'Unsettling the Household: Act VI (of 1901) and the Regulation of Women Migrants in Colonial Bengal', *International Review of Social History*, 41, 1996, pp. 135–56.

61. WBSA, General Emigration, January 1890, A142–4.

62. WBSA, Judicial Police, August 1873, A95–8.

63. Government of India to Secretary of State for India, 22 June 1889, WBSA General Emigration, January 1890, A 145–50.

64. Ibid. Officiating Chief Commissioner of Assam to the Secretary to the Government of India, 26 March 1889.

65. WBSA, Judicial Police, August 1873, A95–8.

66. Ibid.

67. Ibid.

68. Ibid.

69. WBSA, Judicial Police, August 1893, A5–8.

"Left to the Imagination"

Indian nationalisms and female sexuality in Trinidad

TEJASWINI NIRANJANA

This business about the women is the weakest and the irredemable part of the evil... These women are not necessarily wives. Men and women are huddled together during the voyage. The marriage is a farce. A mere declaration by man or woman made upon landing before the Protector of Immigrants that they are husband and wife constitutes a valid marriage. Naturally enough, divorce is common. The rest must be left to the imagination of the reader.

M.K.Gandhi
(Speech on Indentured Labour, 1916)

India in the Caribbean

Contrary to appearances, this chapter is not really about Trinidad/the West Indies; it is primarily an attempt to alter the lens through which we have been accustomed to viewing or framing the emergence of that discursive subject, the modern Indian woman. In analysing the formation of "woman" in India we often use, almost by default, the implicit comparisons with western or metropolitan situations. I want to ask whether our frameworks might look different when the points of reference include other non-metropolitan contexts. Also, what might happen to our terms of comparison when the history of the context being compared with ours is indeed profoundly entangled with our own, in ways that have been made invisible in the postcolonial present? One cannot talk about Trinidad without talking about India, close to 45 per cent of the island's population being of subcontinental origin, the descendants of indentured labourers taken there between 1845 and 1917. The obverse, however, is clearly not true; one can talk endlessly about India without the Caribbean, or most other third world regions, figuring in the conversation. What difference might it make to how we in India think about our past—and perhaps how we think about our present as well—to reflect on that which binds India to a west that is not the West?

One of my motivations for writing this essay is my general interest in comparative cultural analyses, especially those which involve non-first world locations. I have suggested elsewhere that the commonsensical basis for comparative study, in India in particular, has been the implicit contrast between India and Europe (and now North America), and that to alter the primary reference point might yield new insights into and fresh perspectives on our contemporary questions.[1] Searching for relevant and viable frameworks of comparison, I began to think about the possibility of contrasting the formation of the "Indian" in the subaltern diaspora with the hegemonic construction of "Indians" in India.[2]

My interest in Trinidad comes out of my long-time involvement in the teaching of West Indian literature, and dates back to my first serendipitous visit to the island in 1994. I was spending three months in Jamaica, doing research in cultural politics in the Anglophone Caribbean. Having come to understand the West Indies through the reggae of Bob Marley, the poetry of Derek Walcott and Kamau Brathwaite, the cricket writings of C.L.R.James, and through Garveyism and Black Power, like many other researchers I, too, saw the Caribbean as profoundly "African", its otherness from our own Indian context framed primarily in those terms. Of course, the demographic fact that Jamaica, the largest West Indian island, is overwhelmingly Afro-Caribbean in terms of its population only confirmed my conviction regarding the culture of the Caribbean at large. Having heard a great deal about Carnival in Trinidad in the Eastern Caribbean, a five-hour air journey away, I decided to make a short trip there to witness the festival. Before I left, I was told by friends of the stark differences between Jamaica and Trinidad, the Protestant seriousness of the one contrasted with the Catholic exuberance of the other. But nothing had prepared me for the visual shock of seeing a Caribbean population of which nearly half looked like me. In Jamaica, I was, safely, a foreigner, our third worldist solidarities undisturbed by conflicts of race or ethnicity. In Trinidad, I felt claimed by the East Indians as an "Indian", and inserted sometimes into oppositional formations which asserted themselves *against* the dominant "African" culture.

Deeply disturbed at being implicated in this manner, my first impulse was to disavow all the tacit claims made on me, to dismiss the East Indians as a marginal and reactionary group which could only undermine the possibility of conducting dialogue across the South. Much later, however, as I became more familiar with the details of Caribbean history and with contemporary Caribbean politics, I began somewhat unwillingly to recognise the salience of the "Indian" in that part of the world, and to perceive how the dominant narratives of West Indianness excluded a large proportion of the population of at least two major countries, Guyana, and Trinidad and Tobago. As I see it now, one of the main causes of my discomfort in Trinidad was the encounter with "modern Indians" whose modernity did not seem to have been formed by the narratives of nation and citizenship which were part of my own interpretive and existential horizon in India. What I did not seem to understand in particular was the kind of negotiation with the "West" that Trinidadian Indians had undertaken in producing their modernity. Most disconcerting of all was my interaction with East Indian women, the semiotics of whose bodies and lives I could not read.

The aim of this essay, then, is to investigate a conjuncture of modernity, "Indianness" and woman that is radically different from our own in India, in the hope that it will de-familiarise our formation as well as throw some new light on the elements that led to its consolidation. I plan to approach the investigation through an analysis of two "moments": the early twentieth century campaign against indenture by nationalists in India, and a contemporary controversy around East Indian women and popular music in Trinidad. I have chosen these moments for their foregrounding of the question of female sexuality, an issue which is increasingly being seen as central to the formation of gendered citizenship and to dominant narratives of nationhood. Historically, the moments are also those of "Indian" political assertion as well as of the availability of new possibilities for "Indian" women. I use the quote marks for the term Indian to signal its double use: marking in my first "moment" a (future) nationality in South Asia, and in my second, an "ethnic" category in the Caribbean. Much of the current literature, both scholarly and popular, tends to blur the difference between the two usages.

I also argue that indentureship enabled a different sort of accession to the modern for the subaltern diaspora than that which was being consolidated in India in the late nineteenth and early twentieth centuries. I draw here on the West Indian thinker C.L.R.James' notion that Caribbean society, with its plantation system based on the carefully regulated labour of slaves, in place as early as three centuries ago, is in terms of organisation of industrial production and ways of living, the first "modern" society in the history of the world.[3]

To provide a brief historical background to the presence of "Indians" in the Caribbean: when slavery was abolished in 1838, the British colonies expressed a need for sugarcane plantation labour to replace the freed slaves, who for the most part chose to work elsewhere than on the scene of their former labours. A more crucial factor leading to indentureship, some historians have suggested, was the need to depress the wages of free labour, in a context where former slaves had begun to agitate for better wages.[4] About 8,000 African immigrants were brought over to increase the labour pool and resolve the problem, but many more would have been required for wages to come down. Neither increasing African immigration nor initiating immigration from China proved feasible. Eventually, a system was devised for recruiting labourers from the Indian sub-continent, from areas where long spells of drought and famine had pauperised agriculturists and driven peasants away from their villages in search of work. Between 1845-1917, about 1,43,900 Indians were brought to Trinidad (with a total of over 5,00,000 to the Caribbean). While about 22 per cent of emigrants returned to India at the end of their period of indenture, several of them re-indentured and came back to the plantations. Throughout the years of recruitment of indentured labourers, there was a tremendous disparity between the number of men and the number of women; this was mainly due to the planters' reluctance to permit the growth of a permanent community of migrants, a proposition seen as both uneconomic and dangerous. When recruiters attempted to induce more women to migrate, for diverse reasons including pressure from the Government of India, they were usually not able to find "the right kind of women", or the docile labourers the planters wanted. So among the people who indentured themselves, not more than an average of 25 per cent were women.[5] Migration to the Caribbean took place mainly from northern India: 90 per cent of the migrants were from the "Ganges plain", that is, from the United Provinces, Central Provinces, Oudh, Orissa and Bihar; a few were from Bengal, the North West Provinces, and the South (primarily Tamil and Telugu speakers). At first there were two ports of embarkation, Calcutta and Madras, but the West Indian plantation owners soon declared that "the Madrasis were inferior both in health and as labourers", and the agency at Madras was closed down.[6]

The caste-class and religious composition of the migrants reflected, to some extent, the composition in the regions of migration. Historians give us varying figures, but we can conclude that roughly 15 per cent were Muslim; there was a small number of Christians, mainly from the South; among the Hindus 40 per cent were from the artisanal and agricultural castes like the Kurmi and the Ahir, more than 40 per cent from the "chamar" or what were then called the Untouchable castes, and about 18 per cent upper castes like Brahmin and Kshatriya.[7]

We must also remember that subsequent to migration there was a complex process of recomposition of castes in Trinidad, as in other colonies—many people "changed" their caste, often within one generation, and caste endogamy was not strictly practised because of the scarcity of women.[8] What is clear, however, is that most of the migrants were either poor or destitute, having lost their land or never having owned any.

The system of indenture took several years to formalise. Continual problems of illness, desertion and destitution of labourers even led to a temporary halt in immigration during 1848-51. However, it was not until 1854 that an Immigration Ordinance was passed, which regularised the pattern of a three-year contract with free return passage after ten years of residence in the colony. The contract actually ended up being for a period of five years, with two years being treated as mandatory "industrial residence". For a short period between 1869 and 1880, free lots of Crown land were given to labourers in lieu of return passage; but after 1895 full passage, even for those otherwise eligible, was not paid.

On the estate, there was a sexual division of labour in the sense that certain jobs were only done by men; women did weeding, manuring, supplying and cane-cutting, and children also did small tasks. According to Rhoda Reddock, however, this division was not constant;[9] truck-loading, for example, was a heavy male task but many women preferred to do it, too. Men earned approximately 50-70 cents per day and women 25 cents no matter what work they did. Only about 25 per cent of the female immigrants were married; the rest had come to Trinidad as single women.[10] But the wages they earned did not allow them to remain single for long, and most women had to take more than one male protector in order to survive. Prabhu Mohapatra suggests there came into being a variety of households because of the scarcity of women, including those with a single woman with or without children and a visiting male partner or partners. Mohapatra has also studied the phenomenon of "wife murders" common in Trinidad and British Guyana, where there was a high rate of killing of "reputed wives" by "reputed husbands".[11]

Working conditions on the plantations were so poor that hundreds of "coolies" took ill and died, especially in the first years of emigration. Those who survived did so in constant ill-health, often physically punished when the planters decided they were feigning sickness. Many could not earn enough even to pay for their rations, and accumulated large debts to the estate. Labourers were not allowed to leave the estate except for strictly limited purposes. Their living spaces were cramped and unhygienic, having no piped water or arrangements for latrines. Several historians have argued that indenture was just another form of slavery.[12] As Walter Rodney points out, it was "the regimented social and industrial control which caused indenture to approximate so closely to slavery".[13] Anti-slavery societies in England were in fact among the early opponents of indentureship, but it was only after Indian nationalists in India began a campaign against the system that it was finally abolished.

Nationalism and Indenture

Indenture did not figure in early nationalism as a significant anti-colonial issue. On the contrary, as B.R.Nanda points out, in 1893 the leading nationalist M.G. Ranade actually wrote an article on "Indian Foreign Emigration" in which he argued that emigration afforded some "relief" to the growing population of India, and that the expansion of the British Empire could be seen as a "direct gain" to the masses of this country.[14] Eventually, however, due in significant measure to the efforts of a diasporic Indian, M.K.Gandhi, indentured emigration became an important issue for Indian nationalism. In 1896, Gandhi, who was still living in South Africa at the time, had a meeting with nationalist leader Gopal Krishna Gokhale to try and interest him in the cause of overseas Indians. In 1902, Gandhi spent more time with Gokhale, who was to become one of his earliest admirers and supporters in India. On Gandhi's urging, in February 1910 Gokhale piloted a resolution through the

Imperial Legislative Council of which he was a member, calling for a complete ban on the recruitment of indentured labour. In 1911, a ban was imposed on recruitment for Natal, and finally in 1917 it was extended to all overseas colonies, but not before a large-scale campaign had been mounted against indenture by Gandhi and a host of other nationalists.

As historian Hugh Tinker points out, the campaign was, in fact, Gandhi's first big political intervention in India —he gave anti-indenture speeches all over the country, wrote about the topic at length in newspapers, and was able to have an Anti-Indenture Resolution passed at the Lucknow Congress in December 1916.[15] By 1915, "the indenture issue became the central question of Indian politics".[16] Even as emigration itself declined for a variety of reasons, there was widespread nationalist protest, with meetings organised in Hyderabad, Sind and Karachi, Allahabad, Madras, and in parts of Punjab and Bengal.[17] The agitators called for an end to the system which they said was a "moral stigma" for India.

The historical significance of the anti-indenture campaign, suggests Tinker, lies in the fact that "this was the first major Indo-British political and social issue to be decided in dependent India, and not in metropolitan Britain".[18] An examination of the nationalist discourse on indenture would reveal the crucial place occupied in it by the question of women's sexuality, helping us understand why it was believed to be something unspeakable, and why, paradoxically, it needed to be spoken about so interminably.[19] Given this campaign's centrality to nationalist thought, it would be interesting to see how women were represented in the criticism of indentureship. I will take as my point of departure some aspects of Partha Chatterjee's well-known argument about the nationalist resolution of the women's question. Chatterjee has tried to account for the relative insignificance of the "women's question" in the late nineteenth century by suggesting that nationalism was able to "resolve" the question by this time in accordance with its attempt to make "modernity consistent with the nationalist project".[20] In constructing a new woman, the middle-class upper caste *bhadramahila*, nationalism in India was able to produce and enforce distinctions between the material might of the coloniser and the spiritual superiority of the colonised. The new woman was "modern", but not heedlessly westernised. Neither was she like the uneducated, vulgar and coarse lower-caste/class working woman.[21]

The period when indentured emigration to the other colonies began, the 1830s, is also the period of the initial formation, via social reform movements, of nationalist discourse in India. Since for the nationalists official modernity came to be produced through the project of the future nation, there was no room for formations of modernity other than those which involved as its subjects middle class, upper caste Indians. The problem with indentured labourers, both men and women, was that their geographical displacement and the new context they came to inhabit was enabling them also to become "modern". The transformations caused in the lives of the indentured by displacement, the plantation system, the disparate sex ratio, racial politics, etc. had to be made invisible by nationalist discourse. This was accomplished, I suggest, by erasing the difference between the agricultural labourer in Bihar and the one in Trinidad ("Chinitat", as the indentured called it), and imaging the latter, in particular, as victimised, pathetic, lost and helpless. Even when the changes in the emigrant were acknowledged, they were criticised as "artificial" and "superficial"; loss rather than gain.[22] Gandhi writes that the labourer came back to India "a broken vessel", robbed of "national self-respect".[23] Any "economic gain" he might have obtained could not be set off "against the moral degradation it involves".[24]

The indentured woman in particular could not be accommodated in the nationalist discourse, again except as a victim of colonialism. By 1910 or so when the campaign against indenture was gathering momentum, nationalism had already produced the models of domesticity, motherhood and companionate marriage which would make the Indian woman a citizen of the new India. The question of what constituted the modernity of the Indian woman had been put forward as an

Indian question, to be resolved *in India*. What, then, of the Indian women who were "becoming modern", but elsewhere? For nationalism, theirs would have to be considered an illegitimate modernity because it had not passed through, been formed by, the story of the nation-in-the-making. The route to modernity—and emancipation—for the Indian woman in India was well established: education, cultivation of household arts, refinement of skills, regulation of one's emotions. The class-caste provenance of this project, and of the new woman, needs no reiteration here.

What sort of ideological project, then, did nationalism envisage for the indentured woman labourer who was shaping her own relationship with the "West" in a distant land? Reform was not practicable. Disavowal of this figure would not have been possible while the system of indenture still existed. The only solution, was to strive for the abolition of indenture. The manifest immorality and depravity of the indentured woman would not only bring down the system but also serve to reveal more clearly the contrasting image of the virtuous and chaste Indian woman at home. As Gandhi asserted, "Women, who in India would never touch wine, are sometimes found lying dead-drunk on the roads".[25] The point is not that women never drank in India and started doing so in Trinidad or British Guyana, but that for Gandhi and others this functioned as a mark of degraded westernisation and "artificial modernity". The nationalist reconstitution of Indian tradition, I suggest, was not a project that was complete when the new phase of the nationalist struggle, marked by the anti-indenture campaign, was inaugurated.

Although according to Chatterjee the nationalists had "resolved" the women's question without making it a matter for political agitation, with the anti-indenture campaign there seems to have been a refocusing on women. At the end of the first decade of the twentieth century a *political* campaign was undertaken—mobilising "a wider public than any previous protest"[26] against the colonial rulers— to dismantle a system that was said to be turning Indian women into prostitutes. As Gandhi wrote, "The system brings India's womanhood to utter ruin, destroys all sense of modesty. That in defence of which millions in this country have laid down their lives in the past is lost under it".[27] The nationalist discourse on indentured female sexuality, however, veered time and again from denouncing the women as reprobate and immoral to seeing them as having been brought to this state by colonialism.[28] The Indian nationalists were joined by the European critics of indenture, led by C.F.Andrews, Gandhi's associate, who had worked with him in South Africa and had been mobilised by him to prepare a report on Indians in Fiji. As anthropologist John Kelly puts it, Andrews and others "portrayed indenture...as a degenerating force and blamed it for the moral condition of the 'helots of Empire'. But they accepted the claim that the 'coolies' were degraded, and they agreed especially about what we might call the 'harlots of Empire'".[29]

As the campaign against indenture gained momentum, among the delegations which met Viceroy Hardinge to press for action were several organised by Indian women's associations.[30] At the meeting between Colonial Office and India Office representatives on May 9, 1917, James Meston, representing India in the war cabinet, spoke of how "the women of India" felt "deeply on the question [of indenture]". Satyendra Sinha, the other India representative, declared that "there was an intensely strong feeling of concern...[which included] ladies who lived in purdah, but read the news".[31] In spite of Englishmen such as Alfred Lyall, Governor of the North Western Provinces, and G.A.Grierson, who reported on emigration from Bengal and recommended it for its benefits to women, giving a chance for a new life to "abandoned and unfaithful wives",[132] Viceroy Hardinge was not willing to continue supporting a system when... "Its discussion arouses more bitterness than any other outstanding question". Hardinge was convinced that Indian politicians firmly believed that it "brands their whole race...with the stigma of helotry", and condemns Indian women to prostitution.[33]

By mid-1917, the end of indenture was certain. Historians tend to see it as an issue that brought a new focus to nationalist politics in India and gave it a wider base. I would argue that it was not simply that. We need to re-frame the indenture question so that it can be seen as marking for us the consolidation of the early national-modern, a setting in place of new (nationalist) moralities, new ways of relating between women and men, appropriate "Indian" modes of socio-sexual behaviour, the parameters for the State's regulation of reproduction as well as sexuality, as well as the delineation of the virtues which would ensure for Indian women citizenship in the future nation. It should be obvious that the historical formation of these virtues, for example, and the contemporaneity of their description, was obscured by the nationalist presentation of them as the essential, and "traditional", qualities of Indian women.

Chutney-Soca: Ethnicity and Popular Culture

While it is evident that the immigrant female was an important figure invoked by Indian nationalism in India, the centrality of this figure to "East Indian nationalism" in Trinidad has not yet been systematically elaborated.[34] An overview of the cultural history of East Indians, however, suggests that since the emergence of Indians in the Trinidadian public sphere in the 1920s, at no time has the issue of female sexuality been a matter of such heated debate as in the 1990s. One of the reasons for this could be the emergence of new narratives of "Indianness" leading up to and coinciding with the 150th anniversary celebrations of the arrival of Indians in Trinidad. The assertion of an "Indian" ethnic identity has sometimes been seen as the manifestation of "Indian nationalism". Before we go into the validity of this concept, however, it would be worth looking briefly at the significations of nationalism in the West Indies. Here it is a somewhat different entity than that which we find in South Asia, where it is more common to see nationalism as a form of relationship to a nation-state, either one in the making or one that has already come into existence. While Caribbean (particularly elite) nationalism may well take the form of a specifically Jamaican or Trinidadian anti-colonial nationalism, all classes of people often represent themselves as West Indian too. Political movements such as Garveyism in the early twentieth century or midcentury Pan-Africanism, built on perceptions of a shared past of slavery, extended far beyond the Caribbean islands. The short-lived Federation (1958-62) was another attempt to bring together the political units of the region even before the achievement of full independence. The Black Power movement in the 1970s had African-American origins, but resonated powerfully with Caribbean critiques of elite nationalism, such as for instance Rastafarianism.[35]

In spite of the ambiguous nature of the relationship between nation and nationalism in the West Indies, what is evident is the Afrocentric basis of the claim to being West Indian. It is this basis which "Indian nationalism" appears to address, its project not being the creation of an Indian nation-state but one of claiming equal cultural rights *in Trinidad*.

To me, the most salient factor in the East Indian narratives of Indianness in the Caribbean is not the question of producing and maintaining a "colonial" difference—that is, the difference from the colonising European is not the issue, as it would have been with elite Indian nationalism in India; rather, the issue is one of difference from the "African" ("the other race", as East Indians say today). "Indians" have a slight demographic edge over "Africans" in Trinidad, being a little over 42 per cent of the population, while the latter comprise 40-41 per cent, and those of Chinese, Lebanese and West European origin make up the rest.[36]

It may be worth emphasising that the maintenance of distinctions between the "Christianised African Creole" and the "Asiatic coolie" was a matter of some concern for the colonial authorities as well.[37] After the establishment of the republic of Haiti in 1803, the spectre of successful non-white revolt haunted every European in the Caribbean. Any hint of solidarity between labourers, especially of different races, was sought to be speedily crushed. As the planters faced the prospect of the end of indenture, and the imminent formation of a purely domestic labour force, images of the shiftless, lazy African and the industrious coolie circulated with increasing frequency. The colonial construction of "Indian" and "African" continues to inform the contemporary formations of the two groups' identities.[38]

With regard to the indentured woman too, the immediate contrasting image for the colonialist was the African woman, the ex-slave, the urban *jamette* of the Carnival whose sexuality was othered, and sought to be regulated, by the European ruling class.[39] The *jamette* was seen as vulgar, promiscuous, loud and disruptive, and the removal of this figure from the Carnival and related activities became part of the project of creating a new urban middle class in Trinidad in the early twentieth century. Much of the elite's anxiety around the *jamette*, or even the rural Creole woman, seemed to hinge on the fact of her being seen as independent, in both sexual and economic terms. The East Indian woman in post-slavery society, then, brought in to compensate colonial planters for the loss of captive labour, had to be imaged as completely different from the African woman. For this, "Indian tradition" was invoked by different groups, and the lack of conformity of indentured women to the virtuous ideal of Indian culture deplored. For example, the Canadian Presbyterian missionaries who targeted the "Indians" exclusively, attempted to account for the position of Indian women in Trinidad.[40] Sarah Morton, wife of missionary John Morton, narrated her experiences with Indian women: "The loose actions and prevailing practices in respect of marriage here are quite shocking to the newcomer. I said to an East Indian woman whom I knew to be the widow of a Brahmin, 'You have no relations in Trinidad, I believe?' 'No, madame,' she replied, 'only myself and two children; when the last immigrant ship came I took a "papa". I will keep him as long as he treats me well. If he does not treat me well I shall send him off at once; that's the right way, is it not?'".[41] The stories about these immoral Indian women led, in Reddock's analysis, to the construction of a new patriarchy, and to the closure of the question of women's agency, or "freedom denied". The implicit argument here concerns East Indian women in the present, and Reddock's perception that—

like women in India—they do not live lives that are "free". While not wanting to question this rather problematic perception or its underlying conceptual assumptions here, I would merely stress the irreversibility of the indenture experience for women and suggest that it opened up different possibilities, even of self-representation, for succeeding generations of East Indian women in the Caribbean.

Today one cannot speak of how the sexuality of the East Indian woman in Trinidad is constituted except through the grid provided by discourses of racial difference (the question of "the opposite race"); cultural/ethnic difference (the supposed cultural attributes of the "Indian" woman as opposed to the "African"), and caste-class or "nation" (low nation and high nation are terms I have heard used by older Trinidadians to refer to caste).[42] These discourses intersect in various ways with that of "East Indian nationalism" which is often seen as being at odds with "Trinidadian" or "West Indian" nationalism. Unlike in the nationalist discourse in India where East and West were thematised by the race and culture of the colonised and the coloniser respectively, in Trinidad the presence of the "Afro-Saxon" (the term used by some Trinidadian scholars like Lloyd Best to refer critically to the culture of the ex-slave, part Anglo-Saxon and part African) indicates that in many ways the "African", who had been in contact with the West a couple of centuries before the Indians who migrated to the Caribbean, came to stand in for the West as far as the Indians were concerned.[43] We may speculate that contact with the European in India did not affect labour to a great extent partly because the western master belonged to a different social class, and his ways of life were not part of the milieu of the Indian labourer. In Trinidad, however, the African (already part of the "West" in the New World) was of *the same class* as the Indian. The transformations among Indians, therefore, had to do with finding ways of inhabiting, and changing, their new home through a series of complex negotiations with other racial groups, most significant of which was the African. Exposure to "western" ways, therefore, came to the Indian through interaction with the Afro-Caribbean rather than through contact with the European. Even today when Trinidadian Indians speak of westernisation, they often treat it as synonymous with "creolisation", the common term for the Afro-Trinidadian still being "Creole".[44]

It is not surprising, then, that the recent controversy in the East Indian community over the phenomenon of chutney-soca is structured in terms of creolisation and the degradation of "Indian culture". Popular music is one of the most central of West Indian cultural forms, and calypso—which emerged in the late 19th century as a mode of social-political commentary—is one of the most popular of the musical genres. Calypso, which has been sung with a few rare exceptions solely by Afro-Trinidadian men, engages in explicit discussion of current politics. However, there has always been a strand in calypso that comments on relations between women and men.[45] In the 1980s, a new form called soul-calypso or soca emerged, claimed by its inventor Lord Shorty as being inspired by East Indian music. Soca is different from calypso in that it is meant more as music to dance to, and does not usually talk about the political situation.[46] At the end of that decade, several East Indian women, including the versatile Drupatee Ramgoonai, began to perform their own blend of Indian folk music and soca [Drupatee's 1989 song was called "Indian Soca": "the music of the steeldrums from Laventille/Cannot help but mix with rhythm from Caroni...Indian soca, sounding sweeter/Hotter than a chula/Rhythm from Africa and India/Blend together in a perfect mixture"], which came to be known as chutney-soca.[47]

Although "chutney" is also a generic name given to East Indian folk songs, which used to be sung primarily in Bhojpuri or Hindi, of late the term has also been applied to "Indian" songs sung predominantly in English. The word refers also to the "spicy" themes of the songs.

Chutney-soca draws from the folk forms brought to Trinidad by the indentured labourers from rural North India. It is related especially to the *maticore* and *laawa* ceremonies which were performed on the night before a wedding. The participants in the ceremonies were all women, except for the young boys who played the drums, and the songs and "performances" were known to be full of humour and sexual explicitness. Chutney also derives from the songs sung by women after the birth of a child.[48] In the late 1980s, "chutney" came to be performed in public, sometimes with five or ten thousand people present, both men and women.[49] The lyrics are now as often sung in Trinidadian English as in Bhojpuri or Hindi, which accounts for their greater accessibility to people outside the East Indian community, and indeed to young East Indians, most of whom do not speak any "Indian" languages. However, the surprise hit of Carnival 1996 was a Bhojpuri chutney song about a man seducing his sister-in-law, "Lotay La", whose singer—Sonny Mann—reached the National Soca Monarch finals. There were several Afro-Trinidadian calypsonians who did "re-mixes" of Sonny Mann's song, which was also used in the 1995 general election campaign of the People's National Movement (PNM), the African-dominated party. This election, incidentally, brought to power for the first time an Indian-dominated party, the United National Congress, and its leader Basdeo Panday, who became the Prime Minister of the country in late 1995.[50]

As West Indian cultural critic Gordon Rohlehr points out, to be "visible" in the Caribbean is literally to be on stage, to perform.[51] And when East Indian *women* take to the stage as singers or dancers, or as politicians, the protracted struggle over "culture" and "authenticity" takes a new turn, not only in the national arena between different ethnic groups but also within the East Indian community itself.[52] The chutney-soca controversy of the early 90s has provoked some rethinking of what the claim to Indianness involves in Trinidad. The singers, and the (specifically female) participants in the chutney dances, have been denounced by many in the East Indian community for what is termed their "vulgarity" and "obscenity".[53] Leaders of the community have indicated that their objection has to do with the display in a public space of a cultural form that used to be confined to the home. The public sphere is here considered to be an "African" realm, so the making public of chutney (and its Englishing) necessarily involves making it available to the gaze of Afro -Trinidadians. The disapproval of "vulgarity" can be read also as an anxiety regarding miscegenation, the new form of chutney becoming a metonym for the supposed increase in relationships between Indian women and African men.

The responses of East Indians to the public appearance of chutney have been diverse. "Chutney is breaking up homes and bringing disgrace", proclaimed a letter-writer in the *Sunday Express*.[54] "Culture means refinement, and this is not culture", declared a participant in a seminar on the chutney phenomenon.[55] The Hindu Women's Organisation, a small but vocal urban group, demanded that the police intervene at chutney performances and enforce the law against vulgarity and obscenity. The "Indian secularist" position, however, was that chutney was "functional", that it represented "Indian cultural continuity and persistence". Social interaction between boys and girls in an "exclusively Indian environment" was only to be encouraged, argued the secularist. Not only was chutney an East Indian alternative to Carnival, it was also a way of establishing "cultural unity with India".[56] Others accused the "Muslim producers" of some chutney festivals for using tunes from Hindu bhajans, an act they considered sacrilegious.[57] A few East Indian men expressed alarm at what they called the "creolisation" or "douglarisation" of "Indian culture", and alleged that African men were writing the songs for the chutney performers in such a way as to "denigrate" East Indian cultural values.[58] One letter-writer who had attended the opening ceremony of the World Hindu Conference protested against "the lewd and suggestive behaviour of the female dancer" during the chutney part of the cultural programme; "this standard of behaviour", he felt, could not be sanctioned by Hinduism, which he claimed had "high moral and spiritual values".[59]

While one writer contended that chutney represented a unique new *Trinidadian* cultural form,[60] yet another argued that it was self-deluding to think of chutney as creative or unique: "No creation whatsoever has taken place in chutney. The form and content have simply moved from the private domain to the public and from a female environment to a mixed one".[61] "Indianness" is seen in many of these responses to be inextricable from cultural purity, which in turn is seen to hinge on questions of female propriety and morality. In the global context of the reconfiguration of a "Hindu" identity, the chutney phenomenon is inserted by elite Trinidadian Indians into the process which disaggregates Hindus from other "Indians" while at the same time redescribing their space as inclusive of all that is Indian, as being identical with Indianness. Curiously enough, this formation of elite Trinidadian Indian identity today is facilitated not only by organisations such as the Vishwa Hindu Parishad but also by the "secular" Indian state, which intervenes in Trinidad both in the academic and cultural spheres.[62]

A news item in the *Trinidad Guardian* of April 22, 1991, reports the speech of Pundit Ramesh Tiwari, president of the Edinburgh Hindu Temple, who says that "the concept of the liberated woman" had created a "crisis in womanhood" which threatened the Hindu religion, which was "taking steps to reintroduce values to the Hindu woman". Indrani Rampersad, a leading figure in the Hindu Women's Organisation, writes that it is "Hindus" (and not "Indians") who form the largest ethnic group in Trinidad. The HWO condemned chutney performances for their "vulgarity", claiming that, "As a Hindu group the HWO is best placed to analyse the chutney phenomenon from such a [namely, a Hindu] perspective, and as a women's group they are doubly so equipped".[63] The HWO, however, was not supported by some who otherwise shared their position on chutney-soca. East Indian academic and senator Ramesh Deosaran questioned, in another context, one of the objectives of the HWO, which was to "advance" the status of women. Deosaran took objection to the use of this word in a context of "increasing sexual freedom".[64] This freedom, Deosaran argued, had resulted in such things as the "intense gyrations" of chutney dancing, "a serious cause for concern by members of the Hindu and Indian community". Taking issue with this kind of position are some East Indian feminists who see chutney-soca as a positive development, symbolic of the attempts of women to overcome inequality in many spheres.[65]

The resemblance between the vocabulary of the anti-indenture campaign and that of the critics of chutney-soca may allow us to conclude rather misleadingly that what is asserting itself in both is "Indian patriarchy", misleading because elite nationalism in India in the early twentieth century and elite assertions of "Indian" ethnicity in late twentieth century Trinidad are phenomena somewhat different from each other. I have tried to demonstrate that although there is a historical connection between Indian nationalism and indentured labour in the British colonies, the analysis of contemporary Trinidadian discourses of East Indian women's sexuality has to be placed in the framework of the predominantly bi-racial society of the island. Indian tradition (and Indian women) in Trinidad come to be defined as that which is not, cannot be allowed to become, African. While the assertion of a separate and unchanging "Hindu" or "Indian" identity in Trinidad is enabled in part by the colonial and Indian nationalist reconstructions of ethnic and racial identities, reconstructions in which definitions of women and what is "proper" to them occupy a crucial position, it is today part of a Trinidadian reconstruction of such identities, a process whose participants include both "Indians" and "Africans". And while the chutney-soca controversy could be read as marking an attempt to reconstitute East Indian patriarchy, perhaps it could also be read as a sign of patriarchy in crisis. The East Indian attempt to "resolve" the question of women can be seen as aligned with the effort to consolidate the meanings of cultural and racial identity at a time when the new political visibility of "Indians" is providing newer spaces for assertion for women as well as men. Both of these, however, are impossible projects, rendered impossible precisely because of the need to continually refigure the distinctions between the two groups, signified as "Indian" and "African", which share the postcolonial space of Trinidad.

This essay set out to look at the Trinidadian conjuncture of woman, modernity and Indianness, attempting thereby to examine the formation of our own national-modern in India from an unfamiliar angle. This exercise may also yield, I hope, unexpected benefits for those intervening in issues of modernity and gender in Trinidad. The larger project for which this article is an initial attempt to establish a conceptual framework and modes of investigation is likely to address, among others, these questions: what might be the implication for Indian women from India in Trinidadian debates such as the one over chutney-soca? What supposed excesses are sought to be contained by this invocation? What would be the consequences of measuring Indo-Trinidadian women against the Indian national-modern? What specific histories are mobilised in the performance of female desire in chutney-soca singing and dancing? What does the singer's public display or acting out of desire make available for the female audience? How might analysing the chutney-soca phenomenon help us look afresh at women's involvement in popular culture in India? How, indeed, may our contemporary critiques of the Indian national-modern benefit from its illegitimate and disavowed double, "Indian" modernity in the Caribbean?

I am indebted to the work of West Indian scholars such as Bridget Brereton, Kusha Haraksingh, Patricia Mohammed, Kenneth Parmasad, Kenneth Ramchand, Marianne Ramesar, Rhoda Reddock, Brinsley Samaroo, Verene Shepherd and many others who have helped me begin to understand what it might mean to claim India in the Caribbean. I am especially grateful to Kirk Meighoo and Sheila Rampersad for our many thought-provoking conversations. Versions of this paper have been presented in Chennai, Ann Arbor, Cape Town and Durban, with useful critical comments being offered in particular by Ajit Menon and Uma Mesthrie. Thanks also to Mary John, Janaki Nair, Vivek Dhareshwar and David Scott for their suggestions. For not always acting on them I have only myself to blame.

Notes

1. See my 'Alternative Circuits?': Third World scholars in Third World spaces', unpublished paper (1995).
2. I use the term 'subaltern' to distinguish between people of Indian

origin in metropolitan countries such as the USA and the United Kingdom (by and large a product of post-colonial migration) and those in non-metropolitan countries, such as the former British colonies in the Caribbean, as well as Surinam, Fiji, Mauritius, and South Africa.

3. Discussed in James' Appendix to *The Black Jacobins* (1938), London, Allison and Busby, 1980, p. 392.

4. See Walter Rodney, *A History of the Guyanese Working People, 1981–1905*, Baltimore: Johns Hopkins University Press, 1981, and K.O. Laurence, *A Question of Labour: Indentured Immigration into Trinidad and British Guyana*, 1875–1917, Kingston, Jamaica: Ian Randle, 1994, passim.

5. Rhoda Reddock argues that the question of the number of 'Indian women' was 'a major point of contention and policy' from the very beginning of indenture. See her Women, Labour and Politics in Trinidad and Tobago, London: Zed Books, 1994, p. 27. [Henceforth *WLP*.] As she points out, between 1857 and 1879 the prescribed ratio of women to men changed about six times, 'ranging from one woman to every three men in 1857 to one to two in 1868 and one to four in 1878–79'. These changes reflected the difficulties and contradictions in recruiting more women at the same time as recruiting "the right kind of women" (ibid., pp. 27–29). See also Laurence, *A Question of Labour*, especially Chapter 4.

6. Laurence, ibid., p. 104. During years of labour shortage, however, there were a few attempts to recruit workers from southern India and even, in 1884 and once again in 1905, to re-open the Madras agency. These attempts, however, were soon abandoned as unsuccessful.

7. Figures are from Bridget Brereton, 'The Experience of Indentureship, 1845–1917', in John La Guerre (ed.), *From Calcutta to Caroni*, St. Augustine: University of the West Indies Extra Mural Studies Unit, 1985, p. 22. Brereton cautions us against possible errors in these figures due to confusions in record-keeping.

8. See the articles in Barton Schwartz (ed.), *Caste in Overseas Indian Communities*, San Francisco: Chandler, 1967.

9. Reddock, *Women, Labour and Politics*, op. cit., p. 36.

10. Reddock draws our attention to the fact that even as late as 1915 when Commissioners McNeill and Chimman Lal came out to the Caribbean to prepare their report on indenture, they found that only about a third of the women came from India as married

women; the rest were either widows or runaway wives, and a small number had been prostitutes (*WLP*, p. 30). See also Laurence, *A Question of Labour*, op. cit.

11. Prabhu P. Mohapatra, 'Restoring the Family: Wife murders and the making of a sexual contract for Indian immigrant labour in the British Caribbean colonies, 1860–1920' (unpublished paper). Mohapatra argues that the planters' need to create a permanent labour force at the end of the 19th century led to an attempt to reconstitute the Indian family, so that labouring women withdrew from estate work but did unpaid work, both on the land and at home, in addition to reproducing the labour force. It is through the colonial effort to prevent "wife murders" (by passing a series of legislations regarding marriage, for instance), according to Mohapatra, that the Indian family in British Guyana is formed.

12. Among others, see Hugh Tinker, *A New System of Slavery: The Export of Indian Labour Overseas 1830–1920*, 2nd ed., London: Hansib, 1993.

13. Walter Rodney, *A History of the Guyanese Working People 1881–1905*, Baltimore: Johns Hopkins University Press, 1981, p. 39. Although Rodney writes about British Guyana, his analysis is applicable to Trinidad as well.

14. Publishes in the Sarvajanik Sabha Quarterly Journal, October 1893, edited by Gokhale. See B.R. Nanda, *Gokhale*, Delhi, 1977, Bk. IV, Chapter 37.

15. Tinker, *A New System of Slavery*, op. cit., p. 341.

16. Ibid., p. 334.

17. Ibid., p. 347.

18. Ibid., p. 288.

19. In conceptualising this paper, I have found useful the insights provided by the work of Michel Foucault: "The central issue, then... is not to determine whether one says yes or no to sex, whether one formulates prohibitions or permissions, whether one asserts its importance or denies it; but to account for the fact that it is spoken about, to discover who does the speaking, the positions and viewpoints from which they speak, the institutions which prompt people to speak about it and which store and distribute the things that are said." Foucault, *The History of Sexuality* Vol. II, tr. Robert Hurley, New York, 1980, p. 11.

20. Partha Chatterjee, *The Nation and its Fragments*, Princeton: Princeton University Press, 1993, p. 121.
21. Ibid., p. 127.
22. Speech on Indentured Indian Labour, Bombay, District Congress Committee, in *Collected Works*, Vol. XIII, p. 133.
23. Ibid., p. 133.
24. Ibid., p. 249.
25. M.K. Gandhi, 'Indenture or Slavery?' in Gujarati, published in *Samalochak* December 1915. Reprinted in English translation in *Collected Works*, Vol. XIII, Delhi, 1964, p. 1467.
26. John D. Kelly, *A Politics of Virtue: Hinduism, Sexuality and Countercolonial Discourse in Fiji*, Chicago: University of Chicago Press, 1991, p. 48.
27. M.K. Gandhi, *Collected Works*, Vol. XXII, p. 349.
28. Kelly, for instance, points out that in the case of Fiji the critics of indenture stressed the sexual abuse of Indian women (*A Politics of Virtue*, op. cit., p. 30).
29. Ibid., p. 33, C.F. Andrews, Gandhi's emissary on the indenture issue, wrote in 1915: 'Vice has become so ingrained that they have not been able to recover their self-respect... The women of India are very chaste; but these women, well, you know how they are, and how it can be different, situated as they are, living the lives they do, brought up in this atmosphere of vice and degradation?' (cited in Ibid., p. 33–34).
30. Tinker, *A New System of Slavery*, p. 350.
31. Ibid., p. 352.
32. Ibid., p. 267–68.
33. Ibid., p. 340–41.
34. Recent unpublished work by Rhoda Reddock, Patricia Mohammed and Prabhu Mohapatra makes interesting beginnings in this direction.
35. Two major institutions, the cricket team and the university, are shared by all the West Indian countries.
36. There is also a 'mixed' population which is said to be as high as 8–10 per cent of the total.
37. See Walter Rodney, *A History of the Guyanese Working People*, and also Malcolm Cross, 'East Indian–Creole Relations in Trinidad and Guyana in the late Nineteenth Century', in David Dabydeen and Brinsley Samaroo, (eds.), *Across the Dark Waters: Ethnicity and Indian Identity in the Caribbean*, London: Macmillan, 1996.

38. For illuminating discussions of the formation of such stereotypes, see, among others, Ramabai Espinet, 'Representation and the Indo-Caribbean Woman in Trinidad and Tobago', in Frank Birbalsingh, (ed.), *Indo-Caribbean Resistance*, Toronto: TSAR 1993, and Gordon Rohlehr, *Calypso and Society in Pre-Independence Trinidad*, Port of Spain: Gordon Rohlehr, 1990.

39. Rohlehr, *Calypso and Society*, especially Chapter One.

40. The Canadian Presbyterian Mission was founded in Trinidad in 1868.

41. Cited in *Women, Labour and Politics*, pp. 42–43. Sarah Morton's comment implies a willfulness on the part of the Indian women, while East Indian men seemed more inclined to stress her susceptibility to "enticement", as did the colonial authorities who framed the marriage laws intended to reduce the numbers of "wife murders" in Guyana and Trinidad among the East Indians. All of these, however, concurred in the implicit argument that the indentured woman's "immorality" was due to the disparity in the sex ratio. Reddock quotes a petitioner called Mohammed Orfy who wrote, on behalf of the "destitute Indian men of Trinidad", several letters to the Secretary of State for the Colonies, to the Indian Government, and to others. Orfy described as "a perforating plague" "the high percentage of immoral lives led by the female section of our community". In order "to satisfy the greed and lust of the male section of quite a different race to theirs" [he indicts elsewhere the "Europeans, Africans, Americans and Chinese"], Indian women "are enticed, seduced and frightened into becoming concubines, and paramours". These women, according to Orfy, "have absolutely no knowledge whatever of the value of being in virginhood". This makes them, says the petitioner, "most shameless and a perfect menace to the Indian gentry". Cited in Reddock, *Women, Labour and Politics*, op. cit., p. 44.

42. To understand the material coordinates of the construction of East Indian femininity, we would need to build on the work, among others, of Mangru and Reddock. The work of Basdeo Mangru on British Guyana and of Rhoda Reddock on Trinidad indicates that sometimes as few as ten out of a hundred migrants were female [Mangru, 'The Sex Ratio Disparity and its Consequences under the Indenture in British Guyana', in David Dabydeen and Brinsley Samaroo, (eds.), *India in the Caribbean*, London: Hansib 1987; Reddock, *Women, Labour and Politics*].

43. I owe this insight to Kirk Meighoo, with whom I have had many useful discussions on the topic of Afrocentrism in the Caribbean. The term 'Indo-Saxon' is employed to refer to 'westernised' Indians, but it does not seem to be as frequently used as 'Afro-Saxon'.

44. Just as the African in the Caribbean was seen as 'western' or westernised, one can say that the West too was Africanised, and then Indianised, in Trinidad.

45. Several 'African' calypsonians have sung about East Indian women, who appear in the songs as exotic objects of desire. Rohlehr has pointed out that the women frequently appear against a background of the 'Indian feast' that the 'African' is trying to gatecrash (Rohlehr, *Calypso and Society*, op. cit.).

46. As with many musical terms in the Caribbean, however, there is some controversy as to the exact distinction between calypso and soca, although there are separate annual competitions for National Soca Monarch and National Calypso Monarch during the Carnival season.

47. There are also several popular male chutney singers such as Sundar Popo and Anand Yankarran.

48. Narsaloo Ramaya writes: 'About half a century ago, after the birth of a child the women celebrated at the *Chhatti* and sang *sohar*, songs which were like lullabies, delivered in a slow tempo with measured beats and rhythms. After the *sohars*, the women diverted into songs that were spicy with faster beats. They were called chutney because of the hot, spicy tempo.' 'Evolution of Indian Music: From Field to Studio', *Trinidad and Tobago Review*, 14:9, September 1992, pp. 22–23.

49. Much of this information comes from personal conversations with Patricia Mohammed and Hubert Devonish in Jamaica and Rhoda Reddock in Trinidad, February-March 1994. For access to newspaper accounts of the chutney controversy, I am indebted to Rawwida Baksh-Soodeen and the CAFRA archives in Trinidad. See also Baksh-Soodeen, 'Power, Gender and Chutney', *Trinidad and Tobago Review*, February 1991, p. 7.

50. It is a measure of post-Independence racial polarisation in Trinidadian political life that the two major parties, the PNM and the UNC, have come to be identified as the 'African' and 'Indian' parties respectively.

51. Rohlehr, in personal conversation. St. Augustine, Trinidad, February 1994.

52. A 1993–94 controversy surrounds East Indian MP Hulsie Bhaggan, who became the target of political satire in the calypsos of the 1994 Carnival in Trinidad. In 1996, former Speaker of the Parliament, Occah Seapaul, an East Indian woman, was the subject of some calypsos. Given the space constraints of this paper, I will not go into the details of these controversies.

53. Female East Indian singers and dancers, however, are not necessarily a new phenomenon. There appears to be a tradition of women who took part in public performances, such as Alice Jan in the early part of the twentieth century or Champa Devi in the 1940s. But their performances clearly did not evoke the kind of response that chutney-soca has obtained in the 90s.

54. Michael Ramkissoon, letter to the Editor, *Sunday Express*, December 16, 1990, p. 46.

55. Musician Narsaloo Ramaya, quoted in news items, 'Critics Rage over Chutney Wine', *Sunday Express*, December 9, 1990, p. 17.

56. Kamal Persad of the Indian Review Committee, Viewpoint Column, *Sunday Express*, December 16, 1990, p. 43. See also L. Siddhartha Orie, letter to the Editor, *Trinidad Guardian*, January 8, 1991, p. 8.

57. Jagdeo Maharaj, letter to the Editor, *Trinidad Guardian*, July 30, 1990, p. 9.

58. 'Dougla' is the East Indian term for a person of mixed East Indian and African descent. It is derived from the Hindi word for bastard.

59. Kelvin Ramkissoon, 'A Brand of Dancing Not Associated with Hinduism', *The Express*, July 14, 1992.

60. Rawwida Baksh-Sodeen, 'Power, Gender and Chutney'.

61. Indrani Rampersad of the Hindu Women's Organisation, 'The Hindu Voice in Chutney', *Trinidad Guardian*, December 25, 1990, p. 10.

   In this paper, I draw mainly on textual sources for East Indian views on chutney. These probably represent a range from lower to upper middle class. Most of my conversations with women and men from this class background indicate that these views are representative. My recent fieldwork (1997), however, suggests radically different attitudes towards chutney on the part of working class women.

62. The Government of India funds two professorships at the University of the West Indies, one in Sociology and the other in

Hindi. The Indian High Commission also has a Hindi professor to conduct language classes for Trinidadians. In addition, the High Commission helps bring exponents of classical 'Indian culture' to Trinidad.

63. Rampersad, 'The Hindu Voice in Chutney', op. cit.
64. The wording is that of reporter Deborah John of *The Express*, 'Controversy Reigns', October 23, 1991.
65. See Baksh-Soodeen, 'Power, Gender and Chutney', op. cit.

Reproductive Bodies and Regulated Sexuality

*Birth control debates in early
20th century Tamilnadu*

ANANDHI S.

In contemporary debates on population control in India, Tamilnadu figures prominently as a 'success story' of fertility decline. Explaining why Tamilnadu, unlike other regions of India, could succeed in drastic fertility reduction, demographers point to the history of the non-Brahmin Self-Respect Movement (a movement which launched a thoroughgoing critique of Hindu, Brahminic patriarchy in colonial Tamilnadu and emphasised women's control over their bodies). However, while invoking the history of the Self-Respect Movement, such debates silence the issues of women's autonomy and reproductive rights as enunciated by the movement, and reduce its complex discourse on birth control to one of fertility control.[1] In doing so, the links between birth control and patriarchy have been lost sight of in present day policy initiatives, which are now framed in terms of the so-called 'Tamilnadu Model'. Any attempt at re-establishing this critical connection between birth control and patriarchy in contemporary demographic discourse calls, therefore, for a return to the complexities of the birth control debates in colonial Tamilnadu.

In 1930, the Madras Legislative Council witnessed a debate on birth control for the first time. A.B. Shetty, who moved a resolution seeking the establishment of birth control clinics in Madras city, claimed that an increase in population would lead to pressure on food supply, overcrowding, disease and less chances of a decent life. As a solution to these problems, he suggested the propagation of contraceptive methods among "the poor and the ignorant" who were "economically incapable of maintaining a large family of children". He called for government initiatives in this regard through maternity and child welfare centres and the Public Health Department. The Maharajah of Pitapuram seconded the motion and claimed that birth-control had been sanctioned by the *Brahadaranya Upanisad* and the *Yoga Shastras*. He also appealed to the members of the house to join the neo-Malthusian League.

These views did not go uncontested. Disagreeing with the resolution, Muthulakshmi Reddy, a prominent member of the All India Women's Conference (AIWC) and a medical practitioner, felt that "birth-control propaganda was a little too premature". For her, married couples were to be taught self-control and continence instead. Maternity and child welfare centres could teach "mother-craft and child-craft and also the sanctity of motherhood and fatherhood".[2] The issue surfaced once again in the Legislative Council in 1933 with V.M. Narayanasami Mudaliar demanding that the government should propagate birth control methods by opening special clinics in government hospitals on an experimental basis.[3]

What was until then a private initiative of a few members of the Madras elites, became an issue of debate among different sections of the middle class following these interventions in the legislature. The participants in the debate, given their differing ideological locations (nationalist, neo-Malthusians, Self-Respecters etc.), expressed different sorts of anxieties with regard to birth-control. While all of them spoke the language of reproductive control, it was most often mediated by the concerns of maintaining class, caste and other boundaries through regulating women's body and sexuality.

This essay is a preliminary attempt at delineating the essential features of the debate on birth control in the Tamil-speaking regions during the early decades of the twentieth century; it analyses the manner in which the woman's body and sexuality figured in the debate—most often by its absence and sometimes as a trope, but only rarely invested with agency.

The Madras Neo-Malthusian League on Birth-Control

We begin our discussion with the Malthusians and neo-Malthusians who were the first ones in colonial Madras to engage with the question of birth control. As early as 1882, Muthiah Naidu, Lakshmi Narasu and Mooneswamy Naiker, along with a section of the Madras elite, started the Hindu Malthusian League to discuss and propagate methods of birth-control.[4] Though the league had been in existence for many decades,[5] it became more active only during the 1930s when it also acquired a new name as the Madras neo-Malthusian League. The League opened a few clinics to impart the message of birth-control and contraception. It also published a journal, the *Madras Birth Control Bulletin*, and brought out a number of pamphlets containing the opinions of medical experts as well as of lay people on birth control. Though the League urged the common people to join it so as to propagate the message of birth control, it remained an exclusive club of upper caste/class men.[6]

The arguments deployed by the Madras neo-Malthusian League primarily replayed the arguments of its western counterparts. Given the upper class character of its members, the League, first of all, presented a set of economic reasons blaming the poor for their fate.[7] They argued that the impoverishment of the lower classes was a result of their increasing population.[8] Proceeding further, they claimed that a check on population growth through birth control would help improve the standard of living of the poor, and hence argued for the use of contraceptive methods.[9] As one of the propagandists of the League put it,

> The widespread use of contraceptive methods would itself assist to raise the standard of living, for a smaller family [this] means that there is more to go round for each member of it, which in turn means better hygienic and educational opportunities; the two things

are reciprocal. Smaller families bring a higher standard of living and birth-control will enable the masses to produce smaller families.[10]

Along with the economics of 'blaming the victims', the Madras neo-Malthusian League located its arguments in favour of birth control and the use of contraceptives within the eugenic idea of racial purity. This was again a part of the neo-Malthusian tradition in the West.[11] For instance, advocating birth-control for the lower classes, the medical adviser to the League, Dr Murari S.Krishnamurthi Ayyar, wrote,

> As birth control among the well-to-do and the intelligent has come to stay, it is the duty of the politician and the statesman to spread the knowledge of birth-control among the lower classes and afford them facilities for its adoption. It is eugenic to raise people from the lower to the higher state by spreading knowledge among the poor, and dysgenic to bring down the intelligent classes by preventing birth-control among them, though it is an impossible task.[12]

The anxieties of Krishnamurthi Ayyar about the lower classes were best expressed when he wrote about the need to spread education. He argued:

> Before education is given, the people must be examined medically and found fit to receive education and to be benefitted by it...In Madras among the lower class pupils in municipal schools more than 80 per cent were found defective. Either the defects should be remedied or if it is not possible to do so, the education of the defective pupils must not be continued, as there is little use in spending money in educating them.[13]

The neo-Malthusian desire to contain the unbridled sexuality of the lower classes is obvious here.[14]

Who were these "lower and undesirable" classes according to the neo-Malthusians of Madras? Here Krishnamurthi Ayyar's language of class shifts, not unexpectedly, into one about castes through the invocation of Brahminical Hindu texts as advocating the best modes of regulating reproduction:

> As far as India is concerned, when in olden days, the injunctions

laid down by the *sastras* regulating married life were held in great veneration and more implicitly obeyed than at present, birth-control was *unconsciously* adopted by the people at large, though the framers of those injunctions might have been activated by the best eugenic reasons for directing adoption.[15]

In specifying the Hindu textual injunctions which regulated married life and reproduction, he privileged certain upper caste practices of monogamy and forced widowhood, as well as the code of Manu:

> The sex relation in early days was promiscuity which resulted in a large number of offspring. When difficulties of maintaining such large numbers were felt, restriction in production was achieved by replacing promiscuity by polygamy and then by monogamy which restricts one woman to one man. A further step in the direction of restriction was introduced by the institution of Nuns, among the christians and of enforced widowhood and prohibition of widow re-marriage among the Hindus. Besides, in the case of Hindus, according to the Code of Manu, girls with certain characteristics are prohibited from marriage, a sensible rule though not observed at present.[16]

He also added that certain upper caste dietary practices of vegetarianism were inherently capable of regulating reproduction by keeping sexual appetite under control. Validating his argument with demographic statistics, he wrote:

> Taking the people of India, the birth-rate among the Brahmins particularly those of Madras and the other purely vegetarian communities is the lowest except that among the Parsees. The Mohammedans who partake of animal food, have increased by 37.1 per cent from 1881 and 1921...Taking the Brahmins who are purely vegetarians, there was no increase between 1891 and 1921 but a fall of 3.6 per cent.[17]

In the context of such a privileging of the upper caste Hindu as the ideal, we need to remember that Brahminical Hindu texts were more than anxious about miscegeny or the inter-mixing of castes. Women's bodies were thus no more than reproductive bodies with women's sexuality reduced to reproductive sexuality within the family and caste, thus also rendering illegitimate the existence of other forms of female sexuality. According to Uma Chakravarti, "the purity of women has a centrality in brahminical patriarchy...because the purity of caste is contingent upon it".[18] At another level, these normative texts represented reproduction as a desexualised act and the reproductive body as a desexualised body. Significantly for us, this opposition between 'reproductive sexuality' (reproductive body) and other forms of sexuality ('sexual body') informed the version of neo-Malthusianism advanced by the Madras neo-Malthusian League. As Ayyar put it,

> As long as the germ cells belong to the race and human beings are their trusted custodians, birth control should not be resorted to unless it be for considerations of health or economic conditions. If it be practised with the view to shirk responsibility and to lead a life of merely carnal pleasure, it is committing a crime towards the race and shows cowardice on the part of the individual.[19]

In privileging this Brahminical Hindu construction of ideal bodies as reproductive, the bodies of the lower classes/castes were represented by the neo-Malthusians as invested with uncontrolled sexuality requiring outside intervention.[20] As the lower class/castes were incapable of self-discipline or self-control, the agents of such intervention could be none other than upper class/caste men.

Along with envisaging such a control over lower class/caste bodies, the neo-Malthusians accorded women no agency on the question of contraception. For instance, Justice V. Ramesam, the Vice-President of the League, "did not think much of women's knowledge of birth-control or attempt to bring them into leadership positions".[21] In fact, in 1929, he wrote to Margaret Sanger, well-known American birth-control activist who was keen on the participation of Indian women in the International Birth Control Conference,[22] that Indian women were not aware of the reasons for birth control and that only men were qualified to discuss the issue.[23]

The attitudes of the neo-Malthusians should not surprise us.

As demographer Chandrasekhar puts it, "in fact one can read the Essay [on population by Robert Thomas Malthus] from cover to cover without encountering a passage that indicates Malthus ever thought women had anything to do with population."[24] What needs to be emphasised here is the ease with which the upper class agenda of Malthus and the Brahminical Hindu agenda of upper caste Indian men could come together and reduce women to reproductive bodies requiring male control.

Redefining Sexuality: The Nationalist Discourse on Birth-control

The opposition between 'desexualised' reproductive bodies as the ideal norm of 'respectable' female sexuality and 'sexual bodies' as its other, representing 'immoral' and 'disrespectable' sexuality, was articulated by other political groups in colonial Madras. To begin with, the nationalists did not consider birth control as an important public issue. However, during the 1930s, as part of their attempt to redefine middle class sexuality and women's responsibility towards reproduction, the nationalists joined middle class men and women in public debates on birth-control.

As a response to the neo-Malthusian advocacy of birth-control and in opposition to the methods of sterilisation and use of contraception propagated by them, the nationalists articulated their stance on birth-control at two levels. A section among them opposed the very idea of birth-control and argued that procreation was a non-negotiable part of the nationalist agenda. Others criticised the new contraceptive methods and advocated self-control or *brahmacharya* as the only acceptable method of birth-control which would differentiate the nation from its colonisers. However, both these discourses converged in privileging reproductive sexuality and inferiorising other forms of female sexuality—very similar to the terms of Indian neo-Malthusianism. Importantly, in the case of the nationalists, this distinction was tied to their 'politics of difference' where the ideal Indian woman was constructed as a spiritual being as opposed to the western woman, who was materialistic and excessively sexual.[25] Thiru Vi. Kalyanasundaranar (Thiru Vi.Ka), who was a prominent member of the Indian National Congress, an important trade unionist and a Tamil journalist, idealised motherhood and argued that the very purpose of woman's existence was to procreate and attain the status of mother.[26] In his view, a woman was elevated to the status of goddess when she attained motherhood. Since motherhood was the greatest service which only a woman could render to the world, every woman must train herself from birth to become an efficient mother. Women must, from their childhood, think that their "bodies, their beautiful selves and their very being is only for attaining motherhood" and not yield to bodily pleasures for any other reason.[27] As he put it, "[Women's] bodies are meant only for procreation and not for sexual pleasure. Sexual intercourse for women is only an instrument to beget children."[28] Comparing the woman's womb to the earth and sperm to the seeds, Thiru Vi.Ka wrote that the earth would be considered worthy only when the seeds grow into plants. For him, children were not only the "gift of God", but also "the wealth of the nation".[29] In representing the ideal woman's body as reproductive, he declared, "a woman who does not procreate or is unwilling to accept the role of mother is not a woman".[30] Simultaneously he considered those women who sought sexual pleasures but not children, both within and outside the marriage, as equal to 'prostitutes'.[31]

He considered birth-control a western preoccupation when he wrote, "There have been various birth-control methods advocated in the West... I do not appreciate any one of those methods..."[32] But his anxiety was more about those Indian women who came under the influence of the West: "Some of our women who have had western education, adopt birth-control methods due to their ignorance. These women occupy powerful posts. Most of them are teachers. It is the duty of the parents to ensure that their daughters do not get influenced by them."[33]

S. Satyamurthi, an important Congress member in the

Legislative Council, and a Smartha Brahmin known for his extreme conservatism, opposed the concept of birth-control and birth-control clinics on the ground that large families instil 'great virtues' and 'high moral qualities' in people who would ultimately carry these same qualities into public life. For instance, addressing a public meeting in Madras against birth-control, he declared how he himself had benefited from being part of a large family: "I am born in a large family with eight brothers and sisters…Only in such large families can one develop human attributes such as patience, brotherhood and understanding which strengthen familial bonds."[34] According to Satyamurthi, the large family is essentially a realisation of the Hindu concept of *Avibhakta Kudumbam*, a family full of good virtues, which regrettably was being eroded with the emergence of the *Vibhakta kudumbam*. To prevent this, he claimed, women must consider the role of motherhood as a great virtue.[35]

Like Thiru Vi. Ka, Satyamurthi's defence of large families has to be read within the nationalist posing of the 'nation versus the West': Satyamurthi also defended child marriage and the devadasi system as Hindu/Indian institutions while opposing western institutions such as divorce.[36]

On the other hand, prominent nationalist leaders such as M.K. Gandhi did not entirely oppose the principle of birth-control. However, unlike the neo-Malthusians and the eugenicists, they advanced a different set of arguments. Gandhi, for instance, argued that until India became a free nation, men and women must 'cease to procreate' and channelise their physical and spiritual energies into building a 'strong and handsome' nation.[37] Gandhi, was, therefore, strongly opposed to the use of contraceptives and advocated *brahmacharya*, abstinence from sex through self-control, as the only legitimate method. According to him, the use of contraceptives would only lead to uncontrolled sexual desires and the break up of marriages; further, it would result in 'race suicide'. He argued that, "it is…worse for a person to indulge in animal passions and escape the consequences of his acts" through the use of contraceptives.[38]

In his view, the sanctity of marriage could only be retained by self-restraint and control over one's own sexuality.

Gandhi's arguments in favour of *brahmacharya* were premised on nationalist patriarchy's construction of 'respectable' female sexuality as reproductive sexuality. He argued that "the [sexual] union is meant not for pleasure but for bringing forth progeny. And [sexual] union is a crime when the desire for progeny is absent".[39] In marking reproductive sexuality as respectable, Gandhi compared the woman who used contraceptives to a prostitute: "The difference between a prostitute and a woman using contraceptives is only this, that the former sells her body to several men, the latter sells it to one man".[40] Since he considered sexual pleasures as unnatural, he argued that men and women, even in marriage, should desexualise themselves by treating each other as brothers and sisters or as daughters and fathers.[41] Marriage, according to him, could only be "a sacrament [if] the union is not the union of bodies but the union of souls..."[42]

In Madras, somewhat similar arguments were advanced by Annie Besant. After her conversion to Theosophy and with her involvement in nationalist politics,[43] she advocated self-control within marriage as the best method of birth-control. Like Gandhi, she also believed that sexual intercourse is meant only for human procreation and not for sexual pleasure. Besant, for instance, wrote:

> By no other road than by that of self-control and self-denial can men and women now set going the causes which on their future return to earth life shall build for them bodies and brains of a higher type... the theosophists should sound the note of self-restraint within marriage, and the restriction of the marital relation to the procreation of the race.[44]

Besant further argued that the birth-control methods of the neo-Malthusians were 'materialistic' as they treated the body and soul as separate whereas the Hindu regulation of sexuality through the control of bodily passions was 'spiritualistic' and superior as it integrated both the body and soul:

Such is the inevitable outcome of the Theosophic theory of man's nature, as inevitably as neo-Malthusianism was the outcome of the Materialist theory. Passing from Materialism to theosophy, I must pass from neo-Malthusianism to what will be called asceticism...[45]

For Besant, materialism stood for the West while spiritualism stood for India. In other words, the difference between those nationalists who opposed birth-control as such and the others who accepted continence or self-control as legitimate, was only apparent. Both groups constructed the ideal woman's body as a reproductive body and inscribed it as Indian, in opposition to the sexual, materialistic, western woman's body.The nationalists effectively reduced woman's body to a trope in the definition of the nation.[46] This definition was patterned on a Brahminical Hindu construction of sexuality that not only inferiorised the West, but also those within the nation whose sexual norms deviated from what had been valorised as ideal.

Motherhood and Maternal Health: Birth-control Debates in the Women's Movement

Those who participated in the neo-Malthusian and nationalist debates on birth-control, were primarily men and their agenda was one of norming women's bodies as upper class/caste in the cause of the nation. But the invisibility of women in the birth-control debate did not persist. The first wave of feminists in India, who were active in the Women's India Association (WIA) and in the All India Women's Conference (AIWC) soon raised their collective voice on the issue as it affected their reproductive roles. While some women activists echoed the opinions of the neo-Malthusians, they also argued that primacy should be given to women's voices and experiences. For instance, addressing the Indian Economic Conference in 1934, Alarmelmangathayar Ammal, a member of the Madras Legislative Council and of the AIWC, said "the problem of population with its concomitant of birth-control could not be solved by the deliberations of an assembly of males, but as mothers, women must be given a large voice in any future legislative measure on the question."[47]

Similarly, some women activists of the AIWC countered the anti-birth-control campaign of male nationalists, on the ground that they had no experience of childbirth and that birth-control was the right of women to control over their bodies. For instance, Kamaladevi Chattopadhyaya, the first organising secretary of the AIWC and an active member of the Indian National Congress, told Satyamurthi that birth-control was "the sacred and inalienable right of every woman to possess the means to control her body and no God or man can attempt to deprive her of that right without perpetrating an outrage on womanhood."[48] Similarly, in making fun of Satyamurthi's claim that large families instil better moral qualities in people, one Ponnammal wrote in *Stree Dharma*, "A news item was [recently] published that a man had become pregnant...in Rumania. That experience [should happen] at least once for our heroes of the legislature too..."[49]

From 1931 onwards, despite strong opposition, the AIWC passed resolutions in favour of opening birth-control clinics. In the initial stages, influenced no doubt by Margaret Sanger, many AIWC activists expressed support for birth-control as a solution to the population problem. For instance, in 1931 at the sixth session of the AIWC in Madras, Rani Lakshmi Rajwade proposed a resolution expressing concern about the increasing population and growing poverty. The resolution also suggested the appointment of a committee of medical women to study and recommend methods of regulating family size.[50] Following this, in 1932, the AIWC appealed to the public bodies to instruct married couples through recognised clinics about methods of birth-control.[51] In 1933, the Tamilnadu constituent conference of the AIWC at its Salem meeting, passed a resolution, despite severe opposition, welcoming the Madras government's proposal to spread knowledge of birth-control.[52] In 1935, some of the AIWC activists, who joined Margaret Sanger's Family Hygiene Society, argued that the AIWC must open public health clinics.

The women activists who spoke in favour of the AIWC

resolutions on birth-control, emphasised the rights of women as 'mothers' to have information on reproductive control. But they were careful to qualify their statements by adding that birth-control information should be made available only to 'married' women and not to the unmarried, since they considered that the birth-control information might lead to 'immorality' among unmarried women.[53]

In addition, the defenders of birth-control within the AIWC linked the maternal health of poor women to the need for birth-control. Their emphasis on women as mothers, their anxiety about access to birth-control among unmarried women, and their concern about the maternal health of the poor women continued to inscribe women's bodies as reproductive bodies. In other words, though the women of the AIWC spoke in favour of birth-control and critiqued the double standard in middle class sexuality which revolved around the regulation of women's sexuality while naturalising the male claim to autonomy and sexual pleasures, they primarily linked questions of respectable sexuality to marital relations.[54] Despite early feminist claims for an 'equal moral standard' for both men and women, it is obvious in their writings on marriage reforms and reform of prostitution that they consciously demarcated the reproductive sexuality of the middle class women from the sexuality of devadasis and prostitutes.[55]

We may note that in the context of an overwhelming emphasis on the woman's role in nation-building through nationalist patriarchal representations of the mother as metaphor for the nation, early feminists, too, articulated their 'maternal duties to the nation'. In this way, AIWC discourse on birth-control intersected with the nationalist construction of ideal womanhood and respectable sexuality, while celebrating reproductive sexuality.

Those women who opposed birth-control within the AIWC,[56] similarly, advanced reasons not unlike upper caste Hindu nationalists. While some of them were opposed to birth-control on the ground that it was against the Hindu conception of marriage and motherhood, others advocated Gandhian self-control or sexual abstinence. For instance, the editor of *Indian Ladies Magazine* who was an activist in the AIWC, wrote:

> I confess that the suggestion to establish [birth-control] clinics came to me as a great shock... Birth control seems unsuited to India. Is it not self-control that is more necessary? I like to think that such a great soul as Mahatma Gandhi is against birth-control. The only control needed is self-control, according to him. After all, is not birth-control of the very earth, earthly? Does it [birth-control] not argue in a way that people have more body than soul in them, more materialism than spiritualism? And is it not wrong to encourage such ideals?...In the very first place is its adaptability to immorality...Then again, birth-control is against nature and as such, who knows what new diseases will follow in its train?[57]

Similar arguments were made by Muthulakshmi Reddy, a prominent activist of the Women's India Association and the AIWC. She vehemently opposed birth-control clinics and contraceptive methods. Instead, she advocated self-control as a birth spacing method for women: "Self-control and self-restraint should be taught, as continence is conducive to health and long life and the normal growth of the body and mind. These should be taught in home and schools and colleges."[58] In fact, in 1931 Reddy not only opposed Rajwade's resolution on birth-control but managed to pass an alternate resolution which called for the AIWC's initiative in teaching parents about mother craft and brahmacharya. In the AIWC conference, Reddy argued that

> ...parents should teach their children, both boys and girls, without any distinction whatsoever, the great virtue of continence and chastity and the holy object of wedlock... I wish that everyone of us realise that birth-control is an unnatural method of limiting the family, while continence and self-control preserves intact, any tends to raise the moral and the spiritual nature of man and woman.[59]

Reddy's views on birth-control and her advocacy of self-control methods were premised on the idealisation of the Hindu marriage and motherhood:

> One of the objects of marriage according to Hindu conceptions is the production of a progeny, and children are blessings to the

family... let us bring back to our modern society our ancient ideals of chastity, self-control and renunciation, as self indulgence and selfishness bring in their train disease and dirt... we should never advocate early and indiscriminate marriage and at the same time the evasion of its sacred duties and responsibilities by the practice of birth-control.[60]

In other words, although some women of AIWC raised the issue of equal moral standards for men and women and critiqued the imposition of chastity or monogamous fidelity on women alone, their emphasis on the significance of marriage and motherhood for women was similar to those of male nationalists. Once again, the middle-class women in the AIWC reproduced the language of the Indian neo-Malthusians and the language of the nationalists. This was a language which defined an ideal woman as a biological body disinvested of desire and where the most respectable form of sexuality was reproductive sexuality.

The Self-Respect Movement on Reproductive Rights

The representation of women as the guardians of procreation within the family was strongly challenged by the Self Respect Movement.[61] The demand that contraception should become a means by which women exercise control over their bodies and thus free themselves from male domination was a constant refrain of the Self-Respect Movement (SRM). The movement employed different means to propagate this idea. Periyar E.V. Ramasamy, the founder of the movement and an indefatigable propagandist, constantly wrote in the party press and addressed public meetings in defense of birth-control and contraception as a means for women to end their enslavement by men. The party newspapers, *Kudi Arasu*, *Viduthalai* and *Revolt*, frequently carried editorials and articles, including some by women activists,[62] on this theme. The Self-Respect Conferences, Women's Conferences and Youth Conferences of the Movement discussed the issue and passed resolutions in favour of birth-control. In 1936, the Movement brought out a volume on birth-control containing 35 articles defending contraception with a foreword by Periyar. Let us now turn to the views of Periyar and the Self-Respect Movement on birth-control so as to understand the manner in which they differed from the perspectives of others.

First and foremost, Periyar disrupted the commonsensical association of reproduction with women in the endogamous/ monogamous family by preferring a material explanation to a religious one. He began with an elaboration of the emergence of private property in history and the consequent need for male inheritors of such property. Proceeding further, he argued that such historical processes turned women themselves into the property of men, leading to their enslavement within the family. As he put it,

> When people were totally free without landed property, I do not think there were these slavish marriage practices. When there was no concept of private property there could not have been any compulsion for acquiring heirs to inherit family property through child birth. Only with the rise of private property were women imprisoned to protect family property. Once a woman was made the guardian of a man's property by producing heirs for the property, she herself became a property of man.[63]

Further, he argued that the social insistence on the reproductive role of women stemmed from Brahminical Hinduism's requirement of male progeny to conduct the last rites of the father and perform *thithi* year after year, which, according to him, benefited none other than the Brahmin priests.[64]

From such a position, Periyar argued that women had nothing to gain from their role as biological reproducers. Ridiculing those who presented childbearing as the sacred duty of women towards humanity, he noted:

> Some preach that if women stop begetting children, the world and humanity will cease to reproduce... What would be women's loss if the world does not reproduce ? What danger would women face if humanity does not reproduce? or what would be the loss even for those who moralise? [none]...[65]

To Periyar, women did not benefit from childbearing and indeed it came in the way of their freedom. This was because childbearing and rearing was their sole responsibility:

> Pregnancy and child birth for women involve not merely health risks but also deprive women of their rights and freedom. Because, in a Hindu order, male responsibility ends with the act of sexual intercourse and only women undertake the entire responsibility of child bearing and rearing.[66]

In this context, distinguishing between the stance of the Self-Respect Movement on birth-control and contraception and that of others, Periyar noted:

> There is a fundamental difference between our reasons for the necessity of contraception and those of the others. That is, we say contraception is essential for women to be free and autonomous. They say contraception is essential for women's health...nation's economy and to prevent fragmentation and destruction of family property.[67]

He criticised the reluctance of the AIWC to view birth-control as a means for women to exercise their right over their bodies instead of using it for population control:

> First of all, whether a woman needs birth-control or not should be entirely woman's decision...secondly, the objective of birth-control is not to control the growing populace or to advance the economy but to create an environment for women to have rights and decision-making power.[68]

The autonomy and freedom which Periyar spoke about no doubt included women's choices with regard to education and employment and such matters which were by and large monopolised by men. But what is of particular significance in the context of our discussion is that he linked birth-control with the sexual freedom of women, and tried to free female sexuality from its Brahminical Hindu connotations. In other words, his project was one of recasting desexualised reproductive bodies trapped within the endogamous /monogamous Hindu family, as sexual bodies capable of breaking free from such regulations. For him, desire was natural and socially confining it amounted to a form of slavery:

> I don't see any reason why people's love and desire needs to be brought under control and forcibly regulated into certain forms and as [belonging to] someone only. This is so because desire is an inherent [human] quality. To arrest it for any reason is [like accepting] some form of slavery.[69]

He argued that under the present social arrangement, men were not disadvantaged in this regard while women were made to bear the burden through categories like chastity: "We have to end this social oppression of women [which leads to] concealing their true love for some one and living with loveless men for the sake of chastity."[70] He brought this understanding into play while discussing the theme of contraception and argued that it would free women from loveless marriages and make them break away from the monogamous family.[71]

Thus, Periyar's radical departure from others on the question of birth-control and contraception stood the Brahminical Hindu construction of female sexuality on its head. By unmasking the religious aura around the reproductive roles of women, he sought to invest women with control of their bodies. Significantly, he recoded desire as legitimate and endorsed possible transgressions of the monogamous/endogamous boundaries of marriage. Not surprisingly, Periyar identified Brahminical orthodoxy and the nationalists as the two possible opponents of his stance: "There cannot be any objection from anyone other than orthodox Brahmins and their supporters like Gandhi to ending women's slavery through contraceptive devices."[72]

Such a radical consciousness was not evenly present across the Self-Respect Movement. However, even the lower level leaders and cadres of the Self-Respect Movement, both men and women, opposed the religiosity attached to reproduction and viewed contraception as a way of expanding women's freedom.[73]

Female Sexuality in Identity Politics

In this concluding section, let us explore the reasons for the overlap between the positions of the neo-Malthusians, nationalists and the AIWC on birth-control which, as we have seen, privileged women's reproductive role and delegitimised other forms of female sexuality. Also we shall see why the Self-Respect Movement, particularly Periyar, could take a radically different position which discounted the reproductive roles of women and argued for a legitimate space for the prevalence of all forms of female sexuality.

It must be admitted that any delineation of identities (such as caste/class/nation) is predicated upon specific constructions of gender and control of female sexuality. Only by imposing severe restrictions on women's sexuality, may the boundedness of such identities be reproduced.[74] Given this, women's sexuality is viewed as potentially transgressive, a threat that could make identities porous and unstable, so that what is privileged as ideal is the chaste, pure and reproductive woman.

While women are assigned the task of reproducing community identities, their sexuality is contained both physically (the most telling instance being Nazi Germany) and ideologically (as dutiful mothers of male subjects). Both these processes mark out and celebrate the so-called ideal/pure women, elicit their compliance with the patriarchy inherent in identity politics by giving them a sense of pride and participation, while making illegitimate other possible subject positions based on alternate visions/practices of sexuality.

In this context, the neo-Malthusian agenda of containing the growth of the lower classes/castes can be simultaneously seen as an agenda of self-definition by the upper classes/castes. Without presenting a superior self-identity, the upper classes would lack the authority to speak about the Other, the lower classes, as requiring containment. As part of this process of self-definition, the neo-Malthusians valorised the Brahminical Hindu construction of ideal human bodies, particularly those of women. The bodies of the lower classes/castes were therefore marked as inferior, since they were seen as the bearers of excess sexuality that required intervention. The female body and woman's sexuality functioned as a site for differentiating the upper class/caste self from the lower orders.

Though the nationalist project was different from that of the neo-Malthusians, they shared similar ground in so far as they were involved in fashioning a superior self for themselves through a process of Othering. Anti-colonial nationalism needed to invoke the 'rule of difference' so that it could set itself in opposition to the colonisers. By now it is well known that this difference was affirmed by constituting woman as the spiritual bearer of the national self in the uncolonised domestic space.[75] This spiritual quality of the ideal Indian woman was modelled on the canons of upper caste Hindu patriarchy and she was constructed as desiring only a reproductive role unlike her western or lower caste counterparts.[76]

Within this paradigm of national identity, birth-control and contraception emerged as western practices capable of threatening Indian womanhood. Also, in affirming Indian women as non-desiring and reproductive in contrast to the western woman, some nationalists refused to go beyond brahmacharya as the only acceptable mode of birth-control. As in the case of the neo-Malthusians, women's bodies were normed as upper class/caste while the identity of the nation dominated nationalist constructions of womanhood.

As we have already mentioned, nationalism, by invoking chaste/pure women as the bearers of the national self, invested them with the sense of agency and sought their complicity with nationalist patriarchy. Importantly, nationalism endorsed women's public participation only on the condition that they ensured those 'spiritual' qualities which were prescribed for them. As Partha Chatterjee puts it, "No matter what the changes in the external conditions of life for women, they should not lose their essential spiritual (that is, feminine) virtues; they must not, in other words, become essentially Westernised."[77] Given the upper class/caste location of the AIWC women, whose ascribed positions were incorporated as the national norm, public participation conformed to the logic of nationalism. Even when they spoke critically of male nationalists, they were careful to distinguish themselves from public women such as prostitutes and devadasis.[78]

If foregrounding a single bounded identity as the basis of

politics (as in the case of the neo-Malthusians and the nationalists) led to the idealisation of the non-desiring chaste woman, the politics of the Self-Respect Movement was based on a different conception of identity. Identities were multiple and porous. When Periyar broke away from the Indian National Congress and formed the Self-Respect Movement in 1926, his politics was framed by a search for free and equal citizenship for different subordinate social groups such as the Sudras, the Adi-Dravidas and women. Given this concern, he argued that unless the victims of the past become active political subjects, they would not succeed in subverting their positions to become free and equal. Periyar believed that no one else could speak for and represent the oppressed but themselves. For instance, while discounting the efforts of those who emancipated subordinate groups, Periyar argued:

> Can rats ever get freedom because of cats? [Can] sheep and fowl ever get freedom because of foxes? [Can] Indians' wealth ever increase because of white men? [Can] non-Brahmins ever get equality because of Brahmins?...[79]

He addressed this line of argument to different subordinate social groups such as the Sudras, Adi-Dravidas, women, and economically exploited classes, throughout his political career.

In other words, for Periyar, there was a continuum of oppressors and the oppressed, whose location was not fixed but contingent on the context: a Sudra male was the oppressed in relation to the Brahmin, but simultaneously was an oppressor in relation to women. The construction of the Self and its Other was thus fluid, rooted in the concrete and not fixed in terms of any binary such as national versus colonial, Sudra versus Brahmin etc. Thus, the struggle for freedom was multiple, invoking shifting identities and numerous agents of change.[80]

Within such a conception of identities, women were not available as inert bodies to be mobilised in defining identities other than their own. Instead, they too become one of the many active players in the politics of emancipation. In this context, the voice of the Self-Respect Movement was markedly distinct with respect to the politics of birth-control and contraception.

The complexities of the birth-control debate in colonial Tamilnadu and the manner in which sexuality was constructed make evident the limits of identity politics. It also demonstrates that there are alternate ways of fashioning identities by proposing a range of new subjectivities that did not subsume women under the rubric of nation.

Notes

1. T.V. Anthony, 'The Family Planning Programme: Lessons from Tamilnadu's Experience,' *The Indian Journal of Social Science*, Vol. 5.3, 1992; and K. Srinivasan, *Regulating Reproduction in India's Population: Efforts, Results and Recommendations*, Sage Publications, New Delhi, 1995.

2. *Indian Social Reformer*, April 12, 1930.

3. *Swadesamitran*, September 14, 1933.

4. Prior to this, in 1880, Murugesa Mudaliar from Madras became the vice-president of the London Malthusian League and published a journal named *The Philosophic Inquirer* from Madras. Mudaliar's early efforts at propagating birth-control were reported in *The Malthusian*, a journal brought out from London, as "efforts to combat the evils of overpopulation in India... already bearing fruit in that distant land". However, the Hindu Malthusian League is the first ever such organisation to be started in Madras. See S. Chandrasekhar, *'A Dirty, Filthy Book': The Writings of Charles Knowlton and Annie Besant on Reproductive Physiology and Birth Control and an Account of the Bradlaugh-Beasant Trial*, University of California Press, California, 1981, pp. 52–53.

5. One of the founders of this organisation, Muthiah Naidu claimed that "the principles and rules of the new organisation" were to be "the same as those of the parent League in London to which we intend to affiliate". Muthiah Naidu also requested a British medical practitioner to be the patron of this organisation. See Chandrasekhar, *'A Dirty, Filthy Book'*, op. cit., p. 52.

6. *Swadesamitran*, November 20, 1929. The Maharajahs of Pitapuram and Jeypore and few other aristocrats were the patrons of the League. While Sir Dr. P.S. Sivasami Ayyar was its president, three

high court judges, two ex-members of the Madras Council, an ex-president of the Indian National Congress, the Advocate General were life members apart from a few medical professionals, merchants and landowners. See Murari S. Krishnamurthy Ayyar, *Population and Birth-Control in India*, Madras: The People's Printing and Publishing House, 1930, p. XIV.

7. On the class character of neo-Malthusianism, see Mohan Rao, 'An Imagined Reality: Malthusianism, neo-Malthusianism and population myth', *Economic and Political Weekly*, Vol. XXIX, No. 5, (January 29, 1994).

8. The idea of population as the source of poverty had a presence in the Tamil-speaking areas even outside the neo-Malthusian League. P. Thirikooda Sundaram Pillai who was a birth control propagandist, among other things, wrote a book *Vivagamaanavargalukku Oru Yosanai* emphasising the need for birth control for the poor as a way of countering poverty.

9. P.S. Sivasami Iyer's speech quoted in *Swadesamitran*, November 1, 1933.

10. *Indian Social Reformer*, December 9, 1933.

11. For details of the eugenic movement and its ideology see Mohan Rao, 'An Imagined Reality', pp. PE-45–46.

There now exists literature on the anxieties about the inter-mixing of 'races' in different historical contexts. For instance, see Gisela Bock, 'Racism and Sexism in Nazi Germany: Motherhood, Compulsory Sterilization and the State', *Signs*, Vol. 8, No. 3, Spring 1983; Henry P. David et. al., 'Abortion and Eugenics in Nazi Germany', *Population and Development Review*, Vol. 14, No. 1, March 1988; Dennis Hodgson, 'The Ideological Origins of the Population Association of the America', *Population and Development Review*, Vol. 17, No. 1, March 1991; Hanna Papanek, 'The Ideal Woman and the Ideal Society: Control and autonomy in the construction of identity', in Valentine M. Moghadam (ed.), *Identity Politics and Women: Cultural Reassertion and Feminism in International Perspective*, Oxford: Westview Press, 1994; and Ruth Hariss, 'The "Child of the Barbarian": Rape, race and nationalism in France during the First World War', *Past and Present*, No. 141, November 1993.

12. Krishnamurthi Ayyar, *Population and Birth Control*, op. cit., pp. 66–67. Similar views were expressed outside the League, by others like Maraimalai Adigal who wrote that the poor and the

lower castes like "Parayars and Pallars" who are "uncivilised and ignorant" were to be forced to adopt birth control while "the rich and wealthy couples should have at least nine children to save the world". Further he felt that the lower castes and the poor reproduce children who turn out to be "diseased, immoral, drunkards, liars, womanisers and murderers". See, Marai Malai Adigal, *Makkal Noorandu Uyir Vazhkkai*, Vol. II, Madras, Saiva Siddhantha Noorpathippu Kazhagam, 1969 (First edition, 1933).

13. Krishnamurthi Ayyar, *Population and Birth Control*, op. cit., p. 94.

14. Ibid., p. 69. Similar views were found in the columns of the *Indian Social Reformer*. For instance, countering the view that the use of contraceptives lead to immoral activities, one G.R.G. wrote that immorality and crime already existed among the slum dwellers who did not use contraceptives, whereas the upper classes among whom birth control is prevalent have high moral values. *Indian Social Reformer*, December 9, 1933.

15. Krishnamurthi Ayyar, *Population and Birth Control*, op. cit., p. x.

16. Ibid., p. 55.

17. Ibid., p. 72.

18. Uma Chakravarthi, 'Conceptualising Brahminical Patriarchy in Early India: Gender, caste, class and state', *Economic and Political Weekly*, Vol. XXVIII, No. 14, 3 April 1993, p. 579.

19. Krishnamurthi Ayyar, *Population and Birth Control*, op. cit., p. 69.

20. If in the case of upper classes/castes it was women's sexuality which caused greatest anxiety, in the case of the lower classes/castes it was men's sexuality which was presented as particularly threatening. Referring to the children of the lower classes, Ayyar wrote, they are "unwanted and are the result of unwilling submission [of women] to the brutal embraces of their drunken husbands... "(p. 101). By emphasising only the "unwilling submission" of the lower class women and eliding the question of female desire, he presents lower class male sexuality as aggressive. This basically connects with upper caste anxiety about *Pratiloma* marriages.

21. Barbara N. Ramusack, 'Embattled Advocates: The debate over birth control in India, 1920–1940', *Journal of Women's History*, Vol. 1, No. 2, 1989, p. 56.

22. Margaret Sanger was a one-time socialist and a member of the International Workers of the World. In 1920, she wrote the famous eugenic tract, *Women and the New Race*. In 1921, she founded the American Birth Control League which incorporated many of the

assumptions of upper middle-class, including eugenics and 'biological Malthusianism'. For more details, see Dennis Hodgson, 'The Ideological Origins of the Population Association of America', *Population and Development Review*, Vol. 17, No. 1, March 1991.

23. This was despite the fact that women doctors like Mrs D. Devanesan, the Lady Superintendent of the Child Welfare Scheme of the Health Department in Madras, wrote to the government in 1928, on the need for disseminating birth control methods to the poor. Ramusack, 'Embattled Advocates', op. cit., p. 40.

24. Chandrasekhar, '*A Dirty, Filthy Book*', p. 12.

25. Partha Chatterjee, *The Nation and Its Fragments: Colonial and Postcolonial Histories*, Delhi: Oxford University Press, 1995.

26. Thiru Vi. Kalyanasundaranar, *Panin Perumai Allathu Vazkkai Thunai*, Madras: Poompuhar Press, 1986 (13th edition), p. 65.

27. Ibid., p. 104.

28. Ibid., p. 222.

29. Ibid., p. 252.

30. Ibid., p. 253.

31. Ibid., p. 259.

32. Ibid., p. 253.

33. Ibid., pp. 253–54.

34. Satyamurthi quoted in *Dinamani*, 14 January, 1936. See also, Satyamurthi's letter to his daughter, Lakshmi, extolling the virtues of large families. S. Satyamurthi, *Arumaip Padulvikku*, [to dear daughter], Madras, Bharathi Press, 1988, p. 117.

35. Satyamurthi, *Arumai Pudalvikku*, p. 117.

36. Anandhi S., 'Middle-Class Women in Colonial Tamilnadu, 1920–1947: Gender relations and the problem of consciousness', unpublished Ph.D Thesis, Chapter 2, Jawaharlal Nehru University, New Delhi, 1992.

37. M.K. Gandhi, *Self-Restraint vs. Self-Indulgence*, Ahmedabad, Navajeevan Press, 1947 (first edition, 1928), p. 66.

38. Gandhi as quoted in Barbara N. Ramusack, 'Embattled Advocates', op. cit., p. 38.

39. Gandhi, *Self-Restraint vs. Self-Indulgence*, op. cit., p. 51.

40. Ibid., p. 170.

41. Ibid., p. 62.

42. Ibid., p. 67.

43. It is interesting to note that, before her conversion to Theosophy

in 1891, Annie Besant was the secretary of the London neo-Malthusian League from its inception in 1878. In 1877, she published the famous neo-Malthusian tract, *The Law of Population* which, within three years of publication, sold 175,000 copies all over the world. After she became a Theosophist, she disowned her earlier writing and wrote another book, *Theosophy and the Law of Population*, in defence of self-control.

44. Besant, *Theosophy and the Law of Population*, as cited in S. Chandrasekhar, '*A Dirty, Filthy Book*', p. 211.

45. Chandrasekhar, '*A Dirty Filthy Book*', op. cit., p. 211.

46. On troping women in the context of Indian National Movement, see Patricia Uberoi, 'Feminine Identity and National Ethos in Indian Calendar Art', Review of Women's Studies, *Economic and Political Weekly*, Vol. xxv, No. 17, 28 April 1990.

47. *Indian Social Reformer*, 13 January 1934.

48. Kamaladevi Chattopadhyay was an exception in the AIWC who advocated birth control as women's right. Margaret Cousins noted that Kamaladevi had to pay a heavy price by being denied entry into the Congress Working Committee for taking up the cause of birth control and for countering the male nationalists like Satyamurthi. See Ramusack, 'Embattled Advocates', op. cit., p. 54.

49. Srimathi Ponnammal, 'Karpathadai' (Birth Control), *Stridharma*, Vol. XIX, No. 1, July-August, 1936.

50. Barbara N. Ramusack, 'Embattled Advocates', op. cit., p. 41.

51. Aparna Basu and Bharati Ray, *Women's Struggle: A History of the All India Women's Conference 1927–1990*, New Delhi: Manohar Press, 1990, p. 82.

52. *Indian Annual Register*, July-December 1933.

53. *Indian Annual Register*, December 1935.

54. For an account of the AIWC's critique of the double standard in middle-class sexuality and its demand for an equal moral standard, see Janaki Nair, *Women and Law in Colonial India: A Social History*, New Delhi: Kali for Women, 1996, p. 168.

55. Judy Whitehead, 'Modernising the Motherhood Archetype: Public Health Models and the Child Marriage Restraint Act of 1929' *Contributions to Indian Sociology*, Vol. 29, Nos. 1 and 2, 1995.

56. The anti-birth controllers within the AIWC also included some orthodox Catholic Christian and Muslim women who in fact managed to mobilise a sizable number of women against the AIWC's resolution in favour of opening birth control clinics.

57. *Indian Ladies Magazine*, Vol. VI, No. 6, November-December 1933. Elsewhere in India, AIWC activists echoed the nationalists view on birth control by advancing the argument that at this point in history, India could not afford to forego its numerical strength through population control which would lead to the degeneration of the nation.

58. *Women's India Association (WIA) Golden Jubilee Souvenir*, n.d., p. 22.

59. Muthulakshmi Reddy, 'Birth Control Clinics', *Indian Social Reformer*, 11 February 1933.

60. Muthulakshmi Reddy, 'Birth Control', *Stridharma*, July-August, 1936.

61. Revolting against the Brahminical domination of the Tamilnadu Congress, E.V. Ramasamy Naicker along with S. Ramanathan, launched the *Suyamariyadai Iyakkam* (Self-Respect Movement) in 1926. The movement outlined its basic principles as (a) no god, (b) no religion, (c) no Gandhi, (d) no Congress, and (e) no Brahmins. However, its actual politics did not stop with these five goals, but included, in large measure, an anti-patriarchal stance. For details of the Self-Respect Movement's discourse on the women's question, see Anandhi S., 'Women's Question in the Dravidian Movement c. 1925–1948', *Social Scientist*, Vol. 19, Nos. 5–6, May-June 1991.

62. The party newspapers like *Kudi Arasu* and *Puratchi*, carried articles by and public speeches of women activists on the issue of birth control. In 1931, for instance, writing in favour of birth control, Rajammal Vasudevan wrote that in the male dominated social system birth control is a step towards enabling women to have control over their bodies. Similarly, while demystifying the Brahminical Hindu religious notion that motherhood is the sacred duty of women, Indrani Balasubramaniam claimed birth control as the primary right of women.

63. *Viduthalai*, 11 October 1948.

64. *Viduthalai*, 11 October 1948, in Ve. Aanaimuthu, *Periyar Chindanaigal*, Thinkers' Forum, Thiruchirapalli, Vol. I, p. 163.

65. *Kudi Arasu*, 12 August 1928 in Ve. Aanaimuthu, *Periyar Chindanaigal*, Vol. I, p. 107.

66. *Kudi Arasu*, 1 March 1931; for Periyar's views on birth control see also, *Kudi Arasu*, 12 August 1928; *Revolt*, 14 July 1929.

67. Periyar E.V. Ramasamy, *Pen Yean Adimaiyaanaal?*, Madras: Periyar Suyamariyadai Prachara Niruvanam, 1978, p. 78.

68. *Kudi Arasu*, 3 January 1948.

69. Ve. Aanaimuthu, *Periyar E Ve Ra Chindanaigal*, Vol. I, p. 153.

70. Ibid., p. 117.

71. *Kudi Arasu*, 1 March 1931, in Ve.Aanaimuthu, *Periyar Chindanaigal* Vol. I, p. 159.

72. *Kudi Arasu*, 3 January 1948.

73. For instance, see, G.A. Annapurani's speech delivered in Madras Self-Respect Women's Movement on 'birth control and the myth of motherhood', *Kudi Arasu*, 10 January 1932; Janaki's article on 'Sexual Violence, Forcible Pregnancy and Women's Right to Health', *Kudi Arasu*, 10 May 1931; P. Achammal's critique of Hindu religion and compulsions of child birth, *Kudi Arasu*, 8 March 1931.

74. Veena Das, *Critical Events: An Anthropological Perspective on Contemporary India*, Oxford University Press, Delhi, 1995.

75. Chatterjee, *The Nation and Its Fragments*, op. cit.

76. Indian women transgressing 'national' boundaries and entering into conjugal relations with 'others' was a source of great anxiety for Indian nationalism. The best illustration in the case of Madras would be the marriage between the dancer Rukmanidevi and the Theosophist Arundale. The marriage evoked a sharp response from the nationalists and *The Hindu* virulently campaigned against it on a day-to-day basis. Similar was the campaign against the succession of the son of the Pudukottai Maharajah and his Australian wife. S. Satyamurthi characterised the prince as an 'Eurasian Urchin' unfit to be the future 'Brihadamba Dasa' of a Hindu Kingdom. These instances have yet to be fully reconstructed and analysed.

77. Chatterjee, *The Nation and Its Fragments*, op. cit., p. 126.

78. On the AIWC women's hostility towards devadasis and prostitutes, see Anandhi S., 'Representing Devadasis: 'Dasigal Mosavalai' as a radical text', *Economic and Political Weekly*, Annual Number, Vol. XXVI, Nos. 11 and 12, March 1991.

79. Ve. Aanaimuthu, *Periyar Chindanaigal*, Vol. II, p. 673.

80. M.S.S. Pandian, 'Denationalising the Past: "Nation" in E.V. Ramasamy's Political Discourse', *Economic and Political Weekly*, Vol. 28, No. 42, October 1993.

Comrades-in-Arms

Sexuality and identity in the contemporary revolutionary movement in Andhra Pradesh and the legacy of Chalam

U. VINDHYA

Introduction

In contemporary Andhra Pradesh, conceptions about the nature of gender relations, female subjectivity and sexuality, and the democratisation of man-woman relations in cultural and political life revolve around two distinct positions: (a) the political practice of the radical left movement[1] and (b) the legacy of the colonial 'rebel' writer Chalam (1894-1979) that has influenced a burgeoning feminist literature in Telugu as well as feminist political practice. The images of the 'new woman' thrown up by these two positions appear irreconcilable. The conception of 'woman' offered by contemporary revolutionary practice is rooted in the primacy of economism in orthodox Marxist analysis, the consequent neglect of questions of identity and agency, as well as the pressure now generated to respond to feminist critiques and to other emancipatory discourses.

The image of the 'feminist woman', on the other hand is founded on the belief that the personal is the political, a maxim of the western women's movement that privileges private, subjective experiences of individual women in terms of their significance for larger issues. This enables women to "engage in more diversified forms of discursive argumentation and critique which can take into account previously repressed aspects of personal and social life—emotions, desire, the body, personal relations—and which can remain receptive (both) to the specificity of female experience and the need for cultural and group identity."[2] The refashioning of man-woman relations and female sexuality in contemporary Telugu feminist literature does not originate from feminist theory and the women's movement alone but to a significant extent from the space generated by Chalam who, writing between the 1920s and the 1940s had thematised issues like autonomy, sexuality and reproductive freedom for women. What was also distinctive about Chalam was that he had, more than half a century ago, emphasised concrete material changes for women's autonomy, such as economic independence, access to birth-control and abortion, and the protection of women and children outside marriage.

The first part of this chapter explores the terrain of the ongoing debate on femininity, sexuality and the nature of gender relations in the context of the contemporary revolutionary movement. An analysis of Chalam's writings and feminist recuperations of this legacy follows in the second part. Since Chalam is little known outside the Telugu-speaking world, this essay is also an attempt to introduce his radical views about women's oppression and subordination to a wider audience. I shall, therefore, be focusing on his understanding of man-woman relationships as it has influenced the present wave of feminist literature in Telugu.

Sexuality and the Radical Left

In addition to the 'woman question' making its appearance during the social reform and the nationalist period as in several other parts of the country, the Andhra region has a somewhat distinctive tradition. It is now well established that large numbers of women participated in the Telengana People's Struggle (1948-1951) led by the undivided Communist Party against the feudal oppression of the Nizam and the Hindu landlords in Hyderabad state[3] and also in Srikakulam,[4] the first district in Andhra to witness an armed revolt led by the Marxist-Leninists in the 1960s.

The insights of feminist historiography have enabled many

questions to be raised about the inability of the party leadership and the organisation in the earlier Telengana and Srikakulam movements to break with feudal patriarchal norms. However, while these earlier struggles can escape such criticisms of patriarchal attitudes and of historical practices, the present movement cannot dismiss such critique as feminist hindsight. Male dominance and the control and regulation of female sexuality are not confined to revolutionary organisations. The exceptional circumstances of guerilla militancy mean that "revolutionaries' lives are measured not in years but in days and hours",[5] and demands more cautious judgement. But the expectations raised by a movement that is committed to radical societal transformation, which includes having held up the socialist ideal of equality in man-woman relations, make it difficult to ignore criticisms in the name of either political expediency or 'betrayal of loyalty to revolutionary martyrdom'.

Over the past ten years, feminism has emerged as a significant challenge to the existing terms and scope of revolutionary politics in Andhra Pradesh. Questions relating to the sexual division of labour, the role of power in gender relations, female subjectivity and sexuality have been woven into the practice of the revolutionary movement. These questions have not exactly been welcomed with openness by the revolutionary parties, who considered such questions as diversionary, or as belonging to a 'bourgeois feminism' that can only be inimical to class struggle. While the radical left groups in Andhra are not alone in their reactions to feminist ideas and critiques of the 'sex-blindness' of orthodox Marxist analysis,[6] there is a specificity to the manner in which such debates are fought out in the actual terrain of a radical political movement.

It is reported that women now form one-third of the cadre in the CPI(M-L), People's War Group (PWG).[7] This enormous increase in the number of women participants, combined with the emergence of women into a new public sphere and the insistence of the women's movement on the politicisation of personal life has resulted in several noticeable changes. The critiques and challenges of women marginalised by the (predominantly male) leadership within the party may not be loud enough but they are certainly not muted as in earlier struggles. There is therefore both external and internal pressure on the movement to respond to feminist critiques as well as questions of caste, questions that were not confronted in earlier struggles. The impact of these challenges to revolutionary practice has been perhaps to problematise gender as a determining factor in women's and men's lives. A paradox of sorts has emerged. On the one hand, it is only since the mid 1980s that the PWG began to pay attention to the formation of separate women's organisations allied to it and, consequently, a number of these emerged under different names in several cities and smaller towns of Andhra. Interestingly, one of the first issues that these urban-based groups took up was that of violence—individual instances of violence against women in the family, rape and molestation—similar to the one the women's movement had addressed in an earlier phase. The term 'patriarchy' is rather freely used in party documents and other writings to describe the social totality of women's oppression. On the other hand, the PWG has reacted negatively to the current feminist literature in Telugu, with the very term 'feminism' being condemned as diversionary, imported or as concerning a tiny majority unrelated to the reality and struggles of working class and toiling women.

The focus of current feminist theory on previously repressed emotions, desires and aspects of the body and personal relations has been characterised either as an encouragement of licentiousness or as part of a grand imperialist design to dilute the revolutionary movement and erode class consciousness. The politicisation of personal experience and the feminist political analysis of personal life that began to be thematised in creative writing meant that the oppression of women had to be charted where women experienced it most directly: in their daily lives. Such a formulation has been troublesome to the revolutionary left. Issues like sexual abuse, regular harassment of rural and tribal women by landlords, forest guards and police can be unproblematically linked to the broader struggle of the peasantry against the state and powerful sections of the ruling classes and castes. But it is more difficult to accept a politics of sexuality and a politics of housework that challenges a system of domination that is entrenched in every woman's most intimate relation with every man.

In a recent document that reflects on marriages in the party, one of the district committees speaks of the spillover of 'bourgeois and false notions about romantic love, sexual desire and the need for marriage' into the party and decries the 'corrupting influence' of such notions on its members. The document holds that while earlier members considered marriage as 'distracting and harmful' to the interests of the movement, marriages have become more common since the 1990s. The entry of more women as full time members supposedly produces 'a desire for marriage' among the male cadres and is considered by the committee as a major factor in the increase of marriages in the party. The document suggests that the inclusion of a large number of women, while welcome in many ways, has resulted in activities like the pursuit of women (sometimes by men in leadership positions, too) and has even led some cadres (both men and women), to leave the movement because they were not prepared to 'resolve their personal (marital) problems within the framework of the interests of the party'.

The implicit argument in the entire report rests on an acknowledgement of the promiscuity of the male and the unbridled sexuality of both men and women as threatening the very goals of the revolutionary movement. Such tendencies are perceived as remnants of a feudal ideology and speak to the failure on the part of the party to conceive and transmit 'a proper scientific perspective on the man-woman relationship'. What then is this "scientific perspective" to be? And more important, how will it help conquer 'remnants of feudal and bourgeois notions' that are coming in the way of revolutionary transformation? The leadership's appeals not to let personal interests and needs overtake the interests and goals of the movement and its denouncement of these 'aberrations' as 'personal weaknesses' brings to mind Sheila Rowbotham's observation: "A 'scientific' approach to sexuality was to be one of Marxism's most perplexing quests in the twentieth century and one that indicated some fundamental dilemmas."[8] I do not intend to attribute an inability to address questions of sexuality only to the revolutionary movement or suggest that the feminist movement has all the answers, but this persistent confusion about sexuality is due to an unwillingness of socialist practice to balance personal relations and political participation. The tensions involved in this complex intertwining of the two manifest themselves in the party's stand on marriage, children, the regulation of sexuality and appropriate norms of behaviour for women. The discourse on sexuality refers thus to the party's vision of ideologically correct behaviour for both men and women. Furthermore, the current emphasis on the importance of (a man's) behaviour in (his) private world is viewed with apprehension that such an emphasis may be at the cost of public questions.

The organisation, on the one hand, is grappling with the challenge to the tendencies of male authoritarianism and complaints of sexual harassment by holding special conventions of women activists and issuing directives and circulars. While these activities are limited to the underground organisation, the party has had to contend, on the other hand, with the ideological impact of feminist theory establishing sexual politics as a significant area of struggle. If the current wave of Telugu feminist literature[9] explores unequal gender relations and lifts the veil on 'privatised' relationships thereby sketching 'a new feminist woman' emerging from the struggle, the revolutionary movement has tried to counter this feminist focus on the body, female sexuality and personal relations by presenting an image of 'woman as revolutionary subject' in its own literature.[10]

The new woman—militant activist and comrade-in-arms—is fashioned out of the arduous process of struggle to overcome oppression, abuse and neglect in family and society through political action that promises true emancipation. The projection of this militant identity of the revolutionary woman—in harmony with her male comrades and organisation—serves, in my opinion, two purposes. One, it is an attempt to counter the image of 'the feminist woman' who appears bogged down in the realm of subjective experience and two, its depiction of the non-antagonistic nature of gender relations in the organisation attempts to respond to the charges of sexual victimisation of women activists that are increasingly voiced.

The themes of dedicated service to a transcendent cause, sacrifice of personal happiness for the collective good and the exalted value attributed to martyrdom recur not only in party documents but also in the creative writings of the movement. Unity with the 'cause' enables the battling militant, be it man or woman, to soar above vulgar details such as everyday behaviour. Such unity also implies a union of men and women as equals, marching together against a common enemy and underplays differences *between* them. However, as Toril Moi said in another context, 'The two of them may well be one, but *he* is the one they are'.[11]

Adavi Putrika (Daughter of the Forest) is an autobiographical account of the life and experiences of a woman dalam (squad) member, working in the forest region. While this book is the third and the latest in the series within the movement literature that projects the militant identity of woman participants, it assumes significance because it is the only one that has been written by a woman who is directly involved in the movement. *Adavi Putrika* focuses on the transformation of Vanaja (Padmakka in the dalam) from an illiterate, exploited wage labourer to a militant guerilla who can not only read and write (Marxist texts included), but is also prepared to confront the "enemy" with a gun on her shoulder. She is able to achieve this stage within the short span of a year largely due to the help and co-operation of the other (male) members of the dalam. The book contains a graphic and often moving account of the travails of the guerillas across the harsh terrain in thick jungles, the exhausting walks for miles under the cover of night, the endless battle against nature and the seasons, the search for water and food and the constant vigil against police ambush.

In the process of education in revolutionary consciousness and action, Vanaja recounts her formative childhood years, spent in poverty and toil, and her efforts to maintain her dignity and extract a decent wage. She also examines family values and the differential child-rearing practices for boys and girls. Vanaja narrates the attempts made by her family to educate her brother, the only son, while sending out the girls, including herself for daily wage labour. Thrust into the role of wage-earner at a young age because of the death of her father and an ailing brother, she later suffers a short-lived and disastrous marriage to a much older and viciously violent man. She recounts the intervention of the party already familiar to her for its involvement in local/village issues, and her break with her mother and her brother upon joining a dalam, which completes the narrative of her pre-revolutionary life. The rest of the dalam members are very kind to her and keen to provide instruction in a number of matters. In fact, Vanaja narrates how overwhelmed she is at the 'decent behaviour' of the dalam members, particularly the men. She eventually marries the dalam commander, who, though from the middle class and much more politically experienced, is thoroughly patient with her, guiding her at every step. When both of them are asked to join a dalam in Maharashtra, he even teaches her English and Marathi. Yet there is something not quite credible about her account of life in the dalam. Although the harsh and relentless circumstances of clandestine living are undoubtedly authentic, the complete ironing out of any tensions/difficulties she or the other women members might have faced *within* the movement and *with* the men is not very convincing, given the continuous disclosure of experiences of harassment and discrimination in newspaper reports.

Vanaja repeatedly refers to 'maternal bonds' and the heart-wrenching separation from loved ones in her account of her decision to have a baby in an urban hide-out despite her husband's initial reluctance. She tells of her anguish at being separated from her one-year-old son when they were arrested and her guilt about having to send away her baby. While all this makes her only human, her portrayal of her husband as a stoic and unflinching revolutionary who maintains his calm despite the uncertainties of their circumstances compared with an emotionally distraught Vanaja, not only reinforces the image of a strong male militant protector but also reinforces the necessity of subordinating personal needs to a higher, worthier cause. The message to Vanaja also seems to be that she must rewrite her personal identity in relation to a collective identity, in order to contribute to the revolutionary effort.

Vanaja refers to the 'jumper campaign' that the party undertook in the forest regions of Dandakaranya among the Madia tribals. The campaign was directed against the tribal practice of prohibiting clothing on the upper part of women's bodies. Though Vanaja states that the party viewed such practices as patriarchal, there is no reference in her account of the campaign to the obstacles the organisation may have faced from the tribal men or even their reactions to the campaign.

A sharply critical review of *Adavi Putrika* by Vennela, who is herself an activist working in the forest region, points out that the "lack of clarity in revolutionary organisations regarding the sexual division of labour is responsible for perpetuating women's subordinate position, especially in the urban hide-outs."[12] She says those women who joined the movement by defying their families are once again reduced to the role of dependent housewives. In the name of safeguarding their real identity from prying neighbours and others, Vanaja, who shows such confidence and courage in the dalam, is turned into a fulltime housewife with no work apart from household chores. The long hours of anxious waiting for a husband who is always away on 'party work' at odd times and for days on end, reduce her to a weepy, nervous wreck. She is not aware of his whereabouts or even the nature of his work but neither does her husband seem to discuss his work with her. Strangely, at no point in the narrative does Vanaja reflect on the reasons for her present condition. The reviewer faults the leadership for not assigning any work to women like Vanaja in urban dens and points out that such enforced idleness and dependency are an impediment to the growth of women activists.

Vanaja's story does not, of course, end on a note of desolation.

She comes out of prison, realises that her child is better off raised in a 'normal' family and plunges into the civil liberties movement. The journey from victim to heroine is made possible by putting on the armour of the 'Strong Woman' and also upholding its desirability for the rest of the women in the movement. The transformation from a politically ignorant subject to a politically conscious one appears, thus, to bypass the question of gender.

The pressure generated both by external factors like the emergence of the women's movement and internal sources such as the increase in the number of women in the organisation and the consequent focus on the specificity of women's experiences has certainly resulted in 'women's issues' appearing on the agenda of the revolutionary movement. Reference is made to patriarchy as a structure of domination and a lot of discussion is centred (in party documents) around building a strong revolutionary women's movement. Time is spent on concerns like women's health, birth control and the problem of 'feelings of inferiority' among women activists. At the same time there is strong condemnation of the "feminist trends in the country as well as in the party" that are perceived as "anti-democratic, anti-revolutionary tendencies that limit women's struggles to family related issues and target man as the enemy". Significantly, it is also emphasised that women should "fight on economic, political and cultural issues while at the same time taking up women-specific issues, especially against patriarchy". In August 1995, the first women militants convention was organised wherein it was explicitly stated by the party leadership that "there is a need like never before to build a women's movement in order to build a strong revolutionary party". During the convention, several possible impediments to the growth of women activists were discussed. Several women spoke of the necessity of better methods of birth control, claiming it was unfair to impose abortions on them; some of them even said that men should get themselves sterilised if they felt that having children was detrimental to the interests of the underground movement.

Clearly, women are no longer perceived as mere adjuncts to the 'real struggle'. And yet there still appears to be a contradiction between the politicisation of women that the movement is seeking, to enable them to be comrades in a joint struggle, and the glossing over of tension between external and internal forms of domination (as manifested in the areas of marriage, sexuality and children). The increased participation of women in roles that are not merely supportive and, especially, the participation of those women from the most oppressed and marginalised sections suggests that not only are they engaged in struggle against the structures of class and caste but they are questioning accepted roles for women. A resolution of the contradiction is therefore perhaps vital to the relationship between the material and ideological levels of struggle. Two distinct strands make up the radical left's position on sexuality and man-woman relations: (a) Sexuality is more a moral distraction to revolutionary goals than a relationship of power and dominance and (b) the feminist focus on the political character of sexuality is countered by highlighting the image of the 'Revolutionary Woman' who irons out all asymmetries and is glorified because of her participation in the political struggle.

Chalam—The Pioneering Crusader

While the Telengana and Srikakulam struggles as well as the contemporary revolutionary movement enabled women of the most oppressed strata to attain some measure of self-respect, new modes of self-expression and self-determination for women were opened up as a result of a different kind of critical confrontation whose source was the creative writing of Chalam.

Chalam's unique place in Telugu literary and cultural life lies not so much in being the lone voice that was raised decades before its time, but because he successfully initiated debate in which the 'women's point of view' could no longer be ignored, creating a space which the present generation of writers are in the process of enlarging.

Apart from the official token celebrations, Chalam's birth

centenary in the year 1994-95, was commemorated by the Left and more significantly, by a loosely constituted group of women who came together as the *Nurella Chalam* (Hundred Years of Chalam) committee. This group brought out a volume of essays[13] on the enduring legacy of Chalam for feminist politics and organised public meetings in nearly twenty cities and towns in the state throughout the year. This was followed by an innovative scripting and staging of a play called Vallu *Aruguru*[14] (Those Six), in which six major women characters from different novels of Chalam assemble together and share their experiences of oppression in their lives. More important, they realise the difference between the lonely struggle they had to undertake compared with the collective struggle enabled by current feminist political practice.

The centenary year was therefore an occasion to situate the contemporary relevance of the writings of Chalam in the context of the social change and movements that have been gathering momentum throughout Andhra Pradesh, as well as within the issues and concerns that the more serious among the current Telugu writers have been exploring.

Though confined to an educated, middle class readership, and not rooted in Marxist theory, Chalam's writings openly challenged the condition of women in a feudal and patriarchal society. The centrality which Chalam gave to female subjectivity and sexuality formed part of not just a debate on morality but on women's need for freedom from oppression (especially within marriage) and for the formation of an identity that is not repressively feminine. By making his women characters exhibit initiative as well as an aggressive sexuality, Chalam was overturning the traditional ideology of femininity with its long history of self-denial, sacrifice and surrender of personal desire and needs.

The sexual radicalism that Chalam advocated was no doubt heretical to middle class morality; it was also something which the Left could only be ambivalent about. While supporting Chalam's denouncement of the hypocrisy in middle class morals and its denial of freedom to women, the Left could not as readily accept Chalam's emphasis on a woman's right over her own body and sexual pleasure. His depictions of autonomy for women and the democratisation of man-woman relations in the context of personal struggle could only be an individualistic solution and was hence not acceptable to the Left.[15] The discomfiture of the Left could also be traced to what it perceived as the reification of the private emotional realm of subjectivity that Chalam established through the 'romantic ambience' of his novels. It was this ambience that set the stage for Chalam's women characters to explore possibilities for their self-definition, while freeing themselves from the constraints of orthodoxy and convention. Significantly, current radical Left claims on Chalam coincide with the emergence and visibility of the women's movement and literature and the pressure to highlight women's specific oppression, preventing this from being subsumed by other unequal relations in society. Interestingly, the volume of essays edited by a founder member of the Revolutionary Writers' Association and published to mark the birth centenary of Chalam in 1994 is titled *Mana Chalam* (Our Chalam). The continuing relevance of Chalam to the present lies not so much in the strategies for women's liberation that he envisaged and offered through his women characters but in his characterisation of women's oppression and in his passionate belief in equality and autonomy for women as a necessary condition of a humane society.

Chalam was born on May 18, 1894 in Madras to a middle class Brahmin family. His earliest childhood memories, according to his autobiography, were those of regular and severe beatings that he received from his father and the silent suffering of his mother. These memories left a deep and disturbing mark on his sensitive mind. He recalls hiding under his grandmother's bed and resolving never to marry, and never to have children. Even if he did, he would never abuse them physically. As a child, Chalam was weak and sickly, lost forever in daydreams. Religious texts, such as the *Ramayana* and *Mahabharata* exerted a strong influence on him as a young boy, since he was a devout Brahmin. When he was forced to get married at the age of fifteen, he insisted that his wife pursue her studies, carrying her on his bicycle to and from her school despite strong objection from the elders in the family.

As a young man with a keen and inquisitive mind, Chalam was influenced by the reformist movement initiated by Kandukuri Veeresalingam,[16] the late nineteenth century social reformer of Andhra. Chalam was drawn towards the Brahmo Samaj, perhaps the only organisation in which he ever took an active interest, and became one of its 'extremists'. His brief involvement in the Brahmo Samaj came to an end following his disillusionment with the Brahmos, particularly with the rigidity and hypocrisy of some of the leaders.

His open sexuality and his advocacy of 'free love' no doubt accelerated the process of his expulsion from the organisation. He was, by then, already ostracised by his relatives and he refused to make any claims on his ancestral property. As it became increasingly difficult for him to rent a house in the more 'respectable' localities, he moved into huts in the Harijanwadas of the various towns of Andhra where he worked. This was to become a way of life in the years that followed since the only people who let him live among them were Dalits and Muslims.

Chalam worked as a headmaster and later as an inspector of schools. He did not think much of these occupations, given his strong views against the distortions that our education system produces, as borne out in his autobiography. The death of his elder son shattered Chalam and left him a bitter atheist. Later in life, Chalam's relentless search took him to astrologers and holy men. In December 1936, he met Ramana Maharishi at the insistence of one of his close friends and felt strongly drawn towards him. In 1947, his younger son left home and was never traced again. Chalam left for Ramana Maharishi's ashram, Arunachalam in February 1956. He died on 4th May, 1979.

In all Chalam wrote nine novels, 18 short stories and 14 plays. In addition, there were eight other books—four volumes of his letters, a collection of random reflections called *Musings*, a treatise on women called *Stree*, a volume on child rearing *Biddala Sikshana*[17] and his autobiography.

Looking back, it is surprising how Chalam steadfastly refused to be swept off his feet, either by the reform movement, the freedom struggle or the communist movement, all the while retaining an active interest in the changes that were taking place around him. These movements were the major cross currents that challenged the endeavours and aspirations of Telugu writers and intellectuals and soon became integral themes of the more progressive among them. In this respect, the evolution of Telugu literature is perhaps not very different from that of the other Indian languages. Chalam's originality lies more in his ability to see beyond the scope of the social movements of his lifetime and in his consistent refusal to embrace any particular dogma. It is therefore difficult to locate Chalam in any particular school or genre because his concerns cut across the period of colonialism and the discourses it engendered. To the traditionalist he was too radical, to the reformer, too impatient, and to the revolutionary, too sceptical.

Chalam, who attacked the obduracy of orthodox social conventions and traditions, had little enthusiasm for the 'glorious' past, nor did he display an unqualified faith in the future. He does not appear to have made any effort to build an analytical framework or to support existing paradigms. Rather, Chalam seemed to go by what he termed "the common man's rugged common sense".[18]

Chalam's world and work were influenced by Kandukuri Veeresalingam, the late nineteenth century social reformer of Andhra, whom he acknowledged as his 'spiritual father'. He also had a high regard for Gandhi, an interest in the 'Soviet experiment', a reverence for Tagore's poetry and a fondness for both the romantic poetry of Krishna Sastry[19] and the revolutionary thunder of Sri Sri.[20] In his autobiography, Chalam acknowledges the influence of Havelock Ellis and Bertrand Russell as well.

The cultural history of nineteenth century India is generally characterised as one of conflict between social reformers agitating for the improvement of (middle class) women's conditions, and traditionalists who virulently opposed such moves. In attempting to answer the question of how a modern woman should be, the reformers sought to fashion an image of woman in accordance with the newly emerging middle class male consciousness. While responding to the same question, the traditionalists asserted the status quo, and rejected 'westernised' conceptions, attempting to cast the 'ideal woman' in their own mould. What is striking, however, is that today, the contrasting and contradictory images offered by the reformers and the traditionalists appear to be fused. The similarities in their positions are illustrated by the insistence of both the reformers and the traditionalists on the control of women's sexuality, on norms of 'good wifely' behaviour, on women's responsibility towards child bearing and on moulding children as good citizens. The significance of Chalam's writings on freedom and sexuality in women therefore has to be seen against this background and its ideological premises. The distinctiveness of his position lies in his rejection of both the traditional and reformist conceptions of womanhood. Chalam's recognition of the social condition of women (albeit in Hindu and Brahminical society) reveals therefore an unusual male sensitivity to women's oppression.

Chalam began to write in the 1920s and turned his critical and intense passion upon the condition of the polity, and more specifically on the condition of women. What is rather striking about all his novels, short stories and essays is his adversarial view of society, in which individual subjects are irretrievably caught but to which they in no way simply belong. It is only to the extent that the individual (or the woman in this case) lives out this adversarial relation, and fights against the norm that she is a human subject at all.

Chalam's tales of love and power, however, while celebrating women's spiritedness, initiative and aggressive sexuality and decrying repressive social conditions, are rife with ambiguities. Chalam seemed to make an almost heroic effort to reconcile the traditional romantic notion of yearning for external love and the unity of two souls with his belief in freedom. Passionate love, especially for the women characters, uprooted them from the mundane and prepared them for radical options as well as sacrifice. Thus thinking, sensitive women seduce not merely by their beauty and virtue but through their minds as well. But can such an enterprise be successful under feudal patriarchy? While the husbands are rogues, indifferent or just weak-willed, the lovers fare no better. Exposed to the duplicity and cowardice displayed by the men in their sexual dealings, the women struggle to live authentically. Their anguish and struggle to define themselves in the context of the tension between autonomy and dependence, between the need to assert themselves and the need to be overwhelmed, in short, between freedom and control, often end tragically in death, mysterious disappearance or in a self-sabotaging of their love. Yet, the women do not appear as victims alone. "Existentially speaking, under patriarchy, women risk more, fall deeper and rise higher than men."[21] That is why, perhaps, the men in Chalam's fiction pale in comparison to the women; for women, the stakes are higher and there are more victories and more failures than there are for men.

In a booklet called *Man and Woman* written in English in 1926, Chalam says, "[b]ut what is asked for women is not control over the home or the world, but control over herself, her ideas, actions and finance." Again, in the same booklet, referring to the necessity of freedom for women, and the arguments advanced against its advocacy, Chalam writes,

[s]o man controls woman's freedom so that it may not turn into bad ways. Then who controls the man? Society and conscience. Let society govern woman too, why this intervention of man? Is man controlled by woman from turning his liberty into licence? Do men know what is liberty to dictate it to woman? He constructed one code for himself and another for woman. His is God-made, and hers man-made. Any human control over individual rights is odious and unbearable. It is an obstacle in the way of one's natural development...And here is every woman having a man for moral guardian, preserving her purity like pickles in the name of social hygiene, but really for his own private use. This is the wildest, deepest and the most degrading tyranny that has ever existed. The world has not opened its eyes to it as yet.[22]

A theme which keeps recurring in Chalam's writings and which is of relevance to feminist politics is the issue of female sexuality, of women's control over their bodies, and of motherhood. Nowhere have the critiques of Chalam been more highly charged than in his attacks on the theme of sexuality. Throughout his life, Chalam was condemned and ostracised for what people considered to be his advocacy of promiscuity and licentiousness. One may unhesitatingly say that Chalam was a trailblazer in Telugu literature who unravelled the dynamics of female sexuality and desire, and recognised women's right to sexual pleasure. While saying so, one must keep in mind the backdrop to Chalam's writing provided by two different trends in Telugu literature. While the romantic tales sponsored by feudal patronage had elaborate, explicit, and amorous descriptions of women's bodies, the late nineteenth century and early twentieth century literature as well as social reform literature sought to formulate a code of sexual and conjugal morality that mapped women's lives within bounds. Although the latter's representations and reforms were addressed to the oppressive practices that structured the Hindu women's femininity, women were recast in the mould of a conventional femininity, particularly with respect to sexuality. Chalam condemned and attacked both these trends, the one celebrating the erotic, as it were, and the other routinely ignoring women's sexuality and their experience of pleasure and joy. It was especially loathsome for Chalam to accept the culturally cherished notion of the sexually settled, nurturing woman who is so anchored in the socially approved framework of marriage that her sexuality is not a subject for discussion. Neither was Chalam willing to accept the nineteenth century romanticist notion of 'pure love' untrammelled by physical (and hence baser) desire. Through his women characters, Chalam sought to render female sexuality as a normal and natural phenomenon and attempted to exercise the complex fears and stigmas that the theme had so far invoked.

When his novel *Maidanam*[23] was being serialised in a Telugu magazine in 1931, its publication was stopped midway after a section of the readers protested against the brazenness of the story. It is in *Maidanam* that Chalam sought to bring to centre stage several key themes that were of concern to him. Not only was the novel a scathing onslaught on and indictment of the rigidities of caste, religion and the institution of marriage, but it was here that Chalam attempted to explore the possibility of non-exclusive man-woman relationships and the question of women's right to sexual pleasure and reproductive freedom. Implicit in Chalam's rejection of marriage was also his rejection of what he perceived as a (brahmanical) system of values that warped female selfhood.

By presenting sexuality as an arena both of oppressive inequalities and as a strategy towards women's liberation from the weight of repressive tradition, Chalam anticipated several crucial feminist concerns. Firstly, he has shaken our understanding of the 'sexual' by showing that sexuality, gender and reproduction need not be fused; on the contrary, they can be separated into distinct systems of power. Second, in order to talk about sex, we find that we must overcome both internal and external resistance, for we live in a culture that is, in general, inhospitable to critical analyses of sex and one in which female sexuality, in particular, has been simultaneously manipulated by taboo, glorification and degradation. To speak at all, and then to speak in opposition to those manipulative traditions, is to invite strong reactions. Nevertheless, Chalam did venture bravely into this inhospitable terrain. While he sought to expose the double standards of sexual morality, Chalam attempted at the same time to go beyond a critique of patriarchal sexuality. His effort was to raise basic questions about the status of sexuality, power and control in man-woman relations.

Chalam's condemnation of sexual repression and his exploration of the theme of sexual liberation for women meant that he was proposing a social critique, as if it were a precondition for a reordering of the social order. Chalam was more concerned with how to liberate sexuality from power contaminants so that female sexuality is not automatically linked to submission.

Chalam was among the first in Telugu literary and social circles to question traditional definitions of women's sexuality, of women's 'nature', of sexual satisfaction and health on the grounds that such definitions as propounded by men tended only to justify the sexual exploitation of women. Chalam's women characters like Aruna and Rajeswari, through their rebellion against orthodoxy and tradition, appear sexually liberated. However, the point to be underscored here is that their autonomy has led to sexual freedom and not vice versa. Sexual liberation is of little value unless it includes the freedom to reject or enter into sexual relationships fearing neither exploitation nor punishment. It was this freedom (and the attendant anguish) in women like Aruna and Rajeswari that Chalam sought to emphasise to make his point about sexual liberation. He was not interested in proposing new prescriptions for sexuality per se or as a part of a general restructuring of society. By recognising that certain conventions—the double standard, the cult of virginity, and the requirement that female sexuality find expression solely within monogamous marriages—control and inhibit female sexuality as well as support male dominance, Chalam attempted to expose male duplicity. Also, by showing that denial of reproductive freedom and psychological intimidation through ridicule, rejection and isolation are punishments for the sexually active woman, Chalam pointed out the price these women have to pay.

In his collection of essays, *Stree*, and in his volume on child rearing, *Biddala Sikshana*, Chalam also focused on how patriarchy fuses gender and sexuality and how concrete material changes would enable women and men to experience sexuality in ways that were less attached to and formed by gender difference. These changes include economic equality, access to birth control and abortion for women, protection of mothers and children outside of marriage and so on. In fact, if we take into consideration the spirit of Chalam's time (and contemporary middle class attitudes to sexual and conjugal morality) and continuing accusations of sexual deviance that are levelled against Chalam even today, it is almost as if Chalam was trying to say that if we do not demand radical changes and instead concede ground to conventional morality, the margin of what we consider acceptable and proper will shrink further.

Another basic question raised by Chalam concerns women's reproductive rights. At a time when motherhood was seen as instinctively natural and its sanctity was scarcely an issue to be discussed or debated, Chalam's attempts to do so were quite extraordinary. In *Stree*, Chalam sought to expose and condemn the ideological trappings which glorify motherhood while women's position within the family remains subordinate. He wrote about how the societal construction of motherhood is a burden on women and described how young girls, who have scarce knowledge of their reproductive functions, are thrown into marriage and motherhood and the impact this had on their health. Chalam strongly advocated that only those women who are physically and mentally prepared and willing should bear children, and motherhood should not be imposed. In fact, Chalam went so far as to say, "Women must agitate until the state and society ensure that pregnancy does not disrupt women's self-respect, health or economic independence."[24] (*Stree*, 1930, trans) At a time when public knowledge and discussion (and state involvement) regarding women's access to measures like birth-control and abortion were very limited, Chalam was a pioneer in drawing attention to these issues. He considered reproductive health and the need for women to know and claim control over their bodies as integral to the women's health movement of the day, issues that were essential for women's equality and freedom.

The characters created by Chalam, especially the women, are extraordinary beings. Women like Rajeswari (in *Maidanam*), Aruna (in *Aruna*) and Sasirekha (in *Sasirekha*) are middle class Brahmin women who dare to come out of the confines of the family, their stories revealing the exalted heights they reach. When such extraordinary characters enter ordinary lives, the resultant confusion, crisis and absurdities plunge the reader into a self-reflective questioning of basic values and assumptions. Unlike the novelists of this period, in Telugu and other Indian languages, who had to make use of women outside the social order to explore man-woman relations and women's autonomy, Chalam chose to do away with such a ploy. As a result, his women characters cause a greater shock to the upholders of middle class virtues, while at the same time, generating a sense of identification among sympathetic and sensitive readers in the same class. This, perhaps, is at the root of all the controversies that his writings generated during his time as well in the present day.

Conclusion

The space opened up by the path-breaking writing of Chalam combine with the challenges of feminism to provide the context for questions of identity and self determination among women as they are being vigorously discussed in Andhra today. In particular, the debate on the feminist critique of the revolutionary Left and the intensity with which this confrontation is taking place in the political and literary circles of Andhra Pradesh, signal a critical moment in the history of both the revolutionary movement and feminist consciousness and practice. Although the radical left appears to go along with orthodox Marxist analysis of class as the central determinant of power relations, the pressure now generated to respond to the feminist critique is both from within the movement and without. The challenge to the concept of revolutionary identity from feminism lies in that it allows into the political arena problems of sexuality and subjectivity which have so far tended to be suppressed in revolutionary discourse.

While Chalam's emphasis on the need for freedom might have been limited to individual strategies, the microstructure of personal experience as highlighted in some of the current feminist literature has not led to a valorisation of the personal, an exclusionary principle that inhibits other political actions. Feminism is formulated as a political practice in some of the creative writing in Telugu. This implies that no area of experience lies beyond the purview of political intervention. On the other hand, the increased number of women participants in the revolutionary movement in recent years, and the increased politicisation of women that the movement is seeking, suggest that issues concerning sexuality and man-woman relations are the vehicles by which political radicalisation can be extended to the sphere of experience designated as personal. Thus feminist awareness during the process of revolutionary struggle can transform the quality of revolution as well. While the revolutionary movement is perhaps beginning to be alert in recognising that it can no longer afford to ignore the questions raised by feminism, some of the current crop of feminist writing in Telugu emphasises the need for women to challenge the existing structures of authority through political activity. This focus on 'gender specific space' and the politicisation of women constitutes a possible meeting ground between a revolutionary identity and a feminist identity in current creative writing in Telugu.

Notes

1. I use the term 'radical left movement' to refer to the political practice of the CPI (ML) People's War Group and the opinions and statements of the allied writers' organisation called *Virasam* (Revolutionary Writers' Organisation).

2. S. Felski, cited in B.L. Marshal, *Engendering Modernity*, Cambridge, 1994, p. 71.

3. For an account of women's participation in the Telengana struggle, see Stree Shakti Sanghatana, *'We Were Making History': Life Stories of Women in the Telengana People's Struggle*, New Delhi: Kali for Women, 1989.

4. U. Vindhya, 'Women in the Srikakulam Movement', in Ilina Sen (ed.), *A Space Within the Struggle: Women's Participation in People's Movements*, New Delhi: Kali for Women, 1990.

5. S. Rowbotham, *Women in Movement: Feminism and Social Action*, New York, 1992, p. 182.

6. H. Hartmann, 'The Unhappy Marriage of Marxism and Feminism: Towards a more progressive union', *Capital and Class*, No. 8, 1979, 14–29.

7. Vanaja, *Adavi Putrika* (Foreword), Hyderabad, 1995, p. 2.

8. Rowbotham, *Women in Movement*, op. cit., p. 150.

9. See for instance, the anthologies of feminist poetry *Neeli Meghalu*, Hyderabad: Sweccha Prachuranalu, 1993; *Guri Choosi Paade Paata* Vijayawada: Kavitvam Prachuranalu, 1990 and the novels of Volga, *Rajakeeya Kathalu*, Hyderabad: Sweccha Prachuranalu, 1993 and *Prayogam* Hydrabad: Manavi Prachurana, 1995.

10. See for instance, *Vasanta Geetam* Hyderabad: Srujana Prachurana, 1990; *Rago*, Hyderabad: Srujana Prachurana, 1993 and *Adavi Putrika*, Hyderabad: Rago Prachuranalu, 1995 which focus on women's participation in the current armed struggle of the CPI (ML) and the PWG.

11. Toril Moi, *Simone de Beauvoir: The Making of an Intellectual Woman*, Cambridge: Cambridge University Press, 1994, p. 108.

12. Vennela, Review of *Adavi Putrika*, *Andhra Jyoti*, April 14, 1996, p. 5.

13. Volga (ed.) *Nurella Chalam*, Hyderabad: Sweccha Prachuranalu, 1994.

14. Volga, *Vallu Aruguru*, Hyderabad: Feminist Study Circle, 1995.

15. K.V.R. Reddy, 'Chalam—*abhyudaya sohityodyamu*', *Aruna Tara*, May, No. 157, 1994, 5–13.

16. Kandukuri Veeresalingam (1848–1919), a pioneering figure of the renaissance movement in Andhra as much for his varied literary and journalistic activities as for his championing of women's issues. He wrote what is considered to be the first novel in Telugu and the first Telugu books on natural sciences and history. His journal *Vivekavardhini*, started in 1874, was used to promote his views on women's education, widow re-marriage, child marriages, the Devadasi system and so on. In the same year, he established a girls' school, the first such institution in Andhra, at Dowleswaram. In 1883, Veeresalingam started a monthly magazine called *Sat Hita Bohini* for women. His campaign for the rehabilitation of widows, widow re-marriage, women's education and his struggles against child marriage, superstition and the nautch system mark the beginning of the social reform movement in Andhra.

17. G.V. Chalam, *Biddala Sikshana*, Vijayawada: Aruna Publishing House, (1935) 1993.

18. G.V. Chalam, *Musings*, Hyderabad: Chalam Sahiti, 1976, p. 64.

19. Krishna Sastry (1897–1980) was the foremost and perhaps the last

of the romantic poets in Telugu who wrote in the classical mould. He was a contemporary and close friend of Chalam.

20. Sri Sri (1910–1983) is the first truly modern and progressive poet in Telugu who gave new direction to Telugu literature. He was also a friend of Chalam.

21. Moi, *Simone de Beauvoir*, op. cit., p. 72.

22. G.V. Chalam, *Man and Woman*, Vijayawada: Veni Press, 1926, p. 15.

23. G.V. Chalam, *Maidanam*, Vijayawada: Aruna Publishing House, (1927) 1993.

24. G.V. Chalam, *Stree*, Vijayawada: Premchand Publications, (1930) 1966, p. 23.

Sexuality and the Film Apparatus

Continuity, non-continuity, discontinuity in Bombay cinema

RAVI S. VASUDEVAN

This chapter looks at the question of sexuality through the prism of the narrative form of popular Bombay cinema. It will try to develop certain arguments about narrative form and representations of sexuality by looking at a significant 1951 film, *Awara* (Raj Kapoor 1951), hopefully in ways which outline certain more general tendencies within cinematic narration. One of my major concerns will be how the apparent lack of narrative integration of the popular cinema affects perceptions of sexuality or, more precisely, how it affects the dimensions of the sensual and erotic in the field of perception. By lack of narrative integration here I mean the dispersal of cinematic form into a set of relatively separable narrative, didactic and performative units, and also, at a less obvious level, the propensity of scenes and sequences to be composed of a relay of fragments unsystematically coded in terms of temporal development and spatial location. It is only occasionally that such a jettisoning of spatial and temporal continuity may acquire a more purposive feature, as if one logic of construction is being denied in favour of another.

It could be argued that cinema generally constitutes the sexuality of the spectator by channelling the libidinal energy arising from the scopic and auditory drives, the drives to look and to listen. In the industrially regularised production of the filmic narrative form of the classical Hollywood model these drives are controlled by binding the technology of representation to the diegetic field (the field/narrative world depicted), that is, by subordinating relations of space and time to the needs of narrative causality. Shots, spaces and times are not meant to 'stick out', to diverge from the flow of a story. A set of codes related to editing, lighting, sound-mixing and mise-en-scene enabled this streamlined mode of story-telling, a form known as continuity cinema. Through it we are oriented to consume the flow of events that compose a film in terms of the awareness, movement and actions of individual characters.[1]

How does one figure the mode of our attachment to the non-aggregation of popular Indian cinema, where shots are not always, indeed rarely, constituted within a systematic spatio-temporal dissection of scenic space? Gilles Deleuze, setting up a suggestive contrast in the regime of montage forms, compares the organic nature of the American mode emblematised in the work of D.W. Griffith, with a contrasting, or contrary, pathetic articulation of form represented in Soviet work. He contrasts the juxtaposition of complete and inviolate signs, of economic, racial and social difference in the cross-cutting of the so-called organic mode, as in the phenomenon of the last minute rescue, with a figuration which is predicated on the incompleteness and transformability of juxtaposed signs.[2] We may put this contrast to work in a slightly different context. The inorganicity of individual shots assumes a relationality and a dependence leading to an extra term or insight in the signification of Soviet film dialectics. But, if we think of this not as a dialectical integration to a higher power, but as a non-system, or a system of disarticulation, then we may be looking at a rather different set of attachments, in which the libidinal investment of the spectator is fractured into a series of micro-affiliations. As this is a non-systematic arrangement, we are not invited to look at a cumulative impacting of the image-track on spectatorial subjectivity, but to register the disequilibrium of parts as bearing a greater significance than the closed system. That is an extreme statement of the circumstances of narrative construction, to be tested in the following pages through reflection on *Awara*, and in ways which I hope will show how the film apparatus also functions as a highly specific but suggestive and influential way of imagining the transformation of social and political circumstances. Indeed, I will argue that the question of non-continuity and dis-continuity at the level of form allows a series of explorations about narratives of transition.

Sexuality and the Question of Transition

The question of sexuality needs to be explored at a series of levels, of how the narration is constructed, of how certain voices and points of view are advantaged in the relay of events, and how mise-en-scene, literally a particular way of putting objects, characters, light and shade into the scene, engenders a certain aura of sexuality. In a sense my argument here is that one has to think about the representation of sexuality within or perhaps moving against the grain of certain relationships of authority/power. Here, I am particularly concerned with the authoritative field of the father, the various discourses, narrative moves, and sensorial fields that this authority sets up. Central to my argument is that there is a transformation in the fields of authority and sexuality involved here.

The tale of sexual suspicion, modelled on the *Ramayana* in its recounting of the abduction of a wife, and the subsequent doubt cast on her chastity, is integrated into a story of traumatic social transition imagined by the socialist Abbas, the film's script writer. The film's movement from the countryside to the city, and with it the move from an inegalitarian social order to one founded on the contingencies of environment and opportunity simultaneously undertakes a shift from a feudal construction of sexuality to one predicated on notions of chance and of choice.

In terms of socially symbolic narrative, the centering of the transition on sexuality is highlighted in Raghunath's wife, Leela, being a widow. The marriage thus goes against social convention and family wishes. Although this information is only referred to again very indirectly,[3] I suggest it marks a definite disturbance which is structurally central to Raghunath's narrative. It has been pointed out that within Hindu social codes it is quite conventional for a widow to be regarded as an inauspicious figure; she may even be considered to have been untrue to her husband.[4] By marrying Leela, Raghunath then represses connotations of unfaithfulness. However, these charges of unfaithfulness re-emerge—though not, it is true, in relation to her status as a widow, but as bearer of another man's child. Jagga's abduction of Leela and the announcement subsequent to her return that she is pregnant casts doubt on her chastity. The bandit then recovers that which Raghunath had repressed; he even penetrates the Judge's liberality, showing that it overlays a socially conservative viewpoint. The Judge's vision of an invariant social order founded on heredity, summed up in the notion that 'the children of the respectable will be respectable, those of thieves and bandits are destined to be criminals' is communicated back to him by Jagga through Leela. Jagga reminds Raghunath that he has flouted a law which emphasises that the wife must be the indisputable property of one man.[5]

In terms of the underlying narrative organisation, Jagga is not Raghunath's foe. Instead, he focuses the conventional anxieties of Raghunath for his social and sexual standing.[6] In terms of narrative function, he is Raghunath's shadow and, through the course of the story, the two fathers work in tandem to maintain Raj's illegitimacy. This doubling of character functions addresses a family drama rather than the overt social theme, although it also allows the family drama to provide the springboard for an enquiry into social relations.

The figure of the judge is, however, a complex one, suggestive both of a harsh, repressive authority and a much less secure, vulnerable character, notations which are on display from the beginning of the film. In the opening,[7] a geometry of power is constructed around the figure of Judge Raghunath, his gaze functioning in a repressive way to arraign the law on his side and against his assailant, Raj, whom we subsequently discover is his son. There is a disturbance of this field by the incursion of Rita, his foster-daughter and a lawyer in her own right, who declares that she will defend the accused. Under persistent interrogation by Rita of the circumstances in which his wife left home, the Judge finally starts his story of the past, but the sound does not synchronise with the lip movement. The unanchored voice is then implicated in a melodramatic movement from the domain of the public into the register of personal reverie.[8]

That reverie unravels in notations of an authority exercised at the level of narration. Significant here is the deployment of what I have called the narrational song, a song which interprets the meaning of narrative events, past or future. It is performed by characters who are incidental to the narrative, and may not even be 'properly' bound into the space of the fiction. Examples of this are the fishermen's song of warning and the traditional folk song that invokes imagery from the Ramayana to present a narrational stance to Raghunath's eviction of Leela.

The fishermen's song follows upon information presented by the Judge's voice-over, that while he loved his wife, he was not aware of the dangers that were soon to befall them. The song integrates this information through its note of warning, projects it into the immediate narrative, and into the future as well. Its immediate effects are reflected in Leela's anxious look; and it has an anticipatory aspect, for it tells of the dangers characteristic of the area and, metaphorically, of the bandit who will cause upheaval in the lives of Raghunath and his wife. Although the fishermen and the couple are linked by their appearance on the river, they are not shown in the same shot. However, we can imagine the place they occupy because the couple looks off-screen left, and Leela seems to respond anxiously to their warning. This spatially 'unbound' aspect to the fishermen's song reinforces its extra-diegetic resonance; the song appears to be performed in a space outside the couple's but has a prescient knowledge about them, warning them of their destiny.

Despite these features of extra-diegetic authority, the song comes to be associated with a character, Judge Raghunath. I have argued that the 'return of the repressed'—the emergence of the bandit and the 'dishonouring' of Leela—is associated with the Judge's authority. This is indicated by his relationship to the inauguration of the song of warning. For it is the firing of his gun which immediately sets off the fishermen's song, as if Raghunath unconsciously calls up the threatening scenario for his wife. His 'precipitating' of the song of warning is subsequently 'replied' to by another gesture. Celebratory sitar music on the soundtrack accompanies his excited anticipation on hearing Leela has returned after her abduction. A servant begins to light a chandelier with a torch; Raghunath takes this over from him, finishes the work, blows out the torch and flings it away, and the music comes to an abrupt end. The firing of the gun, which inaugurated the disturbance, is here balanced by the extinguishing of the torch; Raghunath's gestural field is aligned with the narration's musical motifs to encompass the period of his wife's trauma.

The alignment between extra-diegetic motifs and a particular character action, in this case, that of the bearer of patriarchal authority, is not a systematic one.[9] But it does suggest how narrative attention is subtly focused around patriarchal authority, and how this has what I would call the effect of involution, a kind of tendency for characters and events to swirl within the gravitational field of the father's authority.

The threat apprehended in the scene on the river unravels immediately, in the wake of a startling moment of transition, one that jars our understanding of the time frame in which action takes place. Raghunath, sprawled on the bed, urges his wife to hurry up and join him. A non-continuity cut follows on from the sexual suggestiveness of this image, thereby allowing for the suggestion of a spatial and temporal ellipsis. Leela goes into another room, where a disembodied hand grasps at her and she screams. There is a cut back to Raghunath, who, aroused from sleep by the scream is disoriented, looking around for Leela in his bed. While the non-continuity cut is a common enough feature of the Bombay cinema's unsystematic narration, it is distinctly disorienting here. It makes the intervening shot of the assault on Leela appear to lie in a temporal and spatial limbo in relation to the shots of Raghunath on either side. The abduction then seems to have taken place while Raghunath is asleep, as if he had dreamt it, and, indeed, it is a figure from his unconscious who is the vehicle of the kidnapping. In terms of the logic of the narrative at this juncture, the judge's sexual advances to the widow have been prohibited, making all preceding sexuality leading to the procreation of the son also subject to a retrospective prohibition; it never really happened.

The doubling of Raghunath and Jagga takes place at the level of the expressionist encounter the two fathers have with the victimized wife in the spaces respectively of magistrate's house and dacoit hide-out. The characters are of course constructed in different ways. Where Jagga is in command in his hide-out, there are involuntary and conflict-ridden elements to Raghunath's behaviour (although, once he acts, then his character becomes fixed, unbudgeable). It is the scene of Raghunath's expulsion of Leela which is particularly interesting, composed as it is of highly non-continuous, fragmentary views of Leela being composed in unbalanced ways, horizontal compositions being juxtaposed with angled shots and close-ups, completely symbolic figures such as a pair of ornamental cherubs being inserted to augment the sentiments being solicited by the musical score.

I would use the category non-continuity here rather than discontinuity as the latter would connote either a systematization of cutting patterns, an active disruption of one mode of representation by another or, if not another, then by a structured intervention such as the tableau which alters the terms, and indeed the rhythms, of perception.[10] The arbitrariness of non-continuity on the other hand expresses a certain fracturing of spectator positioning in ways quite distinct from a cutting pattern tied to the coherent graphics of character perception (the attribution of what we see to a particular character). Subsequently, after Leela's expulsion from the house, the film employs the systematic discontinuity of parallel editing, a mode which conventionally signals simultaneity. The narration moves us amongst three spaces bound into a notional spatial proximity by continuities in the texture of night and of rain, the spaces of Raghunath, of Leela on the street, and of the singing troupe. This set of elements can be conceived of as lying along a linear axis of temporal progression. This is the progression of the narrative events of expulsion and child-birth, but also the narratological event of the song which refers to Raghunath as the unjust King Ram, who doubts the virtue of his innocent wife Sita. However, interestingly, not all elements are comparably structured. Raghunath's image is shown to us from different angles, a way of fashioning the icon, a figure in whom meaning has come to be fixed, and therefore not temporally defined. The judge's double, Jagga, however, is positioned as an image which at once inhabits the time of the sequence, (in that he refers to the event of birth) and also stands outside that time. This is composed as an insert whose knowing presence transcends the immediacy of the event, a function repeated a number of times during the course of the film. These two images could be said to inhabit a spatialised form of narration rather than a linearised, syntagmatic one.[11]

What implications does this have? We have at once the libidinal investment in the onward flow of narrative goals, including the articulation of obstacles and their circumvention, but we also have the emergence of pockets of narrative intransigence, where a character comes to freeze into a strictly delimited representation, one which comes to a halt, rests within the confines of the icon; at a lesser level of narrative weight we have the stereotype of the villain.[12] Arguably, the stringing together of time elements and spatial elements in this sequence liberates the narrative from some of the textual concentration deriving from the oppressive authority the father exercises over the household. The singers refer to Raghunath as king of the universe, and there is a way in which the household can be figured as a form of kingdom, constituting a certain understanding of the natural order as a patrimonial regal order.[13] This autarchic and self-referential sphere is shot through with an authority which also denotes a certain morbid sensuality, inward and claustrophobic. This is the scenic and spatial expression of the overwhelming father, vehicle of an enveloping desire that seeks to contain desire. These cloistered spaces provide the setting for a scene which obsessively recurs across a series of films, that of the father's incestuous drive to hold his daughter within the orbit of his authority.[14] The wife is unceremoniously jettisoned to constitute her own space with her son in a classic formulation of the Oedipus complex.

The father's house, and his image, perform spatialised functions that seek to control the progression of the narrative. We have here a mode of scenic construction in which the image exercises authority, constituting the legitimacy, and perhaps even power, of the beholder, as in codes of looking such as *darsan*. The inertial aspects of the figuration of the judge are elaborated into a full-fledged mode of embodying space. A perceptual field emerges around the judge, centred on a melodramatic stylistics oriented to a plunging below, where signification, here a distinctly theatrical one, impacts on the construction of the image, in intimations not of a realist psychology but of an occulted, dreadful melodramatic one. Here I draw upon Peter Brooks' work in the field of melodrama studies to refer to a system of signification which constantly seeks the perceptual underbelly of relations amongst characters, that which is repressed, which cannot be admitted in everyday perception.[15] The ensemble of melodramatic extremes, and of their gothic variation, course through the crucial moments when characters encounter the Judge, and are invariably focused on interior spaces which provide for a cavernous sense of a terrain normally screened off from view. This is played out not only at the level of darkened sets, but also in the mobilisation of vertical lines through the crane, and extreme psychological states via the low angle shots reminiscent of German expressionism and north American film noir.

A series of narrative images, spaces and scenes emerge in counterpoint to this involutionary space. However, these are not determined by an entirely different dynamic of filmic narration, or distinguished by clearly distinct constructions of character subjectivity and sexuality. Released into the city, the mother and son move within a set of spaces defined by tableau modes of representation. These are the spaces of the slum, the mother's hovel, the schoolroom, remand home and jail, the spaces in which Leela and Raj make abortive attempts to improve their situation, and the space of Raj's subsequent criminalisation. Most significant perhaps is the street, the place of chance encounters that will transform narrative relations.

In contrast to the opening scene in the court, none of these scenes acquire that highly systematic pattern of analytical/ continuity editing aligned to the perception and activity of individual characters. Tableau shots are recurrently employed to highlight circumstances of moral quandary and pathos deriving from the relationship between son and mother, and describing the various travails the son has to face. There is a tendency, throughout the film, to augment such modes of staging with the cinematic flourish of the crane-shot, a movement drawing attention to the film apparatus which writes a cinematic excess into the scene. Such an excess not only seeks to heighten the emotional effects of a scene, as when camera movement follows musicality to draw us into the plight of a character, but they invite us to see apparatus qua apparatus, so that the investment, the libidinal attachment arising from the desire to look is one made in the cinema as cinema and as a mode of omniscient narration. The camera bodies forth a scene, outlining a position of perception that stands above any of the individual characters. The hyperbolic quality to this view from above provides a dimension of expressiveness to the narration and sets up certain recurrent parameters in the field of the visual. There develops an excessive narrational-stylistic echo across the film, matching the emotional extremes of the story with a system of visual excess.

These expressive but highly contained fields are centred on a relay of stable narrative relations. Insofar as a scene is relatively stable, how is a momentum generated by which the separation of the spaces that constitute the integrity of these scenes are bridged, how is a narrative transaction effected? To my mind, there is a characteristic strategy involved here. The scene is almost equivalent to a fixed autonomous shot, but there is an extra drive or element posed in it which sets up a destabilizing dynamic. This follows from the notion of the tableau whose visual logic suggests an image in transit, caught between two moments, implying that an organic, complete form cannot remain.[16] In the opening sequence of the Bombay segment, we are presented with a number of planar blocks that didactically outline the problem of destitute children, their susceptibility to criminality, and the vagabond child's ridicule of those who desire education and social improvement as feminine. The next shot, one of motherly devotion, shows Leela combing Raj's hair, while the boy protests that other children say this makes him look like a girl. The child straining against his mother's ministrations serves as a point of tension within the frame, pushing the scene to unravel in the movement of the child out of the house. There are reverberations here of masculine assertiveness, especially at junctions involving the hero's encounters with women and the domineering father.

The tableau then actually sets up a series of unstable scenic and narrative drives within its equilibrium, and its aesthetic is even used for spaces which should notionally afford a certain dynamic of movement, as for example the street. The street in *Awara* evidently functions like a narrative shifter, a corridor along which figures move from one space to another, generating links between rigidly separated domains. This domain of chance encounters, menacing intimations and criminal drives also stands for the sexuality of the social; for it is in this domain that a chance intimacy with strangers could transform one's life, and present the possibilities of transgressing boundaries of the self, and of spaces to which one is conventionally habituated.

These tableaux, composed in transit and whose limits are defined by the fixed frame, allow us to intermittently focalise characters; unlike the continuity mode, there are substantial gaps in time and space in our sighting of a character. But let me add a rider here. There are instances when such scenes are elaborated by the use of highly structured continuity editing and in the use of point-of-view shots which are especially notable for a very sexually defined way of looking. Such points-of-view work through a series of registers, but most pronounced are two particular usages. One is related to the abduction of Leela, when the Judge is prevented from shooting at the fleeing bandit on learning that his wife is being borne away and could be hurt. The point-of-view shows the Judge looking at the disappearing figures with a certain ambiguous, held-in look, eyes glittering with a peculiar intensity. I use the impressionistic mode here to seek out the particular psychological demeanour of a character split in his outlook, an aura that flows from the particular grid of non-continuity, disjuncture and dream work that I have used to capture the relationship between the Judge and Jagga in their common will to subordinate Leela. There is a somewhat menacing texture to this subjectivity, deriving from that involuted, authoritarian mode of sexual subjection and feudal construction of the woman's body, one which demands that she must remain within the space of the patriarch.

There is a rather different point-of-view shot in Raj's first sighting of the adult Rita. The view does not seek to contain, morally control or punish the woman for her movement out of patriarchal space;[17] instead, it expresses curiosity. There is something sexually perverse in this first sighting, for it metonymises the woman's body into a purse, an object which the man desires to penetrate and gain the secret of. Perhaps it is not insignificant that the object Raj hopes to gain is Rita's car-key, the figural key to an urban mobility that Rita is vehicle of. There is a straightforward narrative function involved in this encounter, that of the sexual allure of class for the plebian man. But the meeting is also a way for the hero to recover his identity within his father's house, access to which Rita is able to provide, but Leela is not. On the other hand, we need to look at mobility itself as invested with a sexuality, defining a particular relation of body to space. It is here, in a set of metaphors linking women, criminality and city, that the hero is afforded entry into a different order of space, providing a release from the involuting series of narrations centred on the sexual orbit of the father's authority.

Insofar as the construction of urban subjectivity is suffused with an opening of body to space, we need to reflect that there is also a holding of body in space, or body by space, and that this derives from a problem in the figurative work of the film apparatus, in the relationship between stasis and movement in its mode of representation. These problems are represented within the diegesis by the mode of representation of the countervailing field of force to the father, the female icon of the mother-daughter figure, Leela/Rita. For this figure is literally an image, alternately an uncued or unsituated insert or even a photograph. The crucial instance, which I have described elsewhere,[18] relates to a scene which constantly collapses, via spatial and temporal ellipses, onto the depiction of a photograph. The photograph is that of the heroine Rita as a child, and is both sign of an innocence that beckons to the now criminalized Raj, and also a displacement of the mother's own view. What is suggestive about this process of scenic collapse and character displacement is the mobility of the fixed image. The photograph functions as a projection of Raj's conscience, emerging at crucial junctures in the moral development of the narrative, moving Raj away from the domain of criminality. But while inserted in the temporal flow of the narrative, it is also a function of a temporality, posed as it is against the movement of filmic representation, and condensing as it does the hero's recovery of a moment of childhood before his access to sexuality and the drives of identity.

If this is a form of immobile mobility, or an insertion into narrative temporality of an image which symbolically demands the neutralisation of time, then we are faced with an implicit reflection on the status of the film apparatus. There is a projection here of the disturbances wrought by the apparatus of the moving image into the body of the diegesis, constituting a reflection on the very sources of the apparatus's foundational discontinuity namely, that of the separate frames which constitute the moving image. The dismemberment of the moving surface by the use of the tableau culminates in an abridgement of that pressure to open out body/space relations within the film, and therefore its constructions of sexuality and sociality. At the end Raj is repositioned as object of a devotional/nurturing kind and the economies of *darsan* are now re-asserted, but with a different figure at their centre.

The desire to return to and relegitimate scopic regimes associated with earlier forms of authority parallels the way in which gaps and discontinuities are created within knowledge. The gap in what characters know about each other has often been noted for the setting up of certain affective dispositions in the spectator. For example, the fact that characters have fallen out because they have been misinformed or inadequately informed generates the pathos of the classical spectatorial disposition, if only they knew... The narration's creation of such gaps, including the manipulation of what we as spectators know about the characters, derives in the popular cinema from a particular symbolic rather than practical or realist economy. This symbolic economy is suggested in the conundrum of the flashback started from a certain character's point of view in which we are shown or told more than the character could know. Thus, in the first instance, in the recounting of Leela's abduction and expulsion, the Judge cannot know all that has taken place, although it is his narration which starts the flashback. Subsequently, it is impossible that Rita can recount the various events of the second flashback. There are ways of cohering this inconsistency of viewpoint and that is by working out certain structural coherences in the work of the narrative whereby characters are symbolically divided, the narrative functions distributed between two characters, so that there is an underlying continuity say, between the Judge and the Bandit, and, in the second half, between the mother, Leela, and Rita.

We need to resituate this problem of narrative voice within the larger frame of the narrative if we recognise that this giving voice and invoking memory is founded on the limits of what characters are allowed to speak or where they are permitted to go. Thus Leela is denied the power to communicate between father and son. Her attempt to do so leads to her death, as if the narrative punishes her for her transgression. The voices pitted against each other have as their implicit object the destiny of the son, ever returned to the scene of aggression of father against mother, in the house of the father, a looming, sexually charged containment by the father of space.

Implicit in my discussion of the film are not only contrasts between an earlier, feudal time and a contemporary urban and modern one and the different constructions of sexuality they carry, but also of the different forms of representation of the urban. The narrative authority of the father, deriving in part from an immovable iconicity, provides the hinge for an enveloping stasis of the urban. In the picturing of the father's house there is a drive to repeat that is not simply a way of remembering but is also a way of sucking the new into the orbit of older ties. Thus the form of knowledge deployed in the film is based not on the possibility of knowing, a verisimilarity of knowledge, but the inevitability of knowing, as it relates to the search for origins. So we have here the overwhelming significance of knowing about blood relations, even if these classically pre-modern terms of identification are meant to be ironically rendered, to show how the certainties of familial origin and of rank can be controverted by the contingencies of environment. There is, despite this irony, a tendency to contravert, or certainly qualify, newer senses of body-space relations and of vision in favour of older ones.

Interestingly, insofar as the structures of family are concerned, they prove rather more complicated than a straightforward change from feudal into modern times would suggest. If we use a grid of contemporaneity for the film, assuming that the story's present time is that of the film's release, 1951, and hazard a chronology for the story in terms of the birth and growing up of the protagonist into, say, his twenties, the original scene, in Uttar Pradesh would take place in the 1930s. The avowedly pre-modern domain of the U.P. countryside and of the Judge's house at the chronological beginning of the story is not as transparently pre-modern as we imagine. In this space, too, there is an attempt to form the modern couple insofar as the marriage has taken place against the norms and prohibitions of the Judge's larger family, in this case the prohibition relating to the remarriage of widows. Further, the space of the couple is at first defined by a space not clearly that of the feudal household, but that of the circuit house which provides temporary dwelling for a bureaucracy in movement. Arguably, there are the residual traces here of a more parcellized overlordship in the demeanour of servants to the Judge; and this is only augmented by the atmosphere of fate generated by the song of warning, something which leaves the husband complacent, secure as he is in his environment, in contrast to the apprehension of his wife.

There is, nevertheless, an attempt here to circumvent the laws of heredity for those of choice and contract. In the chronology I have hazarded, it is perhaps significant that the formation of the modern couple, Mark I, as it were, takes place concurrently with the film industry's first spate of socials celebrating modern love, as in the cycle of films produced by the Bombay Talkies studio, *Jawani ki Hawa* (Franz Osten, 1935), *Achut Kanya*, (Franz Osten, 1936), *Kangan* (Franz Osten, 1939), *Jhoola* (Gyan Mukerji, 1941) and *Kismet* (Gyan Mukerji, 1943), in the period 1936-43. These celebrated the possibilities of modern love being finally reconciled with the dictates of a larger familial norm, as if the family would provide the orbit of social sanction, rather than any extraneous institution such as the state. In the pessimistic versions of that story, it would not be the family but the village hierarchy which would provide the death-knell to such aspirations. *Awara*'s reference to an earlier filmic construction of the social in its initial sequences is reinforced by the presence of Leela Chitnis, star of the early 1940s hits, and by the presence of Prithviraj, the leading romantic actor of that period.

Despite the invocation of an earlier moment in the filmic construction of modernity, *Awara* clearly shows the drive to displace the family itself as locus of resolution and ultimate source of authority. While I have suggested how such a project is in a sense contaminated with the particular scopic and epistemological drives associated with a recovery of narrative into contested patterns of affiliation and authority, there is indeed a positing of the new, now separated out from the familial domain. In the space of the state, the jailhouse where Raj is serving out his sentence, the dismembered family of father and son, and the family of the future, Raj and Rita, are put together in asymmetrical view, the Judge unsighted by the couple and therefore subtly underprivileged in the final symbolic formation. Perhaps we should recall that, in keeping with the chronology we have applied to the film, this symbolism of marginalisation would be ideologically appropriate from the point of view of a Nehruite politics. For this Judge, scion of a landed family and, presumably, sometime absentee landlord, is now a figure who, according to contemporary legislative initiatives in U.P. such as the Zamindari Abolition Act of 1948, should no longer have the material wherewithal nor social authority to be lynchpin of a paternalist resolution of social differences as would have happened in the genre of the social of the 1930s. Needless to say, this is a highly ideological image, that is, an image of what ought to be or must be, rather than a representation of what is. I have tried to suggest here how that project is much more complicated and, indeed, contradictory, if we look at how the transformation of social authority has been constructed within filmic narration.

How could one place these formulations in relation to larger considerations of the cinema as an apparatus of modernity? In his article, 'Cinema and the desire for modernity', Madhava Prasad has argued that 'at the heart of the film industry an informal injunction goes to work to prohibit the representation of kissing and thereby a chain of implied prohibitions unfolds: the prohibition of representations of the private; the prohibition of cinema (at least as Metz defines it); the prohibition, by extension, of the open acknowledgement of the capitalist nature of the new nation-state'. It is the plotting of the latter disavowal which allows Prasad to go on to make the following observation:

> As an effective medium of propagation of consumer culture, popular cinema has managed to combine a reassuring moral conservatism [with] the utopian ideal that consists of not only the pleasures of commodity culture but also the micro-social forms such as the nuclear family which is at once an ideal consuming unit that the industrial economy's logic calls for as well as a desirable alternative to the existing patriarchal enclaves within which subjects are situated... Popular cinema, however, displays no unequivocal

preference for a traditional standpoint in its narratives of conflict between the traditional and the modern. On the contrary, one of its constant preoccupations is with the propagation of commodity culture within the context of traditionally regulated social relations.[19]

These formulations are highly suggestive on the question of the prohibitions surrounding the private, the domain of the micro-social in Prasad's terms, but need to be thought through, in terms of the micro-narrational strategies of cinema. This is in order to locate shifts in the deployment of filmic codes in the process of narration and thereby arrive at a complex sense of how the micro-social is constructed. Thus, in my analysis of *Awara*, I have suggested how a voyeuristic coding is effected via continuity editing, but that there are a variety of other ways of constructing relations of space and time. These are not composed in straightforward opposition to the continuity system; rather these other modes, such as those of tableau framing, have been integrated with continuity narration; in other instances, there has been a relative indifference to continuity editing altogether, shots assembled in a relatively uncoded, discrete way, even if they are assumed to take place in the same space and within a coherent, continuous time.

There are two questions here, and these impinge on the forms of sexuality and commodity culture represented in or operationalised by the cinema. The cinema places the spectator in a characteristically modern imaginary, one constituted by the separation of the spectator from the object which s/he views and hears, a separation not only entailed by the physical separation of spectator from screen, but also because the object whose image s/he views is absent. However, even within the modern phenomenology of the cinematic experience, there are still a series of codes which have developed as signs of modernity, amongst which the most commonplace one is the contract whereby the character on screen does not look into the camera, a contract which ensures the symbolic maintenance of our separation as spectators both from the screen and from each other.

Atomized by the induction of our look into the flow of images on screen, we are constituted as individual viewers. And this position is logically brought under threat when our scopic/auditory drives are thrown out of flow. While this may indeed be so, we cannot assume that this flow can be constituted only by the logic of continuity codes; music is a clear enough instance of how flow can continue even when scenic construction falters. On the other hand, there is also a problem here of what constitutes the modern, how it is culturally fabricated, and how that invites us to assume the position of a bricoleur whose agenda is the fashioning of cultural fragments into new patterns of signification. I have suggested that the sources of dynamism, of social reconstruction and familial nucleation are not inevitably aligned with the mechanics of Hollywood individuation. Indeed, what is being invited is a way of thinking of the modern that does not entirely separate the couple out from certain non- or proto-cinematic conventions of expression which emphasise the stability of the image rather than its constitution of a new dynamic. Significant here, if not entirely systematic or consistent, is the way iconic figures, those of the judge and the Rita icon, representing countervailing pulls, emerge from the narrative process, though in rather different ways. The iconisation of the judge emerges from the pulling apart of the family into separate scenic and cultural articulations. This non-continuous axis contrasts with the way the icon of Rita's photograph seems to disrupt the continuous flow of character actions; but it is crucial to the moral preservation of Raj, and therefore his eligibility to assume the role of the new order. Iconisation is central to the formation of the new family.

This would then suggest that our scopic and auditory drives do not automatically have to be constituted within the voyeurism of continuity cinema in order to address the domain of individuated cognition; instead, such a cognition may be the result of the dialectic of different modes of representation. We may note other instances where conventional codes of looking, for example those associated with an authoritative object-field relationship, are redeployed, as for example in the play associated with the display of the male body.[20]

In terms of commodity culture, we would have to dislodge the associations which have been built up between the seamless narrative constructions of the continuity mode with those of an ideal consumerism by suggesting that it is one form of narrative consumption on offer, rather than the ideal one.[21] What is involved is a more distracted mode of attraction, in which investments range across a series of instances of cultural self-fashioning. As Walter Benjamin noted, this was not bad training for the constellation of sensations that constituted modern experience,[22] something that film studies, at least, has tended to forget in the attention it has paid to the rigorous constructions of the classical mode. Perhaps it will take the experience of third world cultures and their own particular manufactures of modernity to put some of these questions back on the agenda.

Awara (Raj Kapoor 1951), plot synopsis

The film starts as a kind of detective story exploring, through the agency of a woman lawyer, Rita (Nargis) why Raj (Raj Kapoor), a man with a criminal record, assaulted Judge Raghunath, a reputed magistrate. The detective story armature is rapidly dispersed by two flashbacks which compose the body of the film, one recounted by Raghunath, the other by Rita. Raghunath was tricked by the bandit Jagga into believing that his wife, Leela, carries the bandit's child. Echoing the Ramayana narrative, the Judge outcasts his wife who brings up the child, Raj, in the slums of Bombay. In the struggle to maintain himself and his mother, Raj comes under Jagga's influence. A proficient pick-pocket and burglar, Raj comes upon his childhood sweetheart Rita, now a budding lawyer and his (unknown) father's ward. Determined to reform, Raj tries to escape Jagga's clutches but finally kills him to protect his mother. Leela is on her way to explain the circumstances of Jagga's death, but is knocked down by Raghunath's car. On her deathbed, she informs Raj that Raghunath is his father. It is this revelation that incenses the protagonist who now determines to kill Raghunath for the misery he inflicted on Leela. He can't go through with the act and is arrested by the Judge. The revelations about his life-history lead to a suspended sentence for Raj, and to a somewhat ambiguous reconciliation between himself and his now repentant father. Rita promises that she will wait for him to complete his sentence, while our protagonist announces that he will study to become a lawyer.

Notes

1. For a now classic see analysis, David Bordwell, Kristin Thompson and Janet Staiger, *The Classic Hollywood Cinema: Film Style and Mode of Production to 1960*, London: Routledge, 1985.

2. Gilles Deleuze, *Cinema 1: The Movement Image*, Minneapolis, Minnesota Press, 1989.

3. Later, when a person who is effectively Leela's double is introduced. Raghunath speaks with Bhabhi, his sister-in-law; as there is no reference to her husband, it may be inferred that she, as Leela once was, is a widow. 'Bhabhi's' pressure on Raghunath to evict Leela for the suspected sin of extra-marital pregnancy may be seen as motivated to punish Leela for her refusal to accept the role the sister-in-law represents.

4. Veena Das, 'Social Construction of Adulthood', in Sudhir Kakar (ed.) *Identity and Adulthood*, Delhi: Oxford University Press, 1979, pp. 97–98. Conversely, we may observe often enough how the figuring of the widow as object of desire, while maintaining her symbolic exclusion from the domain of the family sets up scenarios of impossible romance. Well-known examples would be *Sholay* (Ramesh Sippy, 1974) and more recently, *Prahaar* (Nana Patekar, 1992).

5. The focus on the women's honour is then displaced by an increasing attention to the oedipal transgression. It is significant that Leela's pregnancy is discovered only when she is transferred from Raghunath to Jagga. The birth's scandalous nature fulfils the metaphorical conditions for oedipal conflict. The male child's intercession between wife and husband contests his father's sexual

authority. Raghunath's anxieties about Leela's faithfulness may be said to cover over the fear that her very motherhood casts doubt on her loyalties.

6. The narrative effectively elides any other motives for his actions. The information we are given about him—that he was convicted by Raghunath simply because he came from a bandit family, and despite lack of evidence of his guilt—is an element in a social discourse of justic which is critical of the rigid, inegalitarian conceptions of the social order associated with Raghunath. But the narrative then 'forgets' this view when situating Jagga's actions; he swiftly becomes a villain, pure and simple. He periodically expresses pleasure at the idea of showing Raghunath that, contrary to his beliefs about the influence of heredity on character, his own son has become a criminal. This social message is retained and is finally conveyed to Raghunath by his son, but Jagga himself never gets around to giving Raghunath the cherished lesson; for all practical purposes he is a malign figure intent on corrupting Raj.

7. *Awara* opens with a court scene which is in many ways exemplary of the codes of continuity editing. It starts with a master-shot or establishing shot, scene dissection via match-on-action cut, transitions via eyelines, point of view, shot-reverse shot. But this is not characteristic of the film as a whole.

8. This is something that is echoed later when the struggle in the Judge's mind over information that Raj is his son is represented by the image of the court-room superimposed on his face, the space of judgement metaphorised as an attribute of the mind, with Raghunath finally crying out his acknowledgement of his son to an empty court-room. This form of discontinuity, in which there is an abrupt move via filmic codes, into a different arena of the diegetic world, the personal and the familial, is a commonplace thematic/ metaphoric shift, as when, for example, there is a metaphorisation of crime as desire, Raj's flight from the police being displaced into an oedipal contest, his escape into the house of the father exchanging one frame of law for another.

9. In fact such associations may be explained in terms of the fact that the narrative invests in disturbance so that it may start its work; and the locus of such disturbance lies in the disruptive authority of existing patriarchy.

10. For a summary of recent discussions of non-continuity, discontinuity

and continuity, see Thomas Elsaesser edited, *Early Cinema—Space, Frame, Narrative*, London: British Film Institute, 1990.

11. Bordwell has noted that 'the temporal thrust of the process of fabula consruction is checked to some extent by the accumulation of "paradigmatic" materials... Throughout the narration will be scattered images and sounds which, by their similarity and their relative independence of immediate context, belong to the same paradigmatic set'. David Bordwell, *Narration in the Fiction Film*, London: Methuen, 1985, p. 317.

12. This is not to underrate Jagga's narratological functions, akin to those of a sutradhar, but only to point to the perfomative fixity of his character, and his narratively subsidiary role all told.

13. For seventeenth century English discussions of families and kingdoms as homologous, Carol Pateman, *The Sexual Contract*, Stanford: Stanford University Press, 1988, p. 46.

14. See, for example, my '"You Cannot Live in Society and Ignore it"—Nationhood and female modernity in *Andaz* (1949)', *Contributions to Indian Sociology*, Vol. 29.1-2, 1995.

15. Peter Brooks, *The Melodramatic Imagination*, New York: Columbia University Press, 1985.

16. For earlier analyses of tableaux in Indian film, see my 'Shifting Codes, Dissolving Identities: The Hindi social film of the 1950s as popular culture', *Journal of Arts and Ideas*, nos. 23–24, January 1993; and 'Addressing the Spectator of a Third World National Cinema', *Screen*, Vol. 36.4, December 1995.

17. In the case of Leela, the widow is already a transgressive figure who has contaminated the patriarchal space to which she has been inducted.

18. Vasudevan, 'Shifting Codes, Dissolving Identities', op. cit.

19. Prasad, 'Cinema and the Desire for Modernity', *Journal of Arts and Ideas*, nos. 25–26, December, 1993

20. In contrast to the authoritarian display of male presence centred on darsan, there are more fluid and playful registers. In *Aar Paar* (Guru Dutt, 1954), for example, there is a playful exchange between Nikki (Shyama) and Kalu (Guru Dutt) as the latter takes a bath, only a sheet separating them. Here the screen provides the axis for a system of permeable difference, if one that finally reiterates the spatial advantage of the hero.

21. Interestingly, it may be a mode which now has a somewhat more systematic deployment in certain works, as for example, those of

Mani Ratnam, Ram Gopal Varma, Raj Kumar Santoshi and Nana Patekar. It should be noted, however, that, apart from Mani Ratnam, the continuity mode is most in evidence in the action genre. Nevertheless, it is possible to hazard that its emphasis on tighter narrative logic and compositional balance may address the desire to reformulate the terms of middle-class subjectivity.

22. Walter Benjamin, 'The Work of Art in the Age of Mechanical Reproduction', in *Illuminations*, London: Fontana, 1973.

Citizenship and Its Discontents

SUSIE THARU

The story to which I will return in this chapter, in loops that mimic the outside-inside-outside structure typical of Saroj Pathak's writing, is called "Dushchakra" which might be translated as "vicious circle", or to put it in a less idiomatic but more evocative form: "evil round". Though her stories have received the acclaim of popular circulation, the critical establishment has not considered her a 'major' writer. All the same, some of Sarojben's stories did catch the eye of the critical world even as they appeared in the early sixties. There is a certain irony here. The stories that attracted critical attention featured protagonists who could be recognised (or indeed misrecognised) as deranged—delinquent, deluded, driven to despair—and therefore lent themselves to readings that affirmed the national-modern as the terrain of the good life. These were invariably also the stories that were anthologised, translated, prescribed for study. Thus, despite the continuing controversies about the aesthetic quality of these works, their melodramatic form and so on, the stories exuded an imperative that has ensured a place for them in the ethico-literary discussions constitutive of the Gujarati public sphere. One of the arguments in this essay is that this recognition—as an almost-but-not-quite-major writer—as well as the initial reading of her work as modernist, has obscured the importance of the more enigmatic, wayward, minor stories such as "Dushchakra", which remained relatively uncommented on until 1987, when Shirin Kudchedkar drew attention to it while we were reviewing her selections from Gujarati for *Women Writing in India*. Among the other Pathak stories on her short-list were: "Whom can I tell? How can I explain?" "Dazed, tormented, terrified", "Divorcee", "Quandary", "The ace of trumps", "Hero/Heroine", and "The vow" (which we finally selected for the anthology).[1]

I recall being disappointed at the time that the author had chosen to call the story "Dushchakra" and not "Ladies tailor" after its male protagonist who, like so many of the characters in her less-known fiction, is so graphically located at the crossroads of class-caste and sexuality at the edges of city life in modern India. The somewhat distanced, documentary voice-over tone of "ladies tailor" as against the analytical "evil round" seemed appropriate for another reason as well. Neither this figure (migrant to the city, a worker from the 'unorganised' service sector, a man in a traditional caste occupation serving a new clientele of urban women) nor his dementia is articulated in a fully psychological, or fully individualist manner. On the contrary she presents him in a mode that invokes the iconography of popular sculpture and film hoarding.[2] Later, as more of her fiction became available to me in translation, it grew evident (and one can also surmise this from the titles listed) that the focus of these stories is actually more on the oscillations, impasses, irresolutions that menace Indian modernity, than on plot or character. There was occasion here, therefore, to return to the history of this immediate post-independence period via an engagement with its forms. Considered thus, Pathak's writing produces a provocative mapping of citizenship and subjection in the modernising sixties, and suggests a reading of sexuality as a form of the Indian state.[3] Emerging alongside and closely related, are issues of narrative structure, address and constituency that put into question dominant theories of the reader-subject and the social contracts of representation in independent India.

The rest of this essay is in four sections. The first addresses literary-biographical accounts of Saroj Pathak's life, and the second her journalism, principally as a means of setting up the concepts that will enable a reading, in the third section, of "Dushchakra" and some of her other short stories. The fourth section reflects on questions of genre, address, subjection and the terrain of the political, that are raised by Saroj Pathak's writing.

I

Going by literary historical accounts—biographical notes, interviews with Sarojben and her husband, tributes and reminiscences by their literary friends—Sarojben's own experiences seem like a testimony to the liberating potential of the independent, modern nation. The early death of her father might well have constrained this upper-caste woman into genteel poverty and over-scrupulous correctness. On the contrary it made "the girls independent and self-reliant", less pressured than they might otherwise have been by the imperative to conform.[4] Her own youthful dreams were not traditional 'feminine' ones of marriage and domesticity, but liberal, modern dreams of achievement that transcend the question of gender. Though not exempt from the experience of conflict between her aspirations and social norms, her own individualism and autonomy appears never to have been undermined or broken by societal pressure. As an intermediate student she made her way into the *avant garde* literary circle around the poet Mansukhlal Jhaveri. In 1949, while still a student, she left secretly for Delhi to marry the Gujarati writer Ramanlal Pathak. It was a registered marriage, conducted without fanfare. She was a Bhatia, he a Brahmin. The couple moved away from Bombay, settling in the capital city and making their living in the institutional spaces opened up by the new state. Their move was a gesture of trust, trust that they would find in the centre a homing space. And they were not let down. During their ten years in Delhi, Saroj Pathak worked as a programmer in All India Radio, as a dancer in the newly-set up Bharat Kala Kendra and as a translator in the Soviet Embassy. Her first book of short stories was published in 1959, around the time she and Ramanlal moved back to Gujarat. Sarojben re-entered university, did her BA, and later her MA, and then worked as a college teacher in Surat until she retired in 1987. The essays in *Samvedana ane Sarjan*, the festschrift edited by Ashwin Desai and presented to her at the time, Shirin Kudchedkar writes, give the impression "of a vibrant passionate human being, with a great love of life." The aura that encircles her marriage is also one of exemplary modernity. In interviews and articles both Saroj and Ramanlal Pathak have described their relationship as "fully supportive yet allowing both of them complete freedom to pursue their own choices", and "in every way satisfying and fulfilling." They were agreed that both commitment and independence must be respected in order to make marriage work. For several years husband and wife worked in different towns though, Ramanlal avers, "in spirit" they were never apart. When he had to stop working on account of a mental illness, he kept house while wife and daughter shouldered the responsibilities outside. Ramanlal accepts that when both partners are writers, one of the two may have to give up something in order to nurture the creativity of the other; this he says he did, willingly, believing her to be the better artist. The wounds that might have marred the perfection of these miraculous lives appear to leave no scar. There is no probing comment on the retreat, inexplicably made by these Gujarati artist-intellectuals, a mere decade after they had arrived there full of confidence, back from the centre, into their region. Ramanlal's "mental illness" is recorded. The stress however is on his sharing of housework, his informed responsibility for the care of their child. An observation that towards the end of her life Sarojben became increasingly pessimistic and preoccupied with death is contrasted in the biographical note by glowing festschrift tributes. Sarojben's own assertion that "from childhood my mind has been rather peculiar, rather odd, my mental constitution never what might be labelled as self-possessed or normal" is predicated by "and this has been of great benefit to me as a creative writer."

We are breathless at the express arrival of this modernity, transfixed by the ease with which its actors drive past the well-regulated crossroads of caste laws, regional difference, the sexual division of labour, the oppression of the family, the contradictions of desire, and even the traumas of breakdown and despair, and come over in a series of punctual and well-contracted stills, prompt, open-to-view, smiling, citizens.

Yet, strangely, we also fall back somewhere, short of the story. They are citizens, but a breed apart. I want to set aside for the moment the familiar diagnoses that explain (away) this effect: the decorum of all public accounts, the less than fully biographical nature of these fragments, their possible inauthenticity; in sum: their "inadequate realism". More significant, it seems to me than the established "inadequacies" of these non-western literary biographies, their lack, is their adequacy as it were, their fullness: What is the secret of the charmed progress of these miraculous lives?

Madhava Prasad has discussed the "failure" of identification associated with popular film by returning to a concept that Geeta Kapur first deployed in her discussion of the "sant" genre: frontality. It involves, according to her, frontality of the image, the design, the formative act. This yields "forms of direct address; flat, diagrammatic and simply profiled figures; a figure-ground pattern with only notational perspective; repetition of motifs in terms of 'ritual play'; and a decorative mise-en-scene" (80).[5] Prasad glosses frontality as "a frontal spectacle in which the performer is the bearer of the message from the Symbolic which must be transmitted through a direct contractual link."[6]

The contrast implicit here is with the disciplinary apparatus of identification in the classic form of realist narrative that emerged and was consolidated in Europe alongside a liberal economy, its democratic order and freedoms of choice. As is now well-known, the crucial problem for this form of realism is one of initiating readers into protocols of attention/interpretation that set up a hierarchy in which the reader's interpretative authority is the principal regulatory factor in the narrative. In painting—as in photography—the problem was addressed principally through a figure-ground relationship that represented perceptual depth. This became the basis of a verisimilitude in which both detail and frame were addressed to, and consequently also configured, and indeed individuated, a situated viewer-subject. In a perceptual as much as in an ideological sense, therefore, the image is mobilised by the reader-spectator's attention and will. In fiction and other realist writing such as history, a cognate effect is achieved through a dominant or controlling narrative perspective that presents everything else 'in citation.' In order to 'make sense' of the account the reader must align with this authority and with the frame of representation that it sets up.

Historically as well as structurally the parallel effort is the bringing into conjuncture of the new sovereign subject—transcendental, agentive, modern—with the citizen who is the elementary term of the abstract (liberal) state.[7] It can be argued that in the laws of attention firmed up by realist narrative, it is this figure, not simply the reader, but the reader/ viewer-citizen, that performs the function of mediating between the epistemological, economic, ethical, juridical and aesthetic subjects; between the state, the nation, the economy and the individual.[8] In the classic (western) form of realist narrative, Prasad writes, the reader/viewer's "interpretative authority brooks no challenge from the frame of representation."[9] Crucial to his argument, however is the fact that this interpretive authority is but a potential and may be acquired only "through the privilege of citizenship." The reader-spectator's exercise of freedom, therefore, "does not jeopardise the process of meaning production because nature—the 'law of attention'—asserts itself. The director, in order to respect the individual's freedom, must curb his own freedom, must merge his own identity into the invisible frame of the state, clearing the ground for the full unfolding of the reality of nation/civil society."[10] The citizen, then, performs the dual function of the voice of narration and agent of the (absent) state.

There are, however, significant differences between this generalised citizen-narrator of the 'classic' form of the liberal capitalist state and that of the narratives of modernisation that we encountered in the literary historical fragments under discussion. Allow me a detour through Etienne Balibar's suggestive work. Balibar carefully disentangles and thematises two senses of the term "subject", pointing to the distinction between the *subjectus* that is subject to the prince, and the sovereign subject, the *subjectum*, that initiates the discourse of modernity. Taking issue with the phenomenologists in general and Heidegger in particular (and implicitly also with Lacan), he argues that the *subjectum* is not a Cartesian concept. The distinctions and oppositions that compel the Cartesian formulation "find their coherence, if not the solution to the enigmas they hold in a nexus that is both hierarchical and causal, entirely regulated by the principle of the *eminent causality*, in God…".[11] It is therefore quite incorrect to work on the premise that the Cartesian *ego cogito* is the forerunner of the sovereign subject. The distinction makes it possible for Balibar to assign the notion of the *subjectum*: transcendental, agential, to Kant rather than Descartes and to draw attention to what he calls a coincidence that intricates the history of epistemology with the history of politics and political thought: "the moment at which Kant produces (and retrospectively projects) the transcendental 'subject' is precisely the moment at which politics destroys the 'subject' of the prince in order to replace him with the republican citizen."[12] The citizen's becoming a sovereign subject, is an additional process; one prepared for by the historical labour of defining the juridical, moral and intellectual individual. In Europe it is a process that begins in the Middle Ages, "but can find its name and structural position only after the emergence of the revolutionary citizen, for it rests upon the reversal of what was previously the *subjectus*."[13] The Kantian subject is concretely linked up with its humanity only within a civic or political frame of universal citizenship—the world-city—and its implied epistemological, ethical and aesthetic rationalities. Conversely, the citizen's housing in and subjection to human institutions, particularly the legal (national) state, is only as a free and autonomous subject. This is only possible "inasmuch as every institution, every state, is conceived of as the partial and provisional representative of humanity, which in fact is the only absolute 'community', the only true 'subject of history'."[14]

The citizen subject then, is at the same time the social

subject-agent (legal, psychological, ethical, imaginary), the obedient subject of the law (including conscience) and the elementary term or the constitutive element of the liberal-democratic polity. Despite the coupling of the terms citizen and subject in the title of his own article, Balibar is cautious about superimposing the figure of the subject onto that of the citizen. Processes of subjectification involve reinscriptions of the revolutionary figure in the rationalities of philosophical and, beyond that, anthropological or cultural space. Further, they also invoke the "defunct subject of the prince even while displacing it."[15] The tensions that cross this figure—*subjectus, subjectum*, citizen, citizen-subject—and maintain it in animation, are further complicated by the fact that while the citizen subject "may become symbolically universalised and sublimated" in the apparatuses of culture and administration it never ceases to refer to a "very precise *history*, where it is a question of progress, conflict, emancipation and revolutions."[16]

Balibar's excavations help us appreciate the historical and structural coordinates of modern western states and cultures as well as the intricate and risk-laden contests that they are engaged in. Not least among these responsibilities is an alert maintenance and renewal of citizens and subjects, and the creation and refurbishment of national genres that endorse and elaborate those figures. The mandate requires action in a variously embattled zone, for it must address the aporias and failures of modernity as well as engage and rework the continuing democratic and egalitarian aspirations of a citizen-figure set loose with the birth of liberal-national states. The state, conceived in this way, is a zone of political struggle, not simply an administrative apparatus or the extension of the ruling class.

I have suggested in an earlier essay on accounts of partition that what is readied in the officiating genres of the immediate post-independence period in India is not primarily a to-be-universalised, sovereign, citizen-subjectum. What we find here is better characterised as a citizen-executive—and pedagogic—authority and its doubles: the subjects of government who are not to be identified with the obedient subjects of either the king or the law. The result is a narrative form and indeed an indigenous, and in many ways different, realism and a naturalised order of things, be it in fiction or in film, that bodies forth this executive avant-garde (experts, artists, modernisers, secular individuals) and invests it with a centrality around which a land and a to-be-governed subject-population is deployed in what emerges as their objective thereness.[17] This avant-garde is an elect body, endowed with auratic, utopic subjectivities and entrusted with governmental responsibilities of administration, reform and development. Structurally, however, these bodies hover in a difficult yoking between their authority and their civic-human equality.[18] The matrix of tensions set up here quite exceed the Balibarian figure.

Each of these dimensions—executive authority, miraculous subjectivity, to-be-governed subject population, indigenous realism—demand more detailed and probing analyses than I will be able to take up in this essay. All the same it might be useful to sketch in the outlines of a gloss since there exists a substantial body of important work that one might reference and draw upon. Though such a reading would necessarily strain against the resolutions imposed by Ranajit Guha's own dominance-without-hegemony thesis (which not only names but also analyses this history as lack), one might well consider his work as setting out a genealogy of this very figure through a series of essays that deconstruct the effects and apparatuses of government in the colonial as well as nationalist state. (In the theatre as liberal mirror for peasant rebellion, in the rule of property, in the prose of counter-insurgency, in a nationalist historiography, in a humanist culture, in Gandhian politics and so on.) Again, if one were to set aside the thesis of the not-quite, or passive, moments in the advent of the bourgeois revolution, one could draw on the writings of Partha Chatterjee and Sudipto Kaviraj to gauge the aporias of a top-down bureaucratic- administrative modernisation.[19] As for the miraculous utopic subjectivities, one might look to Nehru himself and to liberal narratives of self-fashioning that project the attainment of a full-blown individualism and the abstract identity of the citizen as predicated on a mystical transcendence of distinctions based on caste, region, religious community, language or gender.

More immediately related to the concerns of this essay, however, are the developments effected by this figure—citizen/ executive authority—in the structure of narrative and the frame of representation—in the process of firming up an indigenous realism. One might turn here to Geeta Kapur's recent writing which I would want to read as a series of attempts to essay these vexed protagonists of the emergence and consolidation of realism-modernity in twentieth century India: now pressed forward into a larger-than-life frontality and a flatness of surface in direct engagement with the viewer as in the "mythologicals"; now re-turned, as in the films of Satyajit Ray, to the reciprocity of intra-narrative space, embedded in the anthropomorphic scale of deep focus and lyrically exalted; now nominated from within a working class as in the Ghatak oeuvre.[20] The result is a tension and oscillation, in the "officiating" genres of the period, between a frontality through which a message from the modernising Symbolic is directly conveyed, and realist narration, between executive and liberal citizenship, evident as much in literary historical fragments that provided the take-off point for our discussion, as in much of the canonical literature of this period.

Saroj Pathak's journalism and her fiction open out onto this executive centrality on the one hand and the snarled sexualities of subjecthood in a modernizing India on the other. In fact we might think of her fiction as forcing a space in the representational protocols of realism and citizenship for the entry of this subaltern claim.

II

Saroj Pathak traces the origin of her interest in journalism to a specific episode: the suicide of a neighbour harassed for having given birth only to girls. Soon after that she began writing regularly in the established newspapers *Gujarat Samsar*, published from Ahmedabad and *Gujarat Mitra*, published in Surat and widely circulated also in Bombay. It is interesting that the late 1950s and the 60s spawned several initiatives like hers in the regional language press. Books, articles, columns discussed problems, gave practical advice and disseminated legal and medical information. More or less effectively modernised "citizen-women", often with a left-of- centre orientation, took on the responsibility of mediating, on matters related to sexual and family life, between the subject population and the state. In the south the best-known amongst them are probably Rajalaksmi and Anupama Niranjana. Like Saroj Pathak, as writers married to writers, both of these women were also doubly bonded to the institution of literature.[21]

The declared intent of such writing was the establishment of a secular-scientific, contractual approach to issues that concerned women. The columnists dealt with questions of domestic life, sexuality, the pathologies and aesthetics of the body, child rearing, the problems of urban life, the status of tradition and a host of other issues. Not least they took on, especially in relation to the legal advice proffered, the difficult negotiation between the sub-juridical domain of the private and the public legality of contract. The declared thrust of their effort, and indeed their charge, was the invention and securing of a workable form of the national-private and the "conduct of conduct".

Consider first the invention. When advice literature addressed a specific historical problem, it undertook a translation-redistribution of that conflict/contradiction/gap in knowledge. At one level the task involved the creation of interpretative frames in which women and their problems might be recognised as various kinds of pre-and sub-individual figures in relation to nation-state protocols of gender, family, desire, freedom and so on. At another level these executive authorities were actually strategically reworking these protocols in order to provide rational and realist solutions to the problems; they were, as it were, reinventing—each time from scratch—the state as much as they were inventing the rational-real in relation to each problem or problem figure that presented itself to them. Thus, while the columns mapped and maintained outside what would be recognisable by the inside—the inside's outside as it were, they also functioned as a means laying out the inside itself.

The securement takes place in two quite different modes. Shirin Kudchedkar speaks of these columns as "exposing the idle triviality and spite to which women let themselves be reduced and also the forces that strip them of their humanity." It is an astute assessment of the genre which is involved in the strategic designation of enemies (the pre-modern, the feminine) and the field of battle (outside the modern, inside the self). Such designation directs women's own complaints and aspirations away from the modern in relation to which they are only allowed to feel inadequate. A second mode of securement cuts closer to the bone of the advice column. The most straightforward way of characterising the advice column is as an institution designed to recruit subjects into the symbolic order of the national-modern. Yet it may be truer to say that columns such as these assume the failure rather than the success of recruitment; that their actual function is the use of this failure to organise, or better, to re-organise and in so doing reproduce, a national-private. "Women's problems" provide the specific and historical contexts in which these instruments can be engineered and updated such that the frames of analyses that are provided seem true, the explanations correct, the solutions reasonable, if not immediately feasible. Consider for example Saroj Pathak's own ironic replay of the advice column mode in the story "Ace of Trumps". The protagonist there is a single woman in her forties, planning to use the opportunity that has arisen because their block of flats is scheduled for demolition as an excuse to leave the home in which she stays with her brother and his family. She has been feeling badly used and unappreciated and decides to set up on her own, but vacillates with an unreasonable longing "for the tottering old house, for the old skin." An inner voice exhorts:

> When such sweeping changes take place, the old order collapses. If attachment becomes too insistent it should be quietened with a gentle hand on the back, if dismay spreads it should be bathed in

confidence and restored, if tears want to issue forth, they should be spurned, suppressed. And if helplessness or pity peep out, they should be cauterised with a hot brand before they can grow. "Life is a struggle", one should repeat in English, with a dignified and martyred air. It is essential that one's thoughts be 'up-to-date.'[22]

It is possible to argue that this governmental realism and the executive authority it legitimates is not confined to a non-western, developmental modernity. It may be located equally in the heartland of capital.

Historians of photography invariably regard the photo-documentation of the U.S. Farm Security Administration (FSA) as a critical initiative in the making of photographic realism. The FSA was a government department set up in 1935 as part of Roosevelt's 'New Deal' administration. The photographers of the Historical Section of the FSA were to comb the country to supply pictures to New-Deal administrators in various departments. These were then presented in government reports and official exhibits, supplied to the newspapers, and reproduced in popular illustrated magazines. Roy Stryker, who was in charge of the enterprise, actually spoke of his task in grander terms as producing a "pictorial encyclopedia of American agriculture".[23] The shooting script that he circulated among FSA photographers in 1936 is focused on the layout and composition of the picture with the stress on detail. Stryker suggests as themes for the photographs the "relationship between density of population and income of such things as: pressed clothes, polished shoes and so on." He was especially interested in "the wall decorations in homes as an index to different income groups and their reactions."[24] This detail of material life (readied for interpretation as it were) was not only to be lit and brought to the surface in the photograph, it was also to compose the 'natural' setting for a particular kind of figure. One of Stryker's favourite photographers was Russell Lee, about whose work he says: "When his photographs would come in, I always felt Russell was saying: 'Now here is a fellow who is having a hard time, but with a little help he is going to be all right.' And that is what gave me courage."[25] The critical phrase here is: "with a little help." This "little help" is, on the one hand, the exact supplement that writes the New Deal not only into the depth and the governing perspective of the FSA photographs; it is also the bridge that sets up whatever the Farm Administrative Authority had on offer as the meaningful resolution to problems of rural living in the United States. Read the other way, this "little help" is also a modality that defines and fleshes out a subject. It is what will decide the exact constitution of the subject for which the FSA is the perfect predicate. The specifications for this fit-subject-of-government are complex, subtle and intricate.[26] And that is precisely why the figure is best identified/recognised/managed/contained by an aesthetic, in this case the artifice of documentary realism; in other instances narrative realism. Like those who wrote in to Saroj Pathak's advice column and received solutions to their problems, these figures are the inside's outside; appropriately endowed for efficient welfare administration.

The requirements of subjection-subjectification may be equally configured as aesthetic (as in the compositional brief for the photographer) or as psychological (of subtle, but recognisable, qualities of the protagonist-selves.) The photographic aesthetic, then, both creates and documents; in addition it legitimizes, even consolidates and exalts, gives "courage" to, the executive initiatives of the FSA. A year later, following the Pearl Harbour defeat, Stryker was calling for much more programmatic pictures of "men, women and children who look as if they really believed in the US. Get people with a little spirit. Too many in our file now paint the US as an old people's home...just about everyone is too old to work and too malnourished to care much what happens." He asks for: "More contented-looking old couples—woman sewing, man reading."[27] Realism here represents and composes the world and sets into place a frame that brings/forces back into alignment—the US state and the (presumably disaffected) subject-viewer; a figure that is in the singular, yet is, as unit of the enterprise of state, also plural, collective.

It is worth recounting an odd incident mentioned in the FSA records. A few months after a Walker Evans photograph of a cemetery that foregrounded a weather-worn, but solidly upright cross against a backdrop of tenement houses had been issued for circulation, a woman walked into the FSA office and asked for a copy. Stryker records:

> We gave it to her and when I asked her what she wanted it for, she said, "I want to give it to my brother who is a steel executive. I want to write on it, '*Your* cemeteries, *your* streets, *your* buildings, *your* steel mills. But *our* souls, God damn you.'"[28]

Pathak's own oblique and critical relationship to these hegemonic projects is, as we shall find, complexly explored through her fiction, but is evident also in the restraint of her engagement with the conduct-of-conduct mode. Somewhere in an interview she describes the columns as arousing "violently opposed reactions". It will not surprise anyone that the opinions of this modern woman angered those who wanted to preserve tradition. So the threatening letters asking her to "attend to your own husband and home" and not "meddle in other people's business" seem a more or less routine occupational hazard. What is surprising to a reader of her fiction, however, is the example cited as the "success" of the columns. A young woman unhappy with the alliances that were being suggested for her used Pathak's column to discover the address of a women's home where she found shelter. Had it not been for this, she "may have been driven to suicide," Pathak observes.[29]

For one thing, the two sides of the equation seem unmatched. On the one side we have a problem, presented in classical terms: a lone, would-be modern subject battling the multiple-armed forces of a pre-modern regime. On the other side a bureaucratic solution: the provision of a written address, and, at the other end of that address, an institution designed by the state (or on behalf of it) to address this specific kind of problem-population. It is a solution that satisfies a welfarist imagination but requires of its client an impossible/hyper-real (magic real?) courage, resourcefulness and independence of spirit.[30] Pathak does not even attempt to fill out a context in which the action could appear as a human, fully rational, or 'realistic' one. To put it another way, unlike Russell Lee, she does not compose a world in which the action of that client-subject would fall into a 'convincing' depth, one that would, consequently, give her reader the necessary courage. She simply presents the encounter as frontal; her action is a despatch, and she proceeds without further fuss on the assumption that in this situation that frontality is not a despotic but a justified, secular-scientific one. This is why Pathak actually holds up the occasional arrival of a parcel, if not at the destination it was despatched to, at some workable space of the modern, as evidence of the success of advice literature and as a cause of celebration. Given the complexity of the issues she addressed in her columns and the knotted, conflicted anatomy of desire that she documents in her stories, how might we explain/ understand her stolid 'acceptance' of these programmatic solutions?

Two leads might be worth following though of course a question of this kind really has no full answer. The first has to do with the idea of welfare. It is a well-known argument that the welfare state arises in response to the problems of actualising a democratic polity. What the concept enables is a replacement of the contradictory idiom of rights and citizenship, with the homogenising, normalising idiom of statistics, thus making way for what Foucault describes as the governmental logic of the state. As feminist critiques have so graphically shown, the logic of welfare and the deployment of populations is not that of the social contract; the issues here are not ones of sovereignty or of individual rights, let alone of distributive justice. The issues become simply those of a piecemeal restorative justice, taken up by the state in the name of social 'solidarities' or groups and structured in accordance with the state's ideas of social advancement. Welfare then, like pedagogy, names its constituencies and then offers itself as a packaged take-it-or-leave-it complete solution. In fact, one might think of the whole apparatus of welfare as designed to real-ise a republican ideal without confronting in an on-going manner the insurrectionary tensions that mark its origins. To put it somewhat differently, welfare is the attempt to translate, without supplement, the instability that lies in suspense in the figure of the citizen subject. To Sarojben, therefore, it is a welcome, if unexpected, bonus if the proffered solution actually makes a difference to a client.

I think we need to add, however, that Sarojben's somewhat distanced engagement with the project of the modern state makes sense only because she accepts, and in fact through her work affirms and elaborates, the notion of a chasmic divide between a fairly limited area—the territory of the Symbolic and of the civic institutions that house the well-tempered citizen— and deeply disturbing extra-territorial regions where currencies of secular-social contract, of reason or state have little or no purchase. Given a "personal sensibility" that made her less interested in the external events of everyday existence and more in "mental processes", and the uncanny traffic she sets up between her psychological alienation and the socio-political marginalisations of a modernising nation, the rigorous maintenance of the divide has resulted in the extraordinarily suggestive, involved-yet-distanced, analysis of the underbelly of state consolidation in the sixties that may be found in her fiction. Framed in the work of this writer, welfare and narrative declare a certain structural homology. Both address, albeit in radically different ways, an ill-formed and dangerous residue.

III

"Expert Ladies Dressmakers", is a tailor's shop situated on a side street of a large city somewhere on the route between Avanti's school and her house. The shop is in split levels. The Master tailor who takes the measurements and cuts the clothes occupies the street level along with the trainees, who sit by him on a mat and do the hand-stitching: hems, button-holes, buttons. The experienced workers operate machines on the upper level. The camaraderie and competition between the workers, the jokes with which they "relieve the tedium of their lives" revolve around the bodies of their clients who let their sari *pallavs* slip down as their measurements are taken and "expose themselves to the gaze of the tailors as freely as they would to a lifeless mirror." The story consistently pursues the parallels between the two main characters, located on different sides of the caste-class divide. Veerji had joined the shop as a young apprentice, learned the trade and made his way into the adult world upstairs. Once there, the first task assigned to him was the sewing of Avanti's school uniform. The relationship between them grows over the years with Avanti picking Veerji out as her special tailor and Veerji watching out for her as she passes on the way to school in the morning and stops by in the afternoon with ever-more-detailed special instructions about bows and necklines and diagonal cuts. When Avanti is old enough to wear saris and has blouses made to go with them, Veerji experiences a turmoil he cannot comprehend. He becomes obsessed with this girl, he fondles her clothes, talks to her/them while he sews, jealously keeps them and her away from the touch of the others, lavishes his art on every detail. As Veerji "descends deeper and deeper" into his madness, the business waxes. "Because he searched so hard for new fashions for Avanti, more and more customers flocked to the shop." The Master is thrilled with him. Veerji works double shifts, is called out on special assignments, admired for his exceptional skills.

When the story opens, Avanti's marriage has been fixed. The excited young woman orders for a tailor to work all day at her home. No one doubts that Veerji will be assigned the job, but he is torn by the choice that confronts him. The other workers try to ease Veerji's pain by teasing him about the food, festivities and beautiful women. Finally he refuses to go, though he finds it intolerable that his rival in the tailor's shop, Bheemji, will be sent instead. "This will be the last time I sew anything for her", he thinks and as he gazes at the few blouses that remained. Sarojben concludes with what appears at first sight a surprising comparison. Veerji "experienced the kind of anxiety and care that is experienced in a poor household when the bottom of the pot is visible and one must start to pinch and scrape." There is no way out of his predicament. He breaks down. The end of this story is clearly not a resolution. If anything it elaborates the enigma that set the plot in motion. Veerji downs tools. He leaves the shop. The others stop work. But the effect is momentary. The machines soon whirr again. The next day a "new hum joins that humming." Veerji has started up at "Perfection Gent's Tailors." Another round of the story of fashion and tailors, of the sexual underbelly of our capital and its modernity, is set to begin.

Let us pause for a moment to consider the Avanti-figure before moving on to a reflection on the story as a whole. At first glance it would seem that the woman in this story is presented in a less complex mode. We might indeed feel that in comparison to the sensitivity with which the tailor's experience is explored, the life of this exuberant middle-class girl, growing up, becoming aware of her sexuality, preparing for marriage, is presented in an altogether conventional manner. However, a number of things call for attention. The narrative resolutely refuses an appeal to a patriarchal symbolic whose courts would have been only too ready to charge her class-caste arrogance with responsibility for Veerji's misery. Had that happened the story would simply become one of flirtation, exploitation and betrayal, that set up an antagonistic relationship between the middle-class woman and the working class man. Equally interesting is Sarojben's refusal to present Veerji's relationship with Avanti, his secret involvement with her body, his fondling of her clothes, as obscene or exorbitant in the manner of a "spontaneous" liberal feminism. On the contrary, the voice of narration sets itself up in a critical tension, not only from a patriarchal point of view, but also from one that would naturalise Avanti's own urban middle-class femininity. Invoked as she is here, at one edge of her world, with her story told in tandem with that of the tailor, it is difficult to miss the parallels. Avanti goes to school while Veerji apprentices at the tailor shop. Both graduate into the adult world: he to the upper floor to join the machine workers, she into marriage and domestic production. It would appear that her desires will be fulfilled while his dreams are shattered. Yet if we are to go by the structure of the story, there is nothing to endorse that surmise. On the contrary, we are required to stay with the parallels. To ask: How different is Avanti's investment with "clothes and fashion" from that of Veerji? To also ask perhaps: Can we assume that there are no parallels in the relationship between labour and sexuality for these two subjects?

What exactly are the vicious circles here? One of them clearly operates at the level of the plot itself. When Veerji returns to work he does so on the other side of the gender divide. He may believe that the move will solve his problem. However the structural equivalence suggests that there is no guarantee that an identical script of labour, fetishism and despair will not be played out there. An analysis that configures the issue simply as one of sexuality is referenced, but critically distanced. But let us set aside this trail and follow the other one suggested by the ending. What is glimpsed in Veerji's moment of rebellion, his refusal to be "a lifeless mirror", is the insurrectionary citizen; repudiating subjection, confronting antagonism as antagonism, downing tools to lay claim on his desire. The awesome scope of the moment does not go unrecognised by the other workers. The machines stop. There is a minute of silence that is tense with the possibility of another community for protagonist narrator and reader alike. But the hum of business starts up again. The next day Veerji's machine is also a part of it.

A reading attentive to the structure of the narrative opens up a more suggestive direction. In distinct contrast to the confident frontal enunciation that characterises the advice column in which problems/problem subjects are designated for despatch to official institutions; and in contrast also to a classic realist narrative in which the citizen reader's authority over the truth/naturalness of the world is complete, we find in these stories a narrative that inaugurates a different logic. Sarojben follows the protocols of a classic realism. She uses the neutral, "invisible", third person, narrative that presents its objects "in citation", the past tense that opens out onto the territory of completed, already-interpreted events. But as this story grasps itself as real, or more accurately, writes itself into reality, it is caught up in a tension. As authority the narrator stands discredited, no longer capable of shouldering governmental responsibility. The result is a narrative that is realist but does not know how to present an account of desire to avoid deadlock, and a plot that confronts an impasse and viciously circles back into replay. In fact, in a number of Pathak stories—again in contrast to the advice column—the narrative ends precisely at the point that this impasse is erected. Here, the executive centrality, associated with a developmental, welfarist realism is displaced and the reader is thrown into engagement with a discomfiting, difficult-to-interpret, not, or at least not-yet, fully narrativised sexuality; a sexuality no longer set in the Oedipalised spaces of a psychopathology of desire, but in the public arenas of modern Indian history: the new service industry, urban labour, marriage contracts, gendered consumption, and class-caste contradiction. Prefigured here is a frame that displaces the authority of a welfarist realism, and in that critical move also configures an uncanny community of this disaffected writer-narrator, the working-caste man, the middle-class woman and a reader whose response—as was evident in the 'elite' and 'popular' reception of Pathak's stories—would largely depend on his/her social location. Lest I am misunderstood, let me stress that what we find here is not the advent of a counter-hegemonic community in the manner of a 'New Times' utopia. We cannot locate in this fiction a full-fledged map of regions that cannot be charted with the coordinates of classical civil society; the doubles of the citizen that populate Sarojben's fiction are not quite the ones that press in on us today. All we may find here is a critical distancing that suggests another community, just as in Veerji's rebellion we catch a glimpse of the insurrectionary citizen/community, and, in the vicious circling of the plot, a staging of the failure of realism to engage either of these moves.

Nearly all of Pathak's fiction deals with figures animated by a similar logic. There are those whose bids for selfhood (and therefore, also, a fully endowed citizenship) are consistently thwarted; those who remain "caged"; who shuttle, "dazed, tormented, terrified" between incommensurable rationalities, who are summarily, against their own will, "divorced" from the enabling institutions of civil society and wander like ghosts in the solid spaces of the bourgeois family; those whose accounts cannot be rendered, whose stories do not fall into place: "Whom can I tell? How can I explain?" I believe that one of the reasons why this body of work has been so poorly appreciated is because it has been possible to identify a number of Saroj Pathak's protagonists in psychoanalytical or criminological frames: the hysteric, the voyeur; the fetishist, the schizophrenic, the pathological liar, the delinquent; the rowdy—though several others (and Poorbi in "The Vow" is one example) are without any such precedent.

IV

Elsewhere, Tejaswini Niranjana and I have tried to chart and analyse the impasses that confront Indian feminism, compelled as it is to now engage with questions of caste, religious community and the globalisation of capital. Our contention there is that the political movements that emerged in the late 1980s and early 90s had thrown into disarray the liberal national consensuses—on for instance, secularism, planned development, the status of the law. Indian feminism was being propelled into a territory that somehow exceeded and was indeed incommensurable with the classical terrain in which it emerged —that of contractual civil and political rights organised around the humanist subject.

I would like to suggest that the salience Saroj Pathak has for our time is because even in the '60s she was searching out in her fiction an enunciative mode and a narrative strategy that re-engaged these very regions. There is a hiatus in Pathak's work —and one might think of the three genres discussed here as a sort of Deleuzian "Sarojben writing machine"—a hiatus between, on the one side, her journalism, which is taken up by the endowed, responsible, national-humanist, author-citizen of literary history in the interests of a liberal state and of a developmental modernity, and on the other, her fiction, which propels readers onto altogether more unchartered and subversive ground. As she displaces (or evades) the hierarchising discourse of realism and the terms of its fictive contract, she begins to move, inaugurally, into a region where other protocols of signification and address can operate. It is a narrative space in which problems might be posed without being posed as problems for the citizen-reader- executive authority protagonist; and following that, a narrative space in which problems might be posed without being posed as problems for pedagogy or government. As a consequence, ideological relations obscured in the rationalities and consensuses of civil society become visible and demand to be made thinkable. In a commentary on readings of Bhupen Khakhar's painting, "A view from the teashop" Ashish Rajadhyaksha gestures towards a related divergence. 2In earlier readings of the painting—as representing the "common man's" view of the street—the common man, he suggests, was really a substitute for the elite viewer. He goes on to set up frames for reading the painting, alongside others done in the mid-70s as unworking the consensus of realism and inaugurating Khakhar's "slow and painful process of declaring his homosexuality", and proposes the thesis that the "two views provide us with the important lesson that the trajectory of establishing an aesthetic of realism occupies a different space from the trajectory of establishing a language for the contemporary."[31] I would like to think of this paper as part of that larger effort to establish a language for the contemporary that will also open out onto the narrative logics, the generic formations, the perverse figures of the insurgencies that animate the terrain of democracy[32] in our time.

An initial version of this paper was presented in August 1996 at the MIDS workshop on sexuality and at the Aftermath of Empire seminar of the International Institute, University of Michigan, Ann Arbor, October 1996. I would like to thank the audiences and discussants in both places and especially Madhava Prasad, Lakshmi Chandrasekhar and Mary John for stimulating comments.

Notes

1. All these stories have now been translated into English and are forthcoming in *Saroj Pathak: Whom Can I Tell? How Can I Explain? and Other Stories* translated and edited by Shirin Kudchedkar, Calcutta: Stree, 1998.

2. See R. Srivatsan on cinema hoardings in general, and specifically on the 'translation' that takes place when a local hoarding painter 'touches up' the print that the distributors send out from Mumbai or Chennai. *Public Culture*, Vol. 4.1, Fall 1991. See also Ashish Rajadhyaksha on popular stereotypes around the "thematic" domains of Indian nationalism, embodied in toy sculptures. 'The Four Looks and the Indian Cinema: A viewer's view'. Unpublished mss, 1997, p. 11.

3. She is, as it were, making "a map of Thebes instead of performing Sophocles, [making] a topography of obstacles instead of fighting against destiny", G. Deleuze and F. Guattari, *Kafka: Toward a Minor Literature*, translated by Dana Polan, Minneapolis and London: University of Minnesota Press, 1986, p. 32.

4. The citations that follow in this section, except when otherwise referenced, are from Shirin Kudchedkar's introductory essay in *Saroj Pathak* op. cit. The translations are hers.

5. Geeta Kapur, 'Mythic Material in the Indian Cinema', *Journal of Arts and Ideas* 14/15, 1987, pp. 75–108, p. 80. Ravi Vasudevan proposes a somewhat different take on the phenomenon. Analysing a sequence from *Andaz*, he identifies two variations on the mode: brief moments of static iconic frontality and the tableau in which the static formation is infused with narrative value. He interprets frontality as a form of visual address that is attractive because it is "indigenous". See 'Shifting Codes, dissolving identities: the Hindi social film of the 1950s as popular culture,' *Journal of Arts and Ideas* 23/24, 1993, pp. 51–84.

6. Madhava Prasad, 'The State and Culture: Hindi cinema in the passive revolution', unpublished Ph.D. dissertation, University of Pittsburgh, 1994, pp. 36–37. Forthcoming Delhi and Oxford. Prasad goes on to interpret this gaze as a "despotic spectacle" in which the image is "given-to-be-seen" and the subjects witness and affirm the authority of the king. It seems to me that this "darsanic" mode is related to what we find in the literary histories. However, by no means does it exhaust the possibilities of frontality, which

has, for instance been redeployed in the Brechtian epic theatre as an instrument for disrupting the bourgeois mode of narrative production.

7. See Etienne Balibar, 'Citizen Subject', in E. Cadava, P. Connor and J.L. Nancy (eds.), *Who Comes After the Subject?*, New York and London: Routledge, 1997, pp. 33–35.

8. Indeed, there is a sense in which one of the objects of a literary education was precisely the cementing together of these variously formed subjects in an integral (not alienated) national citizen-self. I have tried to trace this genealogy in "Government, Binding and Unbinding" *Journal of English and Foreign Languages*, special issue, "Teaching Literature", nos. 7–8, 1991; also in Susie Tharu (ed.) *Subject to Change*, Delhi: Orient Longman, 1998.

9. Madhava Prasad, *The State and Culture*, op. cit., p. 37.

10. Ibid., p. 38.

11. Balibar, 'Citizen Subject', op. cit., p. 34.

12. Ibid., p. 39.

13. Ibid., p. 45.

14. E. Balibar, 'Subjection and Subjectivation' in Copjec, (ed.) *Supposing the Subject*, New York and London, 1993, p. 7.

15. Balibar, 'Citizen Subject', op. cit., p. 46.

16. Balibar, 'Subjection and Subjectivation', op. cit., p. 7.

17. Ashish Rajadhyaksha writes: "In India it is arguable that if realism constitutes the embodiment of a citizen spectator, who is as it were, charged with interpretative authority over what the text represents, then that authority has been far more acceptable to elite viewers when the Symbolic representation has featured *rural* India,… in short a reality in need of the kind of reformism that realism offers… to undertake." "Revisiting the View from the Teashop", mss p. 4.

18. There is, of course, much debate about the nature of this elite: are they trustees, are they a scientific force with responsibility for development and progress, are they the avant garde, are they secular citizens charged with ensuring the humanity of national culture?

It should be possible to extend the argument here to suggest that different nationalisms are underwritten by different nationalist realisms that were assembled to materialise, and to organise in narrative, their citizens as well as their subject-peoples as individuals and as collectives.

19. Closer to the bone of this investigation is the recent work of Flavia Agnes on feminism, communalism and the law (*State, Gender, and*

the Rhetoric of Law Reform, Bombay, S.N.D.T., 1995); the discussion by the Anveshi Law Committee and others of the debates in the mid-90s around the proposed institution of a Uniform Civil Code (Rekha Pappu, "Rethinking Legal Justice for Women", *Economic and Political Weekly*, Vol. 32.19, 1997, and "Is Gender Justice Only a Legal Issue? The political stakes in the UCC debate", *Economic and Political Weekly*, Vol. 32.9–10, 1997); and Vivek Dhareshwar's analyses of the secular self and its doubles in the *Journal of Arts and Ideas*, nos. 25/26, 1995, pp. 115–25 and *Economic and Political Weekly*, Vol. 30.30, 1995, pp. 104–12.

20. Geeta Kapur, 'Mythic Material', op. cit.; also 'Cultural Creativity in the First Decade: The example of Satyajit Ray', *Journal of Arts and Ideas*, nos. 23/24, pp. 17–50.

21. This paper will have also begun, hopefully, to answer the fascinating question of why these national tasks of pedagogy and maintenance were generally assigned to, and willingly taken up by, left-leaning women like Pathak. The question might be better posed as: What was it that made these women the "elect" organisers, or, in Gramscian terms, the organic intellectuals of the national modern?

22. Saroj Pathak, 'Ace of Trumps' in *Selected Stories*.

23. Roy Stryker cited by John Tagg in Victor Burgin, (ed.) *Thinking Photography*, London, 1982, p. 126.

24. Ibid., p. 126.

25. Ibid., p. 126.

26. In a manifesto-like statement read in 1988 at the inauguration of Anveshi, I characterised our mandate as including the theorising of figures such as the mother of the woman patient in the hospital, shuttling between her modern village and modern clinic, carrying the burden of mediating—a do or die situation here—between these two incommensurable regions. This woman is both the subject of welfare-government and the subaltern (in the sense of not vocabularised, invisible in narrative) as against avant-garde or elite broker of modernity. See Susie Tharu, 'Introducing Anveshi', *Lokayan Bulletin*, Vol. 8.3, 1990, pp. 59–63.

27. Burgin, *Thinking Photography*, op. cit., p. 126.

28. Ibid.

29. Cited by Shirin Kudchedkar, 'Introduction', *Saroj Pathak* op. cit.

30. For another investigation into the epistemological impossibility of this agentive self, see my 'The Impossible Subject: Caste and the

gendered body', *Economic and Political Weekly*, Vol. 31.22, 1996, pp. 1311–315.

31. Unpublished mss. p. 4.

32. In political theory this concept is being invoked today within a forcefield that has suggestive correspondences with the argument here. Partha Chatterjee has recently posited a chasmic divide in non-western nation states beween a small section of 'citizens' who enjoy civil societal privileges and a 'population' which is the target of state policies and programmes. He argues that the mode in which the developmental state relates to the population, is welfare; correspondingly, "if we have to give a name to the major form of mobilisation by which the political (parties, movements, non-party political formations [such as popular cinema, I would want to add]) tries to channelise and order popular demands on the state, we should call it democracy" (pp. 16–17). Today, he concludes, we "may well be witnessing an emerging opposition between modernity and democracy, i.e. between civil society and democracy" (p. 17). For several reasons one must proceed with extreme caution in mapping this civil society/political society distinction onto the divide marked by the effects of Saroj Pathak's journalism and her fiction. All the same, the parallels, I think, are productive. "Two Poets and Death: On civil and political society in the non-Christian world", lecture at Anveshi, Hyderabad, August 1996. A modified (redirected?) version appeared in *Economic and Political Weekly*, Vol. 32.1, January 1997. The citations are from the former version.

Inventing Saffron History

*A celibate hero rescues an
emasculated nation*

UMA CHAKRAVARTI

The Contemporary Context

The nation state in India has been experiencing a prolonged
crisis since the mid-eighties. Regional movements, such as
movements in the north-east, which until then had not
impinged directly upon middle class consciousness made a much
more dramatic impact with what came to be perceived as the
Punjab 'problem'. Operation Bluestar and the assassination of
Indira Gandhi by her own security guards significantly
heightened the emotional appeal of nationalism, especially since
the Congress party effectively played on the theme of
fragmentation of the nation to consolidate itself in power in an
increasingly contested situation. The end of the eighties
witnessed other contests especially around caste with the anti-
Mandal agitation led by upper caste youth in Delhi and other
cities, particularly in north India. Again, the middle class press,
ably assisted by India's 'leading' sociologists, succeeded in
representing the Mandal issue as a 'fragmentation' of the nation.
With the Kashmir situation deteriorating rapidly in the late
eighties, the stage was set for a conflation of an ongoing social
and political crisis with the surfacing of middle class insecurities
about the state of 'their' nation and their hegemonic position
within it. This was the background to a rightward shift of
politics, the rise of a fascist Hindutva brigade and a strengthened
upper caste middle class allegiance to Hindu majoritarian

ideological and political formations. The ideological context for this shift was a crisis of the legitimacy of the state.

A standard and well-rehearsed method of dealing with the crises of the present is to write about or 're'construct the 'nation's' 'glorious' past. Bankim Chandra Chattopadhyaya and R.C. Dutt had, among many others, reinvented the ancient and not so ancient past in the nineteenth century.[1] Today's political and social crisis and the panacea for it, are not being expressed through powerful writing but through the visual media, cinema[2] and television. Highly effective, partly because of its reach, but also because the ideological power of its visual 'message' is much greater as it sediments over weeks and months, television is an extremely significant place to look for reconstructions of the past in its deployments to forge the present and the future. Unfortunately, historians, especially eminent ones, hardly bother with the 'idiot' box. But that is where the real action in terms of 'nationalist' reconstructions of the past and representations of patriotism currently lies.

The late eighties witnessed a spate of serials which responded 'dialogically' to the crisis of the legitimacy of the state: indeed it might be argued that they were sanctioned by state-controlled television for the purpose of ideologically reconstructing the fragmented nation. Some were located in present day India and came in two variants: the first combatted the widespread perception of the corrupt state/government through serials such as *Udaan* on the police, *Sangharsh* on the customs and income tax services and even one on the hallowed Indian Administrative Service. The other set of serials set out to portray the 'real' and uncorrupted people of certain states with separatist movements, such as Punjab and Kashmir. (The north-east is too far from middle class consciousness to merit any such attention.) Popularly dubbed as TV's 'Sarson ka Sagas' Doordarshan weakly and ineffectively tried to combat movements for Khalistan and Azad Kashmir, as well as the ideology and practice of terrorism. These serials were unmitigated disasters: except for *Udaan*, where viewers identified with the crusading female protagonist. The efforts of the other serials to whitewash state institutions and highlight statist ideologies failed to capture the imagination of the audience.

Much more effective were the forays into the past. These came initially in the form of the epics, first the *Ramayana* and then the *Mahabharata*. Both were massively popular and have therefore received a fair amount of attention. The point I wish to emphasise here is the ideological rationale and effect of a fairly conscious move by the state to bring in mega serials on religious themes and beam them into homes throughout the country. In this context Iqbal Masud had, in an extraordinarily sharp and perceptive piece of journalism, suggested that by the late eighties the crisis-ridden post-independence state had taken a *policy* decision to substitute religious for secular features on Sunday morning—the Sunday morning slot was thus to be reserved for hegemonic purposes.[3] The government found that secular serials, especially those that were patriotic, seemed to add to dissent; such attempts to entice people away from discontentment did not appear to work. Turning to religion as an opiate, via television the modern drug, was thus a conscious political act.[4]

Masud also pointed to another more basic motive in the shift to 'religious' serials. Television is, in his view, always 'majority' television. By emphasising ideas of a centralised state through notions of unity, discipline, loyalty (to the king, kingdom or 'nation'), an appeal was being made to the 'silent' majority. Dissent or contestation, whether from contending ideologies, or from people belonging to certain castes, classes or minorities would then be perceived as treason. Masud argues that, seen in this light, the mythologies achieved these dual objectives 'triumphantly'.[5]

In this context it is useful to recall the continuities in the ideological location of the epics and *Chanakya*. The televised epics, though drawing from common reserves of popular tradition, had already begun the process of achieving a certain resonance with contemporary issues by reworking and updating hegemonic epic themes such as threats to state power from the enemy within, the irrationality and tyranny of the people's expectations from their rulers and their easy corruptibility, and the need to re-establish the legitimacy of the state. Principled action was seen as coming *only* from a small elite minority, or from a single individual rather than from people as a whole. The natural saviours were thus a few heroic *men.* The most important echo the epics achieved with the present were in the last episodes of the *Mahabharata,* telecast before *Chanakya,* where, using a very contemporary idiom, it focused on the terrible dangers of disunity and the fragmentation of the land as a consequence of internal rivalries among the ruling elites. Through its handling of the themes of corruption, ego clashes between ruling class members, and *adharma* more generally, *Chanakya* prefigured issues of divisiveness and rivalry leading to fratricidal war and the ruination of the nation. *Chanakya* took off from that last statement and built generally on the theme of a fragmented 'nation';[6] it thus carried the mythological tradition forward in a more focused way, emphasising a joint 'xenophobia' against the enemy within a corrupt, immoral and emasculated king who had turned his back on Brahminic values and espoused a dissenting ideology (conflated in this serial with a 'minority' religion), betraying the nation in its hour of trial, and against a foreign invader violating the very boundaries of the sacred 'Indian' nation.

In another crucial articulation, *Chanakya* was linked to the narratives of the *Ramayana* and *Mahabharata* in the telecast versions through its handling of the theme of the family. It is easy to discern that the epics are essentially 'family' narratives: the *Ramayana* is a narrative of a king's family and the threats to it from within its innermost recesses, from the queen herself.[7] The *Mahabharata* is a narrative of a kingdom and the divided family, threatened and consumed by fratricidal conflict: its message is that when families split and fight each other, a collapse of the nation is bound to follow. *Chanakya* in contrast, but also in continuation, is about threats to the 'united', expanded 'nation', beyond individual kingdoms. The history of this family—the nation—is the attempt to destroy it—its independence and its masculinity—from within by debauched kings like the Nandas, and betrayers like Ambhi of Taxila (followed later by the likes of Jaichand and Mir Jafar), and from without by the territory-hungry Greek invaders (and later by the Muslims and the British). Through its fifty-two episodes *Chanakya* consciously used the memory of a family, standing now for the nation, as an instrument of recall; a straightforwardly linear family narrative was thus recast as a grand national family narrative. Remythologising the identity of the nation and playing upon national 'memory' through a series of symbols of recall which linked the audience of *Chanakya* with the nation he 'created', this serial invented the moment of creation of the first 'Indian' nation, the *ma bharati* or the motherland. As Dwivedi, its maker, stated emphatically, "I am not making a historical film, but interpreting the life of the first man with a national consciousness."[8]

This man, with the fire of the nation burning within him, was created as the archetypal figure of masculine authority. In a far-reaching reinterpretation of *dharma*, the patriotic worshipper of the nation could lie, cheat, bribe, and incite in the cause of dharma where dharma now stood for the securing of the integrity, unity, and Brahminic values of the nation. In the new dharma of the nation the ends justify the means because ultimately real dharma, the regenerated 'independent' nation, will be created. Here, too, there is a link with the *Mahabharata*, where killing and lying are exonerated as part of a Kshatriya 'dharma'. But this is mitigated in the *Mahabharata* by a recognition of ambiguity. In *Chanakya*, however, there are no dilemmas, no moments of self-doubt. The worship of *ma bhoomi* and devotion to the motherland, is the true religion. The regenerated male who worships his motherland, therefore, is not bound by codes, moral or otherwise. Most significantly, in contrast to the Hindutvavadis, *Chanakya* does not use and does not even require gods to worship or mobilise around. In an extraordinarily confident handling of the past, it is human beings who are the main actors. It is not faith but the assertion of a national culture (unambiguously Brahminical despite the divine absence) which is the definitive mobilising force. It is not surprising then, that one of the main characteristics of *Chanakya* is that there are no conventional mythical elements: no *pushpak vimanas*, no star wars, no childish fantasia, no fires that do not burn the chaste, as in the televised versions of the *Ramayana* and the *Mahabharata*. Burning national zeal and masculine valour were enough to build the moral community of the first Indian nation—no other pegs are required (this also makes it much more authentic). Significantly also, *Chanakya's* claim to historical accuracy is thus achieved through its more credible ambience: the 'inventions' of Dwivedi could pass unnoticed and his version of *Chanakya* would be regarded as *the* genuine account of the founding of a 'national' kingdom.

Rewriting Nationalist History

Dwivedi's *Chanakya* was heir not merely to the telecast of the *Ramayana* and the *Mahabharata* but also, and more importantly, drew upon a long history of nationalist writing. In this, too, Dwivedi was expanding on an existing discourse while quite consciously achieving an important shift: the first man with a 'national consciousness' became saffron by Dwivedi's sleight of hand. I outline below the adaptation of various elements from nationalist writing and the process by which Chanakya was transformed into a saffron hero.

A major ideal of the dominant sections of the Indian people and of historical writing in the first half of the twentieth century was that of a strong, centralised empire. This was the counter to the fragmentation and political rivalries that were perceived as the cause of India's subordination. Twentieth century nationalist historians unabashedly wrote their versions of Indian history celebrating military strength. The focus on 'administrator' kings such as Ashoka, Harsha and Akbar by colonial administrators turned historians, such as Vincent Smith, was redeployed by nationalist historians to highlight those phases and figures in Indian history that could epitomise military prowess. The search for heroic figures zeroed in on ancient India: since most of nationalist historiography was a creation of Hindu historians, medieval Muslim India would not do and heroic figures had to be located in the pre-Muslim Indian past. Over the decades, 'nationalist' historians explored a number of figures, finally coming to rest on the dynasty of the Mauryas, and more specifically on Chandragupta Maurya (not Ashoka). This was because Chandragupta Maurya came to power immediately after Alexander's 'invasion'; further, Chandragupta Maurya founded the first empire in India, battled the Greek general Seleucus, 'defeated' and imposed an unequal treaty on him and thereafter ruled the kingdom with an iron hand.[9] In fact, the celebration of the warrior hero Chandragupta was accompanied by a critique of Ashoka for his rejection of war as a valid means of expanding the frontiers of a kingdom. His pacificism was regarded as having 'emasculated' the nation.[10] According to this viewpoint the 'idle' army was unable to defend the frontiers against the Indo Greeks, making India vulnerable once more to foreign aggression because of Ashoka's pacific policies. War and expansion must be a permanent agenda in statecraft; implicitly like Mussolini, the Hindu nationalists believed that war brings out the manly qualities in a people whereas pacificism blunts them, thus weakening the nation.

Jawaharlal Nehru shared some of the concerns of nationalist historians; it is not surprising therefore that his *Discovery of India* has been regarded even by his sympathetic biographer, S.Gopal, as a "version of India's cultural history put together in an astonishingly narrow nationalist tradition".[11] However, though charged with the spirit of nationalism, Nehru was also a little apprehensive about its chauvinist potential. He alone among the nationalist writers privileged Ashoka as the real hero of the Mauryan Empire: while others played on the theme of a strong nation, Nehru dwelt more on the theme of the 'unique' nation, and so for him the idealistic Ashoka who eschewed war was the real hero of ancient India—in a sense a model for all the world's 'heroes' in a post-colonial era where large parts of Asia and Africa had to rebuild their economies and societies ravaged by imperialism.[12]

Dwivedi's *Chanakya* builds on this substratum of ideas and perceptions as most of nationalist writing lends itself quite readily to a saffron agenda. *Chanakya* collapses the strong nation or unique nation theme into a single strand; thus, in the past, India was a strong *and* unique nation with Chanakya not Chandragupta as its archetypal hero (because the former was easier to saffronise). The Chanakyan version ensures that India was at birth created as a strong, unique, spiritual and decisively 'Hindutva' nation.

The Narrative Frame

The opening of the narrative in *Chanakya* is set in Magadha. King Dhanananda is the immoral and debauched ruler who treats the state's resources as something to be dipped into deceitfully whenever he wishes. Only a few upright Brahmins get to know of the corruption. Among them is Shaktar, who takes an open stand against the king and is imprisoned. Immediately after, Acharya Chanak, the father of Chanakya, also boldly opposes the king's plunder of the state. He is jailed but hopes that the people will rise in revolt against its debauched king. They, however, are both too frightened and too caught up in their mundane activities to oppose the tyranny of Dhanananda. Acharya Chanak is subsequently killed. The young Chanakya has watched these events in anguish. Unwilling to live in the midst of tyranny he leaves his widowed mother and his boyhood mates behind as he goes away to Taxila. Dissent has been fruitless in round one.

In Taxila, Chanakya sets up a *gurukul,* an institution where students live with a teacher, and trains young *shishyas* (disciples) in the art of politics and war. Students learn various martial arts and train their bodies to become fitting vehicles of masculine valour. At the same time Alexander and his Greek troops invade 'India'. Chanakya seeks to build a national resistance but fails. In desperation he even travels to Magadha and appeals to the hated king to lead the resistance. Immersed in sensuous pursuits, Dhanananda insults Chanakya, who vows revenge on behalf of the 'nation'.

Before going back to the scene of the 'invasion' he visits his home, now in ruins. His mother has just died and Chanakya performs her last rites. Finding both his home, and homeland, in ruins, Chanakya resolves to rebuild his world. He stumbles upon Chandragupta, the son of a tribal woman who lives with his mother and mother's brother. (Is this a suggestion of a matrilineal household?) Chanakya sees great military potential in Chandragupta and 'buys' him from his greedy uncle. He returns with his protege to Taxila where Ambhi has 'betrayed' the nation by making a deal with Alexander. His patriotic wife, the daughter of Porus in Dwivedi's version, is deeply unhappy at her husband's perfidy. Ambhi's brave sister also refuses to accept Greek tutelage and leaves the kingdom. Porus alone fights but not bravely and sagely enough in this version, so he is vanquished. A Greek garrison is installed and Alexander returns because his men refuse to fight further even though he has appealed to them to carry on until all of India is conquered. (This speech is referenced from its sources in Greek and Roman writings.)

Chandragupta is trained by Chanakya in the martial arts and becomes invincible in the field of military deeds. When Chanakya and Chandragupta have satisfactorily put together a coalition of Indian states and are ready for resistance, a war is fought under Chanakya's moral command. Once the north-west is 'liberated' from 'foreign' thraldom, Chanakya and Chandragupta, along with other kings, strike at Magadha. The king Dhanananda and his male progeny are eliminated. Then Chanakya, through many diplomatic and Machiavellian moves against the coalition partners, secures the throne for Chandragupta. Finding him still vulnerable because of the possibility of resistance built around Dhanananda's minister Raksasa, and Dhanananda's wife and daughter, Chanakya attempts to break the potentially dangerous coalition against the new king by persuading Dhanananda's daughter to marry Chandragupta and thus be the queen consort. He also, by a long and complicated set of moves drawn from Vishakadatta's *Mudraraksasa*, wins the loyalty of the *amatya* (minister) Raksasa for Chandragupta by making the former the chief advisor to the king. Having completed his mission of regenerating the nation Chanakya leaves the capital—possibly for a simple *shikshak's* life, renouncing the arena of power.

The recurrent motifs in Dwivedi's *Chanakya* are the twin concerns proclaimed by the proponents of today's Hindu *rashtravadis*: the need for an "*akhand* Bharat" (undivided India) to combat the fragmentation which lays 'us' open to the external enemy or enemies; and the need to create a new Hindu male to confront the hydra-headed corruption spawned by the illegitimate wielders of state power, the nation's 'internal enemy'. In the portrayal of India in the third century B.C., the petty warring states stand for the first phenomenon and the Magadhan state under the Nandas the second, as corruption and debauchery are both rampant here. Since desperate situations are seen to require desperate solutions, Chanakya has no hesitation in using what may, by the ignorant, be regarded as *kuta niti* (crafty/devious policy)—only, in the hands of the incorruptible Chanakya it no longer remains a kuta niti but is transformed instead into a great moral instrument. In any case, ends justify means whether in diplomacy, negotiations, or in war. Indeed, Chanakya proclaims that corruption can only be destroyed by kuta niti; the policy itself is not 'immoral' but rather is a policy to deal with immorality. Dwivedi uses an interesting distancing device here—he isolates the troubled and 'amoral' passages in the *Arthashastra* and pegs them to the Magadhan state under the Nandas. It is made clear that these aspects are not part of Chanakyan morality or his higher world view. Dwivedi's Chanakya is nevertheless an expert at manipulating people. He also provides for the possibility that all the usual players of his time—villains, heroes turned villains like Porus (in this version), even those who have no love for king or country but only for money—can be redeemed in the holy fire of nationalism through his masterly manipulation. How can this be kuta niti?

In the early episodes of the 52 part serial Dwivedi successfully focuses the narrative on the theme of 'dissent', the conscientious moral opposition to the illegitimate use of state power. This focus achieves a two-fold objective: first, it fixes Chanakya's deployment of kuta niti for moral ends with the imprimatur of a higher legitimacy regardless of whether it meets the requirements of established opinion; and second, it captures the imagination of that group of persons who are ashamed of the rampant corruption prevalent in contemporary India. What is crucial to this unique display of intellectual and moral dissent is that it emanates from a small group of Brahmins. The Brahmins in *Chanakya* are represented not so much in terms of a clearly formulated social class but as *acharyas*, or teachers. Having once made the connection between Brahmin and acharya, the preferred term for Chanakya is shikshak or intellectual mentor of a lost people. This heightens the image of Chanakya as someone who refuses to be part of a corrupt moral order. This way of representing Chanakya is also an appropriation of the Buddha's categorisation of the Brahmins into those moral beings who stand for a higher Brahminism and those other gross materialistic Brahmins who stand for a lower form.[13] In *Chanakya*, however, there is mainly one kind of Brahmin as typified by Chanakya who is not only upright but burns with patriotic zeal. There are some passing suggestions to the 'lower' Brahmins; these are usually men who are in the 'employment' of the corrupt king of Magadha.

This way of representing Brahmins, not as a social group, has a double advantage. It gives the term Brahmin a value by suggestion rather than open allusion, and more importantly, it enables the suppression of caste as a crucial institution of our society, then as well as now. Significantly, the Brahmins are *never* represented as possessing ritual power, or as monopolising knowledge, imparting it only to a select few.

Once the suppression of Brahmins as a social class is complete other castes and classes also become obscured. The serial is marked by the absence of producers; along with this erasure, exploitation also disappears. Thus both caste and class are invisibilised as the account dwells exclusively on soldiers, officials, kings, Brahmins and traders. Since questions of labour and appropriation are suppressed, it is not surprising that the common people are generally missing— not merely as important actors in shaping history, but also in terms of a silent presence.

There is only one 'class' of people who indirectly suggest class and labour—the *dasi*, and even she is present only in the households of the king, and of corrupt officials.

The early part of the narrative also makes it evident that the common people are incapable of moral action: there is almost a similar contempt for them as that displayed by the Greek philosophers for the 'mob'. The people's will simply does not exist—and this is the first lesson the child Chanakya learns, which is an advance on the mistaken illusions held by his father who expects the people to revolt against tyranny. Except for this reference, the 'people' in *Chanakya* is almost deliberately left as a vaguely delineated but homogenised abstract entity—the *praja*. Again, by recall, the praja here is like the praja in the *Ramayana*, self serving and brutish, incapable of conscious moral action, a group on whose behalf the intellectual elite must act. The most significant consequence of this way of representing the chosen few and the larger body of the people is that the serial *invents* a society which has no internal contradictions and no contestations: all its parts and apparently separate units make up a single harmonious economic and social order. There are neither class antagonisms nor is there room for separate gender agendas as I shall try and demonstrate below.

There is, however, one set of exclusions which mark the handling of society in Chanakya. These are not located in the hierarchical order but in a suggested vertical division of society into different sectarian groupings. *Chanakya's* Brahminism is most evident in the way Buddhists in particular, are represented. In two crucial sequences the Buddhist philosophy is trivialised, which I shall return to later. The way the Buddhists are represented here suggests that they are the forerunners of other religious communities like the Muslims and Christians who stand outside Brahminic Hinduism. Through such allusions and through the deliberate use of certain modern terms such as *tushtikaran* (appeasement) which has no equivalent in ancient India and is reserved in the discourse of Hindutva for critiquing the state's alleged appeasement of Muslims by the 'pseudo' secularists today, connections are constantly sought to be made between the events of 'those' days and the events of 'ours'.

Other key terms in achieving this resonance is the repeated use of words like *rashtra, utishtha, swatantrata sangram, seema, sanskriti, beej* and *satta* (nation, arise, war of liberation, boundary, heritage, seed and power). The nation, that is to say, the children of *ma bharati*, are members of one family, one homeland, but it takes a man like Chanakya to foreground this reality to his people. In a powerful sequence set in Magadha after Chanakya has been dismissed by the king who refuses to uphold the honour of the nation in the face of foreign aggression, a voice calls out to him—*tera ghar bhitar se toot raha hai* (your home is being destroyed from within). Chanakya replies—*dekh raha hoon, ghar ko jodne aya hoon* (I can see that; I have come to rebuild it). In the context of a divided and fragmented India, unable to hold together its independent nationhood, Chanakya exhorts his people to recognise that we are all products of a common seed, of common ancestors, that we share a deep bond through a common *sanskriti* which may not be visible because it is obscured by individual greed (*swartha*), but is there nevertheless. It is like a big tree whose roots lie under the ground, whose existence men have forgotten. Divided and fragmented India, with many different *janapadas* (kingdoms) and political formations from Taxila to Magadha, needs to recognise this, then rise and reclaim its sacred space and its nationhood. What Chanakya emphasises is that if the cultural roots are the same from Taxila to Magadha, then the political frontiers *must* coincide with the cultural boundaries. With this Chanakya projects a very high Brahminical notion of culture; the 'one' culture of a people from one beej; the heterogeneous and hierarchised cultures and people scattered over India in the third century B.C. are simply elided. *Chanakya* presumes, for a twentieth century audience, certain cultural frontiers and then insists that the political frontiers must correspond to this mapping of cultural boundaries. The resonance with contemporary Hindutva rhetoric is striking.

Celibacy and Other Sexualities

The whole Chanakyan venture is extremely male. This maleness is evident in the way the narrative unfolds and the manner in which the main characters are delineated. A notable aspect of the handling of maleness, including male sexuality, is its sophistication: it works through suggestion, allusion and subtle body language. It is never gross, overtly sexual or conventionally macho in the way Anand Patwardhan has so superbly captured masculinity in *Father, Son and Holy War*. Almost in contrast, maleness is achieved through the inversion of overt male sexuality. Chanakya uses a highly developed cultural language sedimenting the Brahminical Hindu philosophical view, that it is through a complete control of the senses that a superior kind of *viriya* (strength) is unleashed. Recalling the ascetic/*grahastha* dichotomy and a host of Puranic legends about the need to retain the semen for achieving high levels of *tejas* (brightness, strength), intellectual prowess, mental and physical vigour and spiritual energy, *Chanakya* reiterates the view that celibacy is the preferred state for possessing concentrated masculine vigour.

This masculinity, achieved through renunciate celibacy, is in marked contrast to the Buddhist emphasis on celibacy which leads to escapism and emasculation. The sequence through which this contrast is made is very revealing: The north-western part of 'India' is being ravaged by Greek forces; unable and unwilling to be a mute witness to this violation of the beloved ma bharati, Chanakya is hurrying towards Magadha to seek help against the invaders; as he rushes onward, overwhelmed by anguish, a group of Buddhist bhikshus clad in saffron robes pass him by. Absorbed in themselves, thin, pale and effeminate in their gait and manner they are unmindful, and uncaring, about the great tragedy befalling the nation. In suppressing their sexual impulses they have also been emasculated; turning their backs and fleeing as they are from the arena of conflict, they are reneging on their political duty to the motherland. The Buddhist bhikshus in *Chanakya* thus are feminised, individual soul seekers, not manly redeemers of the collective people. This is in sharp contrast to Chanakya, who has not merely suppressed sexual desire but has transformed sexual energy into real manliness by deploying it for national ends.

The careful containment of male sexuality and its subsequent deployment occupies a key place in the political agenda that Chanakya is engaged in. If one looks closely at the major players in the unfolding drama of the third century B.C. (as invented by Dwivedi) they fall into four archetypes, beginning with the young initiated male, a *brahmacharya* engaged in vigorous physical and mental training which will prepare him for the tasks that lie ahead. This prototype of the brahmacharya applies to all of the students that Chanakya trains in his gurukul, but most effectively to Chandragupta whom Chanakya 'finds' and then shapes as the future ruler. The second archetype is that of the older renunciate male: this figure is the focal point of the narrative in *Chanakya*—that of the protagonist himself, the importance of whose conversion from an ordinary Brahmin to a saffron clad shikshak I have already dealt with earlier. There is only one person in this category in *Chanakya*, making this archetype unique, but it draws upon a well-honed symbolic structure and therefore has a powerful appeal for a certain kind of audience. Both the brahmacharya and the sanyasi or shikshak here are celibate males. In contrast, the third category of persons is the polar opposite of the celibate males outlined above: this is the debauched and over-sensuous male, as typified by Dhanananda and his male progeny; finally, but somewhat marginally, there is the archetype of the grahastha, comprising all the Brahmin householders who are squarely located in the world of administration and governance in the narrative of *Chanakya*. All these categories of men have a distinctive relationship to sexuality: the protagonist Chanakya is depicted as someone who moves from the mandatory celibacy of the brahmacharya of a student to one who chooses a permanent state of celibacy as the sanyasi or shikshak/guru, turning his back firmly on a sexual life of any kind—even one that is deferred to a later point in his life. Since he wears a saffron upper cloth and the *rudraksha mala* it is suggested that he has *chosen* a celibate existence—clearly here also suggesting that no relationship, emotional or sexual, is permissible in Chanakya's singular mission of liberating and uniting his beloved ma bharati.

Heterosexual love, especially when linked to an emotional content, deflects from the service of the motherland especially in moments of crisis.[14] This is part of the reason why Chanakya is not depicted as an ordinary Brahmin; the saffron worn by the shikshak not merely removes him from social class as I argued earlier, but makes him a moral authority figure, a status to which a celibate male is automatically entitled. Once a man can contain his sexuality he achieves great intellectual and spiritual prowess which Chanakya has in abundant measure. Throughout the serial Chanakya's face literally glows with tejas, the quality that comes with complete sexual control. Further, the status of a man who has renounced reproduction and the creation of a family is unimpeachable. Nothing will drag him down since such a figure has no family ties and no irresponsible and corrupt progeny to deflect him from his path of virtuous action.

One highly dramatic moment captures the masculine energy released through the use of a strongly sexual symbolism. Chanakya is in the court of Dhanananda pleading eloquently for help to fight the invading Greek armies. Instead of rising to the occasion, Dhanananda insults Chanakya and personally humiliates him in the presence of the entire court. As an emotionally charged Chanakya vows to avenge this humiliation, which is not personal but the humiliation of ma bharati, he unties his *shendi* (strand of knotted hair on an otherwise shaven head) and proclaims that he will (like Draupadi in the *Mahabharata*) never retie his hair till his country has been freed. Hair is a key indicator of sexuality as Leach and Obeyesekere amongst others have shown.[15] This visual is repeated to recall the Chanakyan mission at different points in the narrative, thus also reiterating its powerful sexual symbolism: as Chanakya's masculinity is insulted, his tied shendi, which stands for a controlled and structured sexuality, is untied to indicate the release of sexual power, in this case transcended to release the full potential of masculinity—physical and mental vigour—through a transformation of viriya or sexual vigour.

The brahmacharya's celibate status and his relationship to masculinity underpins a number of sequences revealing the strongly Brahminical world view of *Chanakya*. The bulk of the brahmacharyas are students of Chanakya at his gurukul in Taxila. While they spend a lot of time learning the texts, chanting sanskrit *slokas* and performing *homa*, there are an equal number of stunning visuals, as young, beautifully proportioned boys wrestle, fence and horse-ride to develop into physically vigorous men. Brahmacharyas are, as is well known, barred from sexual relationships and are required to concentrate their entire physical and intellectual energy in learning the tasks at hand. It is known to be a time when adolescent sexual drives must be deflected and transcended through rigorous physical workouts and focused thinking around an object or mission—in the case of *Chanakya* the mission is to defend the nation. It is not unusual to see the boys in the gurukul dressed in yellow or saffron dhotis, all cleanly scalped, rushing off waving flags in defence of their guru Chanakya, or their motherland ma bharati.

In opposition to the celibate males are the over-sensuous and, therefore, insensate men who are physically and mentally worthless. They are depicted as mostly lying around in a drunken stupor. It is the over-gratification of their sexual drives that has crippled them. As emasculated men, they stand at the other end of the spectrum represented by the masculine vigour of the celibate males. They have literally overspent their semen and so have been emptied of their masculinity. This opposition between masculinity and 'emasculinity' underwrites a lot of nationalist historical writing and is a key theme in the literary exploration of the past. For example, in a powerful nationalist 'historical' play, an adaptation of *Devi Chandraguptam* (the second well known play of Vishakadatta, the author of *Mudraraksasa*), Jaishankar Prasad's *Dhruvaswamini* literally peoples the debauched king Ramagupta's court with dwarfs, eunuchs and hunchbacks. The queen bemoans her fate, where her husband's court is comprised only of emasculated men. The king himself tops the list of emasculated beings.[16] In a recent (and well received) production of this play at a well-known women's college in Delhi,[17] the effeminate king was depicted as staggering about drunkenly, extremely fearful of danger and, most significantly, unable to consummate his marriage. The king is so utterly lacking in manly vigour that he is willing to buy his own freedom (having been unable to defend his frontiers from invasion by a 'foreign' dynasty), and succumbs to the invading king's demand that his wife, the queen consort, be handed over to the aggressor. Ultimately all is saved by the king's younger brother, the epitome of manly vigour who kills the invader and saves his sister-in-law, and thus her kingdom, from potential degradation. Visually, the debauched court of emasculated kings in *Chanakya* and to a lesser extent in *Dhruvaswamini*, suggests standard representations in Hindi cinema of 'Muslim' feudal courts: a central figure of the king or a feudal lord, goblets of wine, women dasis waiting upon debauched men, and the forecourt occupied by curvaceous dancers. Other courtiers lie around the sides of the forecourt, also mostly in various states of drunkenness and lasciviousness. These sequences in *Chanakya* are always cut by scenes of heroic men, resisting or planning resistance to the invaders. The background music also highlights this ambience—even before the court scene comes on, the sound of ankle bells presage the change to such a scene of debauchery.

In *Chanakya* the opposition between the protagonist and the villain is thus strongly laid out as a sexual opposition—the controlled, transcended sexuality of the celibate making for masculine vigour and the over indulgent sexuality of the licentious male whose masculinity has been crippled.

The last category, but somewhat marginal to the visual and symbolic language of the narrative are the grahastha men. (Certain categories of men are left 'unmarked' according to the schema I have outlined; these include figures like the Commander-in-Chief.) The clearly delineated grahastha figures are Brahmin men; some are in the employ of the king as advisors, ministers or councillors; others may be among the conscientious objectors, like Chanakya's father Acharya Chanak.

Their relationship to sexuality is highly structured and is achieved mostly through obscuring the sexual relationships between Brahmin men and their wives in the way the narrative treats these figures. It is almost as if Dwivedi is mindful of the Brahminical textual dictum that Brahmin men must approach their wives only at certain defined times, for the limited (but sacred) purpose of reproducing sons. As figures, these grahasthas do not occupy a clear place in the opposition between the masculinities of celibacy and emasculation.

The elements in the handling of male sexuality in *Chanakya* are linked in two opposing ways—masculinity is equated with physical strength, heroism and patriotism; together they create the epitome of male virility. Its counter elements equate pacifism with cowardice, treachery, debauchery, over-gratification of the sexual drive and emasculation, or the loss of male *viriya*. The major success of *Chanakya* lies in the elaboration of these relational characteristics of masculinity and emasculation as key factors of Hindu nationalist ideologies. This singular focus on male virility is also enhanced by the continuous valorisation of masculine authority. An extremely tight control is maintained in the portrayal of Chanakya, whose central concern is to moralise, uplift, 'nationalise' and make patriotic the spectator; notably, the serial has no 'distractions' of the sub-plot type. For example, there is absolutely no comic relief (the closest to a 'comic' sequence was one where the tightly controlled body language of Chanakya took a loosening; the transformation was required to portray Chanakya as a spy in a brothel—his disguise was a headgear of flowers round his half-shaven head!) Also, and significantly, there is not a single 'romantic' episode in the entire serial—the fuller implications of which I leave for the moment.

But before moving to an analysis of the handling of female characters and female sexuality, which has other implications for the theme of masculinity, a final aspect of masculinity needs to be explored. As a corollary to the absence of 'romance' in the conventional sense, and possibly as a consequence of the focus on celibacy, the only 'emotion' that is privileged in Chanakya is that between men. This is de-eroticised rather than homoeroticised, but is often portrayed in an extremely charged manner, as the atmosphere sometimes literally crackles with suppressed emotions. Male relationships are worked out through rough speech and violent gestures, depicting a 'pure' love, especially in those relationships that hark back to a shared childhood.

A specific kind of male bonding is thus celebrated in *Chanakya* and occurs in four sets of relationships: between childhood friends; between colleagues in the same mission; between father and son; and more often between *guru* and *shishya*. There are shades of the last two of these relationships in a powerful passage where Chanakya tells Chandragupta, '*Mere jivan ke yathartha ho tum*' (you are the truth/reality of my being). In sequences where these four different kinds of male bonding are depicted there is almost an excess of feeling that flows between the individual characters. In contrast, in all the other sequences concerning relationships, especially heterosexual relations, there is almost a clinical ambience—as if emotions are not permissible in such interactions.

Heterosexual relationships are assumed rather than explored and remain unusually desireless in their delineation. Many of the male characters have wives but most of these women remain in the background. I cannot recall even one sequence when there is an indication that a female character is the object of a man's 'feelings'. Yet, significantly, sexuality is assumed to be an innate aspect of a feminine being. What is striking is that celibacy as a stage or a matter of choice, and its transformation into heroism, is *reserved* exclusively for men, while marriage or a heterosexual relationship is a natural given for women. When women are not depicted in a marital situation they are either dasis in the palace, or in taverns and pleasure houses, or in the service of high officials (as stand-ins for wives who are missing). All the 'good' Brahmins have wives to serve them and lend them a sympathetic ear when they are besieged by anxieties. (In fact, they often appear on screen to create the dialogic element so that the audience gets to know what a man is 'thinking' via his 'utterance' to his wife.) In the case of 'bad' characters—those engaged in plotting for power, wives are markedly missing: these characters have dasis to serve them; they are also often found spending their spare time in ale houses or pleasure houses. These spaces are clearly locations where pleasure is available for a price. Visually they are arranged like Roman palaces with fountains and pools; couples dot these interiors, always in recumbent positions, and wine flows all around.

It should be reiterated that while there is an implicit opposition between the good men who have wives and the devious men who have maids or paid companions, there is a certain clinicality in both sets of relationships, and a moral judgement against the paid companions is not in evidence. (In this, *Chanakya* brings the instrumentalism of the *Arthashastra* alive.) A female companion is pragmatically assumed as a natural given for certain men. Sexual services are also assumed in both situations, dutiful in the case of wives and functional in the case of dasis or paid companions. Neither set of characters is important in the narrative: they are simply there, somewhat like props without whom the visuals and situations would be a little incomplete. The presence of the wives, for example, is often reduced to a voice emanating from the inner quarters of the house calling out mundane announcements such as '*bhojan tayar hai*' (the meal is ready). The dasis or paid companions may not have even that one sentence to utter.

Marriage for reproduction is also presumed as the natural order of things, especially when it comes to kingship. Among the elaborate moves that are made by Chanakya for Chandragupta is the negotiation of a suitable marriage alliance for him (Chandragupta's days as a brahmacharya can now end as he has wrested state power and 'liberated' the country). Chanakya's Machiavellian mind considers that the daughter of Dhanananda will be the best possible queen for Chandragupta: through her the king who has overthrown the last Nanda will be a more legitimate ruler and he will be best protected against those who might try to usurp power from him. Dhanananda's daughter, is however, unwilling and makes a spirited resistance against becoming a pawn in a game of moves and counter moves. Unfortunately, the serial rather suddenly drops the issue of marriage and moves on leaving the issue unresolved. The whole episode is characteristically lacking in romantic sentiment—in keeping with the preferred way of treating heterosexual relationships in *Chanakya*.

On the whole there are almost no striking presences of women in *Chanakya* in comparison with the heroic agenda allotted to the men. Even the usual valorisation of mothers is muted. The mother of Chandragupta appears in the narrative in order to hand over her son to Chanakya. Chanakya's own mother also remains a weakly etched character whom Chanakya leaves behind as he goes away to Taxila as a young adolescent after the death of his father. When he returns, his mother has passed away, and the fact that Chanakya could not be with his mother at her death enhances his anger against the corrupt Magadhan king. The anguish of the son for a lost mother, however, easily metamorphoses to anguish for the lost dignity of the motherland and the mother's memory fades away.

Valorisation of a feminine type is reserved for only two women in the 52 part serial: one of them is the sister of the betrayer king Ambhi and the other is the wife of Ambhi. Significantly in this narrative the latter is the daughter of the patriotic Paurava (Porus). These two women conform to an important category of womanhood in nationalist constructions —the *virangana* or the heroic woman, best epitomised by Rani Lakshmibai.[18] Such women participate in whatever capacity they can in the project of resistance or liberation, refusing to accept the aggression unleashed by the foreign invaders. While Ambhi's sister, unable to bear the humiliation of a brother who is willing to sell his honour for the throne, dons male garb and rides off into the wilderness (to join the forces of resistance may be?), Ambhi's wife stays on finally to redeem her husband and bring him back to the path of patriotic duty. There is a suggestion that in the interim period she both denies Ambhi sexual services and womanly solace. Later when doubts besiege him she steers him round to his duty to the nation. Finally, Ambhiraja, too, joins Chandragupta and Chanakya in the task of national regeneration. What is interesting about these female characters is that there is not the slightest shred of historical evidence for either of them. They are inventions to make a statement about the unique essence of Indian women who are heroic and incorruptible even when their male counterparts fail to perform their duty to the motherland.[19] These inventions make it possible to create prototypes of the only legitimate examples of women's agency—women who fight on behalf of the nation, or women who exhort, or even incite, men to perform their manly duty of defending the nation.

The most unique aspect of the deployment of female sexuality in *Chanakya* is, however, the manner in which the prostitute's sexuality is required to achieve 'patriotic' goals. (While it is well-known that nations deploy women's sexuality in espionage, at least one significant strand in Indian nationalism, led by Gandhi, rejected the prostitute's patriotic impulses. To that extent *Chanakya* is breaking a connection between chaste women and patriotism.) If celibacy is the privileged form through which male sexuality is transcended to create real masculine valour, the full and free utilisation of female sexuality is the privileged means through which just ends are secured. In this sense, a woman is essentialised as a sexual being, but because a prostitute or courtesan's sexual services are not confined to a single male but must be available to many men, she is the chosen medium through whom crucial information is gathered, moves and counter moves are made, and the debauched enemy's end may be secured. This is in keeping with the *Arthashastra* where courtesans, actresses and even bhikshunis can gather information useful to the king,[20] and with the *Mudraraksasa* where a beautiful *vishkanya*, a deadly seductress whose poisonous body can kill, uses her body to end the life of the last of the enemies of Chandragupta. What is unique in *Chanakya* is that this is no pragmatic use of female sexuality but is a means through which the embryonic nation can be liberated from thraldom and corruption. The prostitute's kuta niti matches Chanakya's kuta niti; it is a means by which the 'nationalists' can effectively counter the kuta niti of treacherous men who betray the nation. The prostitute's sexuality is thus the structural counterpart of Chanakya's celibacy in the political agenda of redeeming the nation's future.

What could be the contemporary relevance of the narrative strategies of *Chanakya*? In an insightful piece of writing, published soon after the destruction of the Babri Masjid by the Sangh combine, the well known civil rights activist, K.Balagopal, pointed to the complexities of contemporary right wing politics. He suggested that it would be wrong to assume that Hindutva proponents would revert to the prescriptions of the *Manusmriti*,[21] even as sections among the right wing formation do demand a return to the past including the enforcement of the caste system, *pativrata* codes for women, and their exclusion from the public sphere. The political strategies of the Hindutvavadis are amazingly flexible and have a great capacity for redeploying tradition selectively, and innovatively, to forge new meanings.

Hindutva can draw from the cultural repertoire of the past using symbols and figures in ways which may appear to be 'conventional' but have very contemporary political functions. Although *Chanakya's* appeal was limited to an upper caste elite, it was part of a larger process in which a Brahminic Hindu view of history and culture was consolidated along with a rightward shift in politics. Its treatment of women's agency, specifically for political goals, was an extension of the nationalist reconstruction of women's expanded roles during times of 'crisis'. Its handling of sexuality was equally complex and multifaceted ranging from a deployment of culturally loaded symbols to more pragmatic and instrumental uses of female sexuality in particular. In some ways it is a corollary to the way the BJP ideologue, Sadhvi Rithambara wears saffron, the colour denoting celibacy, and uses a sexually charged mode of rhetoric to incite Hindu men.[22] The apparent contradiction nevertheless holds together politically: the complex moves of the Hindu Right are able to contain both Rithambara and Mridula Sinha who emphasises women's domestic functions[23] and thus appeals to a different constituency. *Chanakya's* handling of male and female sexuality has a similar function: male celibacy and male bonding and the judicious deployment of female sexuality are part of the same political agenda—the elimination of political enemies and the establishment of saffron power. Though set in the past, *Chanakya* has considerable political relevance for our times.

Notes

1. Uma Chakravarti, 'Whatever Happened to the Vedic Dasi', in Kumkum Sangari and Sudesh Vaid, (eds.), *Recasting Women: Essays on Colonial History*, Delhi: Kali for Women, 1989.

2. See, for example, the sample of writing on the film *Roja*: Tejaswini Niranjana, 'Integrating Whose Nation? Tourists and Terrorists in *Roja*', *Economic and Political Weekly*, Vol. 29.3, 15 January 1994, pp. 79–82; Venkatesh Chakravarthy and M.S.S. Pandian, 'More on *Roja*', *Economic and Political Weekly*, Vol. 29.11, 12 March 1994, pp. 642–44; Rustam Bharucha, 'On the Border of Fascism: Manufacture of consent in *Roja*', *Economic and Political Weekly*, Vol.29.23, 4 June 1994, pp. 1389–395.

3. Iqbal Masud, 'Images of Dominance', *Indian Express*, 16.8.92.

4. Ibid.; Parita Maitra, 'Master of the Game', *Sunday*, 22nd October-2nd November, 1991, pp. 44–53.

5. Masud, 'Images of Dominance', op. cit.

6. *Chanakya* was telecast in 1991–92. It was directed by Chandraprakash Dwivedi who also featured in the main role. His brother produced the serial and also featured in one of the roles. The initial episodes were extremely gripping and very well crafted. A significant aspect of the serial was its use of detailed research to recreate the past which enhanced its claim to authenticity. Further, many of its characters were well cast, some of the actors having been trained in the National School of Drama. In this the serial was a contrast to the epics on television which conformed more closely to what is described as 'Parsi theatre'. These features might also account for the limited appeal of *Chanakya* mainly to an upper caste, middle class, and a sanskritised Hindi speaking constituency, i.e., the dominant north Indian intelligentsia. The serial was accorded a special status by the *Indian Express* which carried a weekly column on Sunday morning providing a summary of the episode for that week, frequently accompanied by a photograph. It is currently being re-run on Zee TV (July 97).

7. Kumkum Sangari, 'Consent, Agency and Rhetorics of Incitement', *Economic and Political Weekly*, Vol. 28.18, 1 May 1993, pp. 867–82; Kumkum Roy, 'The King's Household:

Structure/space in the sastric tradition', *Economic and Political Weekly*, Vol. 27.43–44, 24–31 October 1992, pp. WS 55–60.

8. Prita Maitra, 'Master of the Game', op. cit.

9. R.S. Tripathi, *History of Ancient India*, Delhi: Motilal Banarasidass, 1937, pp. 146–50.

10. Har Prasad Shastri, *Journal of the Asiatic Society of Bihar*, 1910, pp. 259 ff.

11. Cited in Masud, 'Images of Dominance', op. cit.

12. Jawaharlal Nehru, *The Discovery of India*, Delhi: Oxford University Press, 1982, p. 123.

13. Uma Chakravarti, *The Social Dimensions of Buddhism*, Delhi: Oxford University Press, 1987, pp. 36–39.

14. For a similar argument see Paola Bacchetta, 'Hindu Nationalist Women as Ideologues: The Sangh, the Samiti, and differential concepts of the Hindu nation', Kumari Jayawardena and Malathi de Alwis, (eds.) *Embodied Violence: Communalising Women's Sexuality in South Asia*, Delhi: Kali for Women, 1996, pp. 126–67, p. 148.

15. E.R. Leach, 'Magical Hair', *Journal of the Royal Anthropological Institute of Great Britain*, Vol. 88, 1958, pp. 147–64; Gananath Obeyesekere, *Medusa's Hair*, Chicago: University of Chicago Press, 1981, pp. 33–34; 45–50.

16. Jaishankar Prasad, *Dhruvswamini*, Allahabad: Leader Press, 1974, pp. 22–24.

17. Miranda House Hindi Dramatic Society's production of *Dhruvswamini*, 22–23 December, 1995.

18. For an interesting discussion of the *Virangana* see Kathryn Hansen, 'The *Virangana* in North Indian History: Myth and popular culture', *Economic and Political Weekly*, Vol. 23.18, 30 April 1988, pp. WS 25–33.

19. Paola Bacchetta, 'Hindu Nationalist Women as Ideologues', op. cit., p. 154.

20. R.P. Kangle, *The Kautiliya Arthasastra*, Vol. I, Delhi: Motilal Banarsidass, 1972, pp. 265–67.

21. K. Balagopal, 'Why Did December 6 Happen?', *Economic and Political Weekly*, Vol. 28.17, 24 April 1993, pp. 790–93, p. 791.

22. Kumkum Sangari, 'Consent, Agency and Rhetorics of Incitement', pp. 877–79.

23. S. Anitha et. al., 'Interviews With Women' in Tanika Sarkar and Urvashi Butalia, (eds.) *Women and the Hindu Right: A Collection of Essays*, Delhi: Kali for Women, 1995, pp. 328–35.

Uneven Modernities and Ambivalent Sexualities

Women's constructions of puberty in coastal Kanyakumari, Tamilnadu

Kalpana Ram

Introduction

In a volume that subtitles itself "The Sexual Economies of Modern India", I wish to begin with some reflections on the dilemmas and legacies that derive from debates in Marxist political economy. Tropes such as unevenness when referring to Indian modernity immediately recall debates that have been particularly well elaborated in the Indian context, producing a vocabulary of uneven development and of articulation between capitalist and pre-capitalist modes of production. The debate on political economy has now shifted, in some quarters, to a debate around the cultural components of modernity.[1] Some of the characteristic dilemmas and questions, however, have not changed. The ambiguities once attendant on development, when viewed from the perspective of the 'Third World' rather than from the advanced metropoles of capitalism, are now displaced to the sphere of power (more broadly conceived than before) and subjectivity. Where once we had recourse to notions of articulation between modes of production, or various shades of 'semi-ness' (as in arrested development) in order to characterise Indian modes of production, we now wonder how to characterise a modernity that does not or cannot (depending on the perspective of the theorist) deliver the full emancipatory promise of rationalism, secularism and freedom from the bonds of class, caste and gender.

The problems with utilising eurocentric theorisations of power also persist. Foucault's pioneering insights into the capacity of discourses of power to produce and form subjects are evidently of great use, and in this essay I draw inspiration particularly from his delineation of embodied sites of modernity such as bio-medicine and sexuality, which cannot be reduced to the organisational powers of the modern state. However, while his failure to interrogate the colonial construction of European modernity has been particularly noticeable to those in postcolonial locations, we have yet to trace all the theoretical effects of this failure.[2] To what extent, for example, are some of the problems that haunt his formulations of power an effect of taking the self-sufficiency of European modernity at face value? For all his insistence on the formation of resistance at the sites of power, his metaphors of power and governmentality as "capillary-like" conjure an all-pervasive power that is all the more total for its being de-centred.

Could such a totalising vision of modernity, so all-encompassing, have arisen from the perspective of Indian modernity? I suggest not, if only because modernity in the colonies is characteristically experienced not as a unilinear triumphant conquest over the old, but instead as a contradictory necessity to invoke tradition both as a resource for nationalism *and* as the recalcitrant material that must be opposed, reformed and "recast".[3]

These different subject positions in relation to modernity have in turn shaped social theory in the West and in India. Here I will concern myself with just one dimension of this vast topic, namely, with the conceptualisation of time. In classical western social theory, a certain taken-for-granted homogeneity of the time of modernity is made possible by projecting difference in time on to the colonised other. In my discipline of anthropology, the denial of a time that is co-eval, or shared between anthropologist and the people who are written about, characterises more than the writing practice that Johannes

Fabian has explored.[4] It stems, as Fabian himself would argue, from an older colonising structuration of time as linear, progressive, culminating in the time of European modernity, and of tradition as a time that lingers on in the non-European world. The construction of difference is allied, in this formulation, to the colonial subject's inhabiting of a time outside that of the modern, scientific enquirer/observer. The artifice of an anthropological time-present rests on such bifurcations between the time of the enquirer and the time of the subject of enquiry. Time-present in anthropology does not refer to present time, but rather to an artificial, synchronic, temporal form.[5]

It is precisely the dilemmas of subjectivity generated for the colonised by such formulations of time that have propelled historiography to the fore as one of the master disciplines for Indian nationalism and for the postcolonial state.[6] The overwhelming tendency of Indian historiography to insert Indian life into the cultural and temporal homogeneity of secular-rationalist versions of modernity may be sympathetically understood as an effort to resist colonial versions of difference. However, this effort has engendered its own problems, notably the dilemma that in this secular-rationalist narrative, Indian modernity can never be located in the present. Instead, Indian historiography and social theories of modernisation have typically identified modernity as a mission yet-to-be-accomplished, endlessly deferred to a future that depends on conquering the persistance of tradition.

These differences in turn shape the divergent critiques of modernity that emerge in the West as opposed to India. Where a Foucault can only imagine sites of subversion and resistance which already presume the constitutive power of modern disciplinary formations, resistant historians in India have had no trouble in conceiving of a "subaltern" domain, turning for their subject matter to caste, religion and kinship as so many radical internal differences *within* Indian modernity. Where the enunciation of a *post-* modernity is a radical, if contested gesture in the West, in India an equivalent gesture would be to finally locate modernity in the present, in all its contradictoriness and messiness.

Hitherto representable only in the more imaginative world of literary fiction where a writer like Rushdie can embrace and celebrate India's richness of social relations without any sense of contradiction, a recognition of difference is moving at last into the disciplinary grids of the modernising social sciences and humanities. Tropes of 'doubleness' and 'multiplicity' recur in recent formulations. Veena Das, for example, has argued that major institutions, whether ostensibly traditional, such as caste and religion, or modern like the law courts, are all in fact subject to a double articulation. Each is coloured and re-constituted by the other.[7] Kumkum Sangari pluralises the concept of patriarchy in an effort to represent a feminist reworking of the Indian theme of unity in diversity: namely, multiple patriarchies that are operative in the one social formation.[8]

Representing Sexuality

These developments in social theory represent only partial gains. Our theoretical language does not at present have the resources with which to articulate different temporalities and subjectivities while also being able to show how they are all organised, as well, to co-exist in a single time-dimension. Nevertheless, the partial openings have particular implications for our capacity to represent sexuality. For representations of sexuality, like representations of gender relations more generally, bear the marks of colonial/nationalist history, reflecting the shaping power of the reified polarities of capitalist versus pre-capitalist, or modernity versus tradition. Such polarities allow the rich complexity of domains such as sexuality to evaporate in the very process of achieving representation.[9] Sexuality, and perhaps particularly female sexuality, is organised and discursively produced not through one but a number of competing discursive formulations that bear the mark of diverging social relations (caste, class) that are identifiable not only in terms of space (region), but time (periodicities).

This essay's ethnographic location is among the coastal women of Kanyakumari District, Tamilnadu. Here, discourses of social reform aimed at reconstructing sexuality co-exist, albeit in uneasy fashion, alongside discourses that enjoy archaic, pre-colonial resonances. Discourses of spirit possession, for example, retain their capacity to shape subjectivity and experiences of the body.[10] Yet, such experiences of possession coexist with discourses of social reform that have permeated right down to the rural labouring poor, where they continue to enjoy a lively existence through the efforts of school teachers, doctors, and nurses, non-government organisations and radicalised clergy.[11] These publicly circulating discourses of social reform have been imbibed and turned into the site of individual re-fashionings of the body, particularly in its gendered and sexualised dimensions. Modernity, even among the elites, is internally various, contradictory and selective in the understandings and practices that are assembled. They emerge afresh as ambivalences and selectivities in renditions of both tradition and modernity among rural villagers.

This chapter traces the effects of the doubling and splitting of subjectivity as they are lived by women in a poor Catholic fishing village. In November/December of 1991, I conducted interviews with groups of women I had already come to know well through previous field work in the eighties. I also conducted interviews in the agricultural villages of Chengalpattu district, in order to begin some comparative field work, but these interviews are, inevitably, partial, and only occasionally drawn on here. In addition I sought out women who had attended the health classes run by the local non-government organisation (hereafter NGO), the Kottar Social Service Society, run by Belgian Catholics. Some of the women had been recruited as village level animators for these classes. I also interviewed the teachers at the local village primary school. I was accompanied at my request by an old friend, Stella, who once worked as health coordinator for the Kottar Social Service Society (hereafter KSSS), and is now running her own NGO organisation in Chengalpattu. The questions, loosely taking inspiration from Emily Martin's questionnaire in *The Woman in the Body*,[12] asked the women (among other things) to describe their own experiences when coming of age, and also to consider how they would treat their daughter's coming of age.

What is elicited in our shared interaction is not experience as some raw datum, but the women's explicit attempts to synthesise —at the level of an orally related biography—their past, present and future. Two discourses emerged as particularly significant in their experience of puberty. The first concerns a ritual through which the advent of a fertile sexuality is heralded to the village but more specifically to marriageable kin. The second is a moral discourse which requires the emergent pubescent girl to become a woman through submission to a code of bodily disciplines and restrictions, that accompany her efflorescent sexuality. Before examining the women's negotiation of these discourses, their milieu needs to be situated ethnographically and historically. Responses to a puberty ritual already presume, for example, a construction of female sexuality that is specific to region and caste. I will also attempt to historicise the available ethnnographic representations in order to see how the ritual is located within those wider constructions of masculine power and sexuality that have been given a new life in the politics of Dravidian cultural nationalism.

Anthropological Discourses on Dravidian Kinship and Sexuality

Anthropological discourses on kinship suffer, as Carol Vance has argued,[13] from a tendency to naturalise sexuality in spite of their efforts to demonstrate cultural variability. In what she terms a weak version—by far the most prevalent model—of cultural constructionism, demonstrations of variability in culture co-exist quite comfortably with the assumption of sexuality as an underlying universal substratum that is simply manifested in different ways. I suggest, however, that anthropological discourse on kinship and ritual can, if recast, provide vital sources of insight. I suggest we read these discourses not as pointing to variations on a pre-existing human essence (although I wish to leave open the question of that which precedes, and exceeds the shaping power of culture), but as active sites in which sexuality, desire, and affect, as well as gender specific subjectivities, are produced and renegotiated. Modalities of kinship have been used in anthropological discourse to map out a very specific region in which female sexuality is produced in a relatively public, visible and celebratory fashion in and through a ritual marking of the advent of menarche in a girl. In an extensive across-regional survey of the puberty ceremony for girls, Good[14] maps the region as not only including the four linguistic zones of southern India, but as reaching down into Sri Lanka, and extending north as far as the Madhya Pradesh-Orissa border of central India. This regional mapping is integrally bound, in this view, with the distinctively southern system of prescriptive marriage which, as Louis Dumont put it in his celebrated formulations,[15] means that affinity is inherited, rather than made afresh at the time of marriage.

The culturalist biases of the American school of ethnography have meant that the social basis for Tamil cultural meanings regarding sexuality and gender are seen as located entirely in the sphere of kinship. In my own previous work[16] as in Karin Kapadia's ethnography,[17] we have argued that these symbolic constructions of female sexuality are materially grounded, insofar as they are found not simply in the south, but are particularly elaborated among those caste communities where women also work in the public sphere, as among the Mukkuvars, where women partake of the sphere of trade in fish, or among the Pallars, in rice cultivation. But even this argument, with its exclusive focus on labour and fertility, seems unduly limited to me now.

Anthropologists are being asked to confront the fact that the rituals and kinship systems they document and take to be cultural wholes are in reality nothing more than surviving and rearticulated fragments of more widely articulated systems of power and meaning in pre-colonial societies.[18] In the light of the rich ethno-historiographical work on the late precolonial state in south India,[19] the puberty ritual seems precisely that—a fragment. It is the fragment of a pre-colonial system which constructed both female and male power simultaneously in ritual contexts that ranged from the village rituals of puberty, to the elaborate theatres of power enacted in temples and courts. Even among castes that celebrate fertility as a relatively autonomous female domain within the terms of the puberty ceremony, the mother's brother enacts a model of masculinity that reconstitutes, on a micro-level, more widely employed codes of masculine honour. These codes have a historical depth in Tamilnadu, where kinship has historically been integrated with wider processes of state formation and chiefly authority. The public display of generosity and the privilege of ruling on behalf of a superior were the central modalities through which sovereignty was multiplied, but also regularised in large scale empires such as the Vijayanagara Kingdom, surviving into the twentieth century in princely states like Pudukottai.[20] Such processes were not unified, but rather, segmentary and duplicative.[21] It is therefore not altogether surprising to find a duplication in the ritualised codes of masculinity adopted even by agricultural labouring men who nevertheless enjoy their own little kingdom with respect to the female members of their kin group.

Masculine and Feminine Sexuality in the Construction of a 'Dravidian' Modernity

Such constructions of kingship are not as culturally distant as the historical periodisation of pre-colonial, colonial and postcolonial suggests. Contrasts between Brahminic Hinduism and the non-Brahminic complex have consequencs for the particular versions of modernity that have evolved. In Tamilnadu, the existence of divergent constructions of kinship, sexuality and gender, like the more conspicuous use of language itself, has provided raw materials for the making of a Dravidian modern. The construction of an anti-Brahmin, anti-colonial, avowedly Tamil modernity in this century has breathed new life into these codes of honour and kingship. In contesting the rise of Brahminic power as a professional and administrative elite class under colonial rule in Tamilnadu[22] the bypassed non-Brahmin castes mobilised readily available alternative codes of authority and power. Orators and film makers conveyed to audiences pride in the fact that the great Tamil kings had, after all, been non-Brahmin.[23] In the masculine gendering of the Tamil nation, warrior-king codes of virility, generosity and public constructions of honour, rank and privilege have become markers of successful party leaders, culminating in the apotheosis of "the MGR phenomenon".[24]

How did these redefinitions work in the sphere of femininity and feminine sexuality? The overriding construction of femininity in the Dravidian movement has been that of chaste women and heroic mothers.[25] Women's honour has been represented in terms far more restrictive than men's, tied firmly to their status within kin groups and to the sphere of sexuality. Thus women can only establish their honour in relation to their chastity and their virtue as mothers, while men gain yet another additional sphere in which to provide their uniquely 'Tamil' credentials as defenders of female chastity and maternal dedication. I will not enter here into the lively and ongoing debate as to whether and to what extent the Dravidian movement ever offered women a wider vision of subjecthood.[26] It is important to note, however, that the construction of a Tamil modernity carries within it much more than the politics of cultural nationalism. It also offers a social critique in the name of an egalitarian and rational modernity. The revitalisation of codes of masculine and feminine honour reflects the impact of *both* these strands. Under E.V. Ramaswamy Naicker, *mānam* or honour became redefined as *tanmānam* or the honouring of one's own personal code of ethics; while *mariyātai* or respect became *suya-mariyātai*, or Self-Respect, from which the movement took its name. Such notions of a personalised code of honour departed significantly from codes of honour based on inherited status.[27]

While it is true that these redefinitions of honour still remained a largely masculinist prerogative, they have also inflected the coding of female honour as chastity. After all, the literary classics that the Dravidian movement drew so freely from, display a far wider range of meanings for female sexuality than the motif of chastity will allow. They include, also, a strikingly overt and robust expression of female erotic ardour that was embellished and developed in the court and temple traditions of dance and song. There is, therefore, a selective narrowing in the construction of Tamil tradition. The political context in which chastity was picked out as the defining virtue of Tamil women deserves more recognition. The cultural hegemony of the Victorian-Brahmin reconstruction of patriarchy not only deprived such traditions of female sexuality of their material basis in the courtly-temple nexus, they actively made it impossible to continue a celebration of such values. The controversies around the re-definition of the devadasi tradition as a form of prostitution were complex and need not be entered into here.[28] What is clear is that for the leaders of the non-Brahmin movement—many of whom were sons of devadasis, and, in the case of women like Moovalur Ramamirtham Ammaiyar, themselves ex-devadasis[29]—the reclamation of honour in this politically charged context entailed affirming the chastity of non-Brahmin women. In a future move, the blame for the prostitution of non-Brahmin women was placed squarely onto the Brahminic priestly class as the upholders of such a debased religion.

Most studies of the Dravidian movement have emphasised the emptying out of all elements of radical critique in the quest for nationalism and electoral power.[30] However, in the rural areas of Tamilnadu, agendas of social reform continue to be fuelled by enlightenment critiques. Price[31] finds that when one looks away from the top party leadership to the cadre living in rural Madurai, the message of the DMK continues to be identified above all with having taught certain universalist values.

The Politics of Enlightenment: Sexuality in Christian Kanyakumari

It should be clear by now that I am not arguing for any one set of connections between modernity and sexuality. In some parts of Tamilnadu, the politics of non-Brahminism encouraged wealthy mercantile castes such as the Chettiars to adopt the most elaborate versions of female puberty ceremonies.[32] In sharp contrast, the Christian communities of Kanyakumari, the radicalised clergy and non-government organisations (both Christian and non-Christian) keep alive the kind of peculiar blend of missionary and rationalist scientistic critique of village beliefs that marks the politics of "enlightenment in the colonies".[33] The thrust here is to modernise gender relations into a more egalitarian version of patriarchal norms, based on the mutually respectful couple rather than on the wider kin-based social organisation of sexuality.[34]

The coastal villages of Kanyakumari are located at the regional intersections of Tamil and Kerala politics. In addition to the impact of Tamil modernity, they are exposed to the activist communist traditions of Kerala, particularly notable for its interventions in literacy, health and education. Part of the Travancore kingdom till 1956, Kanyakumari District is heir to an era of reform in public health and land reform that began with the princely rulers of the nineteenth century.[35] Kerala-based social movements represented by such groups as the Kerala Shastra Sahitya Parishad include the Kanyakumari town of Nagercoil in their tours which seek to popularise scientific and rationalist values in the rural population. They find a ready response among non-government organisations in the district, including the radicalised Christian non-government organisations working in the coastal villages, such as the Kottar Social Service Society.

The contrast between tradition and modernity in these discourses of reform emerges most sharply as the opposition between science and ritual. Biomedical discourses, displaying their scientific authority, are opposed to ritual constructions of the body. This opposition radically simplifies the actual complexity of village prescriptions on the body. People refer to local medical discourses as much as ritual ones. When questioned about menstruation, for example, village women point out that without menstruation, "we [women] would get sick, our bodies would become bloated. There would be stomach boils, related to lack of bodily balance and imbalance of heat." As Maria Pushpam put it:

> It is good to have regular periods—it is bad for the body if it does not come.

Another woman, Jeannette, said:

> The blood should flow, or else we have illness.

In reformist discourses, however, such local knowledges, based on a humoral physiology culled from the practitioners of Siddha medical traditions, as well as on village cures, are all ignored. Instead, ritual comes to stand for the entirety of tradition as in the following extract from a girl's letter which is singled out for reproduction in the text of one of the reformist clergy, Fr. Alphonse:

> When I came of age, I was only thirteen. I was devastated by my fear and ignorance of changes in my body. My parents called everyone and had a feast, they decked me with flowers and decoration, jewellery and goodness knows what else. But about the changes in my body they told me nothing. They did not have even a little bit of *arivu* [knowledge].[36]

One of the important elements in the redefinition of local discourse I wish to trace here concerns the redefinition of *arivu* or knowledge. This is a term which is also significant in village women's notions of moral sensibility (see below). In the hands of an enlightenment discourse, it is transformed to mean the use of physiology that will explain the inner workings of the body in a scientific way. Such modern, rationalist redefinitions of knowledge appear also among women who have had lessons from the Kottar Social Service Society:

> **Amala Urpam,** [says she would use menstrual charts to teach her daughters,] I have *arivu* now, which dispels fears. I feel KSSS has made changes to hygienic practices, and brought medical awareness to the coast. Girls need education.

Lourdes: I have learned some things from the KSSS health team, that the menstrual blood comes from the uterus [*karppappai*], that this is the excess, waste blood [*kalaivu rattam*] that comes from there.

Pamela Rose: At college I began to read books about reproduction. I even lent it out to a married woman who was too shy to approach the nuns. Since then I have introduced some element of education on family relations in the catechism class I take in the village. I teach them not only about bodily relations, but about the need for undersanding and mutual acceptance of one another in a marriage, the way Father Alphonse describes it.[37] Some of the village girls show interest, others hang their heads and others never reappear.

I interviewed teachers working at the coastal primary school for their experiences of puberty. Here the impact of a scientific medical discourse was more established, but still occasionally represented by the women as a militant advance on tradition and therefore a source of pride.

Maria Pushpam: [I ask her what she thinks of the questions I am putting to her]. I think your questions are aimed at revealing what girls do and do not know. Girls do not know about their bodily makeup [*utal amaippu*]. I use the rhythm method for contraception, I wait for the safe period. During pregnancies I also have check ups and my children have been delivered in hospital.

Vimla, (Headmistress of village primary school, mother of three): I would teach a girl who has come of age that she is now mature enough to be a mother, that there are changes in the uterus. I am approaching a change now, though my periods have not stopped. These things are all part of nature [*īyarkai*], and we should take it on as such.

It is important to note the double-edged nature of the impact of modernity. On the one hand, women who have been interpellated by the discourse of social reform are empowered with a new professional identity that allows them to intervene in the practices of others and to move into a newly expanded female public sphere. On the other hand, the same process constructs women who speak in the name of older, local knowledges, as traditional and superstitious.[38] The transformative qualities of these discourses of modernity are most apparent among those women who work as mediators between the leadership of NGOs and the less educated village women—known in the jargon of NGOs as animators.

> **Health worker Jeannette,** (village animator): My activities in the village involve educating people about disease, immunisations and injections, hygiene and the treatment for diarrhoea. We hold mothers' meetings, suggest writing to the BDO [block development office] about complaints. We have gone there ourselves with the women, who have broken their water pots outside his office to show they have no water, or have demanded electricity. The changes we advise for the women in the area of health is to boil the water. We get them to drink milk and eat eggs during pregnancy, which they feel might make the baby too big and give them a dificult birth. Seventy five per cent change after asking us questions. They are just superstitious [*mudai nambikkai*], just the society speaking. My sister-in-law burnt herself and her spirit was supposed to come over me, but my tongue has been loosened since going to the KSSS and I ask them all: what ill has befallen me since I have done all the things I should not have?

> **Victoria,** (NGO health worker in Chengalpattu): The sisters at the convent at Porur suggested I train for social work —my parents worked there for the nuns as servants. I was trained in speech and dress, and given a cycle, I was only fifteen then. They taught me not to giggle, but to mix with people, to work diligently. When I went out on my work, people would talk: look at her go with an umbrella, like some teacher. I would ignore them, or talk back: Did you have to pay for my umbrella? I was afraid of men when I first got married, and told my husband quite early on not to insist, or harass me when my body is not right, like during my periods. My husband has agreed. Now he also sometimes says he is tired, or not wanting to, and I feel I can say that too. We use the rhythm method. I learned in workshops, to watch my discharge and avoid the fertile period.

Such a conferral of new, activist identities on to rural women is part of a long history of mission initiatives in the Travancore region.[39] Tracing the contradictory effects of mission discourse, Haggis finds that the very activism demanded of the lady missionary and her Bible women bequeathed a legacy of female professionalism. These Bible women were, like the animators Victoria and Jeannette of our time, recruited from rural castes low in the local hierarchy. Their reports, recorded in 1897, strikingly echo Victoria's account of the taunts she endured for carrying an umbrella, signifier of high status:

> For six months we walked past the mosques without getting permission to go into a single house to teach the women... they would not allow us to carry an umbrella or a bag and sometimes snatched away our books and tore them.[40]

The animators display exactly this mix of daring and resilience enabled by their newly gained position as educators. By contrast, women who have settled into their professional role, employed by schools and hospitals, display more of the other side of modernity. Here, the women's self-perception as bearers of a superior way of life becomes the basis for class distinction. In their self-representation as professional women whose job it is to teach the children of the coastal villagers, the discourses of science and rationalism serve not only to reinforce previously formed inequalities, but to create the means for new class differences. I have argued this elsewhere,[41] and will content myself with just one example:

> **Vimla:** Now the villagers in the coast—they neither take pregnancies as a time to take sensible precautions, nor will they stop having children. To them, it is like eating and drinking and going to the toilet—everyday bodily functions. Yet they complain endlessly of their special burdens. They should see pregnancy as a time of special joys and responsibilities, and should not see themselves as sick patients. As for myself, I have taught at school right uptil the last moment, before the onset of labour in both my childbirths. I have always had a strong will in these matters.

The bulk of the women I interviewed along with my co-interviewer Stella, belonged, however, neither to the category of professional school teachers, nor to the quasi-professionalised category of mediators between non-government organisations and villagers. Rather, they were coastal women who either worked as fish traders, as household managers of finance, or as wives and mothers. They were also a divided stratum, because of their varying levels of education. Their responses, more than any others, have inspired the title of this essay, "Uneven Modernities".

Ruptures and Ambivalences in Female Bodily Hexis

The impact of modernity on the sexual knowledgeability and forwardness of the young was a widely shared object of commentary by older men and women in the villages (both fishing and agricultural), as well as among school teachers. When I asked women if they would give their daughters more information about menstruation and sexuality than they had themselves received, the answer was often:

> Don't our kids know enough already? They see it in all the movies and read it in all the books these days.

> **Beatrice,** the teacher, reports it thus: Today's kids know so much, they know it all. They get ideas from films and books, so that girls won't sit with boys, even as little children—they think it is too much like husband and wife.

Old women also regarded the children of today as knowing a great deal more about sexuality than in their days. While interviewing old women in an agricultural labouring village in the district of Chengalpattu, they recalled their own marriages consummated soon after puberty and contrasted themselves with today's children:

> Today there is *unarchi* [understanding, form of knowing linked with feeling and emotion] and even kids still wearing *pāvatais* [i.e. prepubertal] do not have any shyness.

A Nadar potter of Kanyakumari, inclined to moralism, contrasts the *verkam* or modesty of girls in the old days:

> In the *pandeyakālam* [the days of the Pandian king, old days], the

girl coming of age would be shy, she would be kept isolated. Now there is knowledge and progress. In the old days brides would keep their eyes covered with betel leaf, so that they need not know where they were being taken—today she lifts her head even as the *tāli* is being tied, and all is considered finished once she has done a *namaskāram* to the mother-in-law!

Asked to reconstruct their experience of puberty, and to consider which elements of their treatment they would repeat for their daughters, the coastal women's responses indicated significant ruptures in some elements of generational transmission of the unquestioned, taken-for-granted reproduction of bodily habits. There was a striking selectivity in terms of the way women negotiate more dominant constructions of modernity and of tradition. Some elements were admitted through and were not only valued by the women, but were described as essential aspects they would attempt to pass on to their daughters. Others, however, were minimised, devalued, or rejected outright. The main single element of traditional culture to be minimised or rejected was the puberty ritual. This minimisation took several forms, and I have grouped them under different headings.

Humorous Distancing: Then they came and fed us that "poisonous stuff"

Lourdes is unmarried, 26 years old, and a lively, cheeky young woman, who felt very much at ease with us, being well known to me and related to Stella. Our interview was therefore intimate and often hilarious. She is the youngest of three sisters, and talks about how she knew, from very early, what puberty entailed. She refers to the procedures as "knowing what was in store", humorously re-describing all the main elements of the treatment of puberty. In her version, the seven days of seclusion inside the house becomes rendered as "being shut up and left to rot indoors". The special foods, such as the eggs and the oil brought to the girl to enhance her fertility are rendered as "that poison they bring you". She derived additional mileage out of the fact that they kept up the special diet for seven days instead of three, pointing to her plump form and saying, "Maybe that is why I am like this!" There was no public ceremony performed for her, and asked what she thinks of this, she again makes a joke of it:

> Sure, I'd like one tomorrow! Next month! Get some saris, some jewellery, have some money spent on me!

Lourdes has attended classes on health and reproduction run by the Kottar Social Service Society, and her elder sister was one of the local women coordinating the meetings. She has been influenced by her association with the classes, and told us of the topics covered: social reform, social work, women's liberation, women's rights, sex and reproduction. She tells us she prefers hospitalised births. "New ways and methods are better than old time customs," she tells us. Her elder married sister now lives in Bangalore, giving Lourdes access to the ways of the big city, and she points out that hospital medicines are just as good as village remedies. Here too she gives a characterisistic light touch when talking about what she has learned from KSSS:

> If I was a knowing sort of girl before, KSSS sure spoilt me good and proper! I already knew from shared lavatories and where women wash clothes, about how pregnancy occurs: after marriage, if the flow stops for two months, accompanied by nausea and tiredness, one is pregnant. But with KSSS I was made really "bad"!

Beatrice, the primary school teacher, also reveals a light hearted approach in the way she talks to the young girls in her charge if they look as if they are nearing the time of menarche:

> I say to the girls: Get ready with oil and eggs! No, I don't take it too seriously, I tell the girls, get ready to wear a sari, it won't be long now!

However, such deft and spirited negotiations concerning the ritualised injunctions surrounding menstruation are not restricted to young, more modernised women. Claramma is 66 years old and talks about how she simply used to get around the restrictions on menstruating women by not telling anyone:

> I went to have a bath in Muttom, where they said it was infested with demons. I went at night, with my periods. Nothing happened

—absolutely nothing. I told no one about the periods, or they would not have let me. If I wanted to go urgently to a ritual occasion, it became a nuisance. If one has to go—just don't let anyone know.

Economic considerations

Many women expressed reservations based on the economic costs of holding a public ritual. They made distinctions between the different levels at which it could be celebrated, depending on who, outside the circle of kinship, was invited, whether or not a feast for the wider community was held, whether or not a movie was shown. For most families, holding a public ceremony (*satanku*) meant inviting only kinspeople, not making it a grand affair. The management of expenses and money is a uniquely female sphere in the fishing community, so women who expressed concern over the costs were intimately involved in making ends meet against the fluctuating cycle of the men's catch.[42]

> **Antoniammal:** When it comes to my daughter's turn, I would rather not have the expenses of a *satanku*, I would just call the relevant kinspeople and have a simple affair, not a big feast or anything. There is simply no need for the whole village to know. It was difficult even when I came of age—my father had just died, I did not think we should have the *satanku* because of the expenses involved (Generally, anyway, we wait for the good fishing season before we hold the ceremony for our girls.) But then, my mother needed the support from her kinspeople, as well as the gifts they would give as part of the occasion.

> **Pamela Rose**, (27, unmarried, educated, with B.A. degree in English from Tiruvaiyaru, partly employed): I felt worried and guilty about costing my family so much, at a time when there was such poverty in our midst. I felt, couldn't this have come at another time?

Claramma redirected our discussion of sexuality towards problems of economic burden. She saw no sense in my talk of "freedom". I had been talking of freedom from male-dominated definitions of sexuality and beauty. She transformed this discourse into one based on economic unfreedom:

> In those countries you speak of [where women experience the pressures of having to look young and attractive to men, (i.e. Australia)] there is so much money, the only problem is who to give it away to. Here, I have a handicapped son who needs care, and there is no money for facilities; one unmarried daughter and no money for dowry; and one daughter with five children, who is ill so much of the time, I have to care for the children.

This is women's secret, "peṇkaḷ rahasyam"

The function of the ritual is precisely to render the girl's coming of age a matter of public knowledge. The ritual is a *vilambaram* or advertisement to the public. If the public sphere defined by the ritual was one specific to caste and kinship, today, with the impact of the media, the public is more widely defined as in the practice in larger cities of taking out advertisements in newspapers to announce female puberty in much the same manner as one would advertise marriages, or the death of a significant family member. For those who view the ritual with a newly modern distaste, it is precisely this *vilambaram* or advertising function of the ritualised construction of female sexuality that has become improper:

> **Lourdes:** If I had a daughter, I would keep her only one day at home, and send her back to school the next day. I would not have a *sataṅku*—do not wish to *advertise* it. [Lourdes uses the English word here.]

Some of the respondents made it clear that the public construction of menarche was being judged in terms of its more privatised construction as a feminine secret:

> **Maria Pushpam,** (39 years old Primary school teacher): I would not have any public ceremony for my daughter's attaining age. It is a female secret [*peṇkaḷ rahasyam*]. There is simply no need to inform the whole *ūru* [village, native place] of this matter.

Others made it clear that the transition from public to privatised constructions of female sexuality had strategic value in terms of the economic and cultural shame attached to having unmarried post-pubertal daughters. This is an increasing social problem in the fishing community, and in Kanyakumari District more generally, where there is an unusually high incidence of female literacy and most women marry after they are 19 years of age.[43]

> **Beatrice,** (School teacher): People are starting to wonder about the ceremony—why should we let everyone know? Passing men can then comment and do *keli* [tease, mock]. Hindu customs are there to advertise that our girl has come of age, she is available for marriage. At the same time now if there are two such girls in a family and they are both unmarried, people will talk. So parents worry and grieve over the girls—how are we to marry them? It is better not to have any ceremony, better to keep it to ourselves.

Even the presence of girls in the classroom becomes the occasion for new clashes between the sexualised body of the puberty ritual and the ostensibly ungendered body of the school child. Girls are withdrawn abruptly from the "modern" space of the classroom, inducted into the sexualised space of kinship and ritual, and then have to come back and negotiate the teasing from classmates and from boys.

> **Teacher:** They get teased by the boys. They call out: Has the pot cracked then?

In addition, the church, an overwhelming presence in coastal villages,[44] does not support the puberty ritual—making this the only life cycle ritual that is not officiated by a Catholic priest.[45] There is evidence that for some, the First Communion is beginning to replace the puberty ceremony:

> **Santhoos Mary:** There was no *satańku*—in our family, there is no such custom. We feel it is not right for people to get to know about it. Instead, we had a grand First Communion for me. But even then, my mother resented the big fuss my father's sister made over her contribution to the communion, so we dropped all such celebrations after that.

Moral bodily disciplines in the making of the female sexed subject

Although the anthropological gaze has been fascinated by the ritual, an equally, if not more significant aspect of the transition from pre-pubertal to womanly status is the moral discourse of instructions on bodily disciplines and restrictions, which accompanies the transition. The reason for the neglect of this dimension is quite possibly because it is not available for the anthropological gaze in the way that the more spectacular public ritual is. Even this more limited focus on the ritual has been rendered primarily in terms of the symbolic language of the ritual itself. The subjectivity of the women who undergo the ritual has not, for the most part, been a concern of the anthropological account. The underlying assumption seems to be that this subjectivity can be assumed, as something that can be read off the language of the ritual. We have seen already that this is not necessarily the case at all. We now come to a further complexity. There is a discourse which is not public but which in fact turns out to enjoy far greater shaping power over the subjectivity of women than the public fanfare of the ritual. This discourse revolves around the concept of *kaṭappāṭu*, which may be glossed in English as disciplines, but also as the duties and obligations which are incumbent on the girl after the ritual transition to womanhood. In practice, *kaṭappāṭu* refers to the daily schooling of the female body in keeping one's bodily motility and language under control.[46] The nature of these instructions was conveyed by the women to us in conventionalised, generalised terms:

> Do not go "here and there". [*inge ange pōkāte*]
> There is no need to go out too much any more.
> From now on, learn to behave yourself.

I have noted that the semantic field around the disciplinary tutelage of *kaṭappāṭu* is intertwined with notions of duties and obligations. This intermingling of meanings meant that *kaṭappāṭu* became immune from criticism or resentment. Far from being equated with a loss of freedom, most women and girls saw such restraint as marking the moment at which they stood on the threshold of becoming adult, a properly social occasion. Pre-pubertal childhood is not romanticised but is seen as a time before the advent of good sense, the more conventional meaning of *arivu* and of *buddhi*. Although these are more general terms that can be applied in a non-gender-specific way, they do carry specific meanings for women. They refer to the development of a form of 'self-consciousness', in which the female self is fashioned on the basis of an awareness of her critical role in upholding the family's reputation and honour. In some ways, this consciousness expands to cover nearly all of a woman's sense of social subjecthood.

When I asked women to describe their childhood, there was puzzlement as to what they could describe. The following description comes from **Karpagam**, sixty year old agricultural labourer from Chengalpattu District:

> I would eat the *puli* [tamarind], play under the trees and near rivers. Using a small peanut for currency, I would play, I would play at making rice with a toy stove. *I did not understand anything*. Then as my *buddhi* increased, I was sent to work for a lady in Madras where my relative was a servant. [Emphasis added].

> **Lourdes:** Certain *katappātu* does come with puberty—do not go out too much, do not talk to others too much. But I felt I now had taken no responsibilities for my family, and I must consult my elders before doing things. A girl needs these disciplines. [I ask her if she did not miss her childhood freedoms]. Well, as a child I was just playing around. Now, I had a sense of how to conduct myself with responsibility.

The moral disciplines which surround the embodied transitions from pre- to post-menarche operate in a totalising way, to encompass physiological, moral and cognitive development. The textual traditions elaborate this totalising schema.[47] What flowers at the point of menarche according to the literary, performative and medical traditions, are not merely the reproductive organs and breasts, but a number of quintessentially 'feminine' *kunam* (Skt. gunas): *accam, matam, nānam, payarippu*. These traits, listed in the chapters on reproduction found in medical Siddha texts,[48] are not obscure. On the contrary, they are readily and commonly listed by contemporary Tamils as the traits of femininity. The Tamil Lexicon, itself a thoroughly contemporary endeavour,[49] undertakes to gloss their meaning as: *accam*: dread, terror; *matam*: ignorance, folly, artlessness; *nānam*: shyness, coyness, shame, sensitive dread of evil, keen moral sense, shrinking as does a startled plant or animal when touched; *payarippu*: disgust, abhorrence, delicacy, modesty, shrinking from anything strange.[50]

The *kunam* are therefore simultaneously emotion, forms of ethical conduct, and forms of cognition, all said to spontaneously flower along with the girl's sexuality. These descriptions strikingly resonate with the women's descriptions of their experiences of the transition to womanhood. In particular, the embodied construction of a specifically feminine morality and cognitive maturity [*buddhi, arivu*] stands out in the women's accounts.

However, there are important divergences between the dominant discourse on female sexuality and the discourses of the women. Where the dominant discourse sees female sexuality as flowering spontaneously, there is nothing spontaneous about this production as far as the women are concerned. Femininity is still integrally a morality for the women, but it is a morality produced by acceptance and internalisation of a hard and rigorous disciplining of ones bodily subjectivity. An account offered by Victoria, now working for an NGO in Chenglepet, gives us a glimpse of how shame and self-awareness, supposedly spontaneously flowering in young women, is experienced by the women themselves as a shift in inter-subjectivity, as a consciousness that is produced in the knowing gaze of others:

> I came of age in the hostel. Older girls had tried to tell me what this was, others just laughed. My mother said I was a big girl now, that I should not laugh, talk or move too freely. I felt shame, so this is what it was, I understood, this is how I will be misunderstood by others if I do not do what mother says.

The arrival of *buddhi* and *arivu* entails undertaking observance of these moral disciplines. The result is not only the making of the self, but the making of the self as a socially responsible being, a process whereby the woman comes to see that the family's good name depends on her. Although the advice is worded in generalising terms "Do not go here and there" [*Inge ange pōkāte*], the girl understands the sexual core of the injunction.

> **Pamela Rose:** I knew what was meant—what they meant by not doing wrong involved not becoming pregnant, now that my periods had started.

In a striking demonstration of a selective rendition of modernity, the women, whether or not they expressed ambivalence about the overtly sexualising, public ritualised treatment of girls' bodies, in all cases fiercely retained the importance of the moral discourse of sexually disciplining the self. Over and over again, our questions as to whether they would educate their girls about menstruation was understood and affirmed by the women in terms of the moral discourse of *katuppātu* in sharp variance to the model of scientific education advocated by discourses of reform.

> **Antoniammal:** My school friends had already told me, that this is how it will come, you will find you have a new sense of wisdom, sense [*buddhi*]. *Buddhi* comes from the coming of age. At the time, I felt shy but also a little proud, not embarrassed. But the *katuppātu* came hard to me. They said I was now a big girl, that I should not go out too much, not mix too much with other children, I should cease roaming around, going out to cinemas and such like, and generally not go too far [from the home]. I felt the passing of a period in my life. Then I came to accept it. It meant, after all, that others would see that I was a well-behaved girl, rather than a bad [*moshamāna*, immoral] one.

Antoniammal strikingly expressed the tautological nature of the system of moral reasoning which identifies coming of age with the acceptance of disciplines:

> After all, *Vītile āna piḷḷai vītile tān irrukaṇam. The girl who has become of the house* [i.e. attained puberty] *cannot but stay in the house.* In terms of my daughter, yes, I would teach her. In those days my

mother was not educated and did not, but I am educated and I would teach her. I educate her in other ways, after all, so I would in this respect as well, I would tell her not to run around any more, to mind her step.

Santi, (woman in her forties): Yes I would teach girls about it beforehand, that this is what will happen, and you must not do certain things. Is it not right to instruct a child who might do the wrong thing? [She elaborates on the instruction]: "You are a girl, others will speak ill of you, reform your ways and behave." That is my way, to teach the young. There are those who resent my instructions to their children. But that is my way.

The theme of replacing social control over sexuality with self-control is not limited to the sphere of sexuality. It merges with a broader compaign to get subjects to take responsibility for their actions—as opposed to attributing it to *pēys* or spirit demons. Fr. John for instance, writes tracts that ask people to see their own imagination, their fear and guilt as the only reason for psychological problems.[51] Resonances of their messages are clearly heard in statements like the following by Lourdes. When asked whether she believes in the discourse about *pēys* that are attracted to girls at the time of menarche, she responds:

Well, this is what the grandmothers say—don't throw out the bloodied rags, it will bring the *pēy*. But I think—well, I am the *pēy*, I am the *pishāshu*, so why would they come to me? My mind, that is the reason for these *pēys*.

Conclusion: Feminism and Divergent Regimes of Sexuality

I have argued that the rationalistic, secular, scientific dimensions of the non-Brahmin movement's construction of modernity continue to exercise an important influence, thanks to the ongoing efforts of those who may be regarded, in the Gramscian sense of the term, as state intellectuals.[52] I have traced these effects both in the ambivalence to puberty as constructed by ritual, and in the upholding of puberty as entailing codes of chastity. Even in the upholding of chastity as female honour, the women interpret it in a specifically activist way, embracing it as a personalised code of conduct in which they as women are responsible for family honour.[53] This is the only available alternative, vastly preferable to becoming the passive objects of disciplining by the family, by the neighbours and by society. Many women openly expressed their special pride in never having given their elders any occasion to explicitly instruct them on how to behave. For example, Beatrice said: "There were no restraints placed on me, because my mother had utmost faith in her daughters." Pamela Rose said: "I did not need to be told these things—I was already a quiet type, went only to the next few houses." This active sense of being responsible for the family's honour is in many ways an extension of coastal women's material sources of independence. Chastity becomes yet another way in which women, particularly in the fishing economy, "look after" their families.

At the same time there are wider sources than the fishing economy for such as activist interpretation of female chastity. The poet Tiruvalluvar, writing between AD 400–500, has been widely popularised by the politics of Tamil language-nationalism. His best known work, the *Tirukkural*, is particularly popular, I would argue, due to its being constructed by the Dravidian movement as "secular", compatible with its own preference for a secular-rational modern. In the *Tirukkural*, the poet raises the banner on behalf of women, setting the tone for the parameters of radical debate on female chastity within contemporary Tamil politics:

cirai kākkum kāppu enceyyum makalir
nirai kākkum kappe talai

I translate it thus:

Of what use is it to the girl to protect her by placing her and watching her in a prison-like home?
To control chastity with one's mind, is the highest form of all.

These debates, conducted exclusively with reference to the parameters of Tamil tradition, do not exhaust the meanings of modernity available to Tamil women. The pan-Indian women's movement provides a widely circulating discourse in which a much more radical reconceptualisation of women's embodied rights has been attempted. A recurring motif in these challenges to patriarchal constructions of female puberty is the contrast between the fear and ignorance in which girls experience the changes in their body, and a feminist demand for knowledge and bodily autonomy. The Marathi street theatre play written and performed in the late eighties, *Mulgi Zhali Āhe* [A girl child is born], critically mimics the generalising injunctions thrown at the girl when she comes to puberty:

> Don't lose control, don't give up your woman's vow:
> Don't speak while looking up, stay in the house;
> Bend your head, look down;
> Walk without looking above, don't let your eyes wander.[54]

A Tamil short story, written by feminist author Ambai, highlights a girl's sense of terrified abandonment when even her mother, hitherto the source of female wisdom and nurturance, becomes the mouthpiece of patriarchal injunctions. This is experienced by her daughter as the mother's fall from a near-autonomous power.[55] The circulation of such feminist critiques, more radical than those offered by the Dravidian movement, mean that when women who are already involved in NGO work are given the opportunity to reflexively reconsider codes of chastity, they are capable of shifting their position with remarkable speed. My field work provided the occasion for one such renegotiation. Stella and I conducted the interviews in Kanyakumari together, and would discuss them, while transcribing, late into the night. On her return to Chengalpattu, the first thing she did was to organise a workshop for adolescent girls. Her talent, which resides particularly in language, both in written and spoken form, will hopefully come through even in my hastily translated notes of the speech I heard her deliver on that occasion:

> **Stella:** What do your parents and elders say when they give you that *tāvaṇi*, those two metres of cloth which are handed out as soon as your body changes?

Girl attending workshop: Do not go out too much, conduct yourself responsibly.

Stella: In this fear we come of age. Have they told you what happens in your bodies? As a result of their ignorance we bear the brunt of folly and blame. The boy is not blamed, but we and not only us girls, but our mothers and fathers and grandparents are blamed. The restrictions start even before puberty. Boys can come home at all hours, after the second show [movies], sleep anywhere. Once we start wearing the sari, it cannot be worn anyhow, but just so, tucked in just right, only then is it modest. There are new kinds of work responsibilities, and we are removed from school. Puberty is a time of dreaming as well as of bodily changes. Puberty is saturated with cinema and video images. Physiological maturing does not mean we are ready to have babies. The legal age is high, but in villages girls are marrying at fifteen. It is regarded as a lessening of the parent's duty, their burden is lightened by marrying us off to someone. But girls are not ready for marriage and babies and this leads to many complications as the girl does not have the maturity to deal with the enormous adjustments to the in-laws' houses.

We are seen as easily spoiled. It is as if we are the food that is cooked today—spoiled tomorrow, or like the flower that opens in the morning—spoiled by evening. Even coming late to puberty, or to marriage or to children, is regarded as a scandal. The virtues of femininity—*accam, nānam, payarippu*—only adopt them if appropriate. Only feel shame if you do wrong, not just for being female, or for saying your name to a stranger, like when I asked you all your names this morning. We blame the men. What about our own values? We take the punishment before we have done wrong, we panic and throw ourselves into wells, or take to abortifacients. If a woman questions, we ourselves tell her: sit down and be quiet. If one girl is suffering or questioning, we must all support her. We are bones, flesh, blood, spirit, human, not worms or insects. Say to yourself, I have life and I must live. We must realise we cannot blame society. Society is also us. What is it to be: to walk looking down at our feet, or with straight torso and looking ahead, as Bharatiyar[56] taught us, so that we too will know what is going on in the world?

The persistent appearance of certain sites of resistance in these feminist tracts, widely separated as they are in region and context, testifies to the existence of certain pan-Indian unities in the way that patriarchal codes have constructed the female body. At the same time, we need to remain alert to differences in emphasis and more substantial qualitative differences of style within these patriarchal codes. A good deal of feminist resistance has been directed at the value of impurity, of shame and seclusion which accompany female menstruation and menarche. Yet, in the light of the ethnographic evidence I have introduced in this paper, many of these values emerge as specifically Brahminic and Sanskritic. The existence of alternative, more celebratory codes of female puberty needs to be recognised. The responses of the coastal Christian women do not encourage feminist romanticism about these alternative codes. Rather, these women are caught up in the construction of a different modernity, engaging the values more relevant to their caste and class location.

I wish to acknowledge the assistance of the Australian Research Council for funding this research. I thank participants in the workshop *Rethinking Indian Modernity: The Political Economy of Sexuality*, August 1996 for their comments, some of which have generated ongoing discussions, particularly with Mary John and Janaki Nair. I also thank participants who heard an early version at SNDT University, October 1996 in a seminar organised by Sujata Patel. Finally I thank Ian Bedford for his editorial assistance. The system of transliterations of Tamil words adopted here is that of the Tamil Lexicon, University of Madras, 1982. Certain names of individuals have been altered to make them less identifiable.

Notes

1. See for example, S. Banerjee, *The Parlour and the Streets: Elite and Popular Culture in Nineteenth Century Calcutta*, Calcutta: Seagull Books, 1989; T. Niranjana, P. Sudhir, V. Dhareshwar, (eds.) *Interrogating Modernity: Culture and Colonialism in India*, Calcutta: Seagull Books, 1993; K.N. Panikkar, *Culture, Ideology, Hegemony: Intellectuals and Social Consciousness in Colonial India*, New Delhi: Tulika, 1995.

2. See for example, A. Stoler, *Race and the Education of Desire*, Durham and London: Duke University Press, 1995. Here I wish rather to highlight problems that exist in Foucault's more general conceptualisation of power itself.

3. I allude here to the title of the pioneering text, K. Sangari and S. Vaid, (eds.) *Recasting Women: Essays in Colonial History*, New Delhi: Kali for Women, 1989.

4. J. Fabian, *Time and the Other: How Anthropology Makes its Object*, New York: Columbia University Press, 1983; J. Fabian, 'Of Dogs Alive, Birds Dead and Time to Tell a Story', in J. Bender and D.E. Wellbery, (eds.) *Chronotypes: The Construction of Time*, Stanford: Stanford University Press, 1991, pp. 185–204.

5. D.W. Cohen, 'La Fontaine and Wamimbi: The anthropology of 'time-present' as the substructure of historical oration,' in J. Render and D.F. Wellbery, (eds.) *Chronotypes*, op. cit., pp. 205–25. The quoted phrase is from p. 211.

6. See for example, Partha Chatterjee's discussion of the urgent call from Bengali nationalists, "We must have a history", Chatterjee, *The Nation and Its Fragments: Colonial and Postcolonial Histories*, Princeton: Princeton University Press, 1993, pp. 76ff.

7. V. Das, *Critical Events: An Anthropological Perspective on Contemporary India*, Delhi: Oxford University Press, 1995, p. 53.

8. K. Sangari, 'Politics of Diversity: Religious communities and multiple partiarchies', Parts I and II in *Economic and Political Weekly* (henceforth *EPW*), Vol. 30.51, 1995, pp. 3287–310, and Vol. 30.52, pp. 3381–89.

9. On this point, see N. Seremetakis, *The Last Word: Women, Death and Divination in Inner Mani*, Chicago and London: The University of Chicago Press, 1991, especially pp. 217ff.

10. See K. Ram, *Mukkuvar Women: Gender, Hegemony and Capitalist Transformation in a South Indian Fishing Community*, New Delhi: Kali for Women, 1992, Chapters 3 and 4; see also K. Ram, 'The Female Body of Possession: A feminist phenomenological perspective on rural Tamil women's experiences', paper presented at Anveshi conference, *Women and Mental Health*, February 1996.

11. For a full discussion see K. Ram, 'Rationalism, Cultural Nationalism and the Reform of Body Politics: Minority intellectuals of the Tamil Catholic community', in P. Uberoi, (ed.), *Social Reform, Sexuality and The State*, New Delhi: Sage Publications, 1996, pp. 291–318.

12. Emily Martin, *The Woman in The Body: A Cultural Analysis of Reproduction*, Boston: Beacon Press, 1987.

13. Carol Vance, 'Anthropology Rediscovers Sexuality: A theoretical comment', *Social Science and Medicine*, Vol. 33.8, pp. 875–84.

14. A. Good, *The Female Bridegroom: A Comparative Study of Life-crisis Rituals in South India and Sri Lanka*, Oxford: Oxford University Press, 1991.

15. L. Dumont, *Affinity as a Value: Marriage Alliance in South India, with Comparative Essays on Australia*, Chicago and London: The University of Chicago Press, 1983, p. 14.

16. K. Ram, *Mukkuvar Women*, op. cit., pp. 202ff.

17. K. Kapadia, *Siva and Her Sisters: Gender, Caste and Class in Rural South India*, Colorado: Westview, 1996, p. 252 and pp. 166ff.

18. See T. Asad, 'Two European Images of Non-European Rule', in T. Asad, (ed.) *Anthropology and the Colonial Encounter*, London: Ithaca Press, pp. 103–18. N. Dirks argues this position for the south Indian context in *The Hollow Crown: Ethnohistory of an Indian Kingdom*, Cambridge: Cambridge University Press, 1989.

19. See for example, Dirks, ibid.; A. Appadurai, *Worship and Conflict Under Colonial Rule: A South Indian Case*, Cambridge: Cambridge University Press, 1981; S. Bayly, *Saints, Goddesses and Kings: Muslims and Christians in South Indian Society 1700–1900*, Cambridge: Cambridge University Press, 1989; V. Narayana Rao, D. Shulman and S. Subrahmanyam, *Symbols of Substance: Court and State in Nayaka Period, Tamilnadu*, Delhi: Oxford University Press, 1992.

20. See Dirks, *The Hollow Crown*, op. cit.

21. See Burton Stein on the segementary state, in *Peasant State and Society in Medieval South India*, Delhi: Oxford University Press, 1980, See also Dirks, ibid.

22. See E.F. Irschick, *Tamil Revivalism in the 1930s*, Madras: Cre–A, 1986 and K. Nambi Arooran, *Tamil Renaissance and Dravidian Nationalism 1905–1944*, Madurai: Koodal Publishers, 1980. On colonial- Brahmin alliances as a pan-Indian phenomenon, see L. Mani, 'Contentious Traditions: The debate on sati in colonial India', in K. Sangari and S. Vaid, (eds.) *Recasting Women*, op. cit., pp. 88–126.

23. See Pamela Price, 'Revolution and Rank in Tamil Nationalism', *The Journal of Asian Studies*, Vol. 55.2, 1996, pp. 359–83. See also S. Ramaswamy on wider Tamil nationalist representations of

kingship: 'The Nation, the Region, and the Adventures of a Tamil Hero', in *Contributions to Indian Sociology*, (n.s.), Vol. 28.2, 1994, pp. 295–322.

24. See M.S.S. Pandian, *The Image Trap: MG Ramachandran in Film and Politics*, New Delhi: Sage Publications, 1992.

25. D.S. Lakshmi, 'Mother, Mother-Community and Mother-Politics in Tamilnadu', in *EPW*, Vol. 25.42, and 43, 1990, pp. WS 72–83; J. Pandian, 'The Goddess Kannagi: A dominant symbol of south Indian Tamil society', in J.A. Preston, (ed.), *Mother Worship: Theme and Variations*, Chapel Hill, University of North Carolina Press, pp. 177–91.

26. See the contributions by M.S.S. Pandian, Anandhi S. and A.R. Venkatachalapathy, 'Of Maltova Mothers and Other Stories', in *EPW*, Vol. 26.16, 1991, pp. 1059–64; Anandhi S., 'Women's Question in the Dravidian Movement, c. 1925–1948', *Social Scientist*, Vol. 19.5–6, 1991, pp. 24–41; see also Anandhi S. 'Reproductive Bodies and Regulated Sexuality: Birth Control Debates in early 20th century Tamilnadu', this volume.

27. See the extended discussion on this aspect in Price, 'Revolution and Rank in Tamil Nationalism', op. cit.

28. See Amrit Srinivasan, 'Temple 'Prostitution' and Community Reform: An examination of the ethnographic, historical and textual context of the devadasi of Tamilnadu, India', unpublished Ph.D. Anthropology Department, Cambridge University, 1984; Kalpana Kannabiran, 'Judiciary, Social Reform and Debate on Religious Prostitution', in *EPW*, Vol. 30.43, October 1995, pp. WS 59–69; Janaki Nair, 'The Devadasi, Dharma and the State', *EPW*, Vol. 29.50, 1994, pp. 3157–168.

29. See Anandhi S., 'Representing Devadasis: *Dasigal Mosavalai* as a radical text', in *EPW*, Vol. 26.11 and 12, 1991, pp. 736–46.

30. Compare MSS Pandian's 'Denationalising the Past: Nation in E.V. Ramaswamy's political discourse', in *EPW* Vol. 26.42, 1993, p. 2282–87; with *The Image Trap*, op. cit., and 'Jayalalitha: Desire and political legitimation', *Seminar* 401, January 1993, pp. 31–34.

31. Price, 'Revolution and Rank in Tamil Nationalism', op. cit., p. 15.

32. Kapadia, *Siva and her Sister*, op. cit., p. 114.

33. See Partha Chatterjee, *Nationalist Thought and the Colonial World: A Derivative Discourse?* London: Zed Press, 1986, p. 168.

34. K. Ram, 'Rationalism, Cultural Nationalism and the Reform of Body Politics', op. cit.; also K. Ram 'Maternity and the Story of

Enlightenment in the Colonies: Tamil coastal women, South India', in K. Ram and M. Jolly, (eds.) *Maternities and Modernities: Colonial and Postcolonial Experiences in Asia and the Pacific*, Cambridge: Cambridge University Press, 1998, pp. 114–43.

35. Robin Jeffery, *Politics, Women and Well-Being: How Kerala Became a Model*, London: Macmillan Press, 1992, esp. pp. 56f.

36. T. Alphonse, *Anpu Idayankal, Inpa Utayankal*, Trichinopoly, Holy Family College, 1991, p. 229.

37. See T. Alphonse, ibid. His text is discussed further in my 'Rationalism, Cultural Nationalism and the Reform of Body Politics', op. cit.

38. On conflicting knowledges and practices surrounding the medicalisation of childbirth, see Kalpana Ram, 'Medical Management and Giving Birth: Responses of coastal women in Tamilnadu', in *Reproductive Health Matters*, no. 4, November, 1994, pp. 20–26; and K. Ram, 'Maternity and the Story of Enlightenment in the Colonies', op. cit.

39. Robin Jeffery describes the particular attraction of Christian missions to Travancore who were drawn by the presence of much older Christian communities, R. Jeffery, *Politics, Women and Well Being*, op. cit., pp. 96ff.

40. J. Haggis, '"Good Wives and Mothers" or "Dedicated Workers"? Contradictions of domesticity in the "mission of sisterhood", Travancore, South India' in K. Ram and M. Jolly (eds.) *Maternities and Modernities*, op. cit., p. 94.

41. K. Ram, 'Maternity and the Story of Enlightenment in the Colonies', op. cit.

42. See K. Ram, *Mukkuvar Women*, op. cit., for details, Chapter 6.

43. Ibid., on the importance of an educated strata among the village women, pp. 222ff. According to statistics from the 1981 census, literacy rates are 78 per cent, as against, 22 per cent for the state as a whole less than 5 per cent of women in the age-group 15–19 are married, as against 22 per cent of women for the state as a whole. See also, P. Swaminathan, 'The Failures of Success? An analysis of Tamilnadu's recent demographic experience', Working Paper No. 141, Madras Institute of Development Studies, July 1996, esp, pp. 10ff.

44. K. Ram, *Mukkuvar Women*, op. cit., chapter 2.

45. See also Kapadia, *Siva and Her Sisters*, op. cit., p. 112.

46. See also K. Ram, *Mukkuvar Women*, op. cit., Chapters 3 and 4;

Seemanthini Niranjana, 'Femininity, Space and the Female Body' for a convergent discussion, in M. Thapan (ed.) *Embodiment: Essays on Gender and Identity*, Delhi, Oxford University Press, pp. 107–24.

47. See Kalpana Ram, 'The Female Body of Puberty: Tamil linguistic and ritual perspectives on sexuality', Forthcoming in P. Komaseroff, (ed.) *Sexuality and Medicine: Bodies, Practices, Knowledges*, n.d.

48. Du. Mu. Venukopal, *Cul Maruttuvam*, Madras: Office of the Text Book Committee for Sidda Medicine, Tamilnadu Sidda Marutuvam Corporation, 1986, Chapter 2.

49. For the Tamil nationalist politics surrounding the publication of the Tamil Lexicon, see K. Nambi Arooran, *Tamil Renaissance and Dravidian Nationalism*, op. cit., pp. 110ff.

50. *The Tamil Lexicon*, Madras: University of Madras Press, p. 22.

51. See K. Ram 'Rationalism, Cultural Nationalism and the Reform of Body Politics', op. cit., p. 302ff and K. Ram, 'Maternity and the Story of Enlightenment in the Colonies', op. cit., p. 122ff for a discussion of Fr. John's tracts.

52. See K. Ram, 'Rationalism, Cultural Nationalism and the Reform of Body Politics', op. cit.

53. For a similar argument in relation to female interpretations of honour in the context of Bedouin women, see L. Abu-Lughod, *Veiled Sentiments: Honor and Poetry in a Bedouin Society*, Berkeley and Los Angeles: University of California Press, 1986.

54. Translations from Marathi to English are by Leela Dube, cited in Martine Van Woerkens, 'Dialogues on First Menstrual Periods: Mother-daughter communication' in *EPW*, Vol. 25.17, 1990, pp. WS7–14, p. WS-11.

55. See Ambai, 'My Mother, her Crime', in Ambai, *A Purple Sea: Short Stories by Ambai*, trans. by L. Holmstrom, Madras: Affiliated East-West Press, pp. 11–21.

56. Stella draws here on the familiarity of Tamils with the Tamil nationalist poet Subramania C. Bharathi (1882–1921).

On Bodily Love and Hurt

V. GEETHA

Introduction

This essay attempts to make sense of the phenomenon of woman-battering which takes place in the family. My knowledge of battering comes out of the work that I did with other women in Snehidi, a support group for women who have survived such violence. It seems to me that rather than being exceptional, battering is symptomatic of the sexuality of everyday life, as women live it in the context of marriage and the family. I would like to interrogate this sexuality for what it tells me about men who hurt women.

The women who came to us were mostly from the lower middle class and working sections of the population. A number of them were from the 'other backward castes' and dalits. They were domestic helpers, petty vendors, construction workers, and workers in small business concerns and household industries in the city of Chennai. Very few were literate. A significant proportion lived in bustling working class neighbourhoods and slums. Middle class, upper caste women came to the centre as well, but in smaller numbers. Many from this group were educated, at least up to high school, and a few held jobs in the service sector.

Snehidi offered these women a space where they could talk, question, introspect and argue, with others and themselves, over the choices they had made in love and marriage. We were ourselves a group of disparate women, bound by a common faith in female comradeship. We worked with the Tamilnadu State Free Legal-Aid Board, and found ourselves suggesting options which the Board did not always approve. But we also learnt the value of the sort of counselling which the Board provided the women and men who approached it. In their attempts to come to terms with the stories they heard, the Board's counsellors would locate the problem of family disharmony and violence in the context of the extended family, the caste group and the religious community to which the petitioners belonged. This interpretative exercise was useful and relevant, since a woman's —and a man's—understanding of marital discord heeded behavioural norms and expectations which, in several instances, were largely caste and community specific. In a sense, we functioned as a medial group in the interstices between legal institutions and civil society. We translated legal choices and their implications into the language of the everyday for the women who came to us and relayed their anxieties and fears to the Board's counsellors and lawyers.

Yet it was clear that we were not mere translators or mediators. We were listeners whose presence and vocation—as self-confessed feminists—implicated us in the tale a woman narrated. Sometimes, a woman's narrative reached into our own biographies and we were forced to recognise the fact that as women, we shared a common location. We all possessed bodies which could be violated, dispossessed of their rights and controlled by men. Revealing ourselves to be as vulnerable as those who had endured a particular kind of violence committed us to the woman's testimony. We also helped make the story. Our listening presence helped a woman elicit forgotten moments from her past in such a way that she could name her anger and discontent with her life situation to herself.[1]

Our work as a support group obviously went beyond listening and helping to render tales of hurt coherent: it did not merely address the body in pain. In this sense a women's centre is the opposite of a clinic. It also negotiates those structures and contexts which surround and exercise their command over women's lives. The courts, money-lenders, caste panchayats, schools, labour unions, the woman's friends, her employers, the man's factory or shed: often, we traversed one or more of these worlds to further enquire into the problem, listen to the complaints of others, besides the aggrieved woman; place the child of a battered woman in school, or coax her husband, his family, or even his employers, to give her a regular sum of money so that she could continue to live.

While our understanding of women's hurt derived from a certain sense of ourselves and our location within a common female body, our support work addressed the problem (and possible resolution) of sexual hurt in terms of its structural constituents. Whenever we had to negotiate larger social and cultural contexts and structures, such as community and caste organisations and informal neighbourhood panchayats, we found ourselves using our education, training and knowledge of legal and civic structures in ways which were simply not available to the women with whose lives we were engaged. We could and often did hold out legal and punitive warnings to offending husbands and their families and kin; we cajoled personnel officers in companies and factories to make sure an abusive husband paid his wife her monthly maintenance claim; we countered community pressure on the woman to adapt herself to an existing situation with promises of seeking civil or secular resolutions to the conflict at hand.

Thus, in spite of the deep-felt and shared poignancy of being women together, our differences—from the women who came to the centre—were germane to our very existence as a support group. This meant that we were acting and working from within two contexts. One was anchored in shared notions of discrimination, harassment and hurt. The other was defined and structured by class and caste. Often class and caste positions, our own and those of the women who came to us, informed our own responses to battering. We were also acutely aware of the fact that these positions could not be easily transcended, though in the realm of conversation, confession and the intimacy of a women's group, such a transcendence was achieved, even if temporarily. Caught between two sorts of work, between a mode of listening and a mode of acting, we were—and continue to be—faced with questions regarding the nature of the violence we had to engage with: Is it a function of complex patriarchal structures, and, therefore, an uneven experience which affects different women in different ways? Or is violence an essential aspect of a problematic and unregenerate masculinity, a general masculine way of being, for which one may construct a common grammar, a masculine competence, so to speak, which expresses itself in and through different sorts of performances? More importantly, what was the relationship of violence to love and desire?

In trying to answer these questions for this essay I started with the stories we had heard in Snehidi. Recalling various tales, I discovered that a tale narrated by a battered woman was neither simple nor linear. For one, the protagonist of the tale was always absent, because he was to be protected, and his 'unnameable' acts often remained just that. Women could not and, in some instances, would not distinguish the hurt they endured from the promises of love whispered eagerly into their ears by their husbands. Besides, for many poor women, the experience of conjugality seemed no more or less dehumanising than, say, struggling to earn enough to eat. In a limited situation, where there were so many mouths to be fed, the husband, however mean of temperament and violent he may be, became yet another hungry soul whose claims could not be overlooked and punished, because he beat the life out of her the night before. Besides, it became clear that most women (and their men) lived in habitual intimacy—bred by proximity, a restrictive physical space and social codes which privileged the monogamous family. This intimacy, hedged-in and claustrophobic, and relieved by those moments of sensuality, unaccompanied by violence, made it difficult for most women to be objective about their husbands. Therefore, talking about husbands did not come easy to women. Invariably, they talked of others, of mother-in-law, brothers-in-law, a tiresome father-in-law, a gossipy neighbourhood. When husbands did enter the conversation, it was almost always in the context of responsibilities owned or shrugged away. Resentment against the husband was expressed mostly covertly: "The child sleeps between us these days."

I was thus faced with the task of 'recovering' the husband from these tales of hurt. How would I do this? What precedents existed? And what did I want to recover? The answers did not come easy. Even after I had mentally accounted for structural and psychological differences which determined the nature of the hurt endured by the women, I could not satisfactorily explain, either to myself or to others, a particularly perverse intent, an insistently repetitive act of physical violence, or even that most commonplace form of abuse directed against women, chronic suspicion. Nor could I comprehend entirely that interplay of fear, love and desire which held a woman to an abusive relationship. On the one hand, I was unwilling to surrender the question of intention to pathological explanations, or essentialist ones. On the other, I felt the need to account for a violence which was clearly intentional, being, at almost all times, initiated by self-conscious agents. Violence as an experience seemed to me to represent a point of intersection, of trajectories of hurt, touch, love, fear, hunger and shame. It seemed to inhere as much in the grime of everyday life, in habitual tone, gesture and touch, as it did in the particular and determined act of violence. In short, violence and battering existed as inalienable aspects of conjugal love, markers of the conjugal bond. I felt the need to interrogate this conjugality in terms of its characteristic expressive forms and ask if they added up to a generalised masculine sexual competence, or if they were themselves overdetermined.

As for Method...

Looking for ideological and political affiliates who would help me address these concerns did not prove easy. Much of the writing on battering in India deals with questions of legal claims, rights and redressal. A victimised female sexuality is taken for granted in much of the writing by those groups, including Snehidi, that have worked on family violence. It is almost always considered an aspect of social structures—either of kinship, caste, class or community. Publications and papers put out by the

Forum Against Oppression of Women, Women's Centre (Mumbai), Saheli (Delhi), Vimochana (Bangalore), by groups such as the Lawyers Collective, and articles which have appeared in journals such as *The Lawyers*, are detailed with respect to particular cases, discuss the practical aspects of dealing with wife-rape, battering, sexual assault and work out legal possibilities that women's groups may use. But very few of them have attempted to grapple with the question of sexuality in the context of battering. Assessing my own encounter with readings on sexuality, I recall being impressed by western texts from the 1970s and the 1980s which were either produced during the so-called Anglo-American 'second wave' of feminism, or inspired by it.

To this category of texts belong the work of Germaine Greer, Kate Millet, Susan Brownmiller, Adrienne Rich, Andrea Dworkin, Mary Daly and Catherine Mackinnon. I consider this corpus invaluable because it attempts to account for the intentionality of violence and, more specifically, sexual violence in the context of everyday sexual life and behaviour. Besides, it forces masculine behaviour, thought and action into the public realm in an insistent sort of way, and is fearless in its conviction that while patriarchy is a complex and uneven structure which implicates men and women in its workings, it yet allows, at every level, the routine and habitual violation of the female body.[2]

There is another set of texts which have proved equally germane to my understanding of the social dynamics of sexual violence, and which have helped me theorise an approach to issues of sexuality sensitive to the articulation of gender with other social categories, such as race, for example, but which retains the validity of gender, as an experiential marker, a point of dialogic contact with other women. I refer here to African-American debates on race, class and sexuality, and particularly to the work of bell hooks, Cornel West and the fiction of Maya Angelou, Ishmael Reed, Toni Morrison and James Baldwin. This body of work has proved particularly instructive—both for the passion with which they interrogate structures as well as for the radical, complex, inward-looking self-criticism they exhibit in their reflections on sexuality, gender, violence, race and community.[3]

Readings in these literatures have helped make sense of narratives, of their implication in complex linguistic and social structures. They have also helped me stay close to the stories, and their tellers, helped me sustain my engagement with a work that is often frustrating and exhausting. For, more than anything else, both categories of writers breathe a passion and energy, and exhibit a degree of involvement with what they write about that is intimate without being obsessive. In different ways, they trace out a political location that stays accountable to its premises, and thereby avoid the sterile, rarefied spaces of contemporary high theory which, in some instances, has fallen prey to that very masculinist discourse it started out to criticise.

Understanding Masculinity

From the stories we had heard in Snehidi, it seemed clear to me that husbands sought to represent their familial, economic and social status and power, in short their sense of themselves as men and husbands, through a complex of acts and statements. Many of these had to do with loving, but also controlling, desiring as well as hurting, relishing and possessing the body of the wife. Suspicion and sexual love, possession and desire, authority and affection: by exhibiting these traits in tandem and often acting on them, husbands spoke and enacted a language of love which was also, simultaneously, a language of terror.

a. Suspicion and sexual love

Let us consider suspicion and sexual love as these express themselves in the context of an embattled conjugality. Often, we found that suspicion was an exhibition of sexual love. Suspicion was, in many instances, part fantasy and part incitement. It was as if it cajoled into existence a particular vision of the erotic: the more violatable the wife's body, the more the enhancement of conjugal excitement and pleasure. Otherwise it is not really easy to explain why a man suspects his wife as a matter of routine.

When we once persuaded the women at the centre to do a play on suspicion, they performed with gusto the scene of a man suspecting his wife of infidelity, because she had risen from bed earlier than usual and was found sweeping the front yard a little before dawn. His reasoning was, she had done so with the express purpose of 'showing herself off' to those men who may be lolling about the street at that time of day. Talking an extra minute to the man who sells vegetables, wearing an unusual earring, visiting her mother's house once too often—any of these could provoke suspicion. If she is better educated, holds a better job, if her natal family is exceptionally affectionate and supportive, if she has friends or is gregarious and hearty, she immediately becomes suspect in her husband's eyes. Her gifts, her richness of being cause him to feel deprived, her felicity of tongue offends his sense of propriety and the love she is capable of incites his anger. It is as if the husband is fearful that the object of his persistent wants will disappear. He fears her independence, the fact that she has an identity of her own, outside that of marriage, and, on that account, considers her a recalcitrant and unyielding wife, and beats her, forces her to have sex, when she obviously does not want to, demands that she not see anyone else, be it her mother or her friends or the next door neighbour.[4] One man's suspicion of his cheerful wife led him to accuse her of incest. He insisted their children had been fathered by her brother and all her explanations, arguments were to no avail.

Sometimes, a reason, an occasion, a context may not even be necessary for a man to suspect his wife. It would seem as if the woman's irreducible otherness, evident, for instance, in her self-absorbed relationship to her children and housework, provokes him to test her.[5] Unable to possess her entirely, troubled and agitated by her sexual being, he resorts to what he assumes to be his prerogative: he seeks to wilfully re-affirm his legal possession of her body by accusing it of violations which, he claims, she had invited and permitted. To punish her, he may snip away at her hair if she wears it long, lock her up, force her into sexual acts which she experiences as degrading; alternately he may accuse her of promiscuity, call into question her 'honour', her competence as a good, chaste wife and dutiful mother, and keep the children away from her. The husbands of women who have come to the centre with tales of suspicion have done any or all of these. The husband's power to judge his wife, to mark her body as clean or unclean, her sexual being as legitimate or illegitimate in the context of marriage, allows him mastery over his anxieties regarding her sexual being.

As for the woman, who is the object of suspicion and sexual jealousy: she either suffers guilt, cultivates self-denial and, in some instances, self-loathing; or she actively reworks his suspicion into the terms of their conjugal relationship to the extent that she eroticises it. His suspicion and power to hurt become indices of his complete interest in her and her alone, and an affirmation of his monogamy. Even today, we cannot recall except with a shudder, the tale narrated us by a woman who chose to misread her husband's violence, born largely out of suspicion and paranoia, during intercourse, night after night, as an expression of his love for her. When she came to us, they had been married eighteen years and after listening to her over many days, we realised that she dared not admit to herself that the life she had led thus far was a lie. After several weeks of talking and discussion, we knew that she was now looking for an opportune moment to let go of her good faith and break down; and break down, she did. She burst into expressions of disgust and hatred for the man who, until recently, could do no wrong in her eyes.[6]

Suspicion is never merely a matter of consciousness. It may emerge, for instance, out of a context of felt deprivation. If the marriage happens to be a hypergamous one, where the wife is from a relatively wealthier family or from a caste higher in the hierarchy, her love and loyalty need to be tested, proven and re-tested. Or, if the marriage is hypogamous, where she happens to be from a lower caste or from a poorer family, she needs to live up to expectations whose boundaries she cannot really determine, shifting and arbitrary as these are. Nothing she does is right and she is suspected of doing wrong and ill, almost as a matter of course.[7]

In one instance, the woman's relative affluence and the privileges her natal family enjoyed fuelled the husband's resentment and, sometimes, greed. The husband kept her from visiting her family, or referred to them in derogatory terms. Or else he taunted her with her changed status. Since she could not really hope to recover her 'lost' caste status, it became clear that she was beholden to him. The woman, for her part, brought her caste and class power to bear on her relationship with him. This power—expressed usually through accusations, directed at the husband and his family, of low and unseemly behaviour, unclean habits, and, of course, avarice—did not enable her to negotiate his sense of a lack, and the violence which flows from it, in any effective sense. Yet, it allowed her to experience a sort of pyrrhic victory, in that she took consolation from his 'lowliness'; she reasoned that she cannot really expect anything better from him and left him. But there are also wives who feel hurt and ill-used, who suffer from a sense of guilt, both for having betrayed their 'origins' and for being unable to sustain that love, which had occasioned the betrayal in the first place. Such women keep at the marriage, enduring humiliation, feeling inadequate while living with fear and pain. The point is, whichever way the wife reacts, she is vulnerable to sexual hurt. His mediation of his lower caste status takes place in and through her body, even as her rejection of him, on the grounds of caste status, leaves behind on that self-same body, what seem to her, distasteful marks of violation.

In the other instance, where the wife is from a lower caste or class, her husband routinely humiliates her, often charging her with 'immodest' behaviour. He may accuse her of exhibiting low and coarse habits, of habitual promiscuity and trace these to her origins. Or else he may boast of his superior virtues, his given virility, and claim he can marry any number of women, if he so chooses. For her, conjugality appears hedged in by fear and self-loathing. She cannot be good enough, even if she wanted to, and it is in such contexts that women misread hurt as dutiful love. Sometimes women fight back, no doubt, displace accusations of negativity on to the men and come away, defiant in their independence and sexual autonomy.

Where economic inequality, rather than caste, locks husband and wife together in a relationship of uneasy conjugality, a slightly different pattern emerges. Where a man feels he had entered into an economically unprofitable marriage, he seeks to exact his rightful surplus through other means. He suspects his wife's fertility, her fitness for 'family life'. Her body comes under surveillance, is brought under a regime of control exercised by doctors, priests and family elders. (On one occasion, we witnessed the sickening sight of a father and son discussing the son's wife's menstrual periods in a family counselling centre. The father-in-law claimed he had maintained a record of her menstrual cycle, because he had doubts over her fertility.) In such instances, the wife's body is sought to be 'punished' for its refusal to yield evidence of its 'disease', and, covertly, for its inability to bring in more money. Thus, she is subjected to a perverse and painful sexual violence which seeks to represent her and her sexual being as worthless, corrupt, and therefore replaceable. It is not accidental that dowry demands are never simply that: they inscribe themselves literally and metaphorically on the wifely body. They constitute this body as a thing, which may be discarded if it cannot yield its essential 'use' value. Otherwise, one cannot really explain the characteristic gratuitousness of this kind of violence, which possesses all the solemnity and timing of a carefully rehearsed ritual. The discourse of law, and the insistence with which women translate a complex of violations they had endured into the language of the *Dowry Prohibition Act*, do not allow either the women or the state to raise the question of the body.

Where women are richer than their husbands, they pay for it—again, through practices of the body. They cultivate the virtue of self-denial, and express it in curious ways. Either they assume an innocence and passivity in the realm of conjugality, thereby affirming their husband's manliness, or else they negate their own desiring selves and let their conjugal life be ruled by a logic of money. The husband, in the second instance, becomes an object of contempt, to whom the wife, nevertheless, feels tied because of the children. The children replace the husband as the focus of the woman's attentions and maternal love often becomes dangerously eroticised. Yet the successful, moneyed woman refuses to name her loneliness, or if she does, and takes a lover, she finds herself implicated in a drama of subterfuge and shame.

Men's suspicion brands the female body as essentially vulnerable, and besides, marks it as a space, a topos on which patriarchal structures may map their vicious logic of domination. More specifically, in the context of conjugality, suspicion helps men play out a life-long drama of fidelity and familial worth in which they emerge as well-meaning protagonists. It allows them to declare loftily that it behoves a woman to remain loyal to the marital bed, as well as damn her for her chronic inability to practise this loyalty. Further, it enables them to experience a measure of righteous sexual and moral prowess. Since it is the woman's ostensible sexual misdemeanours that undermine familial honour, men feel secure in their lapses into promiscuity as well as in their wilful seeking of multiple partners. Meanwhile, they remain committed to the ideology of the family and to the notion that it is really the woman's business and duty to keep this institution in place. This also serves to infuse guilt in women who may be venturesome, and effectively prevents them from acting on their own sense of dignity. Paradoxically, then, the patriarchal family belies its own claims of being given and natural. For, if it needs to be shored up by active acts of surveillance then, obviously, it conceals at its very core an illegitimacy, a fiction, which, as it happens, has writ itself large— and there is a further paradox here—on the substantiality of the female body.[9]

b. *Possession and desire*

It is clear that exhibitions of paranoia and fears of the female otherness of the wife are, ultimately, expressions of power. It is this assumption of power, to name, mark and control the body and being of women which has enabled the emergence of a masculinity, that not only orders the conjugal world on its own terms, but which re-inscribes terror as love, fear as eros and aggression as pleasure. That women, too, accept these definitions is, of course, an index of the naturalisation of the norms of masculinity.[10]

How does masculine desire express itself in the context of marriage? Usually through sexual demands made on the wife at any time of the day or night. Women who came to the centre rarely spoke about this, except to say that men generally do not and cannot observe sexual propriety, that their lust awaits neither time nor place. Or they would lament the fact that even after having borne several children, their bodies know no respite, and are seldom left alone. In those instances where the battering had to do with the ostensible inability to 'perform' adequately, women do talk of how they feel disinterest, are tired, would rather hug their children and go to sleep. Their husbands, on the other hand, would read their wives' indifference as an unsaid indictment of their virility and perversely seek to 'prove' it, through violent sexual acts. For most women, to somewhat paraphrase and re-deploy Andrea Dworkin's telling observations, violence was the context in which intercourse takes place, whereas for most men, intercourse was the context in which the conjugal relationship assumed form, coherence, and significance.

Women feel this violence with a particular intensity when their indifference to intercourse or lack of desire fuels men's suspicion and sexual jealousy. For many women, this indifference arises from a tired familiarity with pregnancy and the horror that is visited on them, should they try and use contraceptives. A woman who returned to her husband after a period of separation was so tormented by fears of getting pregnant that she would beg us to tell her of 'safe' and discreet methods which would enable her to have sex and not worry about conceiving. Her situation was particularly poignant because, obviously, she felt love, affection or, perhaps, merely bodily desire for her husband, but there was no way she could tell him of her wants and get him to take her fears seriously. For, as she told us sorrowfully, should she suggest that either of them use a contraceptive, he would question whether she had been seeing another man; or why else would she be afraid? It is in such instances that one notes the essential linearity of masculine desire, which seems so wrapped in itself, and constantly looks to its own fulfilment, its own exhaustion and is constitutively unmindful of female wants and needs.[11]

As far as masculine desire and its manifest forms are concerned, they suffer a complex of mediations in their deployment. There is family and community on the one hand, and an all-male solidarity on the other, those 'blood brothers', peers at work, friends. These institutions chart out specific courses for the passage of masculine desire and, by doing so, instruct notions of the male body and self which, in turn, help shape the trajectories of desire.

The family has a clear stake in male virility in that he has to produce progeny, both to perpetuate his line of descent, and to add to the family workforce. Manliness and the identity of the patriarchal family are so closely interwoven that the former is an essential condition of the latter's existence. The father's conspiratorial, 'we are men together' intimacy with his son, the mother's anxious, watchful pride in his existence, a pride which in our cultures manifests early and is so evident in such practices as kissing the male child's genitalia, praising it, and bragging about it, a sister's dependence on her brother's protection and largesse—all these help to foster and nurture a particular kind of masculinity, and one which rests on the valour and virility of the young male. Often, this masculinity comes to rest on the adequacy or otherwise of his sexual performance. The mother-son relationship is a curious one in this regard. The mother stands in for a femininity that is at once grasping, possessive and self-denying. On the one hand, this femininity, grounded in sacred notions of motherhood, and actual practices of child rearing, denies the existence of female sexuality; yet, on the other, it manages to impress on the act of sex, notions of contempt, guilt and fear. It is not accidental that women at the centre have tales of watchful mothers who disallow their sons from sharing rooms with their wives during the difficult first months of marriage. (In one instance, the mother perversely insisted they share a room, but keep the doors to it open.) Women have confided that they actually saw their husbands sleep with their mothers. One woman told us of how her mother-in-law would insist on sleeping between herself and her husband. Sometimes, the husband and his mother would share the only available bed in the house, leaving the hapless daughter-in-law to sleep on the floor or in the ante room. In all these instances, the men went along with their mothers' decisions and orders. All this makes for a masculine desire, which, given the conditions of its emergence, cannot really afford to respect female otherness, or love and empathise with it on mutual, coeval terms.

Further, in our context, a man's sense of his own sexual importance is inextricably tied up with his community status and identity, as much as with his family. Caste and Brahminical patriarchy seek to 'emasculate' men of lower castes by holding captive their labour and the sexual as well as working rights of their women. Men who are, thus, structurally and bodily dislocated, express their sense of a hedged-in masculinity in and through a rhetoric of sexual aggression and anger, usually directed against the sexual 'honour' of upper caste women. But, this aggression also expends itself on wives and sisters, whose hard-earned earnings are often taken away, whose bodies are often battered. Male anger and violence in these instances are compounded by the fact that women 'allow' these expressions of rage and hurt, legitimise them in the name of community integrity and unity. Sometimes, this thwarted masculinity can be so thoroughly trapped by the vicious logic of caste which works its effects on women's bodies, that it fails to recognise a fellow victim. In one instance, a dalit girl who had married outside the caste, but who discovered the horrors which attend an intercaste marriage, wanted to return to her natal home. Her brothers forbade her from doing so and said that she had chosen her life and must therefore face the consequences of her choice. The girl was eventually killed by her husband. The girl's mother, however, defended her sons' decision and argued that they had acted in the name of family honour. Besides, as men, they knew what would happen to those who broke caste taboos and hence they were justified in keeping their sister out. They did not want to invite aggression from the other castemen.

Conversely, upper caste men brag about their superior sexual prowess, their 'cleaner, unpolluted seed', so to speak, and claim God-given rights over the bodies of lower caste women. By the same token, they are jealous of their women's 'honour' and displace their anxieties about its possible and imminent violation rather violently onto the body of the lower caste man. Upper caste women internalise notions of their own vulnerability and either respond with aggressive and contemptuous anger towards lower caste men or express fear. Lower caste male sensuality gets mythicised and is alternately reviled and feared. What we have here is a general sexual culture that enables men acting with, or on other men, to decide the coordinates of sexual desire and identity. Women's bodies, even where the women are from the upper castes, come to exist as tokens of community identity on the one hand and objects of desire and possession on the other.

Finally, it seems, men derive their sense of sexual worth from the relationships they forge with other men. Men do look for approval from others of their sex and their masculine performative powers are often defined in the context of taunts, challenges and contests among male friends. The passion men have for each other is almost always expressed through a language of filiation, and being 'men together' in various contexts, from the workplace to the playing fields to sex markets, obviously fosters in them a sense of identity which is far more significant to their sense of self than the relationships they forge with women. It is not surprising that, often, battered wives point to 'bad company' as a reason for the violence they endure. And it is not entirely accidental that women sometimes complain of 'being sodomized'. It is possible to read in such acts, a subterranean homoeroticism, which women understand for what it is. But they seldom name it as such, and, instead, speak angrily of how much time a man spends with his friends. While this may be a general complaint against male non-accountability in matters of housework, there is an added edge to these complaints, an expression of a definite sexual resentment of their husband's friends.

Masculine desire is linear and mindful of its structurally determined objectives, yet possesses a certain autonomous resonance, a constitutive aesthetics, best embodied in those masculine, social and sexual performances which are commonplace in our cultures. A performance demands a space and a body and if we were to consider masculine sexual performance in these terms, what insights may we glean?

For many of us, nothing captures men's relationship to space as much as the image of the man urinating unconcernedly on a busy thoroughfare, next to a girls' school building, at a street corner where buses turn, in a public park. Consider flashers: what is it that makes them flash their organs at women, at girls? What notions of intimacy drive men to whisper obscenities into the ears of girls and women on a crowded bus and train? Or pinch their breasts and behinds? Why do men's hands stray, almost unconsciously, as it were, to their crotches, even if they are at a public meeting and on stage? (Women, on the contrary would, pull their saris tighter over their breasts.) It is as if the public space they claim so effortlessly as their own was defined by their penis and its vagaries. It is as if a man prescribes not only those territorial norms which define home and the world, but he prescribes them in such a way, that he is able to inscribe on to either, literally and ideologically, the mark of the phallus. This mark represents an intersection of the body and consciousness, and its substantive and symbolic significance is, everywhere and always, backed by the threat of violence which is no idle threat. Such an exhibition of sexual desire (and power) insists on drawing attention to an unselfconscious, and, therefore, 'naturalised' male sexuality, and covertly registers penile penetration as a natural and necessary act and one that follows from and defines the condition of being male.

In turn, men's relationship to their bodies derives from their sense of space. If space is defined by the trajectory marked by the penis, the male body, by the same token, is defined in synecdochic terms: the penis is the body. In fact, male body language, if carefully studied, will indicate how a man often presents himself as a penis writ large. It is not to be wondered at, that for most men, women's bodies exist as breasts, hips and vaginas, but mostly as hollows which are interchangeable. The passivity of women is not only assumed and enforced by a language and imagery which celebrate the forward, outward trajectories of male sexual expression, but is thereby actively inculcated and accepted by women themselves.

c. Authority and affection

It is clear from these observations that masculinity possesses an inner logic to it and one which, in turn, affects the specific forms of its existence in history. It seems to me that this logic expresses itself most forcefully when it re-defines male (and husbandly) authority as an exercise in concern, pleasure and affection. I remember a man asking, rather piteously, "Can't I beat my wife even once?" and a wife arguing that a man beats his wife only when she 'does wrong'. The naturalisation of authority as affection leads men to hurt women with impunity and 'enables' women to remain submissive and accepting.

Consider, for instance, how men handle romance. Often, as popular representations of romance have it, on film and in weekly magazines, they consider romance a matter of combat, a contest among men who will be boys. A wife or a lover is deemed a prize catch, an object of prey that has been successfully ensnared to the eternal glory of the hunter. Since submission follows capture, it is assumed to be the natural mode of existence of a woman who has chosen marriage. Passivity becomes a favoured erotic trait in women and the more inert her body, the easier and more pleasurable it is for masculinity to stake its claims to supremacy, and flaunt power as an instance of love. A certain university professor married one of his bright young students. It was a union 'of love', though the first few weeks of marriage revealed them to be different in many ways. He forced her to cut her hair, when her beauty was her long, lovely hair which she loved to wear braided. He insisted she paint her lips and face, though she repeatedly exclaimed she preferred herself the way she was. Gradually, as he succeeded in his attempts to undo her, she lost her hold on herself and the world outside. She began to experience bouts of insanity and took to claiming she was pregnant, when it was clear she was not. She had to make sense of the many demands made on her person and the only legitimate justification for these demands seemed to lie in the fact that her husband loved her. Hence, the desperate affirmation, to herself, of his love: the insistence on pregnancy.

The eroticisation of power on the part of the husband often takes perverse forms, as when it insists on a restitution of conjugal rights even in cases where the relationship has broken down, and ceased to exist. When a wife decides to walk away, then begins the stalking, the waiting at public spaces for her, harassing her at her place of work, writing her letters signed in blood, the accusations of adultery. Such accusations as we have heard, are lewd in their observations and the accuser becomes a voyeur who delights in his own warped sense of the sexual. A young woman had left her husband after a few years of marriage and come away with their little son. He was in the army, and, after having completed his commission, came back to claim his conjugal rights. She refused to live with him and filed for divorce. In response, he filed a complaint with the police that his wife was seeing another man and even had her abducted when she was on her way home from work. The hapless woman was not only mocked by the Assistant Superintendent of Police for thus falling foul of her wifely duties, but was warned by her husband to return to him, for otherwise he would drag her to court on charges of adultery. The man knew that his wife was not going to come back, yet he persisted in thus harassing her. It was as if in and through this demonstration of his rights to her body, and his accusations of being robbed of such rights, he experienced not only a sense of power, but pleasure as well.

In other instances, wives do not let go, ask to go back to bad marriages, abusive homes, chiefly because they cannot bear to think of breaking the conjugal bond. It is not simply fear of being alone and lack of support systems, both social and financial, which make them go back, but a power, exercised over their bodies and minds, which they have internalised, to the extent that they claim an identity only in and through its workings on their bodies and beings. Love and sacrifice, desire and denial exist as correlates of each other in a woman's consciousness, emotions which inform each other mutually. Even when a woman decides to end her marriage, she rarely thinks of love and desire as emotions which have been returned to her and with which she may re-build her life. It is not uncommon to hear women tell us that they want to join Snehidi and do 'social service'. Affection is to be exercised only at the behest of an authority or else it is to be transmuted into one of its ostensible nobler forms: selfless love. Even young women, educated, confident of living on their own, seldom imagine they may after all start all over again, love and be loved better than before. In such instances, self-denial becomes a means of defining one's new non-marital subjectivity. Fear of men, disgust over what had happened to them, exhaustion—all these, no doubt, play a part in their practice of a certain austere lifestyle. But very deeply felt and held beliefs regarding the legitimate forms of love and desire are equally fundamental to their choice of values and lifestyles.

There are differences, of course: women from the working classes (and castes) are less bound by the dictum, 'having loved once, I will love no more'. There is a frank acceptance of the pertinence of sensuality, of the importance and possibilities of love. Working caste (class) women are more likely to defy husbandly authority and less likely to read anger as affection or power as love. They are also more likely to leave an abusive relationship faster, and on their own initiative. It is believed that lower caste and working class men are less patriarchal, and relationships in these households relatively more egalitarian. But matters do not appear that clear-cut. Working class men also invest in masculinity, in an ethics of the self, devoted to style, sexual prowess and male comradeship.[12] Their vision of the erotic is as much informed by notions of the primacy of male pleasure and their right to it on their own terms. There may be a greater tolerance of female desire—or promiscuity, as it is more usually identified—but one cannot, therefore, say there is a greater respect for the female person.

Masculinity and the Erotic Principle

It is clear that conjugal relationships are embattled ones. Conjugal love is not merely an instance of sex turning violent. Violence is the form assumed by sexual love in a conjugal context. Enabled into existence by a complex hermeneutics of suspicion and structured by a social and economic order which privileges the monogamous, patriarchal family, conjugal love heeds an ethic of identity which celebrates masculine selfhood. In turn, this selfhood sets itself up as a norm, against which all attempts at expression by a subject may be tested, validated and affirmed as socially and culturally significant. Masculinity has also appropriated and defined the sensual and erotic realms on its own terms. Desire and its satiation heed, as we have seen, a logic of power and authority and a will to control and possess.

Masculine sexual and erotic norms are not simply imposed or thrust on passive female victims, though one cannot therefore assume that force does not essay a role in anchoring masculine selfhood in female subordination. Force may not be determinate in all instances, especially since women consent to be victims, assent to being stokers of masculine egos and persuade themselves to accept violence as an enduring aspect of sexual love and conjugal good faith, as they experience it. What is at stake in this matter for feminists is, of course, the realm of female desire. Yet, given the complex and cunning articulation of structure, consciousness and practice in the workings of masculinity, one cannot merely ask for an inversion of the erotic, as it obtains, under the sign of man. While one desires to privilege an eros which is less linear, more playful and flexible in its workings and claim it for the sphere of female sensuality and love, as an experience which answers to notions of mutuality and female self-knowledge, this still does not help us liberate the erotic from its masculine, structural logic. If one were to speak of female desire—to speak thus seems a misnomer, for it seems, as yet, an experience in search of a name, unless it accepts to be considered a variant of homoeroticism—one is immediately catapulted into the realm of personal lifestyle choices, into texts, into defiant assertions of promiscuity. Since almost all of these exist as exceptional instances, at the margins, they indicate the possibilities of personal choice, of the viability of a private erotics, and, meanwhile, the interlinked realms of the family, community and the economy, remain impervious to such actual transformations as may be wrought by those brave women who have disavowed the ethic of monogamy and compulsory heterosexuality.

So, what is it we want? I think the issue is one of re-inscription. Eros has to be rescued from the domain of the family and conjugality, from its imbrication in those frontier zones which divide castes and communities, and returned to a public sphere—of dialogue, interlocution and democracy. Politics is its legitimate site, the necessary space for its unfolding, since it is as crucial to acts of resistance, as, say, caste, class, language, faith and ethnicity. The right to be free from sexual hurt, from an ethic which translates pain as pleasure, the right to demand in the most intimate of human relationships, an accountability to freedom, equality and dignity: this requires a multiplication of spaces, where sensuality can be made manifest, active and dialogic. As James Baldwin remarked of the sensual basis of African–American survival and resistance strategies: "To be sensual, I think is to respect and rejoice in the force of life itself, and to be present in all that one does, from the effort of loving to the breaking of bread."

Notes

1. Listening constitutes a political and epistemological activity, which is radical in that it helps restore voice and tongue to those who are rarely expected to wield either while telling stories of themselves. Feminist listening allows a woman to narrate her tale in a context which is essentially dialogic: other women who may be in the centre at that time come up with their own stories. Advice is freely offered, refused, argued about. A tale may be interrupted—by visitors, children and the fatigue of the listeners themselves, then resumed.

Each time, the woman traces the events in her life afresh and rehearses a new subjectivity. Tales are initially generic: the elements are clearly pre-given. Stock situations in films, the language of advertisement, neighbourhood gossip and the ubiquitous discourse of law and government—all of these serve to preface a tale in particular ways, such that the story ceases to be exceptional and becomes one that could have happened to every woman. In the second phase of the telling, we encounter self denial on one hand, and fantasy on the other. "It is all my fault, if I had been different..." is followed by "Oh, we were happy once, we did good to one another until..." Later, as the dialogic context of the centre assumes the familiarity of a home for the woman, she feels emboldened to talk of things, "which I have not even told my mother". It is in this sense that a community is forged in language. It is not accidental that feminist events and happenings privilege testimony and have created specific modalities for expression, communication and listening as, for instance, in multilingual translations, group conversations and public hearings.

For a definition of listening as epistemology in the context of psychoanalysis, see Peter Gay, *The Bourgeois Experience: From Victoria to Freud*, Volume I, *The Education of the Senses*, London: Oxford University Press, 1985, p. 166: "Freud ... was one of the great listeners in history. Dreams, slips, gestures, symptoms, silences, served him as unwitting, but once recognised, informative guides to the retreats of inner life where sexual desires had taken refuge... The freedom for interpretation that his decoding of mental messages granted—in fact imposed—on healers and researchers provided a historic opportunity to read erotic experience, in all its complexity, more completely than it had ever been read before."

2. The 'Second Wave' is suspect today: it appears too embarrassingly focused on the self; too pointed and, therefore, unnuanced in its accusations of men and masculinity; naive in its assumptions regarding femininity and its deployment of the category of Woman, and, impolitic in its insensitivity to race and class. I have in mind the following books. Susan Brownmiller's *Against Our Will: Men, Women and Rape*, Harmondsworth: Penguin, 1977; Mary Daly's *Gyn-Ecology: The Metaethics of Radical Feminism*, London: The Women's Press, 1979; Andrea Dworkin's *Women Hating*, New York: E.P. Dutton, 1974 and *Pornography: Men Possessing Women*, London: The Women's Press, 1981; Germaine Greer's *The*

Female Eunuch, London: McGibbon and Kee, 1970; and Kate Millet's *Sexual Politics*, London: Sphere Books, 1971.

To the Second Wave is counterpoised a new epistemology of gender and sexualities which looks to the political economy of sex, to the production of identities and constitutions of sexual taste. Yet, in spite of their slips—and there are many—the feminist writers of the Second Wave are relevant to my purpose. It seems to me that one may read them for not merely what they said, but how they said it, where they spoke from and who they addressed. Dale Spender, writing of Millet and Greer, notes that it is "as much the style as the content of their protest which is responsible for (their) force and this too casts considerable light on contemporary feminist theory." See Dale Spender, (ed.), *Modern Feminist Theorists: Re-inventing Rebellion*, London: The Women's Press, 1983, p. 372. This style is peculiarly suited to illumine that critical area where "consciousness and physical reality meet" (ibid., p. 374). It is at once interested and clinical, passionately determined to explode those rationalisations which women construct to explain and justify their own subordinate lives and yet relentlessly methodical in its assembling of evidence to show why women do this and what men, in turn, do to them.

The style and its location—in an interlocutory, public context— aligns these feminists, objectively, with African Americans. The latter, too, write in and, indeed, inaugurated, the testimonial tradition, "bearing witness", in Henry Gates' memorable phrase, to their maimed lives, so that they may finally break bread in the togetherness of a community which has resisted and survived. In diferent but intersecting ways, Kate Millet and Toni Morrison, Adrienne Rich and bell hooks have freed women's voices: to name, argue, be partisan, declamatory, angry.... These intersections are extremely interesting and significant, as when Rich writes poignantly of the need for white feminists to define their "politics of location" in terms of their privilege, on the one hand, and in terms of their spelt-out filiation to black and working class women, on the other; hooks and West refuse to subsume gender as a category in discussions of the interplay which yokes race and gender together violently. (See, for instance, bell hooks and Cornel West, *Breaking Bread: Insurgent Black Intellectual Life*, Boston: South End Press, 1991 and Cornel West, *Race Matters*, Boston: South End Press, 1993).

3. Same as 2.

4. In 'Compulsory Heterosexuality and Lesbian Existence', *Signs* Vol. 5.4, 1980, Adrienne Rich has persuasively argued that heterosexual norms are enforced and sought to be naturalised by force, because of the threat female comradeship and love represent for patriarchy. She observes that the pleasure women experience in each other's presence and company has been compulsorily rendered invisible and illegitimate by an array of practices and ideologies. In our context, these observations need to be tested and critically examined for their relevance. In our work we have heard men accuse a woman's loud-mouthed female friends for making her cussed; we, ourselves, have been blamed for making women raise their voices and speak. Given the fact that women are actively encouraged to invest all their emotional and empathetic energies in their relationships to their husbands and children, it should not be too difficult to detail those strategic norms, taken for granted in matters of love and sexuality, which render heterosexuality (and monogamy) compulsory options for women.

5. Beginning with the work of Nancy Chodorow (*The Re-production of Mothering: Psychoanalysis and the Sociology of Gender*, Berkeley: University of California Press, 1978), several feminists have tried to account for male 'otherness'—locating it in practices of motherhood and child rearing, often using the language of psychoanalysis to strengthen their arguments. Others, including Dora Russell and Mary O' Brien, have pointed at how the material reality of reproduction is different for the two sexes and that this gives rise to different forms of consciousness. Dora Russell speaks of how men experience a "flight from the body" in relation to the experience of reproduction and suggests that this removes from their thought and action elements which are messy, inchoate and stubbornly resistant to instant abstraction and ratiocination. Mary O' Brien talks of how men and women experience, what she calls, "species time", a time of the body, akin to Jung's lunar time, whereas men order their lives to calendrical, linear time (Dale Spender, *Modern Feminist Theorists*, op. cit., pp. 368–80).

These attempts to account for female otherness and the threat it possibly holds out for men, focus on the latter's experience of a lack, and help us comprehend the nature of male aggression, which is at once intentional and determined, linked as it is in crucial ways to a sense of the self that is economically and socially privileged and which yet has to force its presence into social and political attention.

6. This raises the hugely significant question of whether conjugal love represents a perversion of the erotic or is itself the form the erotic assumes within the context of marriage. As Kumkum Roy's paper in this volume shows, in a world ordered by power, privilege and control, the erotic is necessarily an adjunct to authority and in fact a particularly prersuasive expression of it. In the particular instance I have referred to here, the pleasure the woman experienced in her marriage was necessarily sado-masochistic, and it was not until the hurt threatened to kill that the fiction of marital love exploded into her consciousness and enabled her to name her pain for what it was.

7. In caste society, as in a racially divided society like the United States of America, sexuality is defined in terms of a semantics of honour, violation and aggression, in which women figure as valued tropes, which bespeak liminality. Their bodies constitute frontier zones, which mark the limits of the violable and the inviolate. In societies which fear miscegenation, suspicion exists as a primary structure of sensual feeling. In the old American South, "reckless eyeballing", the eyeing of a white woman by a black man for more than the "prescribed" movement was construed a crime punishable by death through lynching. Suspicion attaches itself in such instances to the body of the victim, marking it as sensually erroneous. In caste society, with its graded inequalities, suspicion has attracted to itself a virtual hermeneutics—how else may one describe the *Manusmriti* —which not only instruct norms to regulate and direct sexual and erotic energy but which induce and create such sexual acts and intentions which may fall within the realm of this hermeneutics. And so, the vicious circle is kept in place.

8. The theme of an upper caste, usually, Brahmin woman, falling in love with a 'shudra' who rescues her from a sexually unfulfilling marriage, has been explored in Tamil cinema. Such films as *Savitri*, which attempts to portray the sexual loneliness of the young Brahmin bride married to an ageing priest, seek to appeal to the sexual voyeurism of caste society, as do a variety of text-image pornography whose protagonists are Brahmin women. The point is that these essentially furtive attempts at 'subversion' provoke anxieties of violation, rather than encouraging or enabling them, thus rectifying the upper caste woman's fear and loathing of the lower caste male, as well as the latter's angry will to violate her. It

is small wonder that in intercaste marriages, fear, loathing and self-disgust erupt into the forefront, once the sensual excitement of contact has been explored and done with.

9. Political responses to battering have not adequately addressed the issue of sexual rights in the context of conjugality. Feminists have been speaking of the necessity of rendering marital rape an offence and, more recently, have initiated a proactive campaign for rights to different sexualities and living arrangements. Stree Sangam and Forum Against Oppression of Women from Mumbai have, in different ways, been working at bringing to public focus and debate issues of sexual preference and conjugal rights and the suggested specific legal means through which such claims and rights may be formulated. Such initiatives, which question the 'naturalness' of the monogamous, patriarchal family, have served to draw attention to the fact that narratives, notions and practices of pleasure and sexuality, as much as the structures of the economy and society, help naturalise the idea of marital and familial love.

10. What is at stake here is a matter of epistemology: of the status of women's knowledge and pleasure in a context which actively persuades them to view their subordinate role in the relationship as given, natural and, therefore, acceptable and enjoyable. Even when one does not subscribe to the notion that women are victims, one is still left with the significant problems of her material situation, which she often experiences as limited or limiting, and her determined ignorance. While she may have recourse to the so-called 'weapons of the weak' to quarrel with and resist domination, these do not, except at opportune historic moments, when they are strategically deployed, explode the frontiers of her life and disciplined body. Women's consent to their own humiliation is a vexed question and one that is not merely determined by her place and location in an unequal social and economic order. Some feminists, such as Catherine Mackinnon, argue that women secure their survival rights thus, allowing themselves to be possessed and violated in order that they may live. Mackinnon adds: "Because the inequality of the sexes is socially defined as the enjoyment of sensuality itself, gender inequality appears consensual. This helps explain the peculiar durability of male supremacy as a system of hegemony as well as its imperviousness to change once it exists. It also helps explain some of the otherwise more bewildering modes of female collaboration. The belief that whatever is sexually arousing

is ipso facto empowering for women is revealed as a strategy in male rule. It may be worth considering that heterosexuality, the predominant social arrangement that fuses this sexuality of abuse and objectification with gender in intercourse, with attendant trauma, torture and dehumanisation, organises women's pleasure so as to give us a stake in our own subordination," in *Feminism Unmodified: Discourses on Life and Law*, Boston: Harvard University Press, 1987, p. 7.

11. Women's response to sensuality in the context of motherhood, their sense of their own bodies during the crucial periods of pregnancy and child-rearing, need to be understood in greater detail and in a historical context. Peter Gay has attempted to do this for the high bourgeois age in mid and late Victorian England, America, Germany and France. Working with diaries, letters, medical history, history of ideas and institutions, he shows how practices of childbirth affected and redeployed sexual energy during the period he is concerned with. Quoting the example of one Eleanor Rogers who left behind ample evidence of her experience of pregnancy and childbirth, both of which she considered so painful that she would forego the pleasure which they occasion and are occasioned by, Gay observes: "Eleanor Rogers's manifest affection for her husband— who was, after all, the author of her ordeal—is beyond doubt. But so is her rising up against the consequences of acting on sexual urges. She loves Will but hates what he has done to her. It is nothing less than intercourse that her crusade against marriage is intended to check. The risks of pregnancy put the pleasure of sex into question." (Peter Gay, *The Bourgeois Experience: From Victoria to Freud*, op. cit., pp. 229–30).

12. See my article on Prabhudeva, 'Two Heroes of our Time' in *Seminar* No. 452, pp. 14–15, for a discussion on motherhood, poverty and style.

Enforcing Cultural Codes

Gender and violence in northern India

PREM CHOWDHRY

Most family related crimes like dowry, bride-burning, rape and incest are well-recognised. They are given enormous publicity and draw social and academic interest, attention and condemnation. One crime which continues to go neglected and underreported relates to the violence inflicted on those who risk inter-caste and intra-caste marriages which infringe on cultural norms and practices. Such marriages are frequently runaway marriages or elopements. Moreover, they are not uncommon, and have shown a tendency to escalate over the years. Most of them result in acts of direct violence inflicted by male members of the family on the couple generally and on the girl specially. Although regarded as a private family matter, which must be hushed up and kept confidential, some cases spill over into the wider community domain. It is through this process that they have attracted media attention.

The following analysis of this widespread phenomenon in rural north India throws up aspects of caste, class and gender which are crucially inter-connected.[1] As marriage provides the structural link between kinship and caste, marital alliances are coming under closer surveillance. Kinship linkages by marriage, and relations established through marriage, give a caste group its strength, recognition and leverage in the wider society and polity. Any breach in these caste linkages brings down the status not only of the immediate family but also that of the clan and finally of the entire caste group. This factor was and remains a potent consideration in the enforcement of strict caste and sexual codes.

At the centre of these codes, therefore, lies the control of female sexuality, since its bestowal in marriage is so crucial to patriarchal forces, given their concern with caste purity, status, power and hierarchy. Those who infringe caste and kinship norms in marriage meet with extreme violence. Although the kind of emphasis placed upon caste, gender and sexual codes by upper caste and lower caste groups differs significantly, resulting in ambiguous responses, any infringement of the prescribed codes commonly evokes a violent response.

A challenge to these codes has come repeatedly both from within the caste and outside it. Processes of democratisation and the opening up of economic opportunities have altered the dynamics of power relations, making for complex interaction between members of different caste groups as well as between members of a particular caste. In the former, the growing resentment and assertiveness of subordinate lower castes and classes has often resulted in inter-caste liaisons which breach upper caste norms and sexual codes. In the latter, younger members are challenging the caste/kinship ideology upheld by senior male members by questioning sexual codes and taboos, defying demands of status, hypergamy or village exogamy, and discarding notions of honour. In the face of these challenges, emanating mostly from the rural periphery and semi-urban linked social groups, influenced by the kind of urbanisation which this region has undergone, earlier domains of flexibility are becoming constricted.

In a situation of drastic social and legal change, such infringements are sought to be controlled by invoking claims of tradition, culture and honour. Honour is enforced through the use of power—whether that of caste, class, gender or seniority—and, finally, through violence. The more vocal opposition and acts of violence are traceable to those social groups which stand to benefit the most by bolstering these cultural ideas. Violent reactions can also be traced to the increased insecurity caused by women's—especially a daughter's—legal right to inherit family property. The tensions between caste and class have generated anxieties and reinforced certain concerns which are being voiced in terms of tradition and caste codes. With the emergence of new socio-economic opportunities, educational advancement and apparent modernisation, new upwardly mobile groups express a fractured response to these codes. Some show defiance, yet others lead in upholding caste/community norms and practices. Both these responses result in furthering caste solidarities as well as caste hostilities, with one feeding the other.

However, a successfully forged alliance between cultural codes, honour and violence justifies the violence and results in a broad complicity that cuts across social groups, gender and age. Yet others may be coerced by the collective pressure of the community, exercised by the caste or village *panchayat*, which stands over and above the individual family. This pressure is aided and abetted by local state agencies which effectively support the gender and caste codes upheld by the caste/community leadership. Their joint patriarchal surveillance allows the perpetrators of violence to go scot free. This pattern has been repeated and sets up a spiral: ideological beliefs and violent practices are validated, which in turn reinforce cultural codes and make their infringement less acceptable, thus producing infinitely more violent reactions.

Case Studies in the Use of Violence

Some of the most talked about incidents are concentrated in rural north India and belong to western Uttar Pradesh, Haryana and the rural belt of the national capital.[2] Perhaps the most shocking of them all was the Mehrana murder case of March 1991.[3] Roshni, a Jat girl of village Mehrana in western UP, ran away with Brijendra, a low caste Jatav boy, assisted by his friend. The three of them were caught and the Jat *panchayat* sat in judgment on them. Under its decree, they were tortured the whole night, hanged in the morning and then set on fire, while two of them were still alive. The entire village was witness to this savage and brutal murder.

A month later in April 1991, in village Khedakul of Narela (north Delhi), Poonam, a Jat girl, was shot dead by her uncle in broad daylight for having an 'illicit relationship' with another Jat boy of the same village.[4] Again, several villagers were witnesses. The father and the uncle declared it a 'heinous crime', with death the only punishment. "Her action had soiled our honour, our pride," the father reportedly told the police. In August 1993, in village Khandravali in Muzzafarnagar district, western UP, a low caste girl, Sarita, having made a runaway match, was axed to death along with her husband Satish,[5] who belonged to her own caste group but hailed from an adjacent sister village[6] and was also distantly related to her. The families of both the victims were bricklayers; it was at a brick kiln in Haryana that they grew intimate and finally eloped. All attempts to trace them failed. However, when they allegedly returned of their own volition, five months after the elopement, they were beheaded in the village *chaupal* by the girl's uncle. Their 'grave social violation' was compounded by their returning to the village, where, according to local opinion, they 'dared to flaunt' their 'disdain for social norms'. The crime was witnessed by the whole village. This was the third elopement within its low caste community. Nothing is known of the other couples. The elders were concerned about protecting the *izzat* (honour) of the village. The brutal hacking was to be a "lesson to others", said Om Pal, the village sarpanch (headman). In this incident, the girl was blamed by the villagers for 'luring' the young man. The grandmother of Sarita openly declared: "Our name is mud. Can I look anyone in the eye now?"

Asha was brutally killed by her kin along with her lover Manoj in March 1994 in village Nayagaon in Haryana.[7] Asha belonged to the numerically and economically strong Saini caste in the village, locally considered to be a higher caste in relation to the Ahirs—the caste group to which Manoj belonged. The boy was declared to be an 'upstart' by the Sainis. According to local accounts, Asha openly asserted her right to choose her life partner. She reportedly told her family members not to interfere.

In June 1994 in village Hendigara in district Hazaribagh,

Mahavir Prasad, a low caste youth was lynched for marrying Malati, a Kurmi girl who was stripped by her own caste men and beaten publicly.[8] The villagers confided to the press reporters that Puran Mahato, Malati's father, who was economically hard up, had personally never objected to his daughter's 'love affair'. He was, however, under great pressure from fellow Kurmis to marry his daughter within the caste. The girl resisted this openly, by running away with Mahavir. On discovering this, the Kurmis convened a *panchayat* and imposed a fine of Rs. 5000 each on the families concerned. However, a more drastic punishment awaited the runaway couple.

More recently, in June 1995, in Bhagalpur, Bihar, Bijoy Kumar Bind, a low caste boy, was publicly lynched for his involvement with an upper caste girl.[9] The rest of the story follows a familiar pattern. Such examples could be multiplied many times.

During my own field work in Haryana (1985-90), I came across several cases which were narrated to me in confidence. Except for minor details, these bear a striking similarity to the above incidents and project similar attitudes. In order to throw some light on this growing social phenomenon, I shall rely on my knowledge and understanding of rural Haryana. The running thread of family and community honour, cultural and customary practice, moral and sexual codes, caste panchayats, caste purity and extreme violence, is noticeable in all of them. Therefore, for fear of repetition, I am not recounting them here. In fact, in rural Haryana, reported cases of kidnapping, rape and abduction are tabulated as 'sex crimes', and are even officially acknowledged to be "nothing but cases of love affairs with abducted women being the consenting party".[10] Most of them result in the physical elimination of the girl and the boy. If the boy escapes for some reason, the girl is almost always done away with. In an unusual case like that of village Kheri in district Bhiwani, the girl was caught, brought back and remarried to an old man despite her four month pregnancy, which was aborted. Significantly, the girl was an adult and all protests to the police and district administration were ignored. The whereabouts of the low caste boy are not known or disclosed; the Jat *biradari* remains tight-lipped. He is rumoured to have been disposed off by them.

In most of these cases, the crimes have been committed in public. Yet, the police is neither willing nor able to prepare the *challan* to document the crime or muster evidence from the villagers. A few cases which reach the stage of a court trial result in the perpetrators being let off for lack of evidence. Ultimately no one gets punished. In a candid remark, the Bahadurgarh police station officer, Risal Singh, opined that the police close their eyes to such incidents, all too many in Haryana, and let them go unreported.[11]

Upholding Honour: Individual and Community Concerns

There is, indeed, complicity between the perpetrators of violence and the police about 'justice' done for the sake of 'honour'. The police force in northern India, heavily drawn from dominant upper caste groups, is avowedly casteist. Moreover, its criminalisation and commercialisation are well known: monetary considerations overrule merit in recruitment, promotion and transfer. In keeping the law, the socio-political role of such a force has proved to be highly dubious. In their opinion, social issues must be resolved by caste leaders or the caste *panchayat* and not according to the law of the land, which applies a different criterion of justice.[12] Police action or inaction has also created nervousness among different communities (specially the lower castes) who fear both the open partiality and hidden biases in reporting a case, as well as the consequences of not obeying the decision of a powerful high caste panchayat. In the worst cases, the community leaders assert: "The police can do whatever they want, but we have to punish the culprits in our own way."[13]

Rural opinion is heavily in favour of punishing those who 'violate social norms' so that 'others learn a lesson'.[14] This attitude is condoned by the peer group. In the case of the Mehrana murder case, for example, Mahendra Singh Tikait, a noted Kisan leader from Western UP, publicly maintained: "I should have done the same. What was done was right."[15] He openly defended the right of the peasantry to punish anyone who breaks caste rules. Caste members view the killings as 'executions' and 'just punishment' for breaking caste norms and boundaries.[16] In all such cases the village or caste izzat is prioritised by the villagers in general and by leaders in particular.

The greatest danger to the ideology of izzat is seen to come from women. A woman dishonours her family, clan, caste and community by her shameful conduct. For example, in the case of village Mehrana, a local Jat woman opined: "*va chhokri ki shadi hone wali thi, par rand phir bhi jaa ke Jatav chhoran ke laagi. Jaton ki naak kata di vaa ne,*"[17] (that girl was to be married soon. Even so, the slut had to elope with a Jatav boy, she has brought shame to the Jats). Thus, dishonorable conduct on the part of a daughter is seen to ruin the family for ever, leaving the parents unfit to show their faces to the *biradari* (community), justifying in their eyes even the extreme step of killing her. Sociologists such as Veena Das believe that this concept of honour operates at the expense of human sentiments and values. According to Das, it demands a sacrifice of the natural ties created by biology, so that kinship morality stresses their transcendence for the higher ends of morality and the maintenance of 'honour'.[18] This behaviour is grounded in the belief that, like the social order, individual personality is also purified and lifted from a 'lower' to a 'higher' self by means of sacrifice.

Considered to be a commonly shared ideology, such notions are said to guide the social behaviour of people in the whole of northern India. However, this concept of caste/community honour is mostly appropriated by the upper castes. After all, the honour of lower caste groups is not recognised by upper castes in the first place. Given their weak socio-economic position, lower castes are also unable to claim any such honour specially in relation to the higher castes. They may vaguely share in the honour of the village as a whole. This identification may mean going willingly or unwillingly along with the dictates of the upper caste leadership as in the case of Mehrana village, where even the Jatavs were reported to have been compelled by dominant Jats to support the decision of the Jat panchayat. Interestingly, some of the earlier media reports had shown a unanimity of opinion between the two.

The only 'honour' which lower castes in the north may 'honourably' claim, it would seem, is in relation to their caste members and lies in their ability to enforce codes within their own caste group. In Khandrawali village, for instance, the infringement of 'incest' taboos by the low caste couple of the village, declared to be a slur on their honour, led to their public beheading. Denied any claims of honour in relation to higher castes, the lower castes, therefore, can become hypersensitive in defending it within their own caste. Such a concept of honour may not only be claimed, but also defended and implemented. Significantly, both the lower and the upper castes do not extend this concept to incest within the family involving senior males and junior females or any other prohibited category of people.[19] Quite clearly, the concept is neither accepted nor applied uniformly by all caste and status groups. Any infringement of this selectively prescribed code invites group pressure and violence. Violence therefore, underlines the existing ideology of honour.

Tabooed Alliances: Enforcing 'Traditional Norms'

Those marriages or associations which activate the interconnection between honour and violence relate not merely to inter-caste factors but also to intra-caste ones which upset certain traditional prohibitory taboos. They breach those customary rules which are subject to the *gotra* or *got* (as it is known in rural north India) rule of exogamy. (*Gotra* are exogamous patrilineal clans whose members are thought to share patrilineal descent from a common ancestor). For purposes of marriage, certain prohibited degrees of kinship have to be avoided. As a rule, three or four *got* exogamy is followed by most castes groups, both upper or lower.[20] A person is not permitted to marry into his or her caste *got*, nor with the mother's, the father's mother or the mother's mother. The last bar is however not universal and the restriction is apparently lessening. In anthropological terminology, *got* rules, in effect, prohibit marriage with either parallel or cross first cousins.

Writing about this taboo, J.M. Douie, the British revenue administrator, had observed in 1892: 'intercourse with a girl of the same *got* and tribe would be considered incest as all the landowners of one village are generally of one *got*.'[21] This is enlarged to include the entire village, as inhabitants of one village are considered to be theoretically related to each other. Cross-caste ties in a village experienced through fictional kinship are particularly valued.[22] North India has a clear preference for distant marriage alliances,[23] with caste groups such as the Jats expressly forbidding marriage into any village which shares even a border with the natal village,[24] or in which other clans of one's village are well represented.[25]

Consequently, village exogamy, which is observed by virtually all northern caste groups, high or low, introduces greater complexity to marriage prohibitions and notions of incest. According to Paul Hershman,

> [i]deally a man is the guardian of the honour of any woman who is related to him as 'sister' whether real or classificatory and therefore both sex and marriage are taboo between them. All men and women of the same clan, same localized clan and same village are talked of as being bound by the morality of brother-sister and therefore both sex and marriage are prohibited between members of any of these units.[26]

Culturally, therefore, incest as a category of sexual and marital prohibition is used as a wider social category to embrace not only a real sister but also classificatory sisters within and outside the caste, extending to the entire village. Significantly, terms like *bhai* (brother) and *behan* (sister) in villages are even used for persons who are not related to each other. Transcending ties of biological kinship, they embrace all males or females of the village of one's own generation, notwithstanding caste divisions. An important connotation of the term *bhai* is that a *behan*'s care and protection are entrusted to him. Although clandestine sexual relations occur quite commonly between classificatory or village brothers and sisters, any social approval of them in the form of marriage is considered an approval of incest and therefore violently resisted. Semi-secret liaisons tend to be overlooked as they require no realignment of social relations; as marriage is forbidden, the relationship is also necessarily of a limited duration. Marriage, on the other hand, affects relationships between groups; it has to be publicly validated by overt transactions and can provide a precedent for similar arrangements in the future.[27] The rejection of marriage in these cases is therefore related to the importance of establishing inter-group relationships by the exchange of rights in women. Moreover, in cases such as these (and not in others as will be shown later) a demarcation exists between private and public morality; morality which spills over from the realm of the private into the public impinges upon 'honour', both private and collective, necessitating drastic action. The Khedakul and Khandrawali episodes, cited above, become intelligible in this context.

The violent reception of such prohibited alliances also commonly results in the self-infliction of violence, namely, the suicide of the couple or at least of the girl.[28] However, just as often, the alleged suicide of the girl (by jumping into a well), is actually a case of murder. Tacit approval exists and the 'suicide' is even officially corroborated and accepted.

Yet, there are also cases like Khandravali, where, despite the knowledge of potential violence, the couple comes back to the village. The return of the couple can best be explained in terms of the viability of personal networks. As described by M.N. Srinivas,[29] this network can include members of diverse castes and status affiliations. Those who have the advantages of urbanisation and education have more heterogeneous networks than others. In cases of elopements, these support groups can work in extremely complex ways, becoming both structures of support and betrayal. The tension between overriding caste-kin connections on the one hand and these socially more heterogenous networks on the other, produces certain structural impediments to their utilisation. Consequently, the success or failure of these networks may compel the couple to return sooner, later or not at all. For example, in the Khandrawali case, Satish and Sarita had been reportedly 'lured' back to the village by this very network with certain promises and threats, where 'justice' was then inflicted upon them for breaking caste codes. Other couples who have fled the village and whose whereabouts are not known or disclosed, have broken off all connections with the village, including ostensibly with their families. Any connection, if reestablished, is not acknowledged. For all purposes they are considered dead.

Caste/Community Pressures: Status Concerns

Certain restrictions are now being slightly relaxed. The principle of village exogamy and even the prohibited degree of *got* are, on occasion, breached and the breach is overlooked.[30] Considerations of class and status have indeed intervened to allow flexibility in this respect.[31] But they remain mostly confined to urban areas or to families that are not under the kind of collective community pressure characteristic of a rural situation. Yet even here it does not go uncontested or uncensured. It remains a point of attack by the caste/community if and when it so desires.[32] Consequently, urban incidents show varying degrees of success. Rural opinion in general, however, not only disapproves strongly of such alliances but maintains a greater surveillance of such breaches. In connection with the tightening pressures of caste/community, I wish to examine two recent cases from Haryana that I am personally acquainted with, which throw a great deal of light on the specificity of rural situations.

In November 1993, in village Pehtavas, district Bhiwani, confrontation and violence among Jats occurred on account of the infringement of certain clan taboos. The two groups of Jats involved in the marriage belonged to the Punia and the Sangwan *got*. Bakhtawar Singh Punia got his two sons married into the Sangwan *got* of the Jats. A *khap panchayat* (multi clan council) of forty villages met on 14 March and held the alliance to be incestuous; it decreed the marriage void. When Bakhtawar Singh Punia refused to accept the verdict, a social boycott of the family was ordered.

Normally, the Sangwans and the Punias can and do intermarry. But because of a tradition, unique to the village, marital alliances between them were considered 'sinful'. During the 1850s, the first important settler of the village, Chaudhary Chet Ram of the Sangwan *got,* had adopted Dhod Ram Punia as his son. The Punia sub-caste thus merged with the Sangwans. The two clans from then onwards became adopted brother *got.* However, the alliance began as one between a higher status brother and a younger, weaker brother. Over the years, some of the families of the Punias migrated to the city, left farming, and took up urban professions. Bakhtawar Singh Punia was one such man. He joined government service as a police inspector. His sons Mahender and Rajesh both grew up to take urban professions. Living in an urban centre allowed Bakhtawar's family to escape the direct ire of the caste panchayat's decision. But the Punia families who were based in Pehtavas and who had participated in the wedding were targeted in the village. These families, fourteen of them, were driven out of their homes in April and attacked repeatedly thereafter. Their houses were stoned and even partially burned. One of them was very seriously injured. Only after the eighty year old Punia patriarch and the first cousin of Bakhtawar Singh Punia apologised publicly to a massive gathering of the *sarv-khap panchayat* (all-clan council) were they allowed to return to the village after eight months. A pledge was made on behalf of Bakhtawar that neither he nor his sons would return. The situation continues to remain tense between the two clans as the Punias have lost lakhs in property. The administration and politicians have watched silently as they want this 'social matter' to be settled by the panchayats.

In May 1995 in village Salani of Rohtak district a similar confrontation took place, despite the marriage being an intra-caste one. Naresh of Bairagi *got* married Santosh of the neighbouring Patoda village in April 1995. Santosh belonged to the Chahar *got*. The Chahar *got* families in Naresh's village are relatively prosperous, and consider their *got* to be higher than the Bairagi *got* of Naresh. They were, therefore, angered that a 'low caste' man (low in terms of social and economic status) had married one of their *got* women, thus bringing down the status of the entire *got*. A panchayat of the Chahar *got* met in the presence of some residents of Patoda village and annulled the marriage. They turned down Naresh's father's suggestion that the couple be allowed to leave the village and settle down elsewhere.

Significantly, Naresh's father did not directly challenge the verdict of the panchayat, but took the plea that, as the marriage had already been consummated, nobody was likely to marry the girl. This plea was not accepted. The panchayat also reportedly forced Naresh's father, Toohi Ram, and his uncle Omal, who had played an important role in finalising the match, to blacken each other's faces, and fined them Rs 2100 each. When Naresh complained to the district authorities about this high-handedness, a social boycott of his family was also announced. A fine of Rs 500 was imposed on anybody disobeying the panchayat's ruling. The couple is now rumoured to have fled the village and their whereabouts are not disclosed.

Both these cases, with distinct parallels to the Khedakul and Khandrawali cases discussed earlier, require a somewhat complex reading. Opposition to the marriage emanates from norms of village exogamy, incest taboos, along with the distinct shades of hypergamy, by which a girl from a lower clan can marry a man of a higher clan while the reverse is prohibited. Significantly, there is no identifiable concept of hypergamy in Haryana. The claims of higher and lower clans among the Jats seem to be more economic and political and are not traditionally defined. Therefore, the attempt to equate status and clan are possible signs of Rajputisation: the symptomatic drive of an upwardly mobile group to claim higher status within a caste.[33] These two cases also reveal attempts at either claiming a higher status or at retaining one's status in the face of challenges and erosions effected by other clan groups within the caste fold. As marriage alliances are a significant means of establishing one's status in society, they assume great importance and demand sharp vigilance. The contradictory reactions of certain groups to the demands of caste status are an indication of the contemporary multi-directional pulls within a caste, accounting for the confrontation and violence in intra-caste marriage alliances.

Transgressing Caste Norms: Challenges

It is inter-caste marriages or rather elopements, however, which evoke the most violent condemnation. These are frequently village affairs and transgress the rules of village exogamy. An overwhelming 93.6 per cent of different age and sex groups, according to a 1982 study, are said to be against inter-caste marriages in rural Haryana.[34] The factors operating behind this disapproval range from considering such marriages to be 'short-lived and impermanent', given to creating problems of adjustment due to 'dissimilarity of culture' and 'problems of identity for future generations', to the essential ones of keeping 'purity of blood'. Yet, the large evidence of runaway marriages suggests something to the contrary and contests this cultural ideology. The agency adopted by the young towards their sexual and emotional fulfillment contradicts the normalised ideals of behaviour which they may otherwise voice.

This region, in fact, abounds in folk tales regarding women of the dominant high caste who run away with low caste men. Such narratives may indeed be drawing upon aspects of existing social practices, given all the examples I have been discussing. High caste women, because of their work in the fields, are considered specially 'vulnerable'. Exclusively female songs celebrate sexual liaisons with lower caste men. This subversion of the sexual prowess of high caste men by their women in folk songs acts as a taunt and possibly underlines upper caste male fears about the unharnessed sexuality of their women and the potent virility of low caste men.

Such liaisons are surfacing more frequently due to the new social pressures generated in the wake of the growing democratisation and greater opportunities for lower caste groups.

Sharper caste contradictions are now emerging due to economic growth, which is benefiting some but not all lower caste groups. The upwardly mobile among them have taken significant initiatives in several pockets of north India.[35] For example, in western Uttar Pradesh, Jat and Jatav rivalry has seen violent conflict over material interests.[36] The Mehrana case is symptomatic of this rivalry where the upper caste woman was used to settle wider issues which had been brewing for some time. This violent gendered response of the upper castes in a bitter struggle with lower caste groups for power and domination has its parallel in other parts of India as well.[37] In north India, many of the lower castes who have advanced economically and are more assertive live either in towns or on the periphery of the towns with strong village links. This situation makes them both somewhat independent as well as vulnerable to the dictates of the wider community. Such contradictions make for a potentially violent solution to any transgression committed by them.

The power dynamics between different caste groups, particularly between dominant and subordinate castes, which has assumed a more threatening form today, has always been potentially explosive. The region of Haryana, for instance, has witnessed severe caste confrontations between dominant and low caste groups even in the colonial period.[38] Nowadays, newspapers more frequently highlight the growing incidents of upper and lower caste/class confrontations in north India.[39] If, on the one hand, this power dynamics shows a new kind of assertiveness among lower castes, it also shows a new determination on the part of the dominant castes, made rich through green revolution technology, to keep their status and position intact. Such occasions are used as an opportunity by the higher castes to assert their hegemony and to 'teach a lesson' to those who wish to challenge them.[40] Significantly, the new assertiveness of the latter is reflected in their relationship with high caste women, witnessed in attempts at elopement and marriage. As a Jat woman opined in the aftermath of the Mehrana murder case: '*In Jatavan ne to haad he kar di. Badmas to ve the he, hamari chhorian pe bhi haath maran lage.*'[41] (These

Jatavs have gone too far. They have always been crooks, and now they have even started pawing our girls).

If high caste women are considered 'vulnerable' to low caste men, the sexual abuse of low caste women by high caste men, extending from rape and sexual exploitation to liaison, remains an ever-growing phenomenon.[42] The case of Phoolan Devi in this respect is internationally known. It is not as if the lower caste women *lose* their 'purity' and 'honour' by mating sexually, willingly or unwillingly—in the eyes of upper castes, they have no 'purity' or 'honour' to begin with.[43] Declared to be 'sexually promiscuous' by upper castes groups, the onus is firmly on these women for inciting upper caste men. One frequently voiced opinion in rural Haryana is: *'yo to hoven he aise hain, mahare ladakon ka ke kasur.'* (These women are sexually promiscuous. What fault is it of our boys?)

This rampant sexual exploitation, largely born out of the work situation and power relations subtending their lives as agricultural labourers, underlines the inability of low caste men to 'protect' their women. This inability is frequently used by landowning castes as a powerful tool of domination. The spiralling effect of this is noticeable in the growing resentment of lower caste groups, the eruptions of violence, the sharpening of caste consciousness and the enforcement of caste/customary codes by all castes, high or low, often as a form of offence as well as defence. In this connection it is significant to note that the extreme left Marxist-Leninist groups in Bihar have successfully used the resentment and resistance of lower castes to the sexual exploitation of their women by higher caste landowning class men as a strategy for mobilisation.[44] The sexuality of women, of both high or low caste groups, has, therefore, assumed an added dimension in the modern context. The pressures against inter-caste alliances have strengthened rather than weakened.

Constricting Opportunities: Primary and Secondary Alliances

Inter-caste alliances were not entirely uncommon in the colonial period. However, more often than not, they were confined to a secondary alliance. In the subsistence level economy of this region, with its highly adverse female-male sex ratio,[45] those agriculturists who were hard pressed economically were known to take recourse to wives from among the lower castes as well. Malcolm Lyall Darling, the famed writer-cum-civil administrator of Punjab, maintained that a Jat would marry almost any woman he could.[46] Frequently, these were women from the Chamar caste. However a faint pretense was kept up that the girl was of his caste and an equally faint acceptance followed. A local belief maintains: *Jat ek samunder hai aur jo bhi daruya es samunder mein parti hai wo samunder ki bun jati hai.* (The Jat is like an ocean—whatever river falls into this ocean loses its identity and becomes the ocean itself). The children of a *Chuhri* or *Chamaran*, accepted in marriage by a Jat, were called Jats though they were often ridiculed as *Chuhri ke* or *Chamaran ke.*[48] Accounts of Brahmins marrying low caste women are also available in folk tales found in UP and Haryana.[49]

North India is indeed rich in folk tales, still popularly recounted, of low caste women marrying higher peasant caste men, as well as Kshatriyas and Rajas.[50] A popular tale tells of a *bhangan* (a sweeper) who married a *kisan* (peasant), but, being accustomed to receiving *rotis* (unleavened whole gram bread) from the hands of *kisani (kisan's* wife), she was unable to get rid of this habit. She therefore started to put *rotis* in all the *allahas*(alcoves) of the house and then make loud requests: '*kisani, roti diyo*' (give me *roti, kisani*). Her low caste origins were soon found out, but she was happily accepted and told to behave herself.[51]

By and large, the agricultural castes did not really look down upon lower caste women who became their wives. This is aptly expressed in a local proverb still quoted extensively in Haryana: *beeran ki kai jaat*[52] (women have no caste). Yet it is significant to note that in no way was it considered an upward move for the natal family of the low caste woman. For all purposes, she was not only purchased from her parents, but was also made to terminate all connections with them after this marriage. This was essential to keep the myth of her belonging to a higher caste.

It was also clear that the social groups involved in such duplicity could not afford to and indeed did not attach undue importance to caste purity if it was breached by a man. This social practice was rationalised by maintaining that : '*roti to bun jagi, naam to chul jaga, dono ka guzara ho jaga*'[53] (At least the food will be cooked, the family name will be carried on; both will some how manage to live together).

British officials have confirmed the existence of this practice. But they greatly frowned upon it and declared it 'a kind of disreputable matrimonial agency'.[54] Given to applauding the 'magnificent physique' of the so-called superior agriculturist castes in agrarian and military professions, they actually bemoaned its biological 'deterioration' because of this practice.[55]

Taking wives from lower castes, however, never became a norm as such, nor was it practised on a wide scale. Moreover, this practice did not go unchallenged, specially from the late nineteenth century onwards when attempts were made to move the court in those cases of *karewa* (widow remarriage),[56] where caste endogamy had not been observed. A series of such cases were brought to the courts in the early nineteenth century. In the case of *Sahib Ditta* vs. *Musammat Bela* in 1900, the reversioners (male heirs of a diseased owner's property) challenged the Brahmin widow's *karewa* marriage to a Jat and sought to deprive her children of their inheritance on the grounds of illegitimacy.[57] It was made out that 'if a Brahmin widow cannot marry a Brahmin, how can she marry a Jat'. The attempt was clearly to invoke the Hindu law applicable to women to refute customary law which was the operable norm in colonial Punjab. The colonial government, for reasons of its own, was more anxious to enforce *karewa*;[58] the case was judged in favour of Jat custom, which recognised such unions.

The same position was held in a series of cases involving lower castes like the Chamars.[59] It was acknowledged that any Hindu widow, from a Brahmin to a Chamar, could be married to men of agriculturist castes by *karewa*.[60] The coupling of these two caste groups, high and low, is significant. In this region, norms were dictated by the dominant agriculturist castes—the chief being the Jats. Consequently, the higher ritual ranking of the Brahmin dropped when confronted with the harsh reality of existence in which the Brahmins were an agriculturist rather than a priestly caste. Moreover, in relation to the Jats they were numerically and socio-economically, far inferior.[61]

New norms, claimed on the basis of caste purity, custom and tradition, sought to invalidate inter-caste marriages. It is clear that British courts represented a higher authority, and had opened a way for people to claim certain rights which could not be claimed through the traditional panchayats. Interestingly, the situation is reversed now, as the traditional panchayats are being used to impose a doubtful tradition.

It must be remembered, though, that all these cases relate to the *karewa* marriage which was inter-caste and not the first *biah* or *shadi* (marriage). It is only in subsequent associations that the propertied classes were opting for lower castes or inter-caste marriages. Primary alliances of these kinds remained confined to lower economic groups. Alliances with lower castes and classes, however, came to be disavowed by certain sections of the landowning castes/classes seeking to maintain caste purity not for property reasons alone but also in order to achieve upward mobility. Caste purity thus became linked with higher status and upward mobility in Haryana, and restrictions upon marriage tended to be accepted.

In the changed socio-economy of the post-colonial period such breaches among the dominant upper caste groups are no longer socially acceptable. Both men and women are under pressure to remain within the caste, though the pressure on men is not as intense. The persistence of a highly adverse male-female sex ratio—874 females per thousand males in 1991[62]—has meant that a large number of men remain single. The Census statistics show that the proportion of 'never married' males in Haryana in 1981 was more than the married males in all the districts of the state.[63] This is reversed in the case of women where the absolute number of married females is more than that of the married males.[64] Also, men remain single for a longer time so that their age at marriage is comparatively much later.[65] As a result, upper caste endogamy has led to a constriction of opportunity not only for men but more importantly for lower caste women who earlier had the facility to marry into castes above them. The likely difficulties in arranging marriages for the children of such alliances and for other members of the family (not noticeable earlier), are also freely and frequently voiced.[66]

Assertions of Power: Enforcing Complicity

As seen above, however, it is not as if these norms are not broken; the imposition of restrictions do not go unchallenged. But any open dissent, complicit or implicit sanctions towards this stand, or even the inability to punish those who break this norm, are not easy to live down. There is the very genuine fear of *hukka pani band* (social ostracism), as the village community is united in not accepting such matches. The open taunts '*tu ke bolle sai tere beti ne aisa kiya*' (what can you say, your daughter behaved like this), are much harder to live down as derogatory epithets become permanent social fixtures to their existence. In many instances entire families have tended to leave the village, as the runaway woman is considered to have *munh ko kalkh laga gai* (blackened the face of the family). It alludes to the old time punishment when a man was shamed by blackening his face— the ultimate infamy.

In fact, when the parents are unwilling to act in such cases, the caste biradari takes over, as in the case of Mehrana, where the Jat panchayat took the decision. In the words of Bihan (Roshni's mother): 'The *panchayat walas* stepped in...they said to me that *ladkiwalas* did not have a say in the matter and that they alone would decide what punishment was to be meted out to the girl. They took her away and hanged her.'[67]

The caste panchayats are indeed intervening frequently to impose justice according to their own definition. Although very little is known about the working of caste panchayats, they remain an active force in rural north India.[68] They have been generally known to award minor punishments which humiliate rather than injure. Punishments include fines, orders to give obligatory village feasts, rubbing one's nose in the dust before the aggrieved party or even the entire gathering or touching their feet, shaving one's head, and drinking or dipping one's nose in the urine of one or more persons.[69]

The more recent exhibition of the power of public stripping, awarding the death penalty and carrying out executions by the panchayat is closely linked to growing urbanisation and consumerism. There has been a steady process of urbanisation in Haryana within twenty years; between 1961–81, the total number of towns in Haryana has increased from 61 to 81.[70] During this time the index of growth of the urban population has more than doubled. Yet despite extensive urbanisation, the distinction between urban and rural is not watertight, with considerable overlap between the two. For example, it is estimated that more than one lakh people from inside the rural and semi-urban areas of Haryana commute daily to Delhi. There are trains from Rohtak, Gurgaon, Palwal and Panipat scheduled to leave in the morning and return in the evening, keeping to the work schedule of the Haryanavi workers employed in various capacities in the metropolis. These trains are not just full, but overflowing. There are also a very large number of army recruits as well as police personnel, all drawn from rural areas, who have to leave their families in the villages because only insignificant numbers are provided with family accommodation.[71]

This kind of urbanisation is accompanied by the spillover of an urban consumerist culture. The role model is set by the rural affluent classes and their conspicuous consumption is emulated by others. Their ideology, signified by 'a jeep, a gun and a bottle of rum', is in keeping with the image of a virile martial race with a macho culture.[72] There is no place for women in the 'modern' urban ethos which is imitated. Paradoxically, despite being so influenced by the life style and consumerist culture of the cities, suspicions toward the urban value system, its culture and influence are reinforced in rural areas specially in relation to women.[73] So, on the one hand, the reigning ideology sanctions and even desires urbanisation and the consumerism associated with considerations of male status and upward mobility, while on the other hand, it holds the city responsible for the rapidly changing, now idealised 'traditional' cultural norms of rural north India. This contradiction is not uncommonly resolved through violence at an individual/family level, and/or if that fails to materialise, at a collective community level.

The caste panchayats, in other words, seek to counter the failure of the law of the land by protecting an eroded 'traditional value system' as it is perceived to be enshrined in customary practices. For example, except for certain incest taboos, the legal restrictions on marriage under the Hindu Marriage Act, 1955 are almost non-existent.[74] But in rural areas, as we have seen, apart from several restrictions on marriages, the category of incest is a very wide and selective one.[75] Incest, when intra-family or intra-*got*, never meets with similar violence, even when made public. Similarly, sexual codes are sought to be enforced only in relation to upper caste women. The purity of lower caste women, even when breached through rape, is not taken into cognisance.

This intervention of the caste panchayats is also an assertion of the combined power and domination of upper caste senior male members over younger men and women. In a way, it is a direct effort to retain power in the face of challenges by aspirants from different socio-economic strata as well as from the younger generation. The new legal system based upon different principles has also cut into their power base. The colonial masters, on the other hand, had nurtured the caste leadership and helped to maintain and strengthen their power. Their concept of justice gave recognition to customary laws and to ancient texts and implemented them selectively in the courts. For example, during colonial rule, the run-away match of an unmarried girl was not given legal sanction because the 'consent' of the guardian had not been forthcoming.[76] Colonial official attitude was moulded according to local custom whereby minor or adult women were always under the guardianship of some male member. Legally, the situation is now vastly altered as 'minor' or 'major' categories are legal categories, so that anyone above eighteen years is an adult and free to act independently without the sanction of a guardian. The caste leadership and the caste panchayats are ignoring these kinds of legal interventions. Consequently, the ideology of the guardianship of women irrespective of their age and status remains enforceable through caste panchayats on pain of death.

The ideology of female guardianship is essentially an ideology of control. It is closely tied up with the question of the control of female sexuality, particularly in relation to women of upper caste groups. In the high caste Brahminical social order this control is intrinsically connected not only to patrilineal succession but also to the maintenance of caste purity and caste hierarchy. Consequently, miscegeny (the mixing of castes) as well as hypogamy (union between women of a higher caste and men of a lower caste), have been severely condemned and given the highest punishment. In Punjab-Haryana, the Brahminical model was not so strong and the concept of caste purity and caste hierarchy were not the same.[78] At the same time, caste endogamy sought to affirm and maintain caste status. Thus, even though the rules of caste purity were breached by men from agriculturist castes (mostly in their secondary associations), women were never allowed to break caste rules.

The idealised norm of marriage for a woman is signified in the phrase '*Jat ki beti Jat ko*' (a Jat's daughter must wed a Jat). The word Jat may be substituted for any other caste group as well. Yet, the class factor may intervene to determine the applicability of this norm, specially in relation to the lower classes which not infrequently overlap with the lower castes. Among the upper caste groups this rule cannot be breached by women even in their secondary association.

The persistent low female:male ratio has greatly contributed towards keeping the pressure on women to maintain caste endogamy. For example, the remarriage of a widow remains essentially a levirate alliance, even forcibly so, if need be. Only recently have those widows, who for some reason cannot be accommodated by the brothers or cousins of the deceased husband, been allowed to remarry outside the conjugal family, but still very much within the caste.[79] It is only among the lower caste groups that greater flexibility is observed for women, whether divorced or widowed, although there are instances of widows being sold off among lower castes in western UP.[80] In fact, there is so much of a premium on a woman's productive and reproductive potential that it is not allowed to go waste. Among the lower castes and classes, for instance, a widow or a divorcee, particularly if she is of reproductive age, cannot refuse to remarry.

Controlling Female Sexuality: Vested Interests

The question of control of women's reproductive and productive labour is therefore intrinsically linked with the control of her sexuality. The decision for its bestowal is crucial to patriarchal considerations of status and authority. For instance, the bestowal of a daughter in marriage is certainly financially draining due to the escalating consumerist premium on dowry. And yet, the forging of appropriate endogamous marital links is closely linked with status considerations and status formation. Any break in this, however minor, is very threatening. The selection of a life partner by a woman is a display of independence in asserting her sexuality and her preference in relation to a sexual partnership; she is also thereby bestowing her reproductive and labour potential.[81] Such an action among men also shows an independence, which, in local perception, presages a disruption of family ties or the break up of the joint family system.[82] It is indicative of the loss of authority suffered not only by senior men but also by older women over the son and more pronouncedly over the *bahu* (daughter-in-law). This may also explain the complicity of senior women in opposing any such move. In a situation where the settling of a marriage alliance is in the hands of senior men and women, such an assertion also deals a severe blow to the family hierarchy, disrupts power equations within it, and disturbs the social hierarchy outside in the village.

This play of power has come to be intimately connected with post-independent changes in India, such as a woman's legal entitlement to inherit parental property. The Hindu Succession Act of 1956 first made it possible for a daughter, sister, widow or mother in regions like Haryana to inherit land with full proprietary rights at her disposal.[83] This introduced fundamental and radical changes in the law, and a break from the past. Customarily, the land of a village is taken to belong to the male descendants of ancestors who originally settled and worked on it, so that male agnatic descendants alone, as members of the local clan, have reversionary rights to the estate. Land is ordinarily not to be alienated outside this group. The only ideal and *izzatwala* (honourable) pattern of inheritance is by men from men. This basically implies that daughters and sisters who are potential introducers of fresh blood and new descent lines through their husbands are to be kept from exercising their inheritance rights.

As the result, the most virulent objections to breaches of caste/community taboos in marriage come from the powerful land-owning classes of the village. This has introduced anxieties for a number of different reasons, not necessarily out of concern for caste endogamy or village exogamy or the upkeep of tradition per se, even though these anxieties are played out through these concerns and in fact reinforce them. The violent opposition to self-assertion in marriage, therefore, overrides the educational or modernising process that such rural families may have undergone. In fact, opposition is almost always grounded in terms of tradition and culture vs. modernity. Such reactions are, therefore, largely due to the increased insecurity in property matters that has arisen in the wake of this enabling Act.

Rural patriarchal forces have been anxiously devising means to stem the progressive fallout of this Act through a variety of means.[84] One way has been to oppose the inheritance rights of a daughter or a sister to those of the brother. Except in cases where there are no brothers, the sisters either sign away their inheritance in favour of their brother or sell it to him at a nominal price. This code of conduct is observed knowingly by both the natal and conjugal families. Brother-sister bonds of love have also been greatly encouraged, visible in the noticeable revival of the Raksha Bandhan festival and the renewed sanctity it has claimed in north India.

This emphasis on the sanctity of the sister-brother bond is not only ruptured should the girl make an alliance within the village (where theoretically everyone is related), such a decision introduces a rank outsider into the family who can claim the property on behalf of his wife. As an outsider he remains beyond the influence of the family and caste/community rules and ethics which ensure patrilineal inheritance. The location of a married daughter within the natal village also spells danger to patrilineal inheritance as it facilitates and could lead to the assumption of land inherited by her. Thus, the tightening of restrictions on marriage practices emphasising village exogamy and caste endogamy, has the effect of negating the progressive fallout of the inheritance law for women.

The significance of such practices can be easily visualised when juxtaposed to the customs prevalent among the predominantly landless lower castes. These castes allow for flexibility in the rule of patrilocality. In other words, since the land and its ownership is not in question, the family of a married daughter might settle in her natal village, with the result that the *ghar jamai* (resident son-in-law) phenomenon among lower castes is not uncommon in rural Haryana or across the border in western UP.[85] At the time of marriage, however, the principle of village exogamy is as rigorously enforced as the prohibited degree of *got* and other taboos by lower caste groups. Breaches are viewed as incestuous and are violently dealt with. Clearly, then, there are similarities as well as significant differences between higher caste and lower caste groups in observing caste and sexual codes. A comparison of the two remains outside the scope of this essay and will have to await a more detailed study. It may suffice to reiterate here that this complex picture highlights the contemporary flux of the caste system in India, revealing the co-existence of consolidation and challenge, and where class and life styles are also assuming importance in social relations. In fact it is the class and gender components within the caste system which have created inter-caste and intra-caste differentiation and inequalities as well as status distinctions. Yet, these aspects remain comparatively neglected and need to be more extensively probed. The interface of caste, class and gender, as this analysis shows, is crucial to understanding the complexities of the caste system as it exists today.

I presented a draft of this paper at the workshop on *Rethinking Indian Modernity: The Political Economy of Indian Sexuality*, held at the Madras Institute of Development Studies, Madras, August I-3, 1996, which has also appeared in the *Economic and Political Weekly*, Vol. 32.19, May 10-16 1997, pp. 1019-28. I thank the participants for their comments. I also wish to thank Uma Chakravarti, Patricia Uberoi and Leela Dube for making extensive comments, observations and criticisms on an earlier version of this paper.

Notes

1. A recent study sees such alliances solely in terms of love marriages vs. arranged marriages and seeks their explanation in individual vs. social action. The former, unrestrained by group or social pressure is considered dangerous and improper and a threat to group harmony and honour. (See Steve Derne, *Culture in Action: Family Life, Emotion, and Male Dominance in Banaras, India*, New York: State University of New York Press, 1995.) This understanding however is too narrow as it leaves out the wider structures of kinship and caste which play an important role in marriage associations. It is the infringement of these which produces violent responses.

2. Media reportage has its own biases. Experience shows that in the study of incidents of casteism, newspaper reports give weightage to upper caste/class accounts, as police, political and administrative office and press reportage and editing are predominantly upper caste, ruling class preserves. Yet even in these accounts, voices like those of women and lower castes, though marginalised, are not entirely absent. In the cases given above these facts are kept in mind and for purposes of analysis, those marginalised voices are picked out which have echoes and resonance in cases similar to those occurring in rural Haryana and for which extensive field work has been undertaken.

3. For extensive coverage of this case see *The Hindustan Times*, 7 May 1991, p. 1; 29 September 1991, p. 7; *The Times of India*, 11 April 1991, p. 6; 30 March 1991, p. 5; *India Today*, 30 April 1991, pp. 122–25; *The Illustrated Weekly*, 20–21 April 1991, pp. 16–19; *Sunday*, 14–20 April 1991, p. 15.

4. *The Times of India*, 21 and 22 April 1991, pp. 1, 3; *Indian Express*, 21 April 1991, p. 1.

5. *Pioneer*, 11 August 1993, p. 1; *The Times of India*, 29 March 1994, p. 4.

6. The constituent villages were formed in the past due to overcrowding in the parent village by an off-shoot of the dominant proprietary caste group. Tracing their origin to a common ancestor, these villages are tied together by kinship bonds; they act together by kinship bonds; they act together on ceremonial occasions and for panchayat meetings. These are territorially contiguous villages, having been established, as Ibbetson points out, "on the edge of the drainage line from which their tanks would be filled". Locally referred to as 'sister villages' many of these are known by the same name with the addition of the words *Kalan* (big) and *Khurd* (small). See Denzil Ibbetson, *Report on the Revision of Settlement of the Panipat Tehsil and Karnal Pargana of the Karnal District, 1872–1880*, Allahabad: Pioneer Press, 1883, p. 74.

7. *India Today*, 15 April 1994, pp. 78–79; *The Times of India*, 12 August 1994, pp. 7; *Sunday*, 22–28 August 1993, pp. 38–39.

8. *The Times of India*, 14 June 1994, p. 4.

9. *The Times of India*, 3 June 1995, p. 1.

10. *Mahendergarh District Gazetteer*, Government of Haryana, Chandigarh, 1988, p. 233.

11. *The Times of India*, 29 March 1994, p. 7.

12. *The Times of India*, 23 November 1994, p. 4.

13. *Sunday Observer*, 23 September-October 1993, p. 13.

14. *The Times of India*, 29 March 1994, p. 7.

15. Mohender Singh Tikait appeared on the television, *Newstrack*, September 1991.

16. *Pioneer*, 11 August 1993, p. 1; *The Times of India*, 29 March 1994, p. 7.

17. *Illustrated Weekly*, 20–21, pp. 17.

18. Veena Das, 'Masks and Faces: An essay on Punjabi kinship' in Patricia Uberoi, (ed.) *Family, Kinship and Marriage in India*, Delhi: Oxford University Press, 1994, pp. 198–224.

19. This is contrary to the observations of Jack Goody in northern Ghana where such relationships of unequal status, characterised by authority, are likely to be treated with more severity than those characterised by relative equality. See his 'Incest and Adultery' in

his edited work, *Kinship*, Middlesex, England: Penguin Books, 1991, pp. 64–81.

20. Gathered from field interviews. For the same norms in other parts of northern India see Oscar Lewis, *Village Life in Northern India: Studies in a Delhi Village*, New York: Vintage Books, 1958, pp. 160–61; M.S. Pradhan, *The Political System of the Jats of Northern India*, London: Oxford Universty Press, 1996, pp. 89–91.

21. J.M. Douie, *Revaj-i-Am of Tehsil Kaithal of Pargana Indri in the Karnal District, Lahore, Civil and Military Gazette*, 1892, p. 7.

22. Helen Lambert in her study of Rajasthan shows how these fictional relationships established by women with persons from their natal village offer them a support structure in their conjugal home. These cross-caste ties are of strategic importance even for men for political and economic reasons when visiting other villages where their married sisters reside. Other men establish fictional kinship ties of solidarity stretching across caste, class and status through their in-marrying women. See her article 'Caste, Gender and Locality in Rural Rajasthan' in C.J. Fuller, (ed.) *Caste Today*, Delhi: Oxford University Press, 1996, pp. 93–123.

23. For a comprehensive list of reference works dealing with northern India, see Bina Agarwal, *A Field of One's Own: Gender and Land Rights in South Asia*, Cambridge: Cambridge University Press, 1994, pp. 335–36.

24. S.P. Sharma, 'Marriage among the Jats and the Thakurs of North India: Some comparisons', *Contributions to Indian Sociology*, New Series, 1973, Vol. VII, pp. 81–103.

25. Lewis, *Village Life in Northern India*, op. cit., p. 161.

26. Paul Hershman, *Punjabi Kinship and Marriage*, Delhi: Hindustan Publishing Corporation, 1981, pp. 133–34.

27. Goody, 'Incest and Adultery', op. cit.

28. Leigh Minturn, *Sita's Daughters: Coming Out of Purdah*, New York: Oxford University Press, 1993, pp. 212–16.

29. M.N. Srinivas, *Village, Caste, Gender and Method: Essays in Indian Social Anthropology*, Delhi: Oxford University Press, 1996, pp. 134–35.

30. Personal observation in Haryana and Delhi villages.

31. Among the Patidars of Gujarat, for instance, who follow a 'circular' model in marriages, the intermarrying 'circles' often break *sapinda* rules in order to get appropriate status matches. For details see David Pocock, 'The Hypergamy of the Patidars' in Uberoi, *Family,*

Kinship and Marriage, op. cit., pp. 330–40. For more recent examples see Adrian Mayer, 'Caste in an Indian Village: Changes and continuities', in Fuller, (ed.) *Caste Today*, op. cit., pp. 32–64. Even marriage within the *gotra* is sometimes possible. In Maharashtra *gotra* prohibition is circumvented by getting the girl-to-be-married adopted by her maternal uncle or some other relative of another gotra. It is he who acts as the father and performs *kanyadan*. (Personal communication from Leela Dube.)

32. An interesting instance is that of a noted politician of Haryana who infringed the *got* prohibition norms while getting his daughter married in 1958. In the subsequent elections that he fought, this factor was assailed by his detractors.

33. Jonathan P. Parry, *Caste and Kinship in Kangara*, New Delhi: Vikas Publishing House, 1979, pp. 195–231.

34. Sarita Mehta, 'Social Mobility in Rural Haryana', Ph.D. thesis, Rural Sociology, Haryana Agricultural University, Hissar, 1982, p. 175.

35. In north India, the Jatavs of UP have shown dynamic progress over the last decade. Lapoint and Lapoint for instance have discussed how the Jatavs of village Garupur in Meratth district are well ahead of the Jats and other castes in the proportion of people who hold a secondary school diploma. See E. Lapoint and D. Lapoint, 'Socio-economic Mobility among Village Harijans', *Eastern Anthropologist*, Vol. 38, pp. 1–18. Similar trends are available among the Jatavs of Agra and Koris of Kanpur. See O.M. Lynch, *The Politics of Untouchability: Social Mobility and Social Change in a City of India*, New York: Columbia University Press, 1969; S. Molund, *First We are People: The Koris of Kanpur between Caste and Class*, Stockholm: Stockholm Studies in Social Anthropology, 1988.

36. For a discussion of Jat-Jatav confrontations in western U.P. see Owen M. Lynch, 'Rioting as Rational Action', *Economic and Political Weekly*, Vol. 29, November, pp. 1951–56. Also for diferent accounts of their conflicts see *The Hindustan Times*, 28 September 1989; 29 June 1990.

37. For this see a most incisive report by Samata Sanghatana, 'Upper Caste Violence: Study of Chunduru carnage', *Economic and Political Weekly*, 7 September 1991, Vol. XXVI.36, pp. 2079–84; also Vasanth Kannabiran and Kalpana Kannabiran, 'Caste and Gender: Understanding dynamics of power and violence', *Economic and*

Political Weekly, 14 September 1991, Vol. XXVI.37, pp. 2130–33; K. Balagopal, 'Post-Chunduru and other Chundurus', *Economic and Political Weekly*, 19 October 1991, Vol. XXVI.42, pp. 2399–405.

38. The socio-economic issues behind caste confrontations are discussed in Prem Chowdhry, *Punjab Politics: The Role of Sir Chhotu Ram*, Delhi: Vikas Publishing House, 1984, pp. 61–99.

39. On 4 March 1993, in the village of Andua of Mathura district the Jats burnt alive two Jatavs. A Jat panchayat of several villages in the area pledged that 'an Andua would be repeated in every village' if any action was taken by the administration against the Jats who were listed for their crimes in the killings. In the same period 16 Jatavs were killed by a Jat mob in Bharatpur district of Rajasthan. Later, a 46 village *panchayat* sanctioned this killing. See for example, 'Jat-Jatav rivalry in Andua village of Mathura district and village Kumher in western UP', *The Times of India*, 25 June 1992, p. 16; 5 March 1993, p. 4. Also see *Sunday Observer*, 26 September-2 October 1993, p. 4.

40. This is a phrase frequently used by the landowners of Haryana. Personal observation made during my field work in Haryana.

41. Cited in *The Illustrated Weekly*, 20–21 April 1991, p. 17.

42. Although not many cases are given publicity, this remains a well known fact in rural areas of northern India. A popular story going around in Haryana tells of a zamindar (landowner), who, deeply perturbed by the impertinent behaviour of his young *kamin* (low caste) agricultural labourer, hauled up the labourer's father. To the angry complaints of the zamindar, the father replied: "Sir, this impudence is because he is one of you. Had he been one of us, he would not have behaved so." Narrated by Ram Chander, village Bandh, 20–21 August 1988. It is also an open secret that a large number of children among low caste women are fathered by high caste landowners.

43. In this respect the case of Bhanwari Devi of village Bhateri in Rajasthan, who was gang raped on 22nd September 1992 by five high caste men may be noted. The plea made by the defense counsel of the accused epitomises the current attitudes of the upper castes/classes. He pleaded in the court that since the offenders were upper-caste men (Gujar and Brahmin), the rape could not have taken place because Bhanwari was from a lower caste. He thereby suggested that lower caste women had no right to say no to a sexual mating, even if forced. More than three years later the court

acquitted the five accused who were declared 'middle aged respectable citizens'.

44. See People's Union for Democratic Rights, *Bitter Harvest: The Roots of Massacres in Central Bihar*, Delhi: Secretary, PUDR, August 1992.

45. This region shows enormous difference in the male-female sex ratio —the lowest in the whole of India. In 1931 it was 844 females per thousand males and in 1941 it was 869 females per thousand males. See *Census of India, 1991*, India Series-1, Paper 1 of 1991, Provisional Population Tables, New Delhi, Registrar-General and Census Commissioner, India 1991, p. 76.

46. Malcolm Lyall Darling, *Punjab Peasant in Prosperity and Debt*, first edition, 1925, reprint, Delhi: South Asia Books, 1978, p. 51.

47. *Personal interview* with Khem Lal Rathi, Delhi, 24 May 1983.

48. *Personal interview* with Shamsher Singh, Delhi, 23 May 1986.

49. *William Crooke Collections*, MS 124, tale recorded by a teacher of the Bahraich district; also found in Haryana. *Personal interview* with Khem Lal Rathi, Delhi, 24 May 1986.

50. *William Crooke Collection*, MS 124, see a tale of the Holi festival narrated by Nathiya Chandu and recorded by Chhajmal Das, teacher of the Rudayar school, Aligarh district.

51. Narrated by Vidyā Vati, Delhi, 24 December 1987. The same tale was also recorded in 1886 titled: *Ala de nivala* by S.W. Fallon, *A Dictionary of Hindustani Proverbs*, Benaras: Lazarus and Co., 1886, p. 190.

52. Also given in Jai Narayan Verma, *Haryanavi Lokoktiyan: Shastriya Vishleshan* (Hindi), Delhi: Adarsh Sahitya Prakashan, 1972, p. 120.

53. *Personal interview* with Shamsher Singh, Rohtak, 23 May 1986.

54. *Census of India, Punjab and Delhi, 1911*, Vol. 17, part 1, report, p. 216.

55. Darling, *Punjab Peasant*, op. cit., p. 51.

56. *Karewa* was a form of widow remarriage which is now almost totally confined to the levirate. This form of marriage was not accompanied by any kind of religious ceremony, as no woman was allowed to go through the ceremony of *biah* (religious wedding) twice. *Karewa*, a white sheet with coloured corners was thrown by the man over the widow's head, signifying his acceptance of her as his wife. This custom represented social consent for cohabitation. There could be certain variations. For example it could take the form of placing *churis* (glass bangles) on the woman's wrist in full assembly and sometimes even a gold *nath* (nose ring) in her nose.

This could be followed by the distribution of *gur* (jaggery) or sweets. For details of *karewa* marriage see Chowdhry, *The Veiled Women*, op. cit., pp. 74–88.

57. *Punjab Record*, 1900, Vol. XXXV, .case no. 50, pp. 184–46; Vol. XLV, *Masummat Kaur vs. Sawan Singh*, pp. 232–34; 1897, Vol. XXXII, *Chander Singh vs. Musammat Mela*, pp. 334–38; *Indian Law Report*, Lahore Series, 1929, Vol. V, *Sohan Singh vs. Kale Singh*, pp. 372–80.

58. See Prem Chowdhry, 'Contesting Claims and Counter Claims: Questions of the inheritance and sexuality of widows in a colonial state', *Contributions to Indian Sociology* (NS), January–December 1995, Vol. 29.1–2, pp. 65–82.

59. *Punjab Record*, Vol. XLV, *Musammat Kaur vs. Sawan Singh*, pp. 232–34; 1897, Vol. XXXII, *Chander Singh vs. Musammat Mela*, pp. 334–38; *Indian Law Report*, Lahore Series, 1929, Vol. V, *Sohan Singh vs. Kala Singh*, pp. 372–80.

60. M. Douie, *Rivaj-i-Am of Tehsil Kaithal*, op. cit., p. 4. The Jats of Indri in Karnal district quoted a case in which a man was turned out of the *biradari* for marrying a Brahmin woman by *karewa*.

61. For the status of Brahmins in this region see, Chowdhry, *The Veiled Women*, op. cit., pp. 110–11, 225.

62. The 1991 Census figures show Haryana with the second lowest figures of 874 females per thousand males and UP with 882 and Punjab with 888 following closely. *Census of India, 1991*, India Series 1, Paper 1 of 1991, Provisional Population Tables, New Delhi, Registrar-General and Census Commissioner, India, 1991, p. 71.

63. The 'never married' category of males and females in Haryana in the specific age groups shows the following figures for 1981:

age group	females	males
15–19	328,090	649,346
20–24	59,163	275,900
25–29	5,629	65,640
30–34	1,089	18,559
35–39	457	10,680

Source: *Census of Haryana 1981*, Social and Cultural Tables, Part IV-A, pp. 46–47.

64. *Census of Haryana, 1981*, Series 6, Part XII, pp. 52–53.

65. The male age of marriage is calculated to be in the 25–29 age group as compared to females, the majority of whom get married between 10 to 24 years of age. Ibid.

66. A common sentiment expressed by everyone in the villages of Haryana.

67. *The Illustrated Weekly*, 20–21 April, 1991, p. 17.

68. According to Hershman the clan and caste *panchayat* in Punjab have lost all their authority, which they had exercised in the past, when they acted as courts and arbitrators in disputes affecting their members. According to him cases are seldom submitted as they once were, to the elders of the *biradari* or caste *panchayats* to decide. The situation in Haryana and U.P. however remains notably different from that of Punjab. See Hershman, *Punjabi Kinship*, op. cit., pp. 35–36.

69. Vasudha Dhagamwar, 'Meaning of Lynch Justice', *Mainstream*, September 25, 1993, pp. 5, 35.

70. For details of towns and their growing populations see *Census of Haryana 1981*, Part 11-A, and Part 11-B, General Population Tables and Primary Census Abstract, pp. 26, 28.

71. Both the army and police have notoriously restricted family accommodation in the cities, specially in Delhi. According to Lt. General B.T. Pandit, Adjutant-General, only 14 per cent of the lower ranks of the army recruits are provided with family accommodation. *Interview* with Lt. General B.T. Pandit, Adjutant-General's Branch, Army Headquarters, New Delhi, 1 April, 1991.

72. For an interesting contemporary observation of this phenomenon see D.R. Chaudhary's article in *Indian Express*, New Delhi, magazine section, 30 May, 1982, p. 5.

73. A definite ideological barrier exists in Haryana between the urban and rural value system, which inhibits the spread of urban influences in the villages. For further discussion see Richard Lambert, 'The Impact of Urban Society upon Village Life', in Roy Turner, (ed.) *India's Urban Future*, Delhi: Oxford University Press, 1962, p. 117–40.

74. In 1946, *The Hindu Marriages Disabilities Removal Act* was passed, which permitted *sagotra* (same *gotra*) marriages between two Hindus notwithstanding any text, rule or interpretation of the Hindu law or any customary usage. This was followed by *The Hindu Marriage Validity Act, 1949*, which validated inter-caste marriages. In 1955 *The Hindu Marriage Act* (no. XXIV of 1955) was passed, a far more

comprehensive act, which incorporated both these acts and offered more freedom in marriage, separation and divorce. For details of these three acts see Sunderlal T. Desai, *Mulla Principles of Hindu Law*, Bombay: N.M. Tripathi Pvt. Ltd., 1966, pp. 468–69, 616–751.

75. Generally speaking, sexual intercourse in north India among different caste clusters is said to be prohibited with the mother, father's mother, father's sister or her daughter, sister, sister's daughters, brother's daughter, mother's brother's daughter, wife's brother's daughter, daughter and daughter-in-law. Outside these relationships tolerance of sexual laxity is acknowledged. Breaches in relation to daughter-in-law however are known to have existed in the colonial period. See Chowdhry, *The Veiled Women*, op. cit., pp. 84–86, 118.

76. C.A.H. Townsend, *Customary Law of the Hissar District (except the Sirsa Tehsil)*, Vol. XXXV, Lahore: Punjab Govt. Press, 1919, pp. 12–21.

77. Uma Chakravarti defines Brahminical patriarchy as a set of rules and instructions in which caste and gender are linked, each shaping the other, and where women are crucial in maintaining the boundaries between castes. Patriarchal codes in this structure ensure that the caste system can be reproduced without violating the hierarchical order of closed endogamous circles, each distinct from and higher or lower than the other. Brahminical patriarchal codes for women differ according to the status of the caste groups in the hierarchy of castes, with the most stringent control over female sexuality among the higher castes. This set of norms has shaped the ideology of the upper castes in particular. It continues to underpin beliefs and practices among these castes even today, and is often emulated by the lower castes, especially when seeking upward mobility. See her article: 'Conceptualising Brahminical Patriarchy in Early India: Gender, caste, class and state', *Economic and Political Weekly*, 3 April 1993, Vol. XXVIII.14, pp. 579–85. Also see her 'Wifehood, Widowhood and Adultery: Female sexuality, surveillance and the state in the 18th century Maharashtra', *Contributions to Indian Sociology*, New Series, January-December 1995, Vol. 29.1–2, pp. 3–22.

78. For the status of Brahmins in Punjab-Haryana see, fn. 47.

79. Even for this the consent of the conjugal family is needed, which is withheld if it does not approve of the match. In village Asaudha,

district Rohtak, Asha, a nineteen year-old girl became a widow. Her in-laws wished her to perform *karewa* with her much older *jeth* (older brother-in-law), estimated to be about fifty years of age, with a wife and three children. She did not accept it, nor did her father, who settled her marriage elsewhere. Her in-laws, however, refused to allow this and a caste panchayat had to be called. The panchayat sanctioned her marriage elsewhere. But at a crucial juncture, the wedding ceremony was forcibly stopped by the in-laws. Even the panchayat decision was not honoured. Asha remains a widow. Narrated by Dheer Singh, village Asaudha Todran, 9–10 August 1990.

80. Pauline Kolenda, *Regional Differences in Family Structure in India*, Jaipur: Rawat Publications, 1987, pp. 289–354.

81. For the substantial contribution of women of different social strata to the occupational continuity of a caste group as also the taking over of the tasks of their menfolk who may have left their caste occupations, see Leela Dube, 'Caste and Women', in M.N. Srinivas, (ed.) *Caste: Its Twentieth Century Avatar*, New Delhi: Viking Penguin, 1996, pp. 1–27.

82. For similar observations see also Derne, *Culture in Action*, op. cit., pp. 40–47.

83. See *Hindu Succession Act*, no. XXX of 1956, in Sunderlal T. Desai, *Mulla Principles of Hindu Law*, op. cit.

84. For details see Chowdhry, *The Veiled Women*, op. cit., pp. 308–73.

85. See, ibid., p. 342; also see Kolenda, *Regional Differences*, op. cit., pp. 306–07.

Globalisation, Sexuality and the Visual Field

Issues and non-issues for cultural critique

MARY E. JOHN

Introduction

Globalisation in India has rightly been associated with liberalisation and the 'opening up' of the economy to the forces of the international market, after over forty years of autarkically conceived planning and state-led development. Along with such processes, there has been a tangible sense of the 'liberalisation' and 'globalisation' of sexuality. Never before—or so it would appear—have our public spaces been so inundated with sexual images—on posters and billboards, in the cinema and on TV, in glossy magazines, and especially in that hoary middle class institution, the daily newspaper, which has visibly taken on the characteristics of a tabloid. Moreover, if the inroads of multinational capital have been cause for concern, the effects of the sexualisation of the visual field are widely perceived as being positively alarming.

Efforts are on, therefore, to try and curb the onslaught: the *Nikki Tonight* show was scrapped soon after its opening because of its prurient talk; in October 1996 Mohini Giri, Chairperson of the National Commission For Women, was glad to announce that plans to launch a soft-porn oriented *Twenty-One Plus* channel had been successfully scotched. But the show that had everyone's attention for a while, even as people wondered whether it would take place at all, was the Miss World contest held in Bangalore in November 1996 amidst heavy police and state protection. Certain women's groups had threatened that they would turn themselves into suicide squads, if need be, in order to stop what they saw as a degrading event. Clearly, therefore, 'sexuality' in one form or another is in the news, and has become the subject of debate and protest.

This chapter contributes to the growing interest amongst intellectuals and feminists in exploring the contemporary field of sexuality—one that is largely uncharted and clearly in need of our critical involvement, but also of our sympathy and, perhaps, even of our sense of humour. Surely there are few other fields which invite such a variety of unhelpful and unproductive responses, from embarrassment, trivialisation or outright denunciation, to apparently 'radical' assertions about its absolute centrality for any understanding of subjectivity and society.

Instead of getting bogged down in fruitless efforts to determine just how critical the area of sexuality is, by attempting to *rank* this field in relation to others such as, for example, political economy, nationalism or caste, it would be more constructive to proceed from a different angle. How can we render sexuality, or the social frameworks of 'sex', intelligible, and make visible the connections between what appear on the surface to be disparate levels of analysis? That is to say, how can we demonstrate that considerations of sex, of men and women's relationships to one another and to themselves, are articulated through the structures of caste, class, national culture and globalisation?

By emphasising the links and connections forged by sexuality, however, I do not wish to be misunderstood as arguing in favour of the dissolution of sex as an intimate, subjective, bodily experience within a 'wider' network of historically situated social relations and their underlying institutional supports. Indeed, in order to make sense of the specificity of sexuality and its peculiar economy of desire and violence, it is quite crucial not to lose sight of the different levels involved.

There are further implications to the avenues I wish to explore here. Firstly, it may be useful at the present historical juncture to keep a distance from the 'victim vs. agency' approach for tackling issues of sexuality.[1] In the Indian women's movement, not to speak of the world at large, we are more familiar with the objectifications and violence of sex for women, who are at the receiving end of male desire and aggression. *Radical* lines of reasoning have therefore tended to see sex and violence as inherently coterminous. On the other hand, more *liberal* positions have sought freedom for the woman by transforming her from the object to the subject of sex, urging her to break out of submission through an active, assertive sexual agency of her own.

However, if the radical position effectively eschews sex altogether in favour of supposedly more egalitarian, asexual relationships, the liberal strategy will not take us very far either. Not because most of us lack the will, or are too conventionally bound, but because sex cannot be considered an isolated entity repressed by patriarchal forces, awaiting release through the right kind of access. Moreover, and this is my second point, the widespread search for signs of agency and resistance in a world steeped in victimisation does not pay enough attention to the *logic* guiding the search. This is particularly pertinent in the case of the Miss World contest where explicit as well as implicit claims about the 'nation' and 'culture' were deployed in opposition to the 'West' and its globalising powers.

I would therefore suggest a more circuitous route: that we begin to conceptualise the sexual domain as a *force-field*, an intersubjective realm in and by which sexual desire is variously aroused, blocked or violated; and where much more than the freedom or lack of sexual expression is involved. In order to discover what greater sexual agency might promise for women, we urgently require a more effective descriptive apparatus that would provide the ability to name socio-psycho-sexual processes that are historical and mortal.

It is therefore necessary to go beyond unproductive theoretical polarisations, whereby, for instance, theories emphasising the repressive, silencing function of social norms (associated with psychoanalysis) are opposed to analytical orientations (associated with the work of Michel Foucault) that stress modern culture's active production of sexual desire through modes of incitement. Neither position does justice to the great unevenness and heterogeneity of the force-field of sexuality. Not all institutional sites are sexualised in the same way; indeed *both* repressive and productive dimensions may well be present in a given situation. The transformative and liberatory potential of thinking about sex in less pre-conceived and uni-dimensional forms is that this may yield a richer, more grounded sense of how power relations work, and therefore also help to foster the necessary spaces to counter their effects. To address the subject of sexuality, it is not enough to oppose violence and abuse; sifting 'good' from 'bad' sexual images is an even more limited strategy. What is required is a careful consideration of our present political culture and its evolving economies of sexuality, including the possibilities and limits encountered by different categories of men and women today.

The Beauty Business

In one of the few extended discussions on the sexual relations between men and women in the Indian context, Sudhir Kakar has offered an important starting-point for an exploration of the ideology of sexuality—the conjugal couple. Unfortunately though, his analyses (drawn from a wide variety of sources, including literature, film, the personal accounts of two slum women and the life of Gandhi) seem to be driven by the need to make implausible universal claims about a quintessential and singular 'Indian sexuality'. One such unsubstantiated statement concerns "a general disapproval of the erotic aspect of married life, a disapproval which is not a medieval relic, but continues to inform contemporary attitudes." He goes on to add that this is because "sexual time beats at a considerably slower pace than its chronological counterpart."[2]

Historians of sexuality in India would, doubtless, have something to say against such sweeping assertions about our past and present. My own disagreement stems from a reflection on contemporary

India, and the globalising processes of the 1990s that I evoked at the very beginning of this paper. In a situation of unprecedented flux, when the contours of not just the economy, but also of caste, community and gender are undergoing far-reaching national and regional transformations, 'sexual time' as Kakar would have it, is showing few signs of beating at a considerably slower pace.

My preliminary evidence comes from the media. The field of visual representation has long been recognised for its extreme significance regarding questions of sexuality. In its simplest formulation, the difference between the sexes has been associated with visual processes—to be sexualised as a 'woman' is to be objectified as an *image* to be looked at, while the power of 'man' is in his gaze, the pleasure and anxiety generated by the desire of looking.[3] The media's new found power plays a disproportionate role in organising our visual field, and, in the present context, is itself one of the hallmarks of globalisation.

Before going any further into the reasons for my disagreement with Kakar's views on the status of the erotic couple, an examination of recent controversies around sexuality would be instructive. The BJP, and the Hindu right wing more generally, can well be charged with adopting vacillating positions on the liberalisation and restructuring of the Indian economy. (For example, Enron was first chased out with much fanfare, only to be welcomed back. Or consider the discordant voices with which the Swadeshi Jagran Manch and the pro-liberalisation faction speak from and for the same party). However, the BJP has perhaps been more consistent on another score: Its members have been so busy discovering nudity and sexual degradation in public places, that it would not be inaccurate to say that they are *producing* a pornographic vision where it did not exist before. Hot on the heels of the M.F. Hussain controversy, Delhi was witness to objections raised by a group of BJP MLAs over a photograph of the so-called "Dancing Girl" statuette (the well-known small, nude figure recovered in the 1930s from an archaeological site at Mohenjo Daro) that was included in the 1997 Diary issued by the Delhi Tourism and Transportation

Development Corporation. (The Chief Minister, we are told, subsequently provided assurances that the diary would be withdrawn.) Hussain's *Saraswati* has been on display in galleries since the time it was painted in the 1970s; and history textbooks have carried depictions of the Mohenjo Daro figurine for even longer. Neither image has been seen as overtly sexual, nor attracted controversy prior to these recent attacks.

These instances are indicative of the twin processes of production and disavowal, whereby images are first sexualised as pornographic in order then to be disowned or banned from representing 'Indian culture'. (It is also surely not accidental that Hussain was targeted as a Muslim unable to respect the sentiments of Hindu religion, or that the *Dancing Girl*, with its thin frame, wiry hair and strong jaw does not conform to a 'classical' aesthetic.)

By comparison, the desire of right-wing women's groups to protect our culture from the Miss World contest appears more straightforward. As Janaki Nair has summarised it:

> 'Indian culture' here is evoked as a sign of resistance to the hegemonic ambitions of the West, invading and polluting the Indian middle class with movies, television shows and now beauty pageants, that will bring 'nudity', 'dubious morals' and AIDS in their wake.[4]

Feminists have had to become quite alert to the workings of modern history by which a pure desexualised 'Indian womanhood' has come to be emblematic of the nation and its culture. The globalising 1990s would thus seem to be offering yet another lease of life to just such an 'Indian culture' in the face of the latest incursions of an alien sexuality. But although such protests were not the only ones being voiced, the histrionics and statements of right-wing women's groups in Bangalore threatened to steal the show, and made it difficult to appreciate the wide ideological distances separating the spectrum of positions taken.[5]

Jayati Ghosh is one of those who has pointed out that beauty contests are enjoying a resurgence in developing nations and certain erstwhile socialist countries, precisely at a time when they have become 'passé' and 'outmoded' in the first world. Processes of 'social globalisation', whereby everything desirable comes to be associated with the West, are aided by international capital, so that yesterday's western products find a ready market elsewhere. This is especially crucial, as she notes, for the volatile fortunes of the fashion and cosmetics industries. Others, too, have demonstrated how the Miss World contest is really about the 'business of beauty', as Janaki Nair defined it.

We clearly and urgently need to have a better appreciation of how women are addressed by the beauty business: in what ways they consent to the new and impossible standards of sexual attractiveness beamed at them, what levels of consumption are now considered normal if not necessary, or what aspirations lead so many to hone their skills and their bodies in the hope of a modelling career.

However, I remain less than convinced that we would come significantly closer to achieving such aims by levelling our protests against tawdry and predictable extravaganzas such as the Miss World pageant. Let me even go so far as to say that concentrating on the contest itself can too easily turn into an impediment. One possible reason why left-wing feminist protesters could so readily be clubbed together with the BJP is that critiques of the inroads of multinational capital into the domestic consumer market come across as broadly analogous to campaigns calling for the protection of 'Indian culture and womanhood' from the depredations of the West. A more productive point of departure for something as intimate as beauty would be to start at home. How is it, for instance, that international and local standards of beauty seem to mesh as well as they do? An interesting aspect of the coverage of the contest was the brief discussion about its racism and colour prejudice. Contestants from Zambia and Tanzania were upset about the media bias in favour of white contestants; one of them (currently studying for a degree in economics and politics, while the other is training to become a corporate lawyer) put the matter openly yet politely, "Racism exists all over the world. I hope and believe that the judges have a broad concept of beauty."[7] But, predictably enough, the judges in India could find no place for any black aspirants.

A disconcerted college lecturer in Delhi informed me that in discussions about the beauty contest with students, while there were a few who were ready to condemn the Bangalore pageant, none of them saw anything problematic with their own college-level beauty contests, which are enjoying a major resurgence and are hugely popular events. At least in the part of north Delhi where I currently live, hardly a day passes without large half or even full-page advertisements in the daily paper (not to mention the banners across the streets) that beckon women and men to try out the latest in beauty treatments and weight loss programmes. But before too quickly seeing these as simply the successful results of the standards and corporations of the West, a closer look at the detailed services on offer reveals a much more complex picture: One such beauty parlour advertisement, for instance, provides a long itemised list of more than 100 services (complete with prices), in which 'imported' services such as bleaches and perms constitute only about one-tenth of the list. Moreover, the make-up section (with the highest prices) is dominated by special offers for those most thoroughly Indian occasions: engagements, weddings and receptions.

In order words, I suggest we begin by noticing how localised and sedimented the beauty business is. Some of those protesting against the Miss World contest also questioned the state's thoroughly compromised position in offering the police, the armed forces and official support for a privately sponsored event. They held processions with mock 'queens' crowned as 'Miss Disease', 'Miss Starvation', and so on, in order to highlight the more basic priorities of poverty and health care from which the state has been steadily retreating. But one of the unintended effects of such a form of protest is that it then nullifies altogether the aspirations and anxieties symptomatic of the desire for beauty. So too, do loose statements about the 'commercialisation of women's bodies', or the treatment of women as 'commodities' which tend to place the speaker in some disembodied position beyond the circuits of capitalism and its markets.

As one writer on the beauty pageant herself noted with evident regret, what is most problematic of all is that the protests do not seem to have addressed those women who are its most obvious targets—college students and young women with strong professional aspirations of their own (the ones, moreover, who will almost certainly be our first anorexics.) Our own Miss India contestant is on record as proclaiming in righteous indignation:

> Why don't the protagonists of women's rights take up the cause of the unlettered, battered women who need help and not us? Why don't they ask us how we feel?[8]

Visualising Conjugality

In the discussion above, my point has been to question certain approaches to globalising trends; contrasts between 'the West' and 'us' can become especially misleading. The distress of the beauty pageant organisers was understandable—they felt justifiably misrecognised as a foreign, alien force. The cultural economics of beauty requires that women's alienated relationship to their bodies—the fragmentation of body-parts and the splitting of feminine subjectivity into an 'other' who must relentlessly police/appraise the body-self—be disavowed. By placing the onus of such alienation on abstract, malevolent western developments, whether capitalist or cultural, the extent and depth of the processes involved become effectively screened from view. Bodies are materialised within social relations; such relations are especially prone to misrecognition because of the work of ideology. As Althusser phrased it, ideology is "not the system of the real relations which govern the existence of individuals, but the imaginary relation of those individuals to the real relations in which they live."[9] The value of Althusser's formulation of the problem (in spite of its ambiguities) lies both in his insistence that ideology functions by constituting concrete individuals as subjects, and in his suggestion that neither the state nor capital act in a directly repressive manner but require rather the work of ideological state apparatuses such as the family and the school.

This is why I would like to propose a specific entry-point into the force-field of sexuality, one that picks up on Kakar's clue about the conjugal couple, but without losing sight of the ways in which the media has been refining its images in order to be in tune with the 1990s. The following analysis is organised around the visual field so as to interrogate contemporary formations of female sexuality, at some remove from the more familiar opposition to women's 'commodification' and 'objectification'.

The first and in many ways central image to which I wish to draw attention hails from the Kamasutra (or KS) condom advertisements, which first appeared some years ago in magazines and on huge city hoardings. These advertisements carried a photograph of a semi-nude young couple in an apparently heightened state of sexual arousal, accompanied by an equally sensational text along the lines of 'For Your Pleasure'. As might be expected, considerable controversy did ensue, but the advertisements were never banned. In my estimation, they deserve our critical attention for signalling a new public legitimation of sexuality in the form of consensual, mutual, safe and private heterosexual pleasure (heterosexual intercourse, to be precise), in a style not witnessed before. The contrast with the pre-existing Nirodh advertisements couldn't be more dramatic —the all too well-known inverted triangle and the childlike faces of the small 'happy' family promoted by the Indian government. The Nirodh advertisements, once a ubiquitous feature of our national landscape, helped position India as an underdeveloped Third World nation teeming with irresponsible adults and poverty-stricken children, watched over by the all-powerful yet strangely ineffective parent-state. What did the KS advertisements help inaugurate and how might we assess their significance?

In his reformulation and elaboration of Saussure's theory of the linguistic sign, based on the distinction between the signifier (sound-image) and the signified (concept), Jacques Lacan has offered a particularly striking analogy for the structuring effect of certain key signifiers: that of 'the point de capiton' or 'quilting point'. The arbitrary and fluid relationship between the double structure of discourse, constituted by a chain of signifiers and a current/mass of meanings, requires points "at which the signifier and signified are knotted together" and appear united:

> Everything radiates out from and is organised around the signifier [as quilting point], similar to these little lines of force that an upholstery button forms on the surface of the material. It's the point of convergence that enables everything that happens in this discourse to be situated retroactively and prospectively.[10]

By directing these insights to a terrain of signification that is broader than that of language, and, more importantly, by historicising the field, the Kamasutra condom advertisements become an essential 'quilting point' for the discourses of sexuality in India, a palpable element of our experience. With no visible signs of the law, be it in the name of the family or the state, the KS images could be read as promoting untrammelled heterosexual lust. On the one hand, this is obviously part of the break from the regimented world of Nirodh, being the result of a transformed addressee—a new middle class in the throes of self-discovery. But the very ambiguity of the image—how could it possibly be advocating free sex?—reveals the complexity of its function as an anchoring point for the significations of 'sex'.

Such ambiguity—proper, no doubt, to an advertising image —is more obviously regulated in other spheres, such as the cinema. An essential aspect of the globalisation of the media lies in its irreducibly plural, intertextual quality, whereby the worlds of advertising, cinema and TV feed off one another, caught up as they increasingly are in relationships of simultaneous competition and interdependency.[11] Interestingly enough, the cinema, too, has seen breaks and transformations in its sexual economies, as the much-cited demise of the vamp would attest. Today's heroine cannot be a passive object of desire, but displays a responsive, active, and at times disturbing sexuality, of a sort probably first enacted by Sridevi.[12] Contrary to what Kakar has claimed, in the emergent genre of new-middle-class films pioneered by Mani Ratnam, it is the marriage relationship itself which is eroticised. The hero in both *Roja* and *Bombay* (played by Arvind Swamy) displays an unabashed passion for his wife in an almost anti-macho, vulnerable mode. His conjugal desire comes to be fully reciprocated by the wife-heroine, her response being integral to the movement of the narrative in each film. It is important to note that the depiction of their sexual desire for one another is no longer confined to spectacular song-and-dance sequences as was the norm in commercial cinema until recently. Indeed, it is staged in contrast to other kinds of sexual display.[13] Moreover, the wife's sexuality is coded as something positive, and, in distinct contrast to so many earlier popular films, it is never threatening or in turn threatened by the possible sexual violation of others. Though there is great danger to the couples' happiness together, in both films the form and quality of such danger operates on the different plane of terrorism and violence. (What gives these films an ideological edge over other recent box-office successes such as *Hum Aap Ke Hai Kaun* and *Dilwale Dulhaniya Le Jayenge* is the clear pronouncement that love, sex and marriage can flourish in the life of the couple, which must now constitute the heart of the Indian family if that institution is to successfully take on the challenges of the present, be it a besieged Kashmir[14] or a communalised Bombay.)

In tandem with such developments in the cinematic world, notice also how far the world of advertising has evolved from the earlier more obviously degrading if not crude use of women's bodies for male gratification. As active and vital consumers in their own right, women are both depicted and addressed differently. Wholesome and intelligent, her sexuality is often alluded to indirectly. Moreover, as more and more columnists are only beginning to notice, modelling itself occupies a very new place in public culture today—as a highly valued profession, eulogised in the press, bolstered by the full encouragement of family members.[15] Indeed, the nationalist fervour that greeted the two international wins of Miss Universe and Miss World a few years ago have yet to subside. (According to newspaper reports, Sushmita Sen made her appearance during a public rally in Bombay in 1995 waving the national flag in a vintage Daimler

Benz car, originally made to order for Nehru.) One can serve one's country well, it would appear, by cultivating the perfect body-image for the market. The organisers of the Miss World pageant clearly believed that they could extend and build on this new-found market nationalism.

How, as critics, might we interpret such phenomena? What sort of descriptive apparatus must be put together and what types of connections with other issues are necessary to comprehend these changes in the sexual field?

To begin with, we are surely witnessing a new ideological dimension to the growing confidence of middle class men, whereby masculine desire can be displayed in the full expectation of consent and reciprocity. In these media images there are no disappointments, and no signs of submission or explicit patriarchal constraint. The new woman may actively devote herself to her husband and children (as in Mani Ratnam's films), or, as in so many advertisements, be addressed as much more than a smart, sexually desirable homemaker. Interviews with models inform their readers that their careers come first, even as they expect to find love and a family when the time comes. As 'Indian women', they are confident of being able to harmonise home and career.

What sense can one get of this emerging visual ideology foregrounding a conjugal, erotic sexuality? How powerful is it? What counter ideologies might be at work?

In August of 1995, the Maharashtra government forced the withdrawal of a controversial advertisement for jogging shoes, in which two models (Madhu Sapre and Milind Soman) posed together in the nude. According to Kalpana Sharma, a BJP minister's major reason for opposing the advertisement was that the two models were going to get married: "How can we allow anyone to pose in the nude with his wife?"[16]

Are there, then, conflicting positions amongst the competing forces vying for dominance, which set limits to the public legitimacy of the sexual couple? But rather than believe that here, too, the BJP managed to carry the day, I would hesitate in according great weight to the ban. To return to my example, by all accounts, the two models have only grown in popularity since the incident; and at least one of them, Milind Soman, refused to apologise.

One cannot help feeling seduced by the surface attraction of these new sexually egalitarian images. For haven't we protested against the double standard, by which men from dominant groups were granted a sexual license whereas women were split into the chaste wife/debased prostitute? Their appeal appears to be founded on the woman's active consent and the absence of violence, all of which is placed within the overall frame of conjugality. It also makes those who question such images into nothing other than the victims of prudery.

Consequently, it becomes increasingly obvious that one has to go beyond the visual representations themselves to the logics and agendas that mobilise them. Or to put the issue in reverse, isn't the success of the new ideology entirely dependent on what is never explicitly addressed, or is left out of the frame altogether? In what follows I will attempt to broaden and contextualise the field by looking out for links with consumer capitalism, caste hierarchy, and the nexus of fertility/contraception. Such considerations clearly do not exhaust the theme before us. This essay has the limited aim of making a case for the need to create a descriptive apparatus from many vantage points and on different sites. The purpose of such an analysis is not the celebration of the diversity of sexuality in India but the presentation of a more convincing perspective on the powers of globalisation, even as our lives are being visibly transformed.

Sexuality and Consumer Capitalism

The most obvious wider context for the mobilisation of desire is that of consumer culture, with its proliferation of images and commodities, its promise of happiness through the possession of products. Many of the criticisms of the Miss World contest naturally highlighted this. As is well-known, an early and widespread ploy in the world of publicity has been the display of sexuality, especially of women's bodies or body parts, to promote the desirability of a particular commodity. Sexual fulfilment has thus been a unique, if not pivotal fantasy, emblematic of the transformation in social relations that awaits the consumer.

What, then, is the relationship between less objectified and more 'wholesome' body-images of women, on the one hand, and India's recent attempted transition from a 'restrictive' state-regulated form of capitalist culture to a global consumerism, on the other? Can any direct connections be made between my claims regarding the legitimacy accorded to visual representations of the erotic couple and our entry into a new phase of capitalist development? To start off with, one would have to examine the need to recruit the new middle class woman as a 'consuming subject' of local/global products in a vastly expanded market (whether for beauty, fashion or the home), a recruitment that cannot take place without her sexualisation as an actively desiring subject.[17] Further considerations would have to account for the modes by which such sexualisation is regulated and housed—in the current context, I am trying to suggest, this is placing new demands on the institution of marriage.[18]

Questions relating to marriage bring in their wake long-standing debates on the nature and form of the family. In this connection, Madhava Prasad's thought-provoking essay on the symptomatic reasons behind the ban on kissing in Hindi cinema (a ban that was recently lifted) assumes a special significance. According to him, whereas the western modern state rested on the stability of the nuclear family embodied in the private autonomy of the conjugal couple, in India, the transition from the traditional to the modern family has been an "unrealised ideal". The need for the Indian state to make alliances with pre-modern elites whose family structures are authoritarian does not admit "the invention of the private, the zone of intimate exchange and union where ... the members of the couple become as one. Thus while the spectacularization of the female body poses no threat to the informal alliance that constitutes the Indian ruling bloc, ... [a]ny representation of a private space and its activities in the public realm constitutes a transgression of the scopic privileges that the patriarchal authority of the traditional family reserves for itself."[19]

If Prasad's analysis draws on the context of post-independence Nehruvian state-led development and its accommodation of 'pre-modern' elites, then we must ask ourselves what changes amongst the dominant classes, and especially what unprecedented features of the Indian state are suggested by the new public legitimacy being accorded to representations of private intimacy. Considerations such as these would also provide fresh dimensions to debates on the changing forms of and pressures on the joint family in India—where the joint family is at one and the same time a statistical artefact and an intrinsic ingredient of 'our' difference from the West.[20] What fresh contracts are possibly being drawn up between the state (in retreat from its productive economic functions, now actively mediating between the nation and international capital) and the new masculine middle class citizen? (Where does this leave the so-called 'traditional' elites and how should we address transformations in rural family structures and sexual codes?)

Caste, Sexuality and Marriage

One of the most challenging aspects of thinking about visual representations as ideologies is that it becomes imperative to relate their function to practices on the ground. Do we read the images I have been discussing as being indicative of actual trends, leading to, or being a faithful reflection of, the effective normalisation of desire between men and women? Or is it likely that the situation is considerably more complicated, because representations of conjugality may be an attempted resolution of a much more conflicted situation?

I would like to put forward the hypothesis (even if my basis is impressionistic and anecdotal) that the institution of marriage has never been under more strain than it is today, especially in the middle classes. To that extent, the confident projections of a desirable middle class masculinity beholding itself in the mirror of a desiring, reciprocal femininity may be suppressing a whole range of issues.

Given that the new middle class couple being constructed in films and advertisements appears so modern and globalised, just what sorts of exclusions are at work is not always easy to determine. The interesting exceptions are the two Mani Ratnam films, where the heroines are a village belle (*Roja*) and a Muslim woman (*Bombay*). This is significant. For in so choosing, the films effectively update and make glamorous older Brahminical codes for the regulation of sexual relations.

Discussed at length in the Indological and kinship literature on India, concepts such as *anuloma/pratiloma*, or hypergamy/hypogamy have the invariable effect of *distancing* the reader from the subject matter being described, by placing it either in the past or in a rural, ethnic, that is to say, 'traditional' context. In a perceptive, if preliminary essay, André Béteille has argued for greater comparative work between caste in India and race in the United States, on the grounds that *both* concepts require illumination by considerations of gender and sexuality (the inequalities of 'sexual access').[21] Questioning the Indological approach to Hindu culture, by demanding that the present and not the past be the point of departure, his own analyses of contemporary India focus on atrocities in rural India, with no discussion of possible developments around sexuality, caste and gender in the dominant culture of the urban middle class world.

This absence is significant, but also ironic—the relative *invisibility* of the regulation of sexual inequalities by caste within the urban upper middle classes is effectively sanctioned by the sociological literature. Inequalities in such contexts, it would seem, are named and alluded to differently, to which the world of cinema also attests.

I would like to suggest, therefore, that *anuloma*, which permits upper caste men sexual access to women of their own or lower caste rank, is revised by Mani Ratnam, such that the urban, secular upper caste hero can legitimately lay claim to the love of a rural girl or a woman from a minority community. The prohibition and condemnation towards *pratiloma* unions (where the woman is of a higher caste than the man) goes unchallenged. (Moreover, the possibility is never entertained that both the hero and heroine could be, say, Muslim or non-upper caste.)

The dangers of *pratiloma* relationships are, of course, by no means left unaddressed in staple cinematic fare, as the ubiquity of poor boy/rich girl narratives would indicate. These, however, tend to be introduced through 'eve-teasing' sequences, where class and gender are played off one another. 'Happy endings' demand that the heroine has learnt to subdue her 'uppity' ways, while the hero has his family and blood-line, and therefore also, fortune and respect restored to him.[22] In other words, if *anuloma* can appear as legitimate, even progressive love, *pratiloma* is approached through sexual harassment. Where the latter creates a certain sexual disturbance by rendering the play of power visible, the former more easily lends itself to the kind of idealisation of conjugality that is being currently promoted on a number of fronts.

The very legitimacy attached to the representation of an unproblematic, fulfilling intimate conjugality may also not simply be the triumph of modern bourgeois subjectivity over the pre-modern family in India. Another effort towards the resolution of conflict seems to be at work. While class-caste endogamy remains the overall norm, ensuring as it does the very reproduction of the middle class, there is ample evidence that an increasing number of women, especially from professional groups, are not getting married, are prepared to leave their husbands, or have other relationships outside marriage. Even in the conventional setting of an 'arranged' marriage, the search for a 'suitable boy' is becoming noticeably protracted and anxiety-laden. And yet, such pressures on the institution of marriage have not been systematically addressed—neither in the women's movement nor by sociologists. Questions relating to marriage have demanded the attention of activists and intellectuals over and over again in the women's movement, but obliquely. Dowry deaths, the Shah Bano controversy, or Roop Kanwar's sati (to mention just some of the most important campaigns of the '70s and '80s), all of which have exposed the precariousness and violence of marriage in very specific contexts, have largely *assumed* its compulsory, everyday, normalised aspects.[23] This is not to say that this particular institution has remained unaffected by feminist interrogations of modernity. On the contrary, as more and more women respond to the demands of a globalising society and a new national culture, whether at home or in the workplace, women are changing far more than men, (whatever the Raymond's suitings series on the 'Complete Man' might want to claim). Could it be, therefore, that contemporary middle class society is also witnessing a mismatch of sorts, a mismatch that cannot be acknowledged, but must be publicly denied by images promising sexual mutuality if not egalitarianism?

Sexuality/Fertility/Contraception

Let me bring these very diverse, if not rambling comments and questions to a provisional close by returning to the image I began with—the sensational Kamasutra advertisement.

Having drawn a sharp contrast between KS and its predecessor Nirodh, it is possible to come to the conclusion that sexual pleasure is 'in' and population control 'out'. Clearly this is far from the case. Instead what I believe is being set up in the KS condom advertisement is a decisive shift in the relative framing of sexuality and fertility in society.

The earlier, Nirodh advertisements were part of an apparatus for addressing the problem of poverty, understood to be *the* problem of an underdeveloped nation. Opposition to population policies have worked within this interpretive horizon, through arguments that large populations are the effect rather than the cause of poverty. Slogans such as 'development is the best contraceptive' were among the more widespread demands to have been raised. In the meanwhile, the Indian state, castigated for its 'softness', muddled along with ineffective family planning programmes, which came to a head in the fascist sterilisation camps of the Emergency (where recorded deaths alone were close to 2,000), while the middle classes remained on the sidelines. Over the last decade or so, the situation has changed dramatically. The middle classes have come into their own, constituting a clear cultural reference point as they seek to administer a new set of norms and exclusions. While their own family sizes register a drop from one generation to the next, the condom has truly been lifted out of its earlier frame by the Kamasutra advertisers to resignify the right to pleasure of this class; being such an eminently translatable signifier, the *Kamasutra* simultaneously signals the inheritance of a Hindu erotic past and, as *KS*, the pleasures of the global present. At the same time, the apparatus for population control has been thoroughly retooled, modernised and rendered efficient: women are the exclusive targets, not their men, through methods ranging from (hazardous) injectables and new anti-pregnancy vaccines, to literacy campaigns. Simple barrier methods will no longer do for them, let alone fertility-awareness-based contraceptive practices which, as Mira Sadgopal has pointed out, are dismissed because they "require the most personal and dedicated involvement of women and their male sexual partners."[24] A new anxiety grips members of the middle class— even as their lifestyles expand, they fear encroachment by those marked 'other': these are no longer the undifferentiated poor, but (since Mandal and Ayodhya), lower castes and Muslims.[25]

The world historical possibilities inaugurated by contraception are therefore now caught up within new nationalist agendas bearing little connection to development. The demand is, rather, pleasure for 'us' and fertility control for 'them'. In such an over-determined situation, it is difficult, but vital to get a better sense of the very real if different dilemmas and struggles faced by women from all classes and groups over the relationship between fertility and sexuality. The part being played by contraception can by no means be assumed; mechanistic renditions of contraception as having solely to do with the ability to 'break' the connection between sexuality and fertility may, indeed, have little to do with the unequal experiences and responsibilities of anyone except population planners.

It is my belief that since questions of 'our' pleasure and freedom as middle class women are not being defined in isolation, but through an active process of othering, there are no avenues other than collective ones for an exploration of a more genuinely egalitarian sexuality that can radically challenge our times.

Conclusion

In the discussion initiated above, questions of sexuality have invariably revolved around heterosexuality, without further qualification. Recent years have seen invaluable, pathbreaking critiques of the institution of heterosexuality, overwhelmingly pioneered by lesbian and gay scholars.[26] As Jonathan Ned Katz has pointed out, even though 'heterosexuality' and 'homosexuality' were invented around the same time during the late nineteenth century in the West—where the former became the successor to 'Victorian love'—heterosexuality subsequently disappeared in the process of its naturalisation. At a later moment, therefore, it had to be explicitly named and de-universalised by homosexuals, now stigmatised and excluded as 'deviants' from an unmarked norm.[27] Critiques of heterosexuality enabled a unique re-engagement with the feminist slogan 'the personal is the political'; however, I also wonder whether, somewhere along the way, an effective collapsing has not also taken place, such that the political has become purely the personal. In the resulting climate where lesbianism signified 'the politically correct identity' for women, heterosexual feminists, it would appear, found it extraordinarily difficult to analyse their lives and 'choices'. According to Jane Gaines, "not only is heterosexuality politically suspect, it is also unthinkable within feminism in both senses of *unthinkable*—it cannot and it should not be thought."[28] Silence has been followed by pain, guilt and defensiveness. Gaines, on the other hand, has come full circle, and has sought to align an actively *feminist* heterosexual desire with queerness, by calling it perverse.

The above analysis has tried to map the broader political field of heterosexual desire in the Indian context from a standpoint that reconstructs some of the major sites and modes of its contemporary deployment. Such reconstruction, of course, runs the danger of falling prey to its own assumptions. But the opposite danger looms larger, if anything—namely, of laying questionable claim to a position that is somehow outside the subject of critique. (This is what tended to happen in most of the opposition to the Miss World contest.) I have, therefore, sought to bring about our dis-identification from dominant cultural representations of sexuality while recognising our *inclusion* in what is being subjected to interrogation.

According to Judith Butler,

> Although the political discourses that mobilise identity categories tend to cultivate identifications in the service of a political goal, it may be that the persistence of *dis*identification is equally crucial to the rearticulation of democratic contestation. Indeed, it may be precisely through practices which underscore disidentification with those regulatory norms by which sexual difference is materialised that both feminist and queer politics are mobilised. Such collective disidentifications can facilitate a reconceptualisation of which bodies matter, and which bodies are yet to emerge as critical matters of concern.[29]

This essay has attempted two things: Firstly, to denaturalise the production of regulatory heterosexual norms through an active consideration of those institutional sites (of capital, the state, caste and the family) that effectively constitute the very materiality of gender relations. Secondly, my suggestion is that the exclusionary outside of the dominant sexual order (of gender, caste, class, and community), "those 'unlivable' and 'uninhabitable' zones of social life which are nevertheless densely populated by those who do not enjoy the status of the subject"[30] are being produced *within* the heterosexual matrix as much as at its boundaries.[31]

It is only too evident that India is being drawn into a new phase of global capitalism, in which unprecedented faith has been restored and whose end or horizon is nowhere in sight. Distinctions between the 'national' and the 'foreign' are increasingly smudged. The partnership between Indian capital and the state-in-the-making, heralded in the Bombay Plan of 1944, has, after all these years, given way to uncertain alliances with global partners of various kinds.

Under such conditions of flux and potential loss of identity on the economic front, forces from the Hindu Right are endeavouring to reaffirm the purity of Indian culture by cleansing it of 'alien' sexualities. The analysis developed in these pages is in considerable tension with their strategies; but my formulations are also slightly different from western feminist confrontations with heterosexuality. The institution that has come to be repeatedly highlighted in the course of the discussion is that of marriage. In so doing, my purpose is not to shift attention away from what has been the most important site so far in the self-understanding of the women's movement, namely the state. Indeed, it is an essential aspect of my argument that we cannot open up sexuality to further investigation without a fuller exploration of *both* these institutions in their changing relationship to each other. But if claims upon and interrogations of the state have been on the agenda for some time now, theorisations of the social and sexual relations underpinning the critical institution of marriage in contemporary India are just beginning.

This essay has been presented to different audiences at various stages in its development, beginning with the workshop on *Rethinking Indian Modernity: The Political Economy of Sexuality*, at MIDS, August 1-3 1996. Subsequent venues included the seminar on *The Imaging of Women in Myth and History*, Gargi College, New Delhi, November 20-22 1996, the colloquiuum series of the Department of Sociology, Delhi University, February 21 1997 and the *5th Women in Asia Conference*, Sydney, Australia, October 3-5 1997. I am particularly grateful to the group consisting of Kumkum Roy, Kanchana Natarajan, Bharati Sud, Monica Juneja, Ratna Raman and Ratna Kapur for their lively discussion of an early version. Thanks also to Satish Deshpande, Janaki Nair and Madhava Prasad for their comments and encouragement, and to Jacob E. John for help with materials.

Notes

1. A number of feminist scholars have begun to question the unqualified positive valency placed on women's agency, and in contexts that bear interesting connections to issues of sexuality. See, for instance, Kumkum Sangari, 'Consent, Agency and Rhetorics of Incitement', *Economic and Political Weekly*, Vol. 28.18, 1 May, 1993, pp. 867–82; and Rajeswari Sunder Rajan, 'The Subject of Sati', in *Real and Imagined Women: Gender, Culture, Postcolonialism*, London and New York: Routledge, 1993, pp. 15–39.

2. Sudhir Kakar, *Intimate Relations: Exploring Indian Sexuality*, New Delhi: Penguin, 1989, p. 20.

3. Two early, and now classic analyses of the visual field came out of Britain in the 1970s, one by the art critic John Berger and the other by the feminist film critic Laura Mulvey. (John Berger, *Ways of Seeing*, London: Penguin, 1972; Laura Mulvey, 'Visual Pleasure and Narative Cinema', *Screen*, Vol. 16.3, Autumn 1975, pp. 6–18.)
   Using the very different intellectual and political resources of a Marxist critique of private property under consumer capitalism (Berger) and Lacanian psychoanalysis (Mulvey), both critiques highlight the relationship between the active male spectator versus the passive female spectacle/publicity image for the sustenance of the social organisation of sexual difference.

4. Janaki Nair, 'Bachchan and the Battle for Bangalore', *The Hindu*, 8 November 1996.

5. See Janaki Nair, ibid.; S. Bageshree, 'When Malice Rules the media', and Revathi Sivakumar, 'Miss World's Hidden Face', *Deccan Herald*, 17 November 1996; Parvathi Menon, 'The Show Goes On: State-sponsored security for Miss World pageant', *Frontline*, 29 November 1996, pp. 105–07.

6. Jayati Ghosh, 'The Meaning of Beauty Contests', *Frontline*, 29 November 1996, pp. 106–107.

7. Cited by Chetan Krishnaswamy, 'Beauty and Bias', *Frontline*, 13 December 1996, p. 9.

8. Cited in Gayathri Nivas, 'A Contest Mired in Controversies', *Deccan Herald*, 23 November 1996.

9. Louis Althusser, 'Ideology and Ideological State Apparatuses (Notes Toward An Investigation)', in *Lenin and Philosophy*, New York: Monthly Review Press, 1971, p. 165. See also Teresa de Lauretis'

critique 'The Technology of Gender', in *Technologies of Gender: Essays on Theory, Film and Fiction*, Bloomington: Indiana University Press, 1987, especially pp. 6–12.

10. Jacques Lacan, 'The quilting point', in *The Seminar of Jacques Lacan, Book III: The Psychoses '55–56*, J.A. Miller, (ed.), New York: Norton, 1993, p. 304.

11. To take the most obvious example, both Doordarshan and Satellite TV networks feature movies—Hindi, regional, and foreign—punctuated by advertisements, as staple fare. Vivek Dhareshwar and Tejaswini Niranjana have also suggested that films such as *Kaadalan* play with and ironise this situation, visible, for instance, in the depiction of city hoardings within the film. See their essay '*Kaadalan* and the Politics of Resignification: Fashion, violence and the body', *Journal of Arts and Ideas*, no. 29, January 1996, pp. 5–26.

    Television has seen a veritable explosion of soaps and serials with globalisation. All too often, the scripts of the new programmes seem to require avaricious women who will stop at nothing for power—in business and in the family. Though the temptation is great, it would be a mistake to view such shows simply as remakes of *Dallas*. A separate treatment of sexuality on television is beyond the scope of this essay.

12. The Hindi film *Mr. Bechara*, with Sridevi and Anil Kapoor, (though less well-known than the highly successful *Mr. India*), employed suggestive strategies for the introduction and accommodation of this new feminine sexuality. Sridevi's boisterous and directly sexual persona is unmistakably the focus of the film and commands assent, even as viewers are invited to sympathise with the hero's active dislike—even sexual repulsion—of her in comparison with the lingering memory of his first wife. Two themes hold the narrative together—the heroine's successful supplanting of the hero's old love, along with her visible and effective devotion to his young son. In other words, as a potentially unsettling new sexual norm edges out a more familiar older one, the audience is simultaneously reassured that this is accompanied by loving and responsible mothering.

13. The promise and legitimacy of their conjugal sexual relations are signalled and set apart in each film by providing a larger sexualised context as backdrop—the 'Rukumani' song in *Roja* with its somewhat startling depiction of the sexual agency of old village

women, and 'Hamma, Hamma' in *Bombay* where the more predictable gyrations and poses of disco dancers interweave with shots of the couple's delayed opportunity to consummate their marriage. In my view, the overall message is that sex in marriage is not just OK, but an ideal to be striven for.

For other discussions of the erotics of these films, see Tejaswini Niranjana, 'Integrating Whose Nation? Tourists and Terrorists in *Roja*', *Economic and Political Weekly*, Vol. 29.3, 15 January 1994, pp. 89–92; Ventakesh Chakravarthy and M.S.S. Pandian, 'More on *Roja*', *Economic and Political Weekly*, Vol. 29.11, 12 March 1994; Tejaswini Niranjana, 'Banning "Bombayi": Nationalism, communalism and gender', *Economic and Political Weekly*, Vol. 30.22, 3 June 1995, pp. 1291–92; Madhava Prasad, 'Signs of Ideological Re-form in Two Recent Films: Towards real subsumption?' in *Journal of Arts and Ideas*, no. 29, pp. 27–43; Ravi Vasudevan, '*Bombay* and its Public', *Journal of Arts and Ideas*, no. 29, pp. 44–65.

14. Placeless, snow-covered slopes with a tumbling hero and heroine —such a common ingredient in our cinema—are brilliantly temporalised and localised in *Roja* to signify India's threatened Kashmir.

15. "I finally got it. The main difference between the Femina Miss India Contest then and now is a fairly simple word—career." (Shobha De, 'The Making of Miss India', *The Times of India Sunday Review*, 19 January 1997.)

16. Kalpana Sharma, 'The medium is the message', *The Hindu*, 17 August 1995.

17. Poor women—women far removed from the middle class—are also being selectively addressed under the new order of liberalisation and structural adjustment, but not primarily as consumers. Increasingly recognised now for their role in production and reproduction, they are to become the new managers of poverty, the micro-entrepreneurs of the Third World. For a discussion of these issues in the field of development see Mary E. John, 'Gender and Development in India: Some reflections on the constitutive role of contexts', *Economic and Political Weekly*, Vol. 31.47, 23 November 1996, pp. 3071–77.

18. A comparative study of women's magazines in English, such as *Femina* and *Woman's Era*, would, I believe, lend further weight to my thesis. Though *Woman's Era* is of more recent vintage, it enjoys

a much larger readership than *Femina* does. Unlike *Femina*, which is a glamour magazine, concentrating overwhelmingly on fashion and beauty, *Woman's Era* devotes considerable attention to questions of marriage and the family, and is respectably middle class even as it offers explicit discussions of sexual relations. In this connection see Amita Tyagi Singh and Patricia Uberoi, 'Learning to "Adjust": Conjugal relations in Indian popular fiction', *Indian Journal of Gender Studies*, Vol. 1.1, 1994, pp. 93–120.

19. Madhava Prasad, 'Cinema and the Desire for Modernity', *Journal of Arts and Ideas, Special Issue: Careers of Modernity*, nos. 25–26, 1993, pp. 77–78.

20. See especially A.M. Shah, 'Is the Joint Household Disintegrating?' *Economic and Political Weekly*, March 2 1996, pp. 537–43. The burden of Shah's argument is that, at least where the household dimension of the family is concerned, the size of the household has been growing over time—whatever a small, professional middle class would like to believe. Shah's views would be enriched, it seems to me, by taking into active account the family as an ideological construct; after all, the dominant nuclear family in the West has been able to outlive its statistical minority status for decades.

21. André Béteille, 'Race, Caste and Gender', reprinted in *Society and Politics in India: Essays in a Comparative Perspective*, Delhi: Oxford University Press, 1997 [1991], pp. 15–36.

22. An interesting Hindi film in this connection would be *Coolie No. 1*, where the hero played by Govinda—'coolie no. 1' at a city bus station—falls in love with a rich rural girl. His extensive efforts at dissimulation and impersonation—from the predictable (industrial tycoon) to the ridiculous (hospital nurse)—finally bring in rich dividends; meanwhile, the wealthy but foolish father-in-law must be shown up for his gullible money-mindedness.

A very recent Tamil film *Minsarakanavu*, challenges the 'sexual harassment' approach to pratiloma. (I am grateful to Janaki Nair for bringing this film to my attention.)

23. Critics of the commodification of women's bodies, which is said to be reaching new heights under the current invasion of the skies, may want to consider the far more subtle and invidious process of 'objectification' that routinely accompanies the presentation of a potential bride to the gaze of in-laws as they check out girls for their sons in upper-caste arranged marriages. We know far too little about the number of times a woman may have to go through such a

'selection' process, what this does to her self-esteem, the assessment of the body that permeates the occasion, and the interwoven discourses of beauty, health, caste, class and family within which that body is embedded.

24. Mira Sadgopal, 'Women, Fertility and Planetary Sustenance', *FRCH Newsletter*, Vol. 8, 1, Jan-Feb 1994, p. 14, See also the discussion on population control by Susie Tharu and Tejaswini Niranjana, 'Problems for a Contemporary Theory of Gender', *Social Scientist*, Vol. 23, 3–4, March-April 1994, pp. 93–117.

25. Soon after the 1991 Census Report on the break-up of the population by religion was released in 1995 by the Indian government, newspapers were flooded with articles which jubilantly used the fact that the Muslim population had grown faster than the Hindu one between 1981–91 to bolster pre-existing beliefs about Muslim lust, polygamy and the swamping of the nation by Islam. In an extremely useful recent article, Alaka Basu has opened up the essentialist and communal category of 'Muslim religion' to a much richer analysis—such that *regional* considerations turn out to be more salient for understanding fertility differentials. See her 'The Demographics of Religious Fundamentalism' in *Unravelling the Nation: Sectarian Conflict and India's Secular Identity*, Kaushik Basu and Sanjay Subrahmanyam, (eds.) New Delhi: Penguin, 1996, pp. 129–56. Though an indispensable corrective in a number of ways, and indicative of the kind of issues demography should be taking on, Basu's essay relies on a somewhat simplistic conception of ideology as 'uninformed ideology', which, by implication, therefore, only needs the right kind of information to be countered.

26. The classical essay remains that of Adrienne Rich, 'Compulsory Heterosexuality and Lesbian Existence', *Signs* Vol. 5.4, 1980, pp. 631–60, which has since been extensively anthologised. More recent contributions include Jonathan Ned Katz, 'The Invention of Heterosexuality', *Socialist Review*, Vol. 20.1, Jan-March 1990, pp. 7–33; *Heterosexuality: A Feminism and Psychology Reader*, Sue Wilkinson and Celia Kitzinger, (eds.) London: Sage, 1993; Judith Butler, *Bodies that Matter: The Discursive Limits of 'Sex'*, London and New York: Routledge, 1993; Jane Gaines, 'Feminist Heterosexuality and its Politically Incorrect Pleasures', *Critical Inquiry*, Vol. 21.2, Winter 1995, pp. 382–410.

27. Katz, 'The Invention of Heterosexuality', op. cit.

28. Gaines, 'Feminist Heterosexuality and its Politically Incorrect Pleasures', op. cit., p. 383, emphasis original.
29. Judith Butler, *Bodies that Matter*, op. cit., p. 4.
30. Ibid., p. 3.
31. It is hoped that such a denaturalisation of heterosexual hegemony in India may be of value to the lesbian and gay movements as well. (For a discussion of lesbian and gay politics and scholarship in our context see the introduction to this volume.)

Notes on Contributors

UMA CHAKRAVARTI teaches history at Miranda House, Delhi University. She has written widely and her publications include *Social Dimensions of Early Buddhism* (1987), *Rewriting History: The Life and Times of Pandita Ramabai* (1998) and (as co-author) *The Delhi Riots: Three Days in the Life of a Nation* (1987). Her research is concerned with the histories of marginalised groups such as women and the labouring poor. She has been active in the women's movement and the democratic rights movement.

PREM CHOWDHRY has taught history at Miranda House, Delhi University from 1966-88, was a UGC fellow at Jawaharlal Nehru University from 1988-94, and is currently Fellow at the Nehru Memorial Museum and Library, New Delhi. She is the author of *Punjab Politics: The Role of Sir Chhotu Ram,* (1984); *The Veiled Women: Shifting Gender Equations in Rural Haryana, 1880-1990,* (1994); and has numerous research articles in the fields of politics, society, culture and gender. She contributes regularly to newspapers and is currently engaged in an exploration of popular culture in India. Her forthcoming work is *Image, Ideology and Identity: Colonial India and the Making of Empire Cinema.*

MARY E. JOHN is a Senior Fellow at the Centre for Women's Development Studies, New Delhi. She is author of *Discrepant Dislocations: Feminism, Theory and Postcolonial Histories* (1996). Current research interests include the history of the Indian women's movement and the formation of women's studies, international feminism, and problems of globalisation.

JANAKI NAIR is a Fellow at the Madras Institute of Development Studies, Chennai and is currently Visiting Fellow at the Centre for the Study of Culture and Society, Bangalore. She has written on the social, cultural and political history of modern India. Her publications include *Women and Law in Colonial India* (1996) and *Miners and Millhands: Work, Culture and Politics in Princely Mysore* (1998). She has also produced and directed "After the Gold", a documentary history of the Kolar Gold Field (Betacam video, 1997).

TEJASWINI NIRANJANA has been teaching in the English department at the University of Hyderabad and is currently Senior Fellow, Centre for the Study of Culture and Society, Bangalore. She is the author of *Siting Translation: History, Post-structuralism and the Colonial Context* (1992) as well as co-editor of *Interrogating Modernity: Culture and Colonialism in India* (1993); and, in Kannada, *Streevadi Sahitya Vimarshe* (Feminist Literary Criticism) (1994). Her current research interests include the formation of the feminist subject in contemporary South Indian cinema, and questions of gender, ethnicity and popular culture in the West Indies.

KALPANA RAM is currently Research Fellow of the Australian Research Council in anthropology at Macquarie University, Sydney, Australia. She is author of *Mukkuvar Women: Gender, Hegemony and Capitalist Transformation in a South Indian Fishing Community*, (1991), and co-editor (with Margaret Jolly) of *Maternities and Modernities: Colonial and Postcolonial Experiences in Asia and the Pacific* (1998). Her publications are at the intersection of feminist and anthropological theory. Her current work deals with the competing discourses on the female body impinging on women among the labouring poor in South India, and on gender, nationalism and dance in India and the Indian diaspora.

KUMKUM ROY teaches history at Satyawati Co-educational College, University of Delhi. Her publications include *The Emergence of Monarchy in North India*, and a number of research papers. She has also edited an anthology *Women in Early Indian Societies*, (forthcoming).

ANANDHI S. completed her Ph.D. in history from Jawaharlal Nehru University, New Delhi. Her recent publications include the monograph *Contending Identities: Dalits and Secular Politics in Madras Slums*, and articles in the *Economic and Political Weekly* and *Social Scientist*. Currently, she is one of the co-ordinators of the Summer School in Women's Studies organised by the Indian Association of Women's Studies and Asmita Resource Centre for Women, Hyderabad.

SAMITA SEN is a lecturer in history at Calcutta University. She completed her doctoral dissertation in 1992 entitled "Women in the Bengal jute industry 1890-1940: Migration, Motherhood and Militancy" and has also been a Research Fellow at Trinity College, Cambridge. Her current interests include gender and labour with special emphasis on a social history of marriage laws.

SUSIE THARU teaches in the department of literature at the Central Institute of English and Foreign Languages, Hyderabad. She has co-edited, with K.Lalita, the two-volume *Women Writing in India: 600 B.C. to the Present*, (1991), and is the editor of *Subject to Change*, (1998). She is currently completing a book on the genre and the imaginary order of citizenship that she has been working on while she was a Nehru Fellow, 1994-1996.

RAVI VASUDEVAN is Fellow at the Centre for the Study of Developing Societies, Delhi. He has written on the history of Indian nationalism and Indian films and teaches at the Film Studies Department of Jadavpur University. He is currently writing a book, *Melodrama, Modernity and Nationhood in Indian Popular Cinema 1913-1957*.

U. VINDHYA is Reader in the Department of Psychology, Andhra University. She has worked in the areas of domestic violence, mental health, issues of women, the dynamics of the political participation of women in people's movements, and the coping strategies of women. She has published several articles in national and international journals on these themes, and is active in the Civil Liberties movement of Andhra Pradesh.

V. GEETHA is a writer and researcher currently working with Tara Publishing. She has written on Marxism and contemporary Tamil culture; along with S.V.Rajadurai she has co-authored *Periyar: Suyamariyadai Samadharmam* and *Towards a Non-Brahmin Millenium: From Iyotheedas to Periyar* (forthcoming). She is a member of Snehidi, Forum for Women, Chennai.

Index